A History of **Argentina** in the Twentieth Century

A History of
Argentina
in the
Twentieth Century

LUIS ALBERTO ROMERO

translated by James P. Brennan

FONDO DE CULTURA ECONÓMICA

MÉXICO - ARGENTINA - BRASIL - CHILE - COLOMBIA - ESPAÑA
ESTADOS UNIDOS DE AMÉRICA - GUATEMALA - PERÚ - VENEZUELA

Primera edición en español (FCE, Argentina), 2001
Primera edición en inglés (The Pennsylvania State University), 2002
Primera edición en inglés (FCE, Argentina), 2006
Segunda reimpresión, 2010

Luis Alberto Romero
A History of Argentina in the Twentieth Century. - 1a ed. 2a reimp. - Buenos Aires : Fondo de Cultura Económica, 2010.
370 p. ; 23x16 cm.

ISBN 978-950-557-670-8

1. Historia Argentina.I. título.
CDD 982

for *Ana* and *José Luis*

Contents

Preface

In this synthesis of twentieth-century Argentine history, I have not sought—as is generally the case in this type of book—either to prove a thesis or to find that unique and revealing cause of a singular, in this case somewhat infelicitous, national destiny. I have merely attempted to reconstruct the history—complex, contradictory, and unique—of a society that unquestionably has experienced better moments and that finds itself currently at one of the lowest points in its history but whose future is not, I trust, definitively sealed. The questions around which this text is organized—questions born of Argentina's anguished and tumultuous national experience—are only some of the many possible ones; and their explication reveals the individual selection that an undertaking of this kind entails.

The first question posed by the book is what place in the world today exists for Argentina—which so assuredly inserted itself into a very different world order more than one hundred years ago—and what is its feasible economic organization? What kind of economic structure can Argentines strive for that would guarantee some of the country's basic goals, such as society's general welfare, a reasonable degree of economic progress, and a certain rationality in public life? A similar question was asked by Juan Bautista Alberdi, Domingo Faustino Sarmiento, and those who a century and a half ago outlined the design of modern Argentina. But unlike the situation when our founding fathers posed the question, the answer today is neither obvious nor at hand. Today the same question is formulated from a more modest perspective and with fewer illusions than one hundred and fifty years ago because now an *aurea mediocritas* seems to us a more desirable destiny.

The second interrogative refers to the characteristics, functions, and instruments that the state must have to guarantee the common good, regulate and rationalize the economy, ensure justice, and improve social equality. Once again, the interrogative poses, in a much less promising context, questions that Argentine society debated and to a certain degree resolved more than half a century ago, answers that today are outdated or have simply been discarded, but that have not yet been replaced.

The third question concerns the world of culture and intellectuals and the conditions that can foster creativity or ideas that can be simultaneously critical, rigorous, and politically engaged and that fulfill a task that can be useful to society, analyzing social reality and proposing alternatives. Thus it happened in the Argentina of the centennial in 1910, during the fleeting experience of the decade of the 1960s, or for an even briefer moment during the hopeful return to democracy in the 1980s. The latter two experiences are close enough to remind us that such conditions are generally neither common nor easy to obtain.

Looming over these interrogatives are more distressing questions, those that most reveal that Argentina is at a crossroads, questions that concern the intersection of society and democracy. What possibilities are there to preserve or rebuild a democratic society combined with social mobility, one not partitioned into isolated worlds but one that is relatively egalitarian and with opportunities for everyone, based on competition but also on solidarity and social justice? All this constitutes the legacy, today more valuable than ever, built over the course of a century and a half, one that endured until the not-too-distant past, until a mere quarter century ago, at which point the momentum began to break down and reverse course.

Above all, there is the question about what characteristics the political system should have to ensure democracy and make of it a practice with some social meaning. In this case, the past reveals itself rich in conflicts, but it is not easy to find in it very many accomplishments, not even in periods of democratic rule, when there can be perceived *in nuce* the practices that carried to destruction institutions that had never fully matured and whose reconstruction appears now a Herculean task. Perhaps for that reason the last question is today the first one: What is the future of our democracy and of the tradition that nourishes it? We must return to Sarmiento and Alberdi and a task that we a bit naively considered to have been finished and whose accomplishments today seem fragile and vulnerable.

A book informed by such concerns is at once the work of a professional historian and a personal reflection on the present. It could not be any other way. Any attempt at historical reconstruction derives from the necessities, doubts, and preoccupations of the present, seeking a balance between professional rigor and personal opinion, but knowing that the scales frequently tip toward the latter the closer the historian is to the period or the subject under analysis. Indeed, writing this book has led me, in good measure, to abandon a more customary style of work and submerge myself in my own personal story and in a past experience that is still alive.

This was first revealed to me on attempting to make use of the ideas employed twenty years ago when, working with Alejandro Rofman, I sketched an outline of Argentine history and discovered how little use the ideas were to me now. The questions we posed then were aimed at explaining the roots of dependency and their baleful effects on the economy and society. Questions relating to democracy and republican institutions did not seem relevant to us, and, in general, politics appeared as merely a reflection of structural conditions, or conversely as an unstructured place where, through sheer willpower, such conditions could be changed, because in the collective consciousness then the perception of dependency was complimented by the search for some kind of liberation.

This dilemma is, I believe, a good example of a platitude in our profession: Historical consciousness guides historical understanding, and though the latter can impose limits on the former and subject it to the rigors of evidence, it cannot ignore it altogether. In previous years, the central idea in a historical reconstruction of this type would perhaps have emphasized social justice and economic independence, while for an even earlier period it would have been progress, modernization, or even the building of the state and nation. These concerns certainly have not disappeared for the historian and are to be found in this text as they were in their own times as aspirations, ideologies, or mobilizing utopias. The problems that they addressed are also present in today's concerns, but their ranking, connections, and accent are different, as the questions around which this text is organized bear witness. The world in which we live, whose outlines we can only barely see, is radically different not only from that one hundred or even fifty years ago but also from that a mere twenty years back.

It is generally believed that one who writes thinks either implicitly or explicitly of the reader. I began to write this book thinking of my colleagues, but I gradually came to realize that my implicit readers were my children and those of their younger generation, the ones who had almost no information about our recent past, not even of the horrors of just yesterday, because our society less and less preserves its collective memory, perhaps because it presently suffers from a great difficulty in envisioning its future. In various parts of the book, I simply wanted to leave a testimony, perhaps unnecessary for scholars familiar with this history but necessary as a civic act, because I remain convinced that only an awareness of the past permits constructing the future. At a time when the pessimism of reason struggles with the heart's optimism, I want to continue believing in the ability of men and women to make their history, to confront the circumstances in which they are fated to live, and to build a better society.

I am grateful to Alejandro Katz for his confidence that I could write this book and to Juan Carlos Korol and Ricardo Sidicaro for their careful reading of this text and their criticisms. I regret only that I could not have followed their suggestions in all cases. When I began to write this book, I asked Leandro Gutiérrez to play the part of critic, and he promised, as was customary between us, a brutally frank and stimulating dialogue. I am sorry that his death made this impossible, but I am certain that much of his penetrating, even acerbic, but enormously warm critical spirit is present in these pages; from no one, except my father, have I learned so much about history.

Preface to the English-Language Edition

With this book, I hope to offer English-speaking readers a broad overview of Argentina's contemporary history and of the country's current problems, such as they at present appear to be. The book was originally written for students and the general public in Argentina, that is, for people who, it was assumed, knew little about Argentine history. Thus, I have sought above all to explain with clarity processes and events that were enormously complex. I have based my conclusions not only on my own scholarship but also on that of my fellow historians—the best of them—and I cannot say what it is that is original in this book, save a personal viewpoint, a perspective, and a synthesis. I do not know whether I have managed to offer a profound analysis, but I do believe I have succeeded in offering a clear one, a book that can be read to good effect by students and all those interested in the past trajectory and future of Argentina.

This English-language edition coincides with the publication of the second edition of the Spanish-language one. For the second edition, I added a new chapter dealing with the ten years (1989–99) of the government of Carlos Saúl Menem, a decade we Argentines refer to as the *menemato*. This new chapter brings with it the problems that are unavoidable in dealing with so recent an experience. On examining those years, I realized that I lacked the generosity and impartiality that I believe I achieved in analyzing earlier periods, even those I lived intensely. Although if I have detested anything in my life, it is the *menemato*, I am fully aware that such strong feelings are not the best path to understanding. I was helped in overcoming my biases by some recent excellent studies on economic policies and reform of the state during the Menem years. Nonetheless, it was not easy for me to integrate as rigorous an analysis on that other very characteristic dimension of Menem's government:

the dimension dealing with the singular behavior of the ex-president Menem, his family, friends, and cronies, that is to say, the members of the gang that for ten years governed the country. I have simply attempted to provide as much objectivity as I am capable of on these controversial aspects of our recent history.

As I said in the Preface, I wrote this book thinking of my children, of Argentina's students, and of all those young people who needed to know something about what happened in our country, With this translation, I am thinking of those in the United States and those in other countries who are able to read about this history in the English language. We live in a world in which national borders are becoming increasingly blurred. This brings with it both a risk and an opportunity. The risk is the temptation to enclose one-self in what is familiar, whether it be the individual or the nation, and resist those changes, which are indeed in many cases negative, wrought by so-called globalization. The opportunity resides in the quest to understand the other and to struggle together to build a better world. I only hope this book is taken as a gesture in support of that struggle.

James Brennan is one of those who believes in such collaboration across national borders and in the possibility that men and women of good faith can improve this terrible world we live in. He thought he saw something of inter-est in this book and expended great efforts to find a publisher interested in translating it. Most important, he himself accepted the most difficult part of the undertaking: to translate it. Jim is well known to professors and students in Argentina. We value his multilayered and comprehensive studies and also his personal qualities, his generosity and modesty, qualities that are sadly un-common nowadays. I am deeply grateful to him.

Luis Alberto Romero
Buenos Aires, May 2001

one

1916

On October 12, 1916, Hipólito Yrigoyen assumed the presidency of Argentina. It was an exceptional day. A multitude of people filled the Plaza del Congreso and adjacent streets, cheering for a president who for the first time had been chosen in elections with universal adult male suffrage, a secret ballot, and a compulsory vote, as stipulated in the new electoral law passed in 1912, thanks to the efforts of President Roque Sáenz Peña. Following the inauguration ceremony, the crowd unleashed the horses of the presidential carriage and dragged it triumphantly to the Casa Rosada, the presidential residence and seat of executive power.

Yrigoyen's victory, though not a landslide, was decisive and revealed the public's political will. From the vantage point of the period, full compliance with the Constitution—the heart and soul of the platform of Yrigoyen's victorious party, the *Unión Cívica Radical*—was crowned with a representative democracy that put Argentina in the vanguard internationally as far as such democratic experiments were concerned. This peaceful political reform coming to a happy conclusion was made possible by a deep transformation in the economy and society. During four decades, taking advantage of an association with Great Britain viewed as mutually beneficial by both countries, Argentina had grown spectacularly and had become wealthy. Immigrants, attracted by the country's transformation, were successfully integrated into an open society that offered abundant opportunities for all. Though there were tensions and conflicts, these were overcome, and consensus predominated over confrontation. Yrigoyen's decision to modify the traditionally repressive role of the state, using state power to mediate between different social sectors and to achieve an equilibrium, seemed to resolve the one remaining obstacle. In sum, Yrigoyen's assumption of power could have been considered, without greatly exaggerating, as the happy culmination of the long process of modernization that had begun in the middle of the nineteenth century.

Another view of the country was possible in 1916, and many contemporaries adhered to it and behaved accordingly. For them, Yrigoyen resembled a barbarous caudillo, one of the warlords who many had believed were eliminated in 1880 with the end of endemic civil war and the final consolidation of political power in Buenos Aires. A government of the mediocre seemed to stand behind Yrigoyen. The political transition to democracy was viewed with suspicion; those who felt displaced from power demonstrated little loyalty toward the recently established institutional system and longed for a time when a select elite governed. Moreover, the First World War, which had broken out in 1914, offered a glimpse of the end of the era of easy progress, with growing difficulties and more precarious economic conditions, in which the relationship with Great Britain would be insufficient to ensure prosperity. The political and social tensions beginning to spread throughout the world during the final phase of the war, which were unleashed at its conclusion, were also manifesting themselves in Argentina and encouraged those who foresaw a future dominated by conflict. Society was sick, it was said; those who were responsible were foreign organisms; ultimately immigration itself was to blame. Thus an increasingly intolerant attitude grew in the country, expressed in a truculent nationalism.

Both views of Argentina, incomplete and distorted, were present in 1916; each, in its own way, was the result of the great transformation wrought over the previous half-century. For a long time, these images shaped attitudes and actions also influenced by new circumstances that corrected or refined the images bequeathed by the period of economic expansion.

State Building

During the decades before 1916, an era not so distant for the citizenry to have forgotten the rapid pace of recent changes, Argentina had embarked on a program that contemporaries called "progress." The first efforts in pursuit of progress could be traced back to the middle of the nineteenth century, with the great expansion in capitalism as the world began to become fully integrated into the international capitalist system. These efforts had mixed results and for diverse reasons. The greatest problem was the absence of effective institutions. State building was therefore a primordial concern. By 1880, when General Julio A. Roca assumed the presidency, the most difficult obstacles had been overcome, but much remained to be done.

The first task was to assure peace and stability and to assert effective control over the national territory. After 1810 and for some seven decades, civil wars had been endemic. Provincial authorities had fought among themselves and against Buenos Aires. The year 1862 marked a turning point, as the new national state, little by little and with little luck in the beginning, began to dominate those who had heretofore challenged its power, in the process ensuring that the army held a monopoly on the use of force.

Some outstanding problems were resolved during and after the Paraguayan War (1865–70). The province of Entre Ríos, Buenos Aires' great rival in the establishment of a new state, and then the province of Buenos Aires itself—whose rebellion had been defeated in 1880—both had to accept the transformation of the city of Buenos Aires into the federal capital. The state then established its dominion over vast territories inhabited by indigenous peoples. In 1879, the southern frontier was secured, hemming in the Indian tribes there along the Andean foothills; in 1911, the occupation of the northern territories concluded. The territorial limits of the nation were clearly defined, and domestic problems were sharply separated from the external issues with which they had been traditionally linked. The war with Paraguay contributed to delineating the fluctuating borders of the Río de la Plata basin, and the 1879 Conquest of the Desert guaranteed possession of Patagonia, although tensions with Chile remained alive until 1902 and reappeared later.

After 1880, a new institutional framework was created, one that lasted for some time. Bolstered by recent military victories, a central power was consolidated whose juridical basis could be found in the Constitution sanctioned in 1853, which, in Alberdi's words, should uphold "a monarchy dressed as a republic." As the historian Natalio Botana argued, there was thereby assured a strong presidential power, exercised without limits in the vast national territories and strengthened by powers to interdict provincial governments and declare a state of siege. On the other hand, the checks and balances exercised by the congress, above all the prohibition of presidential reelection, ensured that executive power would not become tyrannical. Those who so designed the Constitution were conscious of the long history of civil wars and the ease with which the ruling class became divided and fell into bloody and sterile power struggles.

In this respect, the results met expectations. The rule of law was strengthened by a political system in which the executive, from the apex of power, simultaneously controlled politicians and political influence. In its most extreme form, this practice was called the *unicato,* the period of oligarchical rule between 1880 and Yrigoyen's 1916 election, but in reality it was routinely employed before and after 1916. The executive used such powers to discipline provincial groups but at the same time allowed the latter a great degree of freedom in deciding local matters. Power that had been consolidated in the hands of the dominant groups in the littoral (Buenos Aires and Santa Fe) provinces—including the dynamic Córdoba—found different ways to use prosperity to win the cooperation of the aristocracies of the interior, particularly those of the poorer provinces, and thus to ensure the backing of the local aristocracies for a political order that they were in no position to contest.

Though by 1880 the state's basic structure had been established—its fiscal, administrative, and judicial powers—these powers were often mere ideas of what ought to be done. Lacking the instruments for realizing many of the most urgent tasks such as instituting public education and fomenting immigration, the state was at first the preserve of private interests. Nonetheless, as its resources increased, the state expanded its institutions and acquired a coherency and solidity long before society did. The latter, in a full process of renovation and reconstitution, initially lacked the organization and means for halting the state's advance.

The state acted deliberately and systematically to facilitate Argentina's insertion into the global economy and to find a role and purpose, it was hoped, that perfectly suited it. The chosen path entailed a close association with

Great Britain, the foreign power that had been playing the role of mother country since independence in 1810. At first limited to ties of trade, the association became tighter after 1850, thanks to Argentina's production of wool—the first economic undertaking in the country organized on a strictly capitalist basis—contemporary with the deepening of Britain's industrialization, now converted into "the workshop of the world." At this time, the commercial relations between the two countries deepened, and financial ties became important as well, especially owing to the heavy British contribution to defraying the costs of building the state. True maturation occurred, however, after 1880, during the age of imperialism. In those years, Great Britain, undisputed master of the colonial world, began to face the competition from new rivals—Germany first and then the United States—as the entire globe was divided into colonial empires, formal or informal. When the association with Great Britain was being consolidated, Britain was entering its mature phase, unquestionably still a formidable power but not a very dynamic one. Incapable of confronting the industrial competition of its emerging rivals, it took refuge in its empire and monopolies, opting in favor of their assured profits through its preferred low-risk, high-return investments.

Between 1880 and 1913, British capital in Argentina increased twentyfold. To the traditional British areas of investment such as trade, banking, and public loans were added mortgage loans for land, investment in utilities such as gas, and investment in transport such as streetcars and especially railroads. These investments proved enormously profitable. In some cases such as the railroads, the government guaranteed profits and also granted tax exemptions and land alongside the tracks to be laid.

In subsequent years, these concessions became ever-greater problems, though contemporaries saw the Argentine-British connection in a positive light. Even though the British obtained handsome profits on their investments and trade, they left ample room for local businesspeople, especially for the great landowners for whom was reserved the lion's share of an agricultural production made possible by an infrastructure established by the British. The 2,500 kilometers of existing railroad track in 1880 became 34,000 in 1916, just slightly under the 40,000 kilometers in Argentina's railway network at its highest point. Some of the big spur lines served to integrate the national territory and ensure the authority of the state within its borders. Others densely covered the *pampa húmeda,* the fertile grasslands of the pampa, making possible, along with the port system, the expansion of first agriculture and then livestock, after these same British established the system of meatpacking plants.

This expansion required an ample labor force. The country had been receiving many immigrants in increasing numbers throughout the nineteenth century, but after 1880 the numbers grew dramatically. In Europe, immigration was encouraged by strong demographic growth, a crisis in the traditional agrarian economies, unemployment, and cheaper international passenger rates. Argentina decided to modify the traditionally conservative and selective immigration policy and to vigorously foment immigration via propaganda and subsidized travel costs. Neither of these measures would have been effective if possibilities for finding work had not simultaneously increased. The immigrants showed great flexibility and willingness to adapt to prevailing conditions in the labor market. In the 1880s, the immigrants concentrated in the large cities, working in construction in public works and in all the building that accompanied the urbanization process. Beginning in the middle of the following decade, with possibilities in agriculture becoming available, the immigrants headed en masse to the countryside, both those who came to settle permanently and those who traveled annually for the harvest. This phenomenon, made possible by cheap passenger fares and relatively high local wages, explains in part the strong difference between the old and new immigrants. Between 1880 and 1890, immigrants surpassed one million, with some 650,000 settling permanently, a notable number for a country whose population was approximately two million. In the following decade, after the economic crisis of 1890, immigration declined, and those who returned to their country of origin exceeded the numbers of arrivals with every passing year. The earlier immigration flow patterns were reestablished in the first decade of the twentieth century, when the positive balance of arrivals versus returns surpassed one million.

The active promotion of immigration was only one facet of a series of measures that the state, far from employing the hands-off philosophy of the supposed liberal principles it espoused, implemented to encourage economic growth, break bottlenecks, and establish conditions that permitted the development of private enterprise. Particularly between 1880 and 1890, such actions were intense and purposeful. Foreign investments were enticed and promoted with ample guarantees, and the state assumed the risk in the least attractive investments, only to transfer them to private hands once success was assured. In financial matters, it accepted and encouraged inflation for the benefit of exporters, and public banks handled credit policies very loosely, at least until 1890. Above all, the state undertook the so-called Conquest of the Desert, which resulted in the incorporation of vast expanses of land suitable for cultivation, in which great plots at minimum cost were transferred to powerful private interests and the well connected. Many of these were already or would become landowners, and this policy was a decisive turning point in the consolidation of the landowning class. The land was subsequently freely sold and bought, although its spectacularly high values until 1890—based on the calculation of future earnings guaranteed by the capitalist expansion underway—reduced the number of possible buyers.

Though beneficiaries of the state's generosity—a state controlled by them—the pampa's landowners also displayed great adaptability to economic circumstances in pursuit of the greatest possible profits. In the littoral, where cattle were scarce and produce could move by river, landowners leaned toward agriculture; where the land was cheap, they opted for colonization, which brought land under cultivation; once the land increased in value, they preferred a sharecropping system. In the province of Buenos Aires, great landed estates and wool production predominated, until the establishment of meatpacking plants made the breeding of English blooded cattle stock for export profitable. Subsequently, the need for grazing lands stimulated agrarian colonization; land was devoted alternately to grain cultivation, fodder, and pasture, making agriculture inextricably bound with cattle ranching.

This combination turned out to be most suited to the specific conditions of the time. The productivity of the land ensured high returns on low investments. Moreover, the changing and extremely unpredictable nature of international markets made it prudent to maintain flexibility to choose the most profitable option on a yearly basis. It seemed wise to maintain properties intact so as to be prepared for any scenario and to practice large-scale agriculture. As Jorge Sábato suggested, landowners became accustomed to alternating diverse activities, looking for the maximum degree of profitability in each, without staying with any one for long, the priority being not to immobilize their capital. To investments in agriculture were added urban ventures in real estate, construction, and even industry. Thus, with its base in agriculture, an entrepreneurial class took shape, a class that was highly concentrated but not specializing in one sector, an oligarchy that controlled a vast array of businesses from the halls of power.

These conditions also encouraged speculative activities by the country's small farmers. The immigrants who became sharecroppers during the expansion of agriculture had limited capital at their disposal. They preferred to accept contracts to sharecrop sizable tracts of land for three years rather than to purchase smaller parcels of their own. As migrating speculators, they gambled everything on a few years of intense work, making minimum fixed investments, with the payoff of possible good harvests, only to repeat the gamble later with another sharecropping arrangement.

In this first stage, such highly flexible behavior allowed the landed classes to take advantage of external inducements and made possible a truly spectacular economic growth. Since 1890, the expansion of agriculture had been continuous, and the countryside filled with sharecroppers and agricultural laborers. Between 1892 and 1913, the production of wheat increased fivefold, half of which was exported. During this same period, total exports also increased five times, and imports grew at a slightly slower rate. To wheat were added corn and linseed, the three of which were half the country's exports. Among the rest, besides wool, meat exports began to occupy an increasing importance, especially after 1900, when packinghouses began to export chilled and canned beef to Great Britain. By that point, wool production had been pushed to the southern part of the province of Buenos Aires and replaced by livestock, native cattle mixed with blooded British stock such as Shorthorn and Hereford. On the eve of the First World War, Argentina was one of the world's leading meat exporters.

If the profits of their foreign partners were high in areas such as the railroads, packinghouses, shipping, trade, and finance, so too were the profits of the state, coming mainly from import taxes, and those of the landowning class, who, in view of the advantages they enjoyed with respect to other international exporters, chose to spend the bulk of their profits on consumption. This fact explains the lavish expenditures in the cities, which one after the other went about beautifying themselves, imitating the great European metropolises, a process that had an important multiplier effect on the economy. The state supplied the cities with modern services in public health and transport, as well as avenues, public squares, and ensembles of ostentatious public buildings, not always in the best taste. Private citizens built equally spectacular residences, mansions, or *petits hôtels*. The wealth of the country-side spread to the cities, increasing employment and generating in turn new demands for commerce, services, and eventually industry, because the cities, combined with the towns of the agricultural zone, collectively constituted an attractive market.

The industrial sector reached important proportions and employed many people. Some large establishments, such as those in meatpacking, flour mills, and a few others, produced their goods for export or for the domestic market. Other important industries, such as textiles and food processing, supplied products elaborated with local primary materials. An extensive network of workshops, generally the property of better-off immigrants, supplied the rest of the domestic market. This industrial economy grew in consonance with the agrarian one, expanding or contracting according to the rhythm of the latter and nourishing itself with foreign capital. Through the foreign banks, local landowners or those who controlled foreign trade could also add indus-trial investments to the total of their business undertakings.

The bulk of these changes took place in the littoral (Buenos Aires and Santa Fe provinces), extending to include Córdoba, and deepened the rift with the interior, which could not insert itself into the international market. Neither investments nor immigrants arrived there. The railroad did, however, and in some cases it broke down the region's isolation from markets and thereby affected local society. On the other hand, the state undertook great investments, partly sustaining provincial government and education. What predominated above all was the relative backwardness of the interior and the ever-more-manifest differences between the agitated life in the great cities of the littoral and that of the sleepy provincial capitals.

There were some exceptions. In the northern part of Santa Fe province and southern Chaco province, a dynamic and exploitative British company had established a true enclave economy dedicated to the cutting and processing of the *quebracho* tree (used for the extraction of tanin). The most impor-tant exceptions, however, occurred first in Tucumán and then in Mendoza provinces, centered around the production of sugar and wine, respectively. Both prospered, notably by supplying the growing markets of the littoral, thanks to the market share provided by a state that protected the provinces with high tariffs. The state itself permitted the initial take-off of these regional economies, building railroads and financing the investments of the first entrepreneurs of sugar mills and wineries. In both cases, there were political considerations behind such support. More immediately, the relationships of important businesspeople in the nascent industries—Ernesto Tornquist in sugar and Tiburcio Benegas in wine—with the highest official circles weighed heavily. The faces of Tucumán and especially of Mendoza, where economic expansion entailed the incorporation of sizable numbers of immigrants, were fundamentally transformed. The transformation in some ways defied the norms of the international division of labor—Tucumán's sugar was always much more expensive than the sugar that could be imported from Cuba—but was in accordance with the practices of monopoly profits and the connections between business and the state, which characterized the entire turn-of-the-century economic expansion.

Around the state congregated an important group of speculators, intermediaries, and financiers, all with access to those in power and profiting greatly from the concessions, loans, public works projects, and government sales and purchases, especially in the 1880s, when the state injected massive amounts of credit through guaranteed banks. Contemporaries blamed this speculative fever on the crisis of 1890, which halted for a decade the economy's spectacular advance. The problems, however, were deeper and turned out to be chronic. The close links between the Argentine and international economies made the former extremely sensitive to cyclical fluctuations of the kind that had occurred in 1873. The large international debt made service payments extremely onerous, payable only through additional loans or surplus from foreign trade, both of which were drastically reduced in moments of cyclical crisis, generating a more or less prolonged recession. The international crisis of 1890 had the peculiar characteristic of starting in Argentina and dragging down with it one of the most important British investors: the Baring Brothers Bank. In the short term, the crisis had catastrophic effects, above all for small savers, although by bringing to an end the speculative activities of the 1880s, it encouraged other activities, especially agriculture, and inaugurated their important expansion.

Mass immigration and economic progress profoundly affected Argentine society and, it could be said, transformed it. The 1.8 million inhabitants in 1869 became 7.8 million in 1914; the population of the capital city of Buenos Aires grew from 180,000 inhabitants to 1.5 million. In 1895, two of every three residents of the city were foreigners; in 1914, by which time many foreigners had Argentine-born children, half the population was still foreign. The majority of immigrants were Italians, primarily from northern but also from southern Italy, followed by those from Spain and, in far fewer numbers, from France. But immigrants arrived from everywhere, even if in small contingents, to the point that Buenos Aires was thought of as a new Babel. As José Luis Romero noted, ours was an "alluvial" society, built by a process of accretion in which foreigners appeared everywhere, although not of course in the same numbers.

Few immigrants went to the interior, with the exception of places like Mendoza. In the littoral, many went to the countryside, and the majority of those who did so established themselves precariously as sharecroppers. The country's small farmers and their families were the protagonists of an arduous and risky undertaking. Perhaps because they were interested in quick success, willing to make great sacrifices and to risk their scarce capital on a precarious bet, they preferred to live in rudimentary and spartan shacks, without the minimum of conveniences, ready to abandon their homes when the contract expired. As with all immigrants, they took a chance on rapid economic success, which some achieved and many did not. Ultimately, of those who succeeded, they or their children entered the emerging middle classes; those who did not probably went to the cities or returned to their countries of origin. What is certain is that both contributed to the great profits of the large landowners and the exporting firms that benefited from the advantages of the system but did not participate in its risks.

At first, the majority of immigrants went to the cities, where the greatest demand for workers existed. The big cities, Buenos Aires above all, were replete with workers, most of them immigrants but also some Argentine born, or criollos. Their occupations were as diverse as their working conditions. They were unskilled day laborers (*jornaleros*) who searched daily for a job, skilled artisans, street vendors, domestic servants, and even workers in the first factories. On the other hand, their experiences were similar in many ways. They lived overcrowded in the tenements, or *conventillos,* in the city center, near the port where many worked, or in La Boca neighborhood. They suffered difficult daily tribulations: poor housing, high rents, sanitary problems, instability in their work, low wages, disease, and high infant mortality. All of these combined to create a tough existence from which few escaped. It was a young society and one still in the making. The foreigners were foreign to one another, as not even the Italians—a somewhat artificial category that encompassed people with diverse origins and separated by different dialects—could communicate easily among themselves. The integration of such diverse elements, the establishment of solidarity networks and forms of association, and the formation of collective identities in the world of work were slow processes.

Many of the immigrants, driven by the desire to *hacer la América* and perhaps to return rich and respectable to the towns and villages they had left as wretched emigrants, devoted their efforts to the venture of an individual, or more precisely family, upward social mobility. Those who did not achieve it or who failed after some initial success—and did not return to their home country—remained among the mass of workers, continually replenished with new arrivals. Among these people, solidarity practices were most broadly developed, encouraged by working-class activists. The majority achieved at least some success in the "venture of social mobility." Such success generally consisted of acquiring one's own house and perhaps a small business or workshop as well. Above all, the road to success was traveled by educating one's children. A primary education allowed people to break down the barriers of language that segregated their parents. A secondary education opened the doors to a government job or a teaching post, respectable and well-paid positions. A university degree, with the title of "doctor," was the magic key permitting entry into the select circles of polite society. Such an image is no doubt conventional, propagated by those who triumphed and ignoring those who failed. Nevertheless, the venture of social mobility was real enough that it created a popular social myth with deep roots that would last for years, one that helped establish the broad urban and rural middle classes that characterized in its essence Argentine society.

In summary, a new society had been built, one that was still for years to come in the process of formation and in which foreigners and their children were present at all levels of society, high, middle, and low. This open and mobile society offered great opportunities, yet was also divided in two. On the one hand, there was the modernizing Argentina that stood apart from the traditional interior; on the other, the new society that for a considerable period was separate from both the traditional criollo classes and the upper classes, the latter somewhat traditional but to a great extent themselves new, yet seeking to assert their separateness from the new society.

Whereas in the new society the immigrants intermingled freely with the criollos, creating new lifestyles and a hybrid culture, the upper classes—open to accepting rich or successful foreigners into their ranks without reservation—felt themselves to embody tradition, asserting their "Argentineness" and regarding themselves as masters of the country where the immigrants had come to work. Not all the aristocracy came from old money, and in their ranks there were many upstarts and nouveaux riches, not all of them truly wealthy. Some acquired their wealth through dubious means, thanks to political connections; others could barely keep their heads above water and maintain what was then called a "decent" lifestyle. Yet all of them, faced with a mass of foreigners, displayed a desire to shut themselves off, to evoke patrician backgrounds, to concern themselves with surnames and lineage, and, for those who could, to flaunt a luxurious lifestyle and an ostentation that—though perhaps their European models would have considered them vulgar and in bad taste—were useful for marking off social distinctions. That was the function served by the public places where people went to be seen such as the opera, the Palermo racetrack, and the fashionable shopping street, Calle Florida. The greatest example of this urge was the private club, exclusive and educational at the same time. The Jockey Club was founded by the former president Carlos Pellegrini and the writer Miguel Cané for purposes of cultivating a vast and enlightened aristocracy that "consisted of all cultured and honorable men."

These same men reserved to themselves the control of high politics. This was to be an activity for the "notable" who came from traditional families, decent, well-mannered, though not necessarily rich individuals, because in politics there were ample numbers of parvenus who would make their fortunes there. The political system was impeccably republican, though designed to distance voters from the most important decisions, removing them somewhat from the "popular will." Moreover, the electoral practices of the period, especially the strong interference of the government at every stage, tended to discourage those who might want to participate in electoral competition. At the apex of the political system, the selection of the political establishment came through agreements among the president, governors, and other political notables of recognized prestige. At the lowest levels, competition was expressed by political bosses who mobilized their battle-hardened political machines capable, with the complicity of public authorities, of assaulting voting booths or stuffing ballot boxes. The system—stigmatized later by the political opposition—rested on the scant general will to participate in elections. Isolated from the great democratizing processes taking place in Europe and North America, the formation of a citizenry in Argentina was a slow and difficult process. In this process, the population's immigrant character and disinterest in adopting Argentine citizenship and participating in elections weighed heavily; some were reluctant to lose the privileges and safeguards that their status as foreigners conferred (immunity from military service, for example). Such a situation troubled the most enlightened members of the ruling elite, concerned about establishing the consensual basis of the political regime.

Perhaps the most noteworthy and abiding characteristic of this regime was the absence of competition from alternative political parties and a political structure characterized by a one-party system whose head was the president of the republic. The *Partido Nacional Autonomista* (PAN) was in reality a federation of governors, the provincial heads of the political establishment. The president used his power to discipline them, thereby confusing the state's legitimate functions with strictly political motives. Without state mechanisms for the transfer of power and with limited opportunities for a broad political debate, conflicts were negotiated in small circles between politicians and military officers, the press, and the congress. The system proved efficient in resolving minor differences based on shared convictions—as occurred throughout the decade of the 1880s—but revealed its weaknesses when disagreements became more serious, as they did following 1890. It then became clear that this political regime had no room for divergent and legitimate interests capable of offering differing points of view and establishing alternative alliances. The *unicato,* which had contributed to the consolidation of the state and the ending of long-standing conflicts, revealed its limitations for channeling proposals for change in a society that was taking shape and becoming more diverse and in which varied and contradictory interests were developing.

To shape and organize that society in accordance with deep convictions about progress, thereby fostering the consensus necessary for the great changes taking place—this was perhaps the principal concern of the ruling elite. The panorama was certainly disturbing. A mass of uprooted, atomized foreigners interested only in making money and returning to their homelands sparked the indignation of those who, like Sarmiento, had once seen immigration as the great instrument of progress. On the other hand, in undertaking to shape these masses, a number of important competitors appeared: the Catholic Church, though in Argentina its influence was much weaker than in the rest of Latin America; immigrant associations, especially those of the Italians; and finally the radical political organizations that were beginning to appear, above all those of the anarchists, offering the popular sectors a drastically different social project. Against these, a still weak state fought and triumphed. It gradually extended its hold on society, as much by controlling its organization as by accelerating the changes that ensured the much sought-after "progress."

The Law of Civil Marriage and Registry, inspired by the most progressive European legislation of the day, imposed the state's presence in the most important events in an individual's life—birth, marriage, and death—until then regulated by the Church. Subsequently, this state presence was buttressed by control of public health, influence in the workplace, and above all the Law of Obligatory Military Service, which put all men of a certain age in a situation where they could be controlled, disciplined, and "Argentinized." In the decade of the 1880s, however, the great instrument was primary education, and in that area the greatest efforts were extended. According to an 1884 law, education was to be secular, free, and mandatory. Replacing both the Catholic Church and immigrant associations, both of which had advanced greatly in this area, the state assumed all responsibility for education. Literacy ensured a basic education for everyone and at the same time the integration and nationalization of immigrants' children who, if in their homes they traced their past to some region of Italy or Spain, in school learned that the past dated from the founding fathers, Bernardino Rivadavia and Manuel Belgrano.

Even though the elite were by their very makeup cosmopolitan, critical of the criollo or Hispanic heritage, and open to the progressive influences of Europe, from an early date they were preoccupied with national concerns, as much to affirm national identity as to integrate the foreign masses into the nation. The patrician elite, who felt themselves to be the anointed ones for the construction of the fatherland, proceeded to shape their version of the country's history, as Bartolomé Mitre did in his historical works, a process that was at the same time a self-justification of their rule. With the same concerns in mind, they debated about art, music, or the national language.

These and other subjects were commented on in small circles and in private social gatherings, in the press and its editorials, and among university faculty and in the congress. Some wrote entire books on the subject, which were published in Europe. Although there were no intellectual giants among them, a group of gentleman intellectuals effectively contributed to molding the ideas of their social class. They were familiar with all the latest trends in Europe, for each of which there was a local version: realism, impressionism, naturalism, and so on. The school of thought that best expressed their natural philosophy of life was Positivism, in its Spencerian version, with its emphasis on efficiency and pragmatism, on "order and progress," all things suited to a society that was then—on the eve of its centennial celebrations— characterized by its optimism.

Tensions and Transformations

The centennial of the 1810 May Revolution and Argentine independence was an occasion for the happy and confident country to celebrate its recent accomplishments. The attendance of the infanta Isabel, the aunt of the king of Spain, and of the former president of Chile, Manuel Montt, revealed that foreign enemies, old or new, were a thing of the past. Intellectuals and writers such as Georges Clemenceau, Enrico Ferri, Adolfo Posada, and Jules Huret testified, in their own ways, to the country's spectacular success, as did the poet Rubén Darío in his somewhat pompous *Canto a la Argentina*. Demonstrating the alluvial character of Argentine society, all the immigrant communities honored the country and its spectacular achievements with a monument whose foundation stone had been hurriedly laid that year. The official discourse of the ceremonies, empty, trite, and repetitive, barely managed to conceal the other face of this reality. A general strike, even more bitter than the previous year's, which had culminated in the assassination of the Buenos Aires chief of police by an anarchist, threatened to ruin the celebrations. A bomb placed in the Colón opera house laid bare the tensions and violence, to which polite society replied with the first episodes of state terrorism and a draconian Law of Social Defense.

Beyond the pomp and circumstance of the celebrations, a deep concern about the nation's course overtook the country's most reflective spirits, overwhelmed by a growing sense of pessimism. Employing the models of

Positivist sociology and combining them with history and social psychology, intellectuals diagnosed society as ill. Picking up the introspective intellectual tradition of Sarmiento or Alberdi, ponderous essays, brutal assessments, and daring proposals—such as those of Joaquín González in *El juicio del siglo,* Agustin Alvarez in *Manual de patología política,* Carlos Octavio Bunge in *Nuestra América,* José María Ramos Mejía in *Las multitudes argentinas,* and Ricardo Rojas in *La restauración nacionalista*—appeared. Some of society's evils were attributed to the elite themselves, with their glib conformity and abandonment of patrician tradition and civic-mindedness. The crux of the questioning, however, concerned the cosmopolitan nature of Argentine society, inundated by immigrant masses and led by those who sought inspiration in Europe. All the social and political conflicts, all the questioning of the leadership of the established elite could be attributed to bad immigrants, to "strange organisms," to "destabilizing foreigners," incapable of appreciating what the country offered them.

Yet beyond these extreme declarations, there was concern about the corruption of a national character that some saw embodied in criollo society before the immigration tide; others, more extreme, associated it in a polemical fashion with the rupture with Hispanic tradition. Although this latter position was questioned by those who continued to associate that tradition with intolerance and backwardness, there was nonetheless in the elite's consciousness the image of sullen and sinister masses, lacking any ties to society, of dangerous classes lurking in the shadows and beginning to encroach on those areas until then reserved to the fatherland's children. In response, some adhered to an aristocratic elitism that the Uruguayan writer José Enrique Rodó had made fashionable with his book *Ariel.* Others looked for the solution to the problems in formulas of social engineering, including those experimented with by Chancellor Bismarck in Germany. The majority found a solution in a strident and polemical affirmation of nationality. The solution was to emphasize criollo tradition, to Argentinize the immigrant masses while disciplining them. From the beginning of the century, undoubtedly inspired by the prewar European mood, there began to predominate a chauvinistic nationalism, which José Ramos Mejía of the National Council on Education attempted to inculcate in children's lessons in the primary schools. This nationalism reached its apogee in the 1910 festivities, when gangs of the *niños bien* took pleasure in harassing any foreigner who hesitated to remove his hat when the notes of the national anthem began to sound.

Along with the perception of a sickness in society, a perception given credence by the daily crises, conflicts, and tensions of the most diverse nature, two attitudes appeared among the ruling elite. Some opted for conciliatory behavior, assuming responsibility for society's demands and proposing reforms. Others, however, maintained an intransigent attitude, calling on the state to repress any sign of discontent and, dissatisfied with half-hearted support on this score, organizing themselves to take matters into their own hands.

Some reasons for concern were foretold in the economy's progress, despite the fact that in the first years of the century Argentina experienced its most spectacular rates of growth. In 1914, a renewed spurt of immigration caused the population to reach almost eight million inhabitants, doubling the 1895 figure. The amount of cultivated land attained a record of twenty-four million hectares, and the country became the world's largest exporter of corn and linseed and one of the largest of wool, beef, and wheat. Buenos Aires—which proudly exhibited its new subway system—became the premier city of Latin America. Nevertheless, economic crises in 1907 and 1913, and following the latter, two years of depression resulting from war in the Balkans, reminded everyone of the fragility of that growth. Relations with the international economy were becoming more complex, both because of the increasing participation of France and Germany in trade and investment and because of the ever more aggressive presence of the United States in the areas of public services, electrical utilities, and, above all, meatpacking. Their domination of the technology of chilled beef allowed the North Americans to gain ground in foreign markets. After successive agreements over export quotas, the United States finally controlled three-fourths of the meat trade with Great Britain, though the British continued to dominate shipping and insurance.

These were the first signs of a triangular relationship that deepened and became much more complex once local industry began to demand machinery, parts, and oil, supplied by the United States, or when the use of the automobile was popularized, requiring a more delicate and precise handling of economic policy than previously. These problems were overshadowed by a much more critical situation brought about by the First World War, which disorganized financial and trade networks, led to foreign divestment, and produced a marked increase in the cost of living and difficulties in many industries, though the war benefited those activities, such as the export of canned meat, intended to supply the belligerents. Yet even those who were the beneficiaries perceived this increase in exports to have circumstantial and short-lived effects limited to the duration of the war. The truth is that by the time Yrigoyen assumed the presidency in 1916 few would have subscribed to the optimistic and carefree assessment that prevailed in 1910.

The greatest concerns were those emanating from social tensions, popular demands, and diverse necessities generally expressed in a violent manner by the various social actors who were emerging as society became more diversified but also more established. These tensions did not arise from the traditional, lethargic interior but from the dynamic regions of the littoral. In the rural zones, the first noteworthy manifestation of these tensions was that of the agricultural colonists (*colonos*) of Santa Fe, protagonists of the first agricultural expansion, the majority of whom were small producers who both rented and owned land. A critical economic conjuncture—with its origins in the 1890 crisis—combined with the state's political decision prohibiting foreigners from voting in municipal elections. That same year, 1890, the *Unión Cívica* rebellion occurred, and in following years the *colonos* added their demands—elimination of an onerous tax and reestablishment of the vote in municipal elections—to those of the Radicals, the name given to the members of the redubbed *Unión Cívica Radical.* The Radicals and the *colonos* collaborated in Santa Fe's 1893 uprising in which the "*colonos* in arms"—especially the Swiss—played an important role, only to suffer government repression and the aftereffects of a climate generally unfavorable to the *colonos*.

The next rebellion, quite a bit later, broke out in 1912 and had as its actors the sharecroppers (*arrendatarios*) who had participated in the notable expansion of grain agriculture in the littoral region and the hardworking small farmers (*chacareros*) who, at the head of small family enterprises and with great sacrifice, could at times prosper and consolidate their position. Both were harried by constant pressures, especially those coming from the landowners, who periodically adjusted their rental contracts with the sharecroppers, motivated by the increasing demand for land that resulted from a permanent migratory flow. Both *arrendatarios* and *chacareros* were also subject to the demands of the commercial intermediaries that stretched from the small local store owner to the great exporting firms of Dreyfus or Bunge y Born.

In periods of good prices, the *chacareros* could maintain the balancing act. With the fall of international prices in 1910 and 1911, however, when rents were kept high, the situation of the sharecroppers became critical. On the other hand, the *chacareros* had sunk roots in the country, formed communities, and established their interests, and they were also adversely affected by the fall in prices. Thus in 1912, the *arrendatarios* and *chacareros* found common cause and undertook a strike, refusing to bring in the harvest unless the landowners satisfied certain conditions: longer tenancy contracts, lower rents, and various other demands such as the right to freely acquire agricultural machinery for the harvests and to raise domesticated animals. In the cases of both Santa Fe's *colonos* and the pampa's sharecroppers and *chacareros,* the moderation of their demands—which neither questioned the basic aspects of the system nor proposed alliances with rural day laborers (*jornaleros*)—contrasted with the violent actions of Santa Fe's *colonos* and the organizing activities of the sharecroppers and small farmers who initiated an important cooperative movement and established their own representative organization, the *Federación Agraria Argentina.* Since then, this organization has represented the small landed interests and has constantly demanded concessions and pressured landowners and public authorities.

In the great cities—above all in Buenos Aires and Rosario—the establishment of collective identities was more complex and less in unison, but with more spectacular consequences. Among the popular sectors, linguistic and cultural heterogeneity was overwhelmed by the daily experience of confronting the harsh living conditions, which encouraged cooperation and the founding of associations around which popular society started to coalesce: mutual aid and resistance societies and trade unions. In addition, living together allowed for the spontaneous integration of cultural traditions and the emergence of hybrid cultural expressions of great creativity, such as the tango, popular theater (*sainete*), and even an Argentine slang (*lunfardo*) in which creole influences and the diverse contributions of the immigrants came together.

The Church, the immigrant associations, and especially the state, which combined coercion with education, sought to exert influence on this spontaneous formation of culture. Nonetheless, the state's powerful instrument, public education, clashed in this first period with the mass of adult workers, illiterates who were almost impervious to its message. This situation left open a wide field of action for alternative identities by radical intellectuals and particularly anarchists. These found an appropriate language to address the working masses, dispersed, foreign, and segregated, who to act together needed great mobilizing ideals, such as that of overthrowing the ruling class and establishing a new and just society, without bosses or the state. The general strike and spontaneous revolt that the anarchists successfully directed were the instruments, it was imagined, for bringing together these fragmented laboring masses and making more effective the struggles for the demands specific to each of their unions. Faced with the anarchists, the state redoubled its repressive efforts, and the 1902 Residency Law even authorized the deportation of unruly elements. In a game of reciprocal challenges, the social agitation that began around 1890 became more acute by 1900 and culminated in the great strikes of 1910, the high point of mass agitation and urban revolt—although the groups' organizational strength never matched their mobilizing capacity—and also of repression.

This identity, segregated and antiestablishment, a source of serious concern on the part of the ruling classes, was not the only one that took hold among urban workers. Slowly but surely appeared among them a group of skilled workers, usually with a very basic education, determined to settle in the country and in many cases already Argentine citizens. Among them and also among other popular sectors already integrated into urban society, the Socialists found their constituency. Unlike the anarchists, the Socialists offered a discourse more rational than emotional, calling for gradual improvement of society in which final aspirations would result from the outcome of a series of small reforms. These were in great measure to be achieved through parliamentary means, which is why they urged the immigrants to become citizens. The Socialists always obtained good electoral results in the cities following the 1904 victory of Alfredo Palacios as congressman from Buenos Aires.

Nevertheless, the Socialists had no success in channeling the specific demands of the workers, who, when they did not follow the anarchists, preferred the syndicalists. The latter had a particularly strong standing among the big unions such as those of the railroad workers, the merchant marine workers, and the dock workers. Like the Socialists, the syndicalists favored gradual reforms, but were uninterested in political struggle and political parties and concentrated their actions strictly on trade-union matters. Both the Socialists and the syndicalists contributed—especially after 1910—to directing conflict along reformist lines and to finding common ground and negotiating with the state. The state, for its part, was capable of displaying a more conciliatory attitude, expressed in the drafted labor code of Bismarckian inspiration, proposed in 1904 by Minister Joaquín V. González and written with the collaboration of the most progressive political leaders. The establishment of the National Department of Labor in 1907 was likewise a demonstration of the state's ability to seek compromise and reform.

The unions became definitively established as an important actor with perennial demands. They did not, however, manage to articulate society's other concerns, particularly for those who preferred to attempt the road of social mobility rather than tie their fate to that of the working masses. Social mobility was an attractive and relatively attainable option in a society whose hierarchy was open and fluid. The attainment of economic success was essentially an individual venture, but social prestige and the possibility of gaining access to the redoubts that the upper classes kept closed were collective problems, expressed in political terms even when politics did not encompass all the issues at stake.

The political system designed by the elite, effective as long as society remained passive, began to reveal its weaknesses once new actors made their voices heard. In 1890, the first crack in the system occurred when a dissident faction that emerged from the establishment itself—headed by university students—encountered unsuspected support from a society battered by economic crisis. It is significant that the principal leaders of the new parties—Leandro N. Alem, Hipólito Yrigoyen, Juan B. Justo, Lisandro de la Torre—had fought together in the 1890 Revolution. This blow hurt the profoundly divided political regime, which for three or four years foundered, incapable of finding a suitable response to a challenge progressively more clearly delineated. Around 1895, following a pair of rebellions that were put down and through the efforts of Carlos Pellegrini, the regime's "great operator" in politics, the political establishment recovered its balance, a balance that General Roca consolidated when he reached the presidency for the second time in 1898. Nonetheless, some holdovers were not reabsorbed by the oligarchic regime: the Socialist Party, whose base was the working class, and the *Unión Cívica Radica* (UCR), a political movement still seeking its constituency.

Once the political agitation had passed, Radicalism survived for several years in a state of latency. In 1905, it attempted a revolutionary uprising with both civilian and military supporters, but failed. The attempt had, however, an enormous propagandistic effect, especially because it broke out at a moment when the political regime found itself once again afflicted by a deep division. The origins of this division lay in the incidental rupture between the regime's two leaders, Roca and Pellegrini, but there were deeper divisions. Thus, despite the failure of the 1905 uprising and the harsh repression unleashed against it, the UCR began to grow, to develop its network of party committees, and to incorporate new social groups who had their first political experiences: young professionals, doctors, lawyers, merchants, businesspeople, and, in the rural areas, many small farmers. All these groups made up the world of those who had successfully traversed the first stages of social mobility but who found the doors closed for the exercise of a citizenship that, together with its specifically political dimension, had another dimension entailing social recognition.

Radicalism's program—whose heart was full compliance with the Constitution, the sanctity of the vote, and a certain morality in public life—expressed those common interests, limited but precise. To implement the recommended principles, the UCR, like the Socialist Party, had an organic charter and party statutes, although its leading personalities, the majority of whom had emerged in public life in the 1890 Revolution, always exercised a decisive influence. Above all, Radicalism had a powerful weapon with which to confront what it called "the regime," regarded as "treacherous and discredited." That weapon was "the cause," defined by its intransigence, that is, the refusal to accept any compromise or agreement, a position that explains its policy of electoral abstention. The UCR thus refused to contemplate the eventual establishment of a party system in which the parties alternate and share power and, identifying itself as synonymous with the Nation, demanded the complete removal of the regime that had been constructed on the foundations of the *unicato*. Certainly electoral abstention—perhaps the clearest expression of the incapacity of the political regime to accommodate society's demands—made things easier for the ruling elite, but in the long run the moral condemnation proved effective.

The tensions that society was experiencing, which expressed its growing complexity, and the number of legitimate concerns striving to be heard, appeared more violent and threatening than they really were because of the government's scant ability to make room for them and to find an appropriate space for negotiation. Feeling challenged by the extreme form of their

protests, many leaders opted for a harsh response: to single out "foreign minorities," to ignore, repress, and also to maintain and safeguard privileges.
This is what President Manuel J. Quintana (who succeeded Roca) did
when he put down the 1905 uprising. This position became increasingly attractive, not only because of the magnitude of the societal challenge but also
because of the doubts of the ruling elites and the growing realization of their
illegitimacy, which caused divisions in their ranks and weakened their position, allowing those who urged reform to make advances. Pellegrini's defection to the side of the reformers, at the end of Roca's second presidency, was
a decisive turning point, as was the determination of President Figueroa Alcorta, who assumed the presidency in 1906, to use all the instruments of state
power to dismantle the machine assembled by Roca and also to make possible the election of Roque Sáenz Peña as president in 1910. The most notorious weapons of the old regime were employed in the cause of a transformation that, on adopting the arguments of Radicalism, sought to make politics
more transparent, incorporating the population as a whole in the electoral
process. Proposals for a secret ballot, safeguarded with voter registration lists
verified with the military conscription roll, were intended to avoid any
government interference in elections, whereas the mandatory vote, which
Sáenz Peña translated into the exhortation: "The people must want to vote!"
was meant to incorporate the masses into citizenry status. The masses, nevertheless, despite the preachings of Radicals and Socialists, demonstrated no
great interest in voting.

In addition, electoral reform established the representation of majorities
and minorities, by a proportion of two to one. Those who drafted the bill
were absolutely convinced that the parties representing traditional interests would win a majority with no problem and that minority representation would fall to the new parties—above all the UCR and perhaps the
Socialist Party—who would thus become incorporated into the system and
share the responsibilities. Such a conviction was founded on the simultaneous
decision by a group of reformers to change its own political practices, eliminating the electoral machines that until then had operated—whose archetype
figure was the legendary Cayetnao Ganghi, a political boss from the federal
capital who carried a suitcase full of voter registration cards—and to incorporate everywhere into the political competition figures of sufficient social and

intellectual stature to attract votes without resorting to fraud. The task, in a word, was to eradicate criollo politics and to establish a party of "the noteworthy," an undertaking favored without doubt by the mandatory vote, which would help to break the political bosses' machines that had heretofore been dominant.

After the 1912 reform law passed, the first elections provided a great surprise for those who had designed the reforms. Although the traditional groups who were beginning to be called the Conservatives won in many provinces—and there the governments found a way to continue to wield influence—the Radicals triumphed in Santa Fe and the federal capital, with the Socialists winning second place there. The prospect of victory mobilized many to vote for Radicalism, which in those years became a mass party with a network of committees and ward bosses, imbued with many of the practices of "creole politics." Hipólito Yrigoyen, a mysterious figure who never spoke in public but who was a tireless backroom politician, became a leader of national stature. To confront him, the Conservatives attempted to organize a solid party apparatus on a national scale like the Radical Party, but based on different groups and provinces. Lisandro de la Torre—previously the founder of a "new" party, Santa Fe's *Liga del Sur,* was the candidate of the neoconservative party emblematically called the *Partido Demócrata Progresista.* The success of the undertaking was ever more doubtful, however; many leaders, headed by the governor of the province of Buenos Aires, Marcelino Ugarte, were suspicious about the project of political reform, all the more so behind the leadership of a profoundly liberal leader such as de la Torre. These leaders preferred to propose their own alternative. With the Conservatives divided, the Radicals—who had to grapple with their own divisions—won a narrow victory in an election that, in 1916, inaugurated a markedly new stage in politics and society.

two

The Radical Governments, 1916–1930

Hipólito Yrigoyen served as president from 1916 to 1922, the year that Marcelo T. de Alvear succeeded him in the presidency. In 1928, Yrigoyen was reelected, only to be deposed by a military revolt on September 6, 1930. It would be another sixty-one years before an elected president would peacefully transfer power to his successor. Thus, these twelve years in which democratic institutions began to function normally turned out to be an exceptional period in the long run.

Even though both Yrigoyen and Alvear were Radicals and had shared in the party's many struggles, the two presidents were very different; even more different were the images that had been built around them. That of Yrigoyen was contradictory from the start. For some, he—the model of honesty and rectitude—had come to unmask the ignominious regime and to begin a process of "renewal." There were even those who saw him as a secular saint. For others, he was the ignorant and demagogic politician, an expression of democracy's worst vices. Alvear on the other hand was identified, for better or worse, with the great presidents of the old regime, and his political style assimilated the vices and virtues of the latter.

However different their two personal styles may have been, both had to confront similar problems. Above all, each faced the double challenge of establishing the country's new democratic institutions on solid ground and leading through new avenues of representation and negotiation the demands for social reform, which Radicalism in some ways had assumed responsibility for. This reformist impulse was not exclusive to Argentina. In Uruguay it had its expression since 1904 in President José Batlle y Ordóñez, and in Chile since 1920 in the figure of Arturo Alessandri. In Mexico, with much more dramatic consequences, the revolution that erupted in 1910 and was consolidated in 1917 similarly undertook a deep transformation of the state and society. Other reformist movements, such as the Peruvian *Alianza Popular Revolucionaria Americana* (APRA), though they did not prevail, shook up some of the oligarchic regimes and dictatorships that predominated in Latin America. In all these cases, the demand for political participation was linked to improvements in the situation of various social sectors. That mandate and that public will for reform, which doubtless characterized Radicalism and had emerged during the previous period of economic expansion, had to evolve in circumstances markedly different and infinitely more complex than anyone could have imagined. The First World War especially changed all the variables of reality: the economy, politics, society, and culture. It was not clear whether Radicalism, confronted with the new situation, had the answers or even was prepared to think about possible solutions.

The war itself constituted a challenge and posed problems difficult to resolve. At first, Yrigoyen followed the policy of Victorino de la Plaza, his predecessor in the presidency: a "benevolent neutrality" toward the Allies, which presupposed the continuation of trade with traditional clients and also providing them with credits to help finance their purchases. In 1917, Germany began to attack neutral commercial shipping with its dreaded submarines, forcing the United States to declare war, a war in which the latter attempted to drag along with it the Latin American countries. Argentina had traditionally resisted the appeals to Pan-Americanism, a doctrine that assumed an affinity of interests between the United States and its Latin American neighbors. But the sinking of three merchant ships by the Germans mobilized a broad current of public opinion in favor of breaking off relations with Germany, a policy advocated by the United States and enthusiastically supported by the newspapers *La Nación* and *La Prensa*.

Opinions were divided in a peculiar way. The army—whose professional training was German—was sympathetic to Germany, while the navy aligned itself with Great Britain. The Conservative opposition was generally in favor of breaking off relations, as were most of the Socialists, though after April 1917 a breakaway faction among the latter adhered to neutrality, following the Soviet Union's line. The Radicals were divided on the question, presaging future splits. Outstanding leaders such as Leopoldo Melo and Alvear supported England and France, whereas Yrigoyen, almost stubbornly, defended a neutrality that, if it did not make him an enemy of the Allies, distanced him from the United States. Yrigoyen in fact demonstrated various degrees of hostility toward the United States. In 1919, he ordered a warship to salute the pavilion of the Dominican Republic, a country then under occupation by U.S. marines, and in 1920, he opposed President Wilson's blueprint for the organization of the League of Nations. Yrigoyen also proclaimed October twelfth, the anniversary of Columbus's discovery of the New World, as *Día de la Raza*, thereby opposing Pan-Americanism with the image of a Hispanic America that excluded Anglo-Saxon neighbors.

This decision had a powerful symbolic content that resonated with a widespread sensibility in society, somewhat diffuse but deeply rooted. Anti-North American sentiment had been growing since 1898, when the Cuban War had marked the beginning of a strong phase of U.S. expansionism and had led to a reaction in the form of a Latin American identity. In this sentiment, traditional, advanced, and progressive attitudes were mixed. José Enrique Rodó, a writer of enormous influence, had identified the United States with materialism in his *Ariel* and contrasted it with Hispanic-American spiritualism. Yrigoyen joined those who—distancing themselves from the reigning cosmopolitanism—found Latin American identity in the common Hispanic roots; others distinguished between the predatory "filibustering" of the Yankees and the more tolerable imperialism, discreet and civilizing, of the British. Among other groups, anti-North Americanism was tied to socialist ideas, as with Manuel Ugarte, who in 1924 wrote *La Patria Grande*. Support for a militant Latin American unity against the Yankee aggressor was strengthened by the Mexican Revolution. In 1922, on the visit of the Mexican writer and social critic José Vasconcelos, José Ingenieros and other progressive intellectuals urged a "Latin American Union" that would take up the anti-imperialist sentiments present in another movement that resonated throughout Latin America: the University Reform.

Social Crisis and New Stability

In the highly symbolic and declamatory realm, the Radical government provided original answers, satisfying new expectations. Yet the same did not occur when it confronted more concrete problems, such as those that the First World War unleashed in society. Social conditions, which were already complicated at the moment the war erupted, grew worse because of difficulties in foreign trade and the withdrawal of foreign capital. In the cities, there was inflation; real salaries lagged behind—indeed those of government employees suffered a decline—and unemployment was high. The war hurt agricultural exports, especially of corn, and in the rural areas it aggravated the already greatly deteriorated situation of small farmers and farm workers. Thus a climate conducive to social conflict was established; it remained latent as long as conditions were adverse for the workers, but fully manifested itself after 1917, when signs of economic recovery began to appear. Then began a brief but violent cycle of social conflict that reached a high point in 1919 and lasted until 1922–23.

This wave of protest unfolded as it did elsewhere in the world at that time, first echoing the mobilizations surrounding the 1917 Russian Revolution and then the revolutionary movements that erupted when the war was barely over, in Germany, Italy, and Hungary. The impression that worldwide revolution was imminent served to a certain extent as an inspiration for the workers, but the propertied classes were even more influenced by the specter. Revolution and counter-revolution had a symbiotic relationship, and both combined to inflict a mortal wound to liberal democracy. In the midst of the crisis of values unleashed after the war, liberal democracy was questioned by different political movements and ideologies, ranging from outright dictatorships—such as that established in Spain in 1923 by General Primo de Rivera—to the new authoritarian experiments with a popular base, such as that begun in Italy in 1922 by Benito Mussolini, whose novel character exercised a true fascination for many.

Strikes began to multiply throughout 1917 and 1918, driven above all by the big transport unions, the Maritime Workers Union (*Federación Obrera Marítima*) and the Railroad Workers Union (*Federación Obrera Ferrocarrilera*), whose strength was enhanced by their ability to paralyze the harvest shipments, a tactic they used sparingly but with intelligence. Led by the group of syndicalist union leaders who directed the FORA (*Federación Obrera Regional Argentina*) of the Ninth Congress (to distinguish it from the anarchist FORA), the strikes were successful, thanks largely to the government's changed attitude that eschewed mere repression and persuaded the maritime and railroad companies to accept arbitration. Thus a union strategy that combined confrontation and negotiation coincided with a government strategy that, by simply not resorting to violent repression, created a new balance of forces and placed the state in a position to arbitrate between labor and capital.

The initial successes strengthened the position of this syndicalist FORA, whose membership increased notably in the following years, and established the hegemony of the government strategy of limited confrontation. Nevertheless, the government's predisposition to negotiate was not manifested in all cases. As David Rock noted, the policy seemed directed mainly to the workers in the federal capital—potential *Unión Cívica Radica* (UCR) voters in a district that the Radicals bitterly contested with the Socialists—but did not extend to either the unions with a majority of members who were foreigners or to the workers in the province of Buenos Aires. Thus, the 1918 strike of meatpacking workers, who were overwhelmingly foreigners, was dealt with by using the traditional methods of repression, firings, and strike-breakers. Such methods were also used that same year in the railroad workers' strike, an action that went beyond accepted limits and threatened the shipment of that year's harvest.

Both the syndicalists and the government had very little room in which to maneuver, and the dynamic of social conflict was even more restricted throughout 1919, when a wave of strikes reached its culmination. In January of that year, as a result of a strike at the Vasena metallurgical plant in the working-class neighborhood of Nueva Pompeya, a series of violent incidents took place between the strikers and the police, who abandoned a hands-off policy and unleashed a harsh repression. There were deaths on both sides, and soon the violence spread. A series of unplanned and spontaneous strikes that lacked clear objectives caused the city to be a no-man's land for a week, until the army undertook a full-scale repression. The army counted on the collaboration of groups of armed civilians, organized out of the *Círculo Naval*, who proceeded to persecute Jews and Catalans, regarded as Bolsheviks and anarchists, respectively. At that time, the government could still resort to its contacts with the Socialists and members of the leadership of the FORA to work out an agreement to end the initial strike at the Vasena factory, as well as to negotiate the cessation of a long yet pacific strike of the maritime workers' union simultaneously occurring.

The so-called Tragic Week galvanized the workers of the city and the entire country. Far from declining, the number and intensity of strikes increased throughout 1919. There were numerous work stoppages in which the protagonists were workers who were not members of unions and who came from the most varied industrial and service activities, among whom the catchword of "general strike" helped with identification and unification. This agitation coincided with a new upsurge in rural protest. Small farmers, led since 1912 by the *Federación Agraria Argentina,* demanded better terms in their contracts and undertook new strikes, driven by the difficult conditions created by the war. Their mobilizations coincided with those of the farm workers (*jornaleros*) who labored in the fields and small rural towns. This group was usually mobilized by the anarchists, and the small farmers sought to differentiate themselves clearly from the protests of the farm workers. Despite the fact that the Radicals had sympathized with the farmers in 1912, the government was frosty to their demands and in 1919 accused them of being "maximalists," unleashing a harsh repression against them.

The year 1919 marks a turning point in government policy toward these protest movements. Until then, a rather benevolent and tolerant attitude, complemented by a policy of refraining from the classic methods of repression, such as sending troops, firings, and hiring strikebreakers, had sufficed to permit an outlet for the protest of accumulated grievances and to balance the scales, heretofore heavily weighted in favor of business. Yrigoyen's actions possibly combined, together with much political calculation, a greater sensitivity to social problems and a belief in the role as arbiter that the state, and perhaps Yrigoyen himself, should assume. But this new attitude failed to find expression in institutions, despite the manifest will to negotiate on the part of the union leaders. The advances realized at the beginning of the century, when the Department of Labor was created and a Labor Code was proposed, were not continued. The president could not devise any more original ideas than to turn to the chief of police as final arbiter, responsible since time immemorial for labor problems. Neither did the congress assume that it should intervene in urban social conflicts, regarding them as merely a matter for the police, even though it did ultimately intervene with the small rural producers. In 1921, congress sanctioned a land tenancy law that took into account most of the demands about contracts, a solution that unquestionably contributed—together with a return to agricultural prosperity—to quieting the demands of those who increasingly regarded themselves as small rural businesspeople.

Following the events of 1919 and under strong pressure exerted by some of the reconstituted and galvanized propertied sectors, the government abandoned its flirtation with reform and returned to the classic mechanisms of repression, now in collaboration with a right-wing paramilitary organization, the *Liga Patriótica* (Patriotic League). Such repression was even extended in 1921 to the Maritime Workers' Union, the union with which Yrigoyen had established the strongest ties. By then, for various reasons, the strike wave had petered out in the great cities, although it continued in more distant and less visible parts of the country: in the *quebracho* enclave economy that the British company *La Forestal* had established in northern Santa Fe and its Las Palmas counterpart in southern Chaco, as well as in the rural zones of Patagonia. In those places, the impersonal and unpredictable effects of the economic conjuncture, exploited by the actions of greedy and unregulated companies to the detriment of the workers, caused great strike movements to break out between 1919 and 1921. The government authorized them to be put down by force through bloody exercises in military repression, which attained a justified notoriety, as in the case of Patagonia.

The experience of 1919 had profound effects on the propertied classes. Defeated in 1916, they at first retained a great deal of institutional power, albeit a power that Yrigoyen slowly undermined, and they held onto all of their social prominence. Yet they were on the defensive, with neither ideas nor a strategy for dealing with a political and social panorama that displeased them but that they knew had been legitimized by democracy. In 1919, the specter of social revolution rudely awakened them. The *Liga Patriotica* founded during the agitated days of January 1919 was the first expression of their reaction. In it came together groups of the most diverse nature: the *Asociacion del Trabajo* (an owners' organization that provided strikebreakers); the elite's private clubs such as the Jockey Club; military groups (the *Liga* was organized in the *Círculo Naval*); and the representatives of foreign companies. Conservatives and Radicals were in agreement and mingled together during the *Liga's* first stages—the *Liga's* president, Manuel Carlés, drifted back and forth between the two parties during his lifetime—and the state lent the *Liga* unequivocal support through the police. Most notably, the *Liga* demonstrated the ability in that annus mirabilis to mobilize vast contingents of society, recruited from the middle classes, on behalf of the defense of order and property as well as of a truculent vindication of patriotism and nationality, threatened by foreign infiltration. Also noteworthy was the *Liga's* ability to organize great numbers of "brigades," which assumed the task of imposing order through force—subsequently very actively in the rural setting—and to pressure the government. The government probably took into account the magnitude of the forces polarized around the *Liga* when in the course of 1919 it made a subtle but decisive turnabout in its social policies.

The right had new momentum and a compelling, although still somewhat vague, argument against democracy. Willingly or not, Yrigoyen was suspected of subverting public order. From that point on, there appeared in the country a panoply of the ideological and political tendencies that then circulated widely in the counter-revolutionary world. The *Liga* proclaimed its causes to be those of order and the fatherland. The Catholics combined a social philosophy—capable of competing with the left—with an antiliberal integralism that it began to disseminate through its Courses on Catholic Culture, which were later crystallized in the magazine *Criterio,* established in 1928. Young intellectuals such as the Irazusta brothers disseminated the ideas of the French fascist Charles Maurras and of Leopoldo Lugones who proclaimed the arrival of "the hour of the sword." There were undoubtedly differences among their positions, some of no small consequence (Lugones, for example, was outspokenly anti-Christian). These differences, however, did not concern their audiences, who probably did not take seriously much of what they heard but who took from all the clamor a common message: a rejection of social mobilization and a critical view of liberal democracy.

Alvear's coming to power in 1922 partly tranquilized the propertied classes. The majority trusted once again in the virtues of a liberal and patrician democracy, but the new rightist discourse continued to circulate on the fringes of their ranks. At the same time, other powerful institutions began gradually to invigorate the new movement, to unify its actions, and to endow them with legitimacy while recruiting supporters beyond the propertied classes. The *Liga Patriótica* devoted itself to a "practical humanitarianism," establishing schools for workers and mobilizing the "señoritas" of high society. Much more important was the action of the Catholic Church. In 1919, at the height of the crisis, the Church organized the Great National Collection for purposes of mobilizing the rich and winning over the poor. That year, all the Catholic organizations operating in society, diverse and though with different agendas, were unified in the Argentine Popular Catholic Union, a layperson's army commanded by bishops and parish priests who organized a fullscale war against socialism. They competed head to head in the creation of libraries and soup kitchens, organizing lectures and undertaking development and charity works. In charity work, the activists who had been recruited in the highest social circles became aware of their lofty redemptive mission. Revealingly, the Church—ever more opposed to democratic institutions— dismissed any possibility of forming a political party.

The army, which had been organized since early in the century along strictly professional lines, also finally began to interest itself in the course of political events, perhaps from annoyance at the way Yrigoyen had used it to open and close the escape valve of social control and also concerned by the president's use of political criteria in handling the army, specifically promotions. Distrust of Yrigoyen clearly created conditions that made the army receptive to the general criticisms of the democratic system, heard ever more loudly in society.

The antiliberalism that nourished all of these sentiments turned out to be effective as a weapon, unifying discourse, and battle standard. But the reconstitution of the political right did not end here. No one was under the illusion that things could return to what they had been in 1912. The world had changed greatly since the First World War. It was necessary to discuss Argentina's place in the world, the state's role in social conflicts, how to link together the various interests of the propertied classes, and many other questions that Yrigoyen's government seemed in no rush to find new solutions for. The *Liga Patriótica* organized conferences in which representatives of the most diverse social sectors debated all these questions, as they did in the publications of the Argentine Social Museum or the *Revista de Economía Argentina* founded by Alejandro Bunge in 1918. A different Argentina required new ideas, and in that sense the debate was intense and not confined to the right. In such an environment, some young militants of the Socialist Party—with a solid Marxist formation on economic and social questions—

even thought that the party's platform was too narrow, thereby beginning a dissidence that resulted in 1928 in the founding of the breakaway *Partido Socialista Independiente.*

To what extent were the right's fears justified? The strike wave that culminated between 1917 and 1921 had been formidable but had not been guided by the explicit purpose to subvert the established order. Rather, the strikes expressed, in an undoubtedly violent manner, the depth of the grievances accumulated during a prolonged period of difficulties in the opulent Argentina of those years. Moreover, those who could claim to be the leaders of the protests, those who favored this subversion—the anarchists and then the Communists—had only marginal influence. The strongest and most influential leadership and direction were exercised by the syndicalists and the Socialists; both fought as much for limited reform in a social order whose basic characteristics they accepted as they did for finding the means and issues whereby to negotiate the conflicts. The syndicalists, opposed to working through political parties, placed their bets on negotiations between the unions and the state, a road that the state had proposed since before 1916. This approach, adopted by Yrigoyen, had to be abandoned in the upheavals of 1919, though it remained an inclination that reappeared dramatically at the end of the Second World War.

The Socialist Party—founded in 1896, with a considerable electoral following in the federal capital—was also far from advocating drastic positions. Adhering to the prevailing European trends, socialism was seen as the culmination and perfecting of liberal democracy, as the final stage of a modernization that would sweep away the obstacles of tradition. Among these traditions, the Socialists singled out what they called "creole politics," in which they lumped together traditional conservatism along with Radicalism, which they vigorously opposed. The Socialist Party demonstrated little ability to establish itself in social protest movements. A few successes among the small farmers of the *Federación Agraria Argentina* were insufficient to compensate for the party's negligible influence among trade unionists, who, even if they voted for the Socialists, preferred to follow the syndicalists. Socialism played all its cards in elections; in the federal capital, it secured an important number of votes with which it successfully competed against the Radicals, albeit at the cost of watering down the specific concerns of the workers with a broad ensemble of demands, including those of the middle class. This situation left an open space on the left, which various groups competed to occupy, especially after the tremors of the war and the Russian Revolution. Pacifists and partisans of the Third International and of the Soviet Union finally joined forces in the Communist Party. The Communists had little influence during the 1920s, although they garnered the sympathy of many intellectuals. Other progressive tendencies, of Leninist inspiration, were also expressed in the anti-imperialism of the period and in the University Reform movement.

The Socialists bet on legislative action and on the possibility of fashioning congress into a representative forum. Yet the party had an almost congenital inability to establish alliances and agreements; although it spearheaded some legislative reforms, it did not manage to fashion itself into a vigorous political force, capable of counterbalancing a reconstituted right or even of identifying the central elements of the approaching conflict. The Socialists other long-range bet was the uplifting of the working class, who, it was believed, would become enlightened through contact with science: thus the Socialists' intense educational endeavors through cultural centers, libraries, lectures, theater and choral groups, and the *Sociedad Luz*. The diffusion of certain Socialist endeavors in the great urban centers visibly testifies to the changes that, once the crisis years were surmounted, the workers and society as a whole were experiencing.

The end of intense labor struggles, the decline in union affiliations, and the weakening of the *Unión Sindical Argentina* attest to the waning of social conflict. The *Unión Ferroviaria,* founded in 1922 and transformed into the undisputed head of the labor movement, expressed the new tone of trade-union action: a highly unified union, strongly led in a centralized fashion, negotiating in a systematic and institutionalized manner with the authorities, abandoning the strike as a tactic, and in the process obtaining notable successes. For its part, the state demonstrated its desire to make advances in social legislation—the majority of which were passed during Alvear's presidency—which included such measures as full recognition of the trade unions, retirement plans for commercial employees and railroad workers' unions, regulation of woman and child labor, and establishment of the first of May—turned into a conciliatory Labor Day—as a national holiday.

Beyond the difficult moments and upheavals, Argentine society had experienced profound changes that matured during the war and that explain the state's conciliatory attitude. Although after the conflicts immigration began anew, the population had already become substantially naturalized. Argentine children replaced immigrant parents; immigrant societies began to recede in the face of other groups in which people, without associating by country of origin, grouped together for specific activities; and the "national question" that had been such a concern during the centennial celebrations began to fade away.

This shift was reflected in popular culture. The systematic efforts of the public schools had created a population that was highly literate and with it a new reading public, one perhaps not very discriminating, but avid for publications. The great newspapers, aided by technological advances in Linotype and the rotary press, expanded their readerships. In 1913, the newspaper *Crítica,* which catered to this new reading public and at the same time shaped it, revolutionized journalistic practices, as happened again in 1928 with *El Mundo.* The need for information and entertainment was satisfied by magazines that followed in the tracks of a tradition of general-interest publications such as *Caras y Caretas* and culminated in *Leoplán* or by specialized magazines such as *El Gráfico, Billiken, Tit Bis,* or *El Hogar.* In the years following the war, weekly installment novels—a genre that wavered between romantic and mildly erotic—enjoyed great success, whereas the more sophisticated cultural and political needs were fulfilled first by the Spanish editions of *Siempre* and then by the *Claridad* or *Tor* collections. In a society with an avid reading public, these publications were effective vehicles for diverse cultural and political messages, which also circulated by means of popular libraries and lectures. Many people read for entertainment. Others sought to prepare themselves to take advantage of the multiple new work opportunities, but many others read to lay claim to a cultural heritage—so varied that it included everyone from Plato to Dostoyevsky—which until then had been the patrimony of the elite and propertied classes.

The expansion of a reading culture was part of a process of individual social mobility in a society essentially characterized by growth and opportunity. The fruits of such a society were its vast middle sectors, among whose members could be seen the results of a successful venture in social ascent: the established small farmers, who identified themselves as small rural businesspeople, the small merchants, and the urban industrialists, among whom emerged some important names or great fortunes. Alongside them were a mass of employees, professionals, teachers, and *doctores;* the title of "doctor" continued to represent the culmination, in perhaps the second or third generation, of those professions in which wealth could not be separated from prestige.

Perhaps for that reason, the university loomed as an important issue for this society in the process of expansion. The University Reform movement—a movement that erupted in Córdoba in 1918 and spread throughout the country and all of Latin America—was one expression of the country's transformation. The universities, whose chief purpose was to train professionals, were at the time socially elitist and emphasized scholastic rote learning. Many young students wanted the university to open its doors, to allow them to participate in its administration, to remove professorial cliques, to establish standards of academic excellence and scientific modernization, and to put itself at the service of society's problems. Intense student agitation coincided with the toughest moments of the social crisis between 1918 and 1922, to such a degree that many believed that the student agitation was linked to the social crisis. Others noted that the students' demands were moderate. The reformers received the important backing of Yrigoyen and managed in many cases to have student representatives incorporated into the governing of universities, as well as to have more traditional professors removed, and new curriculum and teaching methods introduced. They also developed a long-range program, which since then has served as a banner of student political activity, an activism that was henceforth the preparation for a political career. University reform was, more than a theory, a sentiment, the expression of a movement of social and intellectual *apertura,* which served to agglutinate the most diverse ideologies, from Marxism to idealism, but which drew above all on a still diffuse Latin American anti-imperialism and on the Russian Revolution, with its appeal to the masses. It was tied to other Latin American sources, creating a sort of pan-Latin American student brotherhood and injecting a new and vibrant current into progressive political movements.

The University Reform also expressed some concerns that society at large was particularly sensitive about. Despite the fact that by the 1920s social protest movements were in decline and a marked social mobility discouraged the class conflict then prevalent in Europe, there was a strong reformist sentiment in society. Diverse experiences of cooperation and change came together—from small farmers grouped in their cooperatives to development societies in new urban neighborhoods—which drew inspiration from socially progressive intellectual currents in Europe and set the tone for a reflective and critical attitude toward society and its problems. This attitude took a concrete form in a certain idea of social justice, probably inspired in turn by more traditional sources—such as the Church—but equally concerned with the necessity of adapting the country's institutions to a changing society. The idea was still vague and did not take a concrete and effective form in political representation, yet it also circulated in the world of the workers. The workers themselves, influenced by social mobility and the popular images such mobility created, increasingly identified less with that segregated sector of society that, at the beginning of the century, had so troubled the intellectuals. It was not easy to distinguish, outside their work, the railroad worker from the office worker or the farmer's daughter from the middle-class schoolteacher. In big cities and in prosperous rural areas, society was characterized more by fluidity than by drastic differences.

The aspiration for individual social ascent and social reform was just one aspect of this new culture that characterized these popular sectors, both middle and working class. Changes in lifestyles were also molding new ideas and attitudes that turned out to be lasting. Having access to home ownership changed the idea of domestic life and placed the woman—often liberated from the obligation of working outside the home—at the head of the family, a family that soon fraternized around the radio receiver. In a complementary development, young women aspired to be able to work, whether in a store or an office, to study, and also to enjoy greater sexual freedom. A certain economic comfort, and the steady reduction of the workday—which together with Sunday began to include the so-called English Saturday on which workers worked a half-day but were paid a full day's wage—increased the amount of free time. This fact explains the success of libraries, lectures, and public readings and also the development of a wide range of cultural offerings to fill such leisure time.

Popular theater had reached its peak by around 1910. In the cities, theater houses had multiplied both in the downtown districts and in the neighborhoods. Actors like Florencio Parravicini were perhaps the first artists to achieve widespread popularity. After the war, tastes turned from the popular theater, or *sainete,* to the new vaudeville shows with cancan dancers and songs. Polite society finally accepted the tango, stripped of any traces of its origins in the brothels. The tango and the phonograph made tango singers popular; sheet music, combined with the unfailing piano, firmly established the tango in middle-class homes. At this time, the popularity of such tango singer-songwriters as Enrique Delfino, Santos Discépolo, and Carlos Gardel was established, although Gardel achieved widespread fame only in the following decade through movies that were filmed abroad. Films—silent until 1929—exercised a strong attraction; movie theaters proliferated in the cities, and the popular culture being fashioned, once perhaps markedly *criollo,* drew on new international influences.

Thus, the new means of communication increased their influence on the lifestyles, attitudes, and values of this growing society. They also influenced attitudes toward sports, associated since the beginning of the century with a *vitalista* philosophy and hygienic concepts as well as with the pleasure of exercise and fresh air, the importance of which the elite had disseminated in society. The creation of athletic clubs was a characteristic expression of the organizational and community impulses prevalent in society at this time. Bit by bit, some sports activities were transformed into massive spectacles, which the media projected from their original local setting to the entire country. In 1931, the League of Professional Soccer was established, and judging by the words of both the press and the radio, the porteño soccer club added a new element to national identity, perhaps as strong as the patriotic symbols or the figure of Hipólito Yrigoyen. Yet the tendency toward the homogenization of society, around a culture shared by diverse social sectors, was accompanied by an equally significant process of differentiation in the function of various activities.

One manifestation of differentiation was the constitution of an artistic and intellectual world that, although propelled by the growing cultural demands of society, defined a lifestyle all its own. As the writer and critic David Viñas explained, unlike the turn-of-the-century "gentleman writers," these artists and writers felt themselves professionals, and some of them thoroughly were. They had their own meeting places—cafes, newspaper offices, art galleries, and literary reviews—and their own critical standards to celebrate excellence and lambaste mediocrity. Since 1924, Buenos Aires had an iconoclastic and combative "vanguard." In that year, Petorutti brought cubism, Ernest Ansermet introduced Impresssionist music, and the literary review *Martín Fierro* was founded. *Martín Fierro'*s avant-garde *ultraísta* aesthetic attracted many new writers, eager to criticize the older generation. Many others embraced the cause of social commitment and the utopia of Communism, and among other groups—identified as the "Florida" and "Boedo" schools—there began a sharp polemic. The points of agreement and friendly exchanges were probably greater than was their confrontation, but intellectuals began to practice in these years a new style of discussion in which the local reality became inseparable from that of Europe, the United States, and the Soviet Union itself, the last of which was perhaps more idealized than understood.

The Economy in a Triangular World

With the First World War—much more than the crisis of the 1930s—a stage in the history of the Argentine economy came to an end: that of relatively easy growth on the basis of what had been a clear model of economic development. From 1914 onward, the country entered a more complex world that required a defter handling of economic policy, and in which the future was relatively uncertain, to such a point that doubts and pessimism predominated. Only in a few circles were such feelings translated into a challenge to search for new solutions.

The war revealed sharply a long-standing weakness: the Argentine economy's vulnerability—whose engine was exports—the dependence on the importation of foreign capital and labor, as well as the continued expansion of the agricultural frontier. The war affected both the size and the price of the country's exports and ushered in a trend toward deterioration in the terms of trade. Agricultural exports first suffered the problem of a lack of transport. Yet with the ending of the conflict, something even more ominous loomed: an excess in supply throughout the world and the existence of permanent agricultural surpluses that caused every government to protect its producers. Even more serious was the fall in the export of livestock products after 1921. During the war, foreign capital was repatriated; at the war's termination, it was apparent that the times of easy foreign investment were over, because Great Britain and other European countries were not in a condition to make investments. Their place was taken by North American bankers, such as J. P. Morgan, who were also committed to loans to Europe. Capital flows were thus conditioned by the international economic situation. Argentina dramatically experienced the effects of the European conjuncture. It lived in a state of severe crisis between 1913 and 1917, recovered between 1917 and 1921 (especially because its wartime commerce stabilized), suffered the jolt of postwar adjustment between 1921 and 1924, and enjoyed a period of tranquillity during the "golden years" until 1929, which were sufficient to set the general optimistic tone of the decade.

The most important novelty was the presence of the United States, which, here as in other parts of the world, occupied areas left open by European countries, to a greater or lesser extent all defeated in the war. The economic expansion of the United States in the 1920s was revealed first by a strong surge in the export of automobiles, trucks, and tires—for which Argentina became one of its principal markets—as well as phonographs, radios, and agricultural and industrial machinery. To ensure U.S. presence in a tempting market as well as to surmount eventual trade barriers, the large industrial firms—General Motors, General Electric, Colgate, among others—undertook important investments, which at first were intended only to locally assemble imported parts. U.S. firms also made inroads into public-service companies such as electricity and streetcars as owners and suppliers, particularly for the State Railways, the only ones to grow during this period. In contrast with the British investments, and with the exception of agricultural machinery, the North Americans did not contribute to generating exports and therefore foreign earnings. Moreover, because the possibility of placing Argentina's traditional exports in the United States were remote (despite some initial expectations), this new relationship created a strong imbalance in the balance of payments, which became an insoluble problem.

On the other hand, the old "special" relationship with Great Britain continued at a basic level: purchases of grains and meat, which the British paid for with the profits obtained through the sale of railroad equipment, coal, and textiles and with the earnings made by the railroads and companies in other services. The British connection's insufficiencies were ever more apparent. The imports were expensive, Great Britain could not supply new consumer demands, and British capital was incapable of promoting the transformations that the North Americans were propelling. At the same time, however, Argentina lacked alternative buyers, especially for meat, especially after 1921. Increasingly under siege by the North Americans—who already before the war had supplanted them in the meatpacking sector—the British could pressure the Argentine government by threatening to shift purchases to Commonwealth countries, an option demanded by those at home who wished to introduce Great Britain into the new world of protectionism.

In sum, as the historian Arturo O'Connell emphasized, Argentina was part of an international economic triangle but could not strike a balance with its trading partners. To maneuver itself between the United States and Great Britain required a skill that Yrigoyen's government seemed scarcely to have.

Alvear was, in this respect, more imaginative and deft, though his government did not offer a solution for the deeper problems and probably did not have one. Moreover, a special competence was needed to confront crisis situations, when conflicts between the various sides were exacerbated and losses fell on the weakest actors: local producers or those who worked for them. Since 1912, these tensions had been experienced in agriculture; since 1921, they had been felt in a much more sensitive area and one that affected more powerful interests: the livestock sector.

Thanks to sales of canned meat, the final years of the war were excellent, benefiting not only the cattle ranchers of the central zone but also those of the marginal areas and even those who bred the rangier creole stock. The situation changed abruptly in late 1920, when the European governments, who had been stockpiling meat, reduced their purchases, leading to plummeting prices and production. The greatest losses were suffered by the cattle ranchers in distant zones, whereas those who possessed good land for fattening cattle and supplied choice beef for the chilled meat trade—for which a quota was maintained—managed partly to get around the difficulties. The crisis ended by defining the differences in the cattle ranchers' ranks between breeders and fatteners and unleashed conflicts that in bonanza times went unnoticed. The Yrigoyen government reacted slowly and ineffectually to these conflicts. In 1923, because of pressure from breeders and with the support of President Alvear, congress passed a series of laws that protected cattle breeders, to the detriment of both local consumers and the meatpacking industry. The opposition of consumers and their political spokespersons—the Socialists—was of little consequence, but that of the meatpackers was devastating: They cut off their purchases and in a few months forced the government to suspend the sanctioned laws.

This episode proved the enormous power of the meatpacking industry and of the big cattle ranchers directly associated with them, a power that was soon demonstrated again. In the early years after the war, cattle ranchers indulged in wishful thinking about the possibility of finding a market for their products in the United States—which would have partly solved the problem with the unfavorable balance of payments—but in late 1926 the U.S. government, using as a justification the danger of foot-and-mouth disease, decided to prohibit imports from Argentina. Great Britain wielded a similar threat, forcing terrified ranchers to accept the idea that a return to bilateral trade was the only solution for them and for the country. The *Sociedad Rural,* the organization that represented the interests of the landed elite, then suggested that the North American presence in the economy in general be restricted and launched the slogan "Buy from those who buy from us," which implied defending British imports and investments and having society collectively pay the costs.

Agrarian issues were the source of many concerns, despite the fact that, as a result of the crisis in the livestock sector, there was a notable shift to agriculture. The pampa's agrarian frontier stabilized at some fifty million hectares; grain cultivation increased there enormously, as did the pampa's contribution to exports. Thus began a long period of stability, an economic plateau that did not demonstrate the spectacular growth of the previous period but in which the stagnation and other problems that would be experienced after 1940 were absent. Expansion was extended to the non-pampa zones in which the government, through the efforts of the minister of agriculture Tomás A. Le Bretón, undertook a vigorous colonization campaign that absorbed the excess rural population of the pampean region as well as new migratory currents. In this way, the fruit-growing region of the Río Negro valley, the yerba maté districts of Misiones, and especially the cotton cultivation in the heart of the Chaco became productive areas; the increase in cotton cultivation later had a decisive influence on the future growth of the textile industry.

Observers did not deceive themselves about this period of calm, because apparent to everyone were the limitations established by a world market ever more competitive, the end of the era of natural comparative advantages, the closing of the agricultural frontier, and the rise in land prices. To these factors was added the lack of investments, except in harvest mechanization, which solved the problem of the reduction in the available workforce arising from the steady decline in seasonal "swallow" (*golondrina*) migrants who formerly came to work at harvest time and then returned to Europe. The rules of the game that made it preferable to maintain capital liquidity and shift back and forth between different investment possibilities—practices established in the previous period and deepened by the diversification of the economy that until then had effectively stimulated growth—ceased to fulfill the same function under the new global market conditions. Tulio Halperín Donghi noted the incipient awareness of problems by a society that, on the one hand, was beginning to become interested in industrialization, and, on the other hand, lacked the propensity to do something to confront its problems.

The war had had strongly negative effects on an industry established in the era of great agricultural expansion. Dependent in great measure on imported primary materials and fuels, industry could not take advantage of the natural protection afforded by the conflict. Yet once the war was over, industry embarked on a steady expansion that lasted until 1930 and was characterized by product diversification, thereby reaching new markets. Contemporaries attributed these changes to a great extent to the increase in tariff duties established by Alvear in 1923, though the previously mentioned North American investments were probably the principal factor in that expansion, encouraging local investors in industry as well. In other similar cases, Bunge y Born, the leading grain-exporting firm, established around this time the paint factory Alba and in the following decade the textile plant Grafa. To a large extent, the new industries were equipped with North American technology. As the new industries simultaneously tried to conquer a tempting market and gain a share of the foreign exchange generated by the exports to Great Britain, the local propertied sectors began to diversify into this activity that seemed more dynamic than the traditional activities.

The issue of industry began to find a place in public debate and constituted the discursive core of the then most lucid analyst of the Argentine economy, Alejandro Bunge, the inspiration for Alvear's tariff reform. As Javier Villanueva suggested, perhaps in a limited way such a reform was intended to encourage—through moderate protection—North American investments without increasing conflicts with Great Britain. The British were worried as much about the final destination of the foreign exchange as by the growing competition in some sectors of their established business interests, particularly textiles. In this way, an incipient industrial current added a new element to the central debate over the relationship between Argentina, North America, and Britain. At least for a moment, some saw in industrial growth the possible road of the future, yet such people lacked the influence to make their convictions prevail. The *Unión Industrial Argentina,* the country's most important industrialists' organization, joined the forces proclaiming "Buy from those who buy from us," a slogan that had been coined by the British ambassador.

Neither the agrarian nor the industrial question was the central concern of those in government; their principal preoccupation was with budgetary problems. The war had exposed the precarious finances of the state, sustained basically with customs duties and consumption taxes and buttressed by successive foreign loans. All these sources were sharply curtailed in the two crisis periods that coincided with the advent of the Radical governments, which for various reasons had to deal with growing expenses. Yrigoyen's government first needed funds for its social policies and then for a broad distribution of government jobs, which constituted a principal political weapon in the final years of Yrigoyen's first administration. Since 1922, Alvear had begun to implement a strict orthodox fiscal policy and sharply reduced government spending until, because of the necessities of the internal struggle with *yrigoyenismo,* he had to resort, albeit in a more moderate fashion, to the same distribution of government jobs as his predecessor. As for Yrigoyen, when he returned to power in 1928, he again made frequent use of this practice. In both cases, state spending increased with respect to previous periods, but above all its very nature changed, with investments declining relative to administrative expenses, in which the public employees' payroll weighed heavily.

It was clear that the state had to look for another way to finance its spending. Taking inspiration from similar reforms undertaken in France and England, Yrigoyen proposed in 1918 a personal income tax. Congress practically ignored the bill and failed to act again in 1924 when Alvear insisted on the idea. On the other hand, there was a broad debate about the issue in those circles where the economy's future was being discussed. Alejandro Bunge, an enthusiastic supporter of the idea, devoted generous space in the *Revista de la Economía Argentina* to it. The *Revista* undertook a lofty and scholarly discussion of economic problems and analyzed them from a philosophical perspective that stressed concepts of freedom, equality, and social justice then being debated in Europe. Possibly in the pages of Bunge's review was generated the consensus that allowed the income tax to rapidly become law in 1931, following the onset of the Depression and Yrigoyen's fall. But the reasons for the parliamentary obstruction during Alvear's administration were more pedestrian. The opposition refused to pass any legislation giving the presidency more resources that, it was assumed, would be directed to electoral necessities.

The Difficult Construction of a Democracy

The failed debate on fiscal policy underlined the difficulties in constructing an efficient democratic system in which ideas could be freely debated and where the checks and balances of the various branches of government worked in a suitable fashion. The electoral reform of 1912 proposed simultaneously to broaden the franchise, safeguard freedom of expression, ensure respect for all political tendencies, and exercise control over those in public office. In none of these undertakings were the results altogether successful. With respect to electoral participation, the immigrant masses continued to fail to become naturalized, which meant that the numbers of those eligible to vote who did not vote were equal to or greater than those who did. This problem was resolved only gradually over time and with the ending of immigration. But even among the eligible voters, participation was not overwhelming; in 1912, perhaps because of the novelty effect of free elections granted by the Sáenz Peña Law of that year, participation reached 68 percent in the entire country, but immediately fell to 50 percent, bottoming out in 1924 at 40 percent. Only in 1928—with the plebiscitary nature of Yrigoyen's election—did it recover in spectacular fashion, at the level that henceforth would be maintained, around 80 percent.

Conceded rather than being won, citizenship was slowly built in society. The multiple and diverse associations that crisscrossed the country, established for specific purposes—from urban development groups to rural cooperatives—contributed to the gestation of first-hand experiences with direct participation and to the development of abilities that politics required: the ability to speak and listen, to convince and be persuaded, and above all to compromise. These associations also contributed another important experience: negotiation with public authorities, mediating between society's demands and political power. A similar role was played by party committees and centers that were beginning to densely cover society as electoral participation became a routine.

Elections to a large extent continued to operate the old way. A caudillo distributed favors—all the bigger the more direct his connections with public authorities—and hoped in this way to influence how his beneficiaries voted. Thanks to official support, the Radicals could easily expand this clientilistic network that had been established while they were still in the opposition. The government itself used party committees to implement some of its big social policies, which although they had clear electoral purposes, hinted at a new conception of citizens' rights: subsidies for meat, or the so-called Radical meat, and also for bread and rents. To a certain extent—above all among the Socialists—the party organizations aimed at the education and integration of citizens and their families in a network of integral sociability: job training, entertainment, and culture. But all these contributed to the development of political skills. In this context, new citizens appeared, educated and aware of their rights and obligations, increasingly aware of the political dimension of all activities, so that gradually the gap between society and the state narrowed.

The parties' growth revealed the extent of the new democracy's hold. Only the *Unión Cívica Radical* achieved the dimensions of a modern political party at the national level. Forged in long opposition, and established to confront the old regime, it could function effectively even when far removed from power. Based on an extensive network of local committees, it was organized step by step until reaching its convention and national committee. An organic party charter laid the foundations of its organization, and its doctrine was nothing less than that of the Constitution, as Yrigoyen liked to emphasize. The party also demonstrated a modern preoccupation for tailoring its platform to people's changing demands. Perhaps the most thorough expression of its modernity was its ability to furnish a national political identity, the first and most heartfelt in a country whose common identifying symbols were still few. Yet this modernity rested on some traditional elements. All the complex organizational structure mattered little when compared with Yrigoyen's leadership; the party's followers' identities were expressed through his person. A silent, shy caudillo, who appeared infrequently and almost never spoke in public, he soon began to inspire a personality cult. His portrait was seen everywhere in the country; images of him adorned medals and even *mates* (the drinking gourd used by the popular classes for drinking the yerba mate tea), leading the people to identify the president as an apostle or messiah.

The Socialist Party also had a formal organization, a thick network of committees, and a platform, but lacked national standing; even though the party achieved something of a following in the provinces of Mendoza, Tucumán, and Buenos Aires, almost all of its power was concentrated in the federal capital. There, thanks to the penetration of its network of party committees and its success in offering an alternative to the government in power, it competed inch for inch with Radicalism, often defeating it. The *Partido Demócrata Progresisita,* for its part, took root among the small farmers of southern Santa Fe and Córdoba, as well as in the city of Rosario. Together with issues of agrarian development, it advanced the cause of electoral honesty and gained a small following in the federal capital. The rightist parties were forces only at the provincial level. Although the *Partido Conserrvador* of Buenos Aires province exercised a recognized leadership, and the various parties of the right reached agreement during presidential elections, they did not manage to constitute a stable force at the national level, perhaps because traditionally this had been achieved through presidential authority.

In national elections, the UCR obtained something less than half of the votes, though in 1928, in elections that were a referendum on Yrigoyen, the total approached 60 percent. The Conservatives combined polled between 15 and 20 percent and the Socialists between 5 and 10 percent, with the exception of 1924—the year of the lowest voter turnout—when their total rose to 14 percent. The Progressive Democrats experienced a similar development, although with somewhat smaller numbers. Thus, the UCR was in reality the only party of national standing and the only one to face an opposition, strong but localized, in each of the provinces, including some breakaway groups from its own party, such as San Juan's *bloquismo* and Mendoza's *lencinismo.*

Political participation finally took root and was expressed through the parties, as the 1928 electoral figures and the previous intense politicization of the entire society bear witness, a society at long last making use of democracy. Yet on the other hand, the delicate institutional mechanism that is also a characteristic of democracy never managed to fully establish itself, and all shared responsibility for that failure.

Electoral reform had foreseen an important role for minority parties and congressional limits on executive power. That ideal, with roots that could be traced back to previous institutional practices, competed with a new one that had to be learned by the president and the opposition. Although the government's relations with traditional sectors were initially not bad—five of the new cabinet ministers were members of the *Sociedad Rural*—its relations with the political opposition were difficult from the beginning. Yrigoyen began his government with a congress hostile to him, as were the majority of the provincial governments, and much of his strategy was directed at increasing his negligible power. To win elections, Yrigoyen made generous use of the national budget, distributing public jobs among his *punteros* or ward bosses, although in Buenos Aires competition with the Socialists forced him to employ more modern methods. In 1918, he was successful in obtaining a majority in the chamber of deputies, but the key continued to be control of the provincial governments, decisive actors at election time. Yrigoyen did not hesitate to interdict hostile provinces and then to organize elections in which his candidates triumphed, thereby considerably increasing his power. He never managed, however, to get control of the senate and ran into unforeseen difficulties in the chamber, where opposing legislators began to find allies among many Radicals who did not accept the president's methods.

Yrigoyen created a problem with the congress from the first day of his administration when, discarding the traditional ceremony of reading the presidential address, he sent a brief message to be read by a minor government official. This symbolically demeaned congress and ignored its authority, which Yrigoyen did every time he attempted to control its procedures. The president and his ministers not only did not respect the congress's prerogatives but refused to allow congressional interference in executive affairs. This institutional short-circuit was even more apparent in the federal interdictions of the provinces. During his six years in power, there were nineteen such interdictions, and only one province, Santa Fe, was spared such a measure. Only on four occasions did Yrigoyen request a law to interdict provinces, all governed by Radicals, to intervene in internal party conflicts. On fifteen other occasions, it was done by decree, ignoring congress, to eliminate opposing governments and to "rectify" provincial problems. Such methods, not at all different from those employed by presidents such as Juárez Celman or Figueroa Alcorta during the oligarchic era, were successful. In 1922, the ruling party lost the election in only two provinces.

If Yrigoyen resorted to firmly established practices, which others would soon make use of, his justification was novel. The president had to fulfill a duty and a mission, a "mending," for which he had been elected, and which placed him above institutional procedures. Perhaps for that reason, the "apostle" began to be deified by his followers. Beyond whatever content this "mending" may have had, democratic procedures unquestionably had a difficult time taking root in this climate of permanent authoritarian removals.

It is curious that those who were elected to be custodians of the country's political institutions were the ones who, on other occasions before and after, displayed little respect for democratic procedures. The truth is that both Conservatives and dissident Radicals—the latter led by the able Vicente Gallo—strengthened themselves through their defense of the institutional order. They did so ferociously, together with the Socialists and Progressive Democrats, and even poured into the streets in the stormy year of 1918 to demand their rights. Thus, while Radicalism and its caudillo made a substantial contribution to the incorporation of citizens into the political life—in a style that was at once traditional and modern—they failed not only to strengthen an institutionalized democratic system but also to establish such a system as a value in and of itself among the citizenry.

Like Sáenz Peña, Alvear benefited from the party machinery that brought him to power in 1922 easily and with little opposition. It is possible that his selection by Yrigoyen was intended to ease some tensions with certain opposition sectors in the party whose importance he recognized. But Alvear advanced much further along this path than Yrigoyen had foreseen. In his cabinet, there was only one *yrigoyenista,* his minister of public works. Alvear limited the creation of new public jobs and accepted checks on executive power that were institutionally the preserve of the congress, relations with whom he nurtured with care. Above all, he did not use federal interdictions by decree. The party apparatus at first reacted adversely because the distribution of minor public jobs was the principal tool of local caudillos.

The "people's man" Yrigoyen was contrasted with the "oligarchic" Alvear. Moreover, Alvear relied on the support of those who on distinct occasions had opposed Yrigoyen or had questioned his methods; the followers of the old caudillo soon established a current increasingly more hostile to Alvear's government. In late 1923, Alvear appeared to cast his lot decisively with the anti-Yrigoyen group on nominating Vicente Gallo to be his minister of the interior. Gallo, along with Leopoldo Melo, led the so-called antipersonalist faction opposed to Yrigoyen. Radicalism's split widened in 1924, when two slates of candidates were put forward and two separate parties soon established. The debate was intense. It included everyone from the so-called genuflectors, characterized by their slavish obedience to Yrigoyen, to the "conspirators," a word suggesting that agreements had been reached between the antipersonalists, the Conservatives, and the Socialists. Minister Gallo tried to resort to the old and proven methods for removing the *yrigoyenistas:* giving jobs to supporters and interdicting hostile provincial governments. But Alvear refused to abandon his principles to such a degree. In July 1925, a bill foundered that would have interdicted the province of Buenos Aires, a key piece in Gallo's strategy, and the latter resigned.

From that point on, Alvear remained in the crossfire between the antipersonalists—who could firmly establish themselves only in Santa Fe—and the *yrigoyenistas,* who ran a good election in 1926, winning seats in a congress converted into an arena of combat between the two factions. The polarization was extreme, with dissident provincial sectors such as the strongly populist *lencinismo* in Mendoza or *cantonismo* in San Juan joining the anti-Yrigoyen group, united with their partners only by their hatred of the Radical leader.

The Conservative right was at that time totally engrossed in preventing the return to power of Yrigoyen, whom the right saw as incarnating the worst vices of democracy. Yrigoyen was presented alternately as a social agitator, an authoritarian caudillo, or simply an expression of the crude and incompetent rabble. Such an image was propagated, with different nuances, by *La Nación* and *La Prensa,* and for the general public, by *Crítica,* the latter converted into a leader in the anti-Yrigoyen campaign. For the moment, this opposition did not imply a questioning of democracy, because all were committed to playing the electoral card, uniting in a broad front the forces hostile to the caudillo, including the group of Socialists led by Antonio De Tomaso and Federico Pinedo, which had just broken away from the old party to form the *Partido Socialista Independiente.*

Unlike 1916, the political right was completely sure of its objectives and of the support it enjoyed among the propertied classes, but it was beginning to demonstrate a certain ambiguity about the means to attain its objectives. If the electoral card failed, another would have to be played, which would, one way or another, put an end to a democracy that did not ensure the election of the better bred. In support of that position were different political groups and ideological tendencies that, although few in number, had contributed to the new galvanizing of the right. From the pages of *La Nueva República,* founded in 1927, youthful followers of Charles Maurras such as Rodolfo and Julio Irazusta or Ernesto Palacio unleashed their battery against universal suffrage and a confused democracy, which should be replaced by a strong leader surrounded by an elite and legitimized in plebiscitary fashion. Soon the *Liga Republicana* that this group formed took to the streets, even when it became clear that it was incapable of reliving the mobilizations of 1919. A "march on Rome" was impossible, and thus all eyes turned to the military, to whom the writer and right-wing intellectual Leopoldo Lugones had already appealed in 1924, in a lecture that the army then published for the consumption of its officers, and which *La Nación* had disseminated. The open adhesion of General José Félix Uriburu, who had just gone into retirement, undoubtedly encouraged hopes for a military coup that would revitalize society; such was the offer that the nationalist groups made to an elite still vacillating between the old liberal republic and the promise of a new nationalist state.

The nationalists' expectations of the armed forces were unrealistic, all the more so when there was no immediate social crisis that justified, as in 1919, a reassessment of the institutional principles in which the military had been educated. If the armed forces experienced various moments of unrest during Yrigoyen's presidency, everything had been solved in the following period. Under the leadership of General Justo, Alvear's minister of war, the military had been adequately rearmed, and its lavish public buildings together with great public war games had given the army prominent social visibility. President Alvear had also shown himself open to proposals from the group of military engineers, who since the First World War had been concerned about "critical dependencies." In 1927, Alvear established the *Fábrica Militar de Aviones* to manufacture war planes, and since 1922, a military man, Enrique Mosconi, had presided over *Yacimientos Petrolíferos Fiscales,* the state-owned oil company created by Yrigoyen when his first term in office was coming to an end. Under the direction of Mosconi—who like Justo was a military engineer—the company expanded oil production and, thanks to the construction of a refinery in La Plata, made advances in the domestic gasoline market, covering the country with its characteristic service-station pumps. Simultaneously, in the midst of the spread of the automobile, great private companies also grew: British Shell and North American Standard Oil, which operated in Salta. As a result, competition with the private firms began to turn oil into a subject of public debate.

The armed forces, particularly the army, occupied an increasingly important place in the state; and as its own interests grew more sharply defined, the military became a significant political actor. The armed forces also had diverse agendas: those stemming from the close relations between their officers and the traditional liberal right, as well as the strict professionalism inculcated by General Justo, though there were also close ties with the *Liga Patriótica* and the strong appeal of the new nationalist ideologies. Yrigoyen's return to power reestablished old resentments—because of Yrigoyen's tendency to handle military promotions with political criteria—and undoubtedly polarized the officer corps, as it did the entire country. Significantly, in the *Círculo Militar's* 1929 elections, the slate of General Mosconi triumphed against one sympathizing with the president's opposition. The figure who was emerging as the natural head of this latter faction, General José F. Uriburu, conducted his affairs from the aristocratic Jockey Club and in reality lacked a solid following in the army, whose behavior was still an enigma.

The Return of Yrigoyen

After 1926, public opinion was polarized on the question of Yrigoyen's return to power, a debate that extended throughout society. *Yrigoyenismo,* led by a band of new leaders, fully developed its network of committees and strengthened the caudillo's mythic image. Although Yrigoyen had traditionally refused to identify his "revitalizing cause" with any explicitly defined platform, on this occasion he used the issue of oil nationalism, together with the slogan of defeating the "conspiracy." Thus a curious situation was created. During his first presidency, the oil issue had not unduly concerned him; the greatest advances in this area unquestionably occurred during Alvear's administration. In a mass democracy, however, slogans are effective in their ability to unify a plethora of political tendencies. In previous years, the oil issue had been inserted into public debate, and the foreign presence was associated with its most aggressive manifestation: the United States, in this case, the Standard Oil Company.

The banner of nationalization coincided with the preaching of the military sectors concerned about ensuring the country's autarchy with regard to strategic resources. Such sentiments were also linked to the landowning sectors' new and potent hostility toward the United States, following the conflict over the meat trade and ultimately with roots in a long-standing anti-U.S. sentiment, which unanimously associated the country with "imperialism." Above all, one has the impression that in some way oil appeared as the panacea that would guarantee the return to prosperity, a source of such abundant profits that with them would be ensured simultaneously the prosperity of the propertied sectors, the state, and society, which, in one way or another, obtained its resources from both the former. It is difficult to know how much the oil debate, a thoroughly modern issue, influenced the election and how much a more personal adhesion to the old caudillo influenced the outcome. What is clear is that Yrigoyen's victory in 1928 was notable in three ways: for the number of people who participated, for the number who voted for Yrigoyen (approximately 60 percent), and for victory having been obtained in the opposition and without the prebends of power or presidential blessing.

The nationalization bill, approved by the chamber of deputies, stalled in the senate, and until the dispute was resolved, Yrigoyen devoted his efforts to another problem that more directly affected his relations with the propertied sectors. Invited by the president, a British commercial mission headed by Lord d'Abernon came to Argentina. The agreement subsequently signed between the two countries provided important trade concessions to the British, guaranteeing them the supply of materiel for the *Ferrocarriles del Estado,* as well as a preferential tariff for artificial silk, in exchange for a promise that the British would continue to buy Argentine meat. This treaty, which granted important concessions without any clear benefit for Argentina, showed that Yrigoyen identified with the prevailing current of opinion among the elite, which emphasized strengthening bilateral relations with Great Britain to the detriment of those with the United States.

This convergence of opinion was insufficient in the face of the exacerbation of political conflict. Embarked on a campaign to conquer the final independent bastion—the senate—the government resorted to the classic methods of political persuasion: ample distribution of government jobs with which it paid its debt to a party apparatus that had been faithful during the years in the political wilderness, as well as the interdiction of hostile provinces. This time it was the turn of Santa Fe, a bulwark of *antipersonalista* Radicalism, and also Corrientes, but above all Mendoza and San Juan; a protracted political dispute regarding the investiture of those provinces' elected senators was unleashed. In those provinces where violent incidents had already taken place, another violent act occurred: the assassination of Carlos Washington Lencinas, the caudillo from Mendoza, in which the federal government appeared involved.

It is probable that the opposition, overwhelmed by the electoral results, may have abandoned hope of dislodging Yrigoyen by institutional means and did not fully fathom the significance of the immediate consequences of the global Depression that began in October 1929. The fall in exports and the withdrawal of North American capital affected the railroad and shipping companies tied to foreign trade as well as the government. The high inflation, decline in wages, and layoffs had immediate electoral repercussions. In March 1930, with the support of the entire opposition, the *Socialistas Independientes* defeated in the federal capital both the Radicals and the Socialists, and in other parts of the country the government also suffered setbacks. Nevertheless, by this point, all the voices of the opposition, from the newspaper *Crítica* to the *Liga Republicana* and reformist university students, were clamoring for the fall of the government. The senility attributed to Yrigoyen and his inability to find rapid solutions to the economic crisis, as well as the public struggle over his successor—either the vice president Ezequiel Martínez or the minister of the interior Elpidio González—provided the opposition with a new and decisive justification for his removal.

Discussion revolved around whether to seek an institutional solution or appeal for a military intervention: whether to reestablish political institutions according to traditional standards or whether the moment had arrived for the new republic, drawing its inspiration from the models then being offered by Europe. The elite probably wavered between both solutions, one faction encouraged by the political leaders and by the military officers who followed General Justo and another by the nationalist ideologues who surrounded General Uriburu. Only after both leaders reached an agreement could the coup d'état take place on September 6, 1930. Government resistance was practically nil (the day before, Yrigoyen had requested a leave of absence from the presidency), but the forces mobilized by the conspirators were also scarce, mostly inexperienced cadets from the *Colegio Militar.* Equally inconsequential was the mobilization in favor of the deposed president, who not long before had been popularly elected.

The indifference with which society received the end of what undoubtedly had been an important democratic experiment calls for reflection about its legacy. In large measure, the democratization process completed a long stage in the opening up and expansion of a society begun five decades previously and seemed its natural coronation. The access of increasingly vast social sectors to the benefits of the established society, which despite the crisis of 1917–21 characterizes this period, implied finally expanding the citizenry, a process initiated at first by the state but ultimately taken up by society, as the spectacular increase in political participation at the end of this period bears witness.

Yet at the same time it was necessary to translate that process into stable institutions, to set in motion the necessary democratic practices and strengthen them in such a way that their exercise would become natural; here the Radical governments failed to make sufficient advances in helping society see such institutions as something valuable that had to be defended. Radicalism failed to abandon the practices employed by the old regime—those stigmatized with that very graphic expression, the *unicato*—and subordinated the development of new practices to old habits. For its part, an often factious opposition did little to make the bitter political struggle resemble a constructive dialogue between the government and the opposition; it did even less to defend to the death those institutions that the propertied classes distrusted from the outset.

The final balance is not complete without mentioning that democracy and Radicalism triumphed at the precise moment that the propitious conditions for their flourishing suddenly changed, however much society may have delayed taking note of the situation. The First World War substantially altered the fundamental rules of the game of the Argentine economy, calling into question the place that the country occupied in the world and unleashing internal conflicts that on occasion manifested themselves violently. Whoever governed the country could not be content with the old formulas and had to invent imaginative responses. Moreover, any political leader who sought to govern democratically had to find institutional forms to resolve conflict, broadening the spaces of representation and public debate as well as state regulatory mechanisms; in both these aspects, the shortcomings of the Radical governments were great. These questions stemming from the economic crisis, as much as or even more than those tied to institutional democracy, dominated the subsequent period.

three

The Conservative Restoration, 1930–1943

On September 6, 1930, General José Félix Uriburu assumed power as provisional president, transferring the office on February 20, 1932, to General Agustín P. Justo, who had been elected, together with the vice president Julio A. Roca, in November of the previous year. In the interim, the provisional government had presided over elections for governor in the province of Buenos Aires on April 5, 1931, in which the Radical candidate, Honorio Pueyrredón, had won, only to have the election annulled. This episode shows the uncertainty with which the government struggled, wavering between "national regeneration" and constitutional restoration.

National Regeneration or Constitutional Restoration

Uncertainty was common among all the social groups that had contributed to overthrow Yrigoyen's government and to interrupt institutional continuity. All were in clear agreement about the first objective and supported the government when it persecuted Radical leaders, fired them from the public jobs handed out by the deposed government, or investigated corruption charges. The majority also supported the hard-line policy toward social movements: the interdiction of ports to dismantle union control there, the deportation of anarchist or Communist leaders—persecuted by the police's new Special Section—and even the execution of the "expropriating anarchist," Severino Di Giovanni. But strictly speaking, unlike 1919, in 1930 the social mobilizations were few. The Depression paralyzed protest; union leaderships, who had hardly identified with institutional democracy, had done little to defend it. Fear of social protest had not been the primary cause of the 1930 revolution, and neither was the global economic Depression, which was absent from the debates and whose tremendous consequences had yet to be seen. For its protagonists, the revolution had been undertaken against the vices attributed to democracy. Once Yrigoyen had been deposed, however, there was no agreement about what to do, and the propertied classes as well as the army, which was slowly becoming a new political actor, vacillated between different courses of action.

The most outspoken group was the nationalists, who rapidly assumed the initiative. Their opinions had been effectively used as a weapon against Radicalism because of their spokespersons' talent for polemics, their ability to articulate diverse discourses that appealed to distinct sensibilities, and their capacity to express and legitimize what others would not admit: an authoritarian elitism in which they took pride. They were also strengthened by the success that these kinds of ideas were having throughout the world, ideas that inspired traditional authoritarian regimes as well as new regimes, successful experiments such as that of Mussolini's Italy. Finally, they could count on some limited but important support from the state. From Uriburu's cabinet of old-style conservatives, they were helped by the minister of the interior, Matías Sánchez Sorondo, a traditional conservative like Uriburu, who sympathized with these new authoritarian forms. They also received the support of some military officers in the president's circle and other high-ranking functionaries, such as the *interventor* of Córdoba, the writer and essayist Carlos Ibarguren, one of the initiators of the intellectual rehabilitation of the nineteenth-century dictator Juan Manuel de Rosas. The nationalist militants themselves, on the other hand, occupied only some positions of minor importance in various provincial governments.

Uriburu nonetheless did everything possible to support the nationalists. He spoke in different forums, principally military, abominating democracy, demanding a deep institutional reform, and preaching the advantages of corporatism and functional representation. But his power and political skills were negligible. Paradoxically, he wagered everything on the elections, trusting in an electoral triumph in Buenos Aires. The April fifth defeat practically turned him into a political corpse. Having failed in his appeal to society, Uriburu tried a second ploy, this time with the army, which he attempted to mobilize through the *Civic Legion,* a civilian guard organized by military officers, supposedly to be the vanguard of the proclaimed revolution but never a significant force.

The nationalists were much more effective at attacking than at building, and their participation in the government hindered rather than helped them. They gradually began to distance themselves from the government, as the influence of those who surrounded Justo and the attraction for an electoral solution to the crisis, which they finally supported, grew stronger. About this time, the nationalists had just finished fashioning their discourse, which they soon employed as much to combat the new government as to appeal, with increasing fervor, to the army. To the traditional criticisms of democracy were added a vigorous anti-Communism and an attack on liberalism, regarded as the root of all of society's evils. Typical for the period, they reduced all of their enemies to one: high finances and imperialism combined with the Communists, the foreigners responsible for national disintegration, and also the Jews, all united in a sinister conspiracy. They demanded the return to a hierarchical society such as had existed in the colonial period, uncontaminated by liberalism, organized by a corporatist state, and cemented by an integral Catholicism. If much of this could be identified with fascism, it lacked its vocation and mobilizing capacity. Rather, the nationalists demanded the establishment of a new governing elite that was national and not beholden to foreign interests. They believed they would find such an elite among the military. The Uriburu alternative having failed, the army became their chief hope.

While the nationalists were proposing a reactionary but new road, the majority of the political class was opting for a defense of democratic institutions, though emphasizing that these should never be subordinated to democracy's excesses. On the contrary, a long experience of how to resolve electoral questions and practices, free from excesses and mediating the popular will, had been inherited from the past. This alternative, which vindicated liberalism's position, was demanded by society and was vigorously defended by the principal organs of public opinion such as *La Nación* or *Crítica,* as well as being endorsed by the political parties that had constituted the opposition to Yrigoyen.

In the meantime, the Socialists and the Progressive Democrats again passed over to the opposition. The parties that in 1928 had supported the candidacy of Leopoldo Melo, in contrast, oscillated between contesting Uriburu's authoritarian and corporatist project and using the government's support for an eventual election that was unquestionably indispensable if the Radicals were to be defeated. Tactical differences deeply divided them. One group established in the National Democratic Federation—decidedly liberal and energetically opposed to Uriburu—suffered the defection of the Conservative Party in the province of Buenos Aires, less hostile to the president's policies. Nevertheless, the party's defeat in the April fifth provincial election—which simultaneously closed off the project of a national "regeneration" and the illusion of defeating the Radicals in clean elections—created the conditions for a regrouping of political forces around the candidacy of General Justo, a candidacy that was already taking shape. The most steadfast sectors of the front were the conservative groups that established the National Democratic Party, a heterogeneous coalition of provincial parties ranging from the more traditional of Buenos Aires to the more liberal of Córdoba or Mendoza. The antipersonalist Radicals, their principal competitor in the front being formed, had fallen apart after many members had returned to the fold of the original Radical Party, now led by Alvear. The Independent Socialist Party had a solid base only in the federal capital and also a group of qualified leaders. These groups united behind the figure of General Justo, but without overcoming their differences, to the point that they supported Justo while presenting two different vice presidential candidates.

Justo—the key figure in this alliance—could present himself as a military man with a civilian vocation, but above all as one who could count on the army's support. After September sixth, he waged a silent war against Uriburu for control of the principal commanders and ultimately emerged the winner. His most faithful supporter, Colonel Manuel A. Rodríguez, not only commanded the country's most important military base, the Campo de Mayo, but was elected president of the *Círculo Militar,* the influential officers' club, a fact that testified to the predominant mood in the army. The officers were courted by different groups of activists: the Radicals, embarked on conspiracies; the nationalists, equally active; and the followers of Justo, who combined the principles of respect for the Constitution with professionalism. Among most of the military there still predominated a distrust of politics and a basically professional attitude that tipped the scales in favor of Justo.

The greatest difficulty was with the Radicals, who had risen like the phoenix from the ashes following their April 1931 electoral victory in Buenos Aires province, along with the return of Marcelo de Alvear, who, with Yrigoyen's blessing, reunified the party. The options were not clear among the Radicals. Many placed their hopes on elections, and others on overthrowing the provisional government with a civilian-military uprising. Many Radical military officers plotted, and the government used the conspiracies as the pretext to undermine its most formidable opposition. In July 1931, a rebellion erupted in Corrientes, led by a Colonel Gregorio Pomar; it was swiftly put down, permitting the government to arrest or deport the military officers sympathetic to the Radicals. Despite such repression, the Radical convention nominated Alvear as its presidential candidate, which the government vetoed on specious constitutional and public security grounds. The Radicals then returned to their former tactic of abstention without abandoning their conspiratorial attempts, leaving the field open to Justo's candidacy, which could be presented as the middle ground between Uriburu's dictatorship and Alvear's extremist subversion.

In the November 1931 elections, Justo faced only a coalition of the Democratic Progressive Party and the Socialist Party, which nominated two prestigious leaders: Lisandro de la Torre and Nicolás Repetto. Although the opposition eventually succeeded, it had the liability of a weak party organization outside the federal capital and Santa Fe province, as well as the well-known anti-Radicalism of its candidates. In November 1931, in a reasonably honest election, the ticket headed by Justo triumphed in a victory that was not a landslide and that permitted the opposition to win the government of one province (Santa Fe) as well as a respectable parliamentary representation.

The country's political institutions were preserved, and the revolution appeared to have found a safe harbor. There were government and opposition factions in the congress; the opposition behaved with caution and was regarded as a formal opposition, perhaps because everyone knew that it was really not a viable contender for power. The Radicals' abstention tactic was later a liability, but for the moment it constituted an advantage, despite the telling spectacle the popular multitude that accompanied Yrigoyen's funeral cortege might have signified for the government; Yrigoyen had died in July 1933.

Organizing the governing party was not a simple task. Justo attempted to balance the participation of different factions in the government, and, although his reserve toward the conservative parties was notorious, they nonetheless constituted his most solid base. Only one of his cabinet ministers—Alvarado of public works—came from conservative ranks; two others, the foreign minister Carlos Saavedra Limas and the minister of the treasury Horacio Hueyo, could in some ways be regarded as belonging to their ranks. The antipersonalists had two cabinet posts—Leopoldo Melo as minister of interior and Simón de Iriondo of Santa Fe in education and justice. The Independent Socialists held one seat: Antonio de Tomaso, one of the politicians most respected by Justo, and the only one of working-class background, who served as minister of agriculture.

Despite the fact that the Independent Socialist Party soon declined politically and was disbanded, its leaders, particularly De Tomaso and Federico Pinedo, played a key role in building the political alliance and in the formation of what was called the parliamentary *Concordancia,* the coalition of pro-government forces, as well as in the drafting of the government's principal policies. The pro-government parties won the elections by using familiar techniques, of which there was a vast accumulated experience, combining the support of the public authorities—particularly the police commissioners—with the system of political bossism (*caudillaje*), and exploiting the multiple collusions between both. As long as the Radicals maintained their abstention policy, these methods served principally to settle conflicts in the ranks of the pro-government parties; but after 1935, they were used to block the road to power for the political party led by Alvear. The city of Buenos Aires—more sensitive to public opinion—was free of such things, and there the opposition always won. In the province of Buenos Aires, on the other hand, the crudest frauds were practiced; a governor, Manuel A. Fresco, categorized them as "patriotic," saying what many others surely thought. Yet perhaps the stigma attached by society to what were very traditional practices is significant, revealing the extent to which a democratic culture had begun to take root in society.

State Intervention and the Closing of the Economy

The government's effectiveness had been demonstrated, to society generally and particularly to the propertied classes, by its ability to deal with a difficult economic situation. The Depression, which had been felt since 1928, persisted until 1932, hitting hard what had been until then—despite the changes experienced in the previous decade—an open economy. The flow of foreign capital, which had traditionally nourished the national economy, ceased, and many immigrants returned to their countries of origin. International prices for agricultural products fell sharply—much more so than in the 1919–22 crisis—and although exports did not decline, the earnings of the agrarian sector, and that of society as a whole, greatly shrank. Because the government opted to maintain service payments on foreign debt, which had become much more burdensome with the decline in revenue, both imports and state spending had to be sharply reduced. Indeed, the state's budgetary deficit became a serious problem.

Moreover, the international economy's problems, already apparent in the previous decade, grew increasingly greater. During the crisis, the industrialized nations used their buying power to defend their markets, ensure the repayment of debts, and protect their investments. Great Britain took refuge in commercial protectionism and established a sterling "zone" for the pound, defended first through exchange controls and later by the inconvertibility of the British currency. Germany and France took an identical road, as the United States eventually did when in 1933 it declared the inconvertibility of the dollar. This changed world required new and imaginative economic policies. Those adopted initially—by Uriburu and by Justo at the beginning of his government—had been limited to the classic pump-priming methods, and these leaders only timidly embarked on new paths. But in mid-1933, with the designation of Federico Pinedo as minister of the treasury, a more novel approach was adopted, with two tendencies that lasted for years: the growing intervention of the state and the gradual closing of the economy. There was also another policy, less permanent but of greater immediate importance: strengthening the relationship with Great Britain.

In late 1931, just before Justo succeeded Uriburu, the government established an income tax, realizing an old project of Yrigoyen's that had been systematically vetoed since Yrigoyen first proposed it. Yet in the new climate of crisis—and in the hands of what was viewed as a trustworthy government—the income tax was accepted without debate by the propertied classes. Public finances ceased to depend exclusively on taxes on imports and on foreign loans. Combined with the initial drastic reduction in state spending, by 1933 the government had managed to balance the budget with its new fiscal policies.

In 1931, exchange controls were also established, through which the government centralized the purchase and sale of foreign currency. This measure had originally been meant to confront the crisis and ensure the availability of foreign exchange for the payment of foreign debt, but such a measure soon constituted a powerful instrument of economic policy. The government could establish priorities for the use of foreign currency, something that concerned not only different domestic economic sectors but also the two great foreign contenders for their use: the United States and Great Britain. In November 1933, a substantial reform established two exchange markets. One, regulated by the state, administered the exchange from the traditional agricultural exports; in the other, originating in loans received or in nontraditional exports such as industrial goods, foreign exchange was bought and sold freely. For the first, devaluation was minimal, although a differential of 20 percent was established between the purchase and sale prices. The state thereby acquired massive resources and could decide their use. Thus was established a series of priorities to sell the exchange the state controlled. Servicing the debt was the first concern, followed by covering the costs of the necessary imports, and finally providing the funds for public-service companies such as railroads. In the second market, the little remaining foreign exchange was freely bought and sold, both for the importation of consumer goods and to pay for the capital goods that companies needed.

An important step in the control of the financial sector was taken in 1935 with the creation of the Central Bank, whose principal function was to regulate the cyclical fluctuations of the money supply, avoiding both excessive supply and scarcity and controlling the activity of the private banks—which participated in its board of directors—above all in the handling of credit. The *Instituto Movilizador de Inversiones Bancarias* assumed responsibility for the orderly sale of banks that had been battered by the Depression. To attenuate the effects of cyclical crises and defend local producers, the commercialization of agricultural production also began to be regulated. Using the funds coming from the exchange controls, the National Grain Board guaranteed a minimum price for rural producers, sparing them from having to sell in the worst moments. The National Meat Board strove for the same objective, though limited to the small sector in the meat market beyond the control of foreign packinghouses. The system was extended to producers outside the pampa zone, such as those of wine and cotton.

Along this path, the state assumed a greater role in economic activity and went from merely managing the economic crisis to defining the rules of the game ever more broadly, according to a model theorized by the British economist, John Maynard Keynes, whose ideas were beginning to be implemented throughout the world. At the same time, the economy as a whole gradually shut itself off from the rest of the world in which relatively closed markets were also clearly emerging. This tendency was still incipient, compelled by conjunctural factors, but was becoming increasingly more pronounced, encouraging changes that were eventually irreversible.

The most important change had to do with industry, whose production began to increase with the outbreak of the economic crisis and continued to do so after the recovery in the second half of the decade. Thanks to the prosperity of the previous decades, an important consumer market had been established in the country. The increasing closing-off of the economy, the tariffs, and the lack of foreign exchange created suitable conditions for the substitution of imported goods by others produced locally, especially if production did not require a very complex technology or if there already existed an industrial base that could be more intensely used. Indeed, the country's base industries had grown throughout the 1920s and continued to expand along the same lines during the 1930s. The textile industry grew notably, but so did the majority of activities directed to the consumer market: food processing, clothing, and diverse chemical and metal products. Big business, until then predominantly linked to export agriculture, increased its industrial activity. The most important export firm, Bunge y Born, which already had industrial investments, in 1932 established the textile firm Grafa in what was then the most dynamic industrial sector. Other traditional economic groups such as Leng Roberts or Tornquist—which combined agricultural, industrial, and financial activities—did the same, as did the new foreign investors.

Significantly, in the mid-1930s three great North American textile firms—Anderson Clayton, Jantzen, and Sudamtex—established plants, to be followed immediately by Ducilo, dedicated to synthetic fibers.

Import substitution industrialization was offered the attraction of an existing and captive market and quick profits. Once a market was saturated, it was better to move into another branch where there was little competition than to deepen the investment in the saturated market. As Jorge Sábato and Jorge Schvarzer demonstrated, the propertied sectors' former business strategy of diversifying into different activities without tying themselves down to any one found a new outlet in import substitution industrialization, subsequently complemented with real estate investments. Moreover, the combination of a protected market and a few great firms per branch or industry made pressures for greater efficiency or lower costs minimal. On the other hand, the rules of the game established by the state were important, whether in the form of tariffs or exchange controls. Thus, industrial growth opened up a new area of negotiation between the propertied sectors and the state.

The changes in the agricultural sector were less notable, especially in the pampa region. Livestock continued to retreat in the face of grain cultivation, just as in the previous decade. Agricultural production did not decline, despite the collapse in prices, although the producers' situation deteriorated appreciably, especially the smaller ones, and conditions were established for a rural exodus, which occurred following the beginning of the Second World War. Until then, the exportation of corn increased greatly, especially in the middle years of the decade—taking advantage of a period of drought in the United States—reflected both in the balanced budget and in the relative prosperity between 1934 and 1937. This prosperity stimulated both industry and construction. The most important change occurred outside the pampa zone and in those areas where some semi-industrial crops grew, geared to the domestic market, especially cotton, which since 1930 was almost totally consumed by the domestic market. The occupation of new lands extended throughout the entire Northeast, a process that was begun in the previous decade and that established a broad sector of small producers dependent on a highly concentrated commercial and industrial sector. There as well, the state intervened to regulate commerce.

In summary, the economic crisis and the immediate responses adopted to deal with it had created a series of new conditions that made a return to the status quo difficult. It could be debated whether the stability and relative prosperity apparent by 1936—reflected in a renewal of union protest—should be attributed to these changes, or whether, as Arturo O'Connell argued, it was merely the result of a temporary prosperity in exports. But the closing-off of the economy, state intervention, and a certain industrial growth seemed to be features that were here to stay.

The British Presence

These changes occurred gradually, without eliciting great debates or polarizing politics. On the other hand, the question of the relationship with Great Britain—which had been under discussion since the previous decade—turned out to be much more controversial. Pressured by the inroads made by the United States, and in the context of the crisis unleashed in 1930, Great Britain opted to concentrate on its empire, strengthening its ties with its colonies and dominions and establishing limits to the U.S. presence there. At the same time, in the context of global financial restrictions, Great Britain proposed to defend its established markets and safeguard its income from loans or investments. Not all these objectives were compatible, and therefore once the priorities were established there was considerable room for negotiation. In 1932, at the Imperial Conference held in Ottawa, the balance was tipped in favor of the Commonwealth members, who would receive export preferences in the British market. Among other measures adopted, members decided to reduce by one-third the purchases of frozen Argentine meat, which could be replaced by Australian meat, and to reduce by 10 percent chilled beef purchases, taking as a base figure the already low 1932 purchases. This was an extremely sensitive point for Argentina, perhaps not so much for its intrinsic economic importance as for the web of interests established in the meat trade: producers, packinghouses, and shipping companies were all capable of exerting strong pressure on the government. At the same time, the Argentine government possessed a powerful weapon. Tariff policies and the control of foreign exchange would give Argentina discretionary powers with regard to imports. Argentina could thus regulate the amount of foreign exchange used to make service payments on the foreign debt with Britain, as well as the amount used to buy British products or to remit the profits of

British companies with operations in Argentina. In a context characterized by a scarcity of foreign exchange and the strong demands of the North American commercial interests, the point became extremely important for Great Britain.

In 1933, a mission in London headed by the vice president Julio A. Roca negotiated the terms for the maintenance of the Argentine meat quota. This was vital to ensure the government's credibility among the diverse sectors tied to agriculture, and in that respect the mission was a relative success. The agreement provided that the 1932 levels would be maintained and that Argentina would be consulted about any eventual later reductions that were necessary. The Roca mission did not achieve much in terms of its second objective: to increase the participation of local producers in the control of exports to negotiate better terms with the packinghouses. The treaty, signed by Roca and the British minister Walter Runciman, limited to 15 percent the share that could be handled by nationally owned packinghouses, among whom, the British feared, might be established a cooperative without profit motives. In exchange for its concessions, Great Britain was guaranteed that the sterling pounds earned by this trade would be spent in their entirety in Britain: in repayment of the debt, importation of coal and railroad materiel and textiles (for which a preferential tariff treatment was established), and remittance of the profits of British companies. At the same time, the agreement stipulated a "benevolent treatment" for these companies, subject as they were to multiple difficulties. The agreement was undoubtedly a great victory for the British. In exchange for maintaining the Argentine presence in the British meat market—a business in which British interests were the principal partners—the British were assured payment for services on their old investments and control of a significant part of the contested domestic market. The North Americans, for their part, discriminated against through tariffs and exchange controls, lost ground in the Argentine market, though they would counterattack with industrial investments that circumvented the tariff barriers. The tendency toward a bilateral relationship with the British, however, had been fully ratified.

The "benevolent treatment" aimed to salvage British firms in difficulties, namely the railroads and urban transport companies. The railroads were squeezed by fixed costs, general reduction in activities, and increasing competition from automotive transport, the latter stimulated by the systematic construction of roads begun in 1928 and vigorously maintained by Justo. Trucks now took the most lucrative part of the freight business and at the same time stimulated the importation of motor vehicles, parts, and tires, all of North American origin. The treaty guaranteed British firms the right to repatriate their profits, but these were minimal throughout the decade. Something similar occurred with the Anglo streetcar company—also owner of the first subway line in the city—which became a victim of the taxi buses, faster and more efficient than the trolleys. The "preferential treatment" in this case consisted of the creation of the *Corporación de Transporte de la Ciudad de Buenos Aires,* a British company representing tramway and subway interests. The creation of this company sparked public indignation without achieving the objective that taxi bus drivers become members and desist in their competition. In the case of both the railroads and urban transport, what was at issue was the fact that companies had ceased to be profitable and had not made the necessary investments to maintain their predominance. "Preferential treatment" therefore sought only to increase some monopoly privileges and to delay these companies' inevitable demise, which is why their boards of directors began to devise a different strategy: to sell the companies to the state.

Despite the fact that the benefits were not equal for all parties, the London treaty was supported by the various propertied sectors. When the treaty was discussed in congress, the only consistent opposition came from the Socialist Party, which was worried about the repercussions of these arrangements on local consumers. Nevertheless, conflicts appeared on the scene almost immediately between the various interests: the packinghouses; the cattle ranchers who operated as "fatteners," and who supplied the chilled beef and had maintained almost intact their quota in the British market; and the majority of the "breeders" who had to choose between the exportation of lesser quality frozen meat or sale to the fatteners or to the domestic consumer market. The most important fatteners closely tied to the packinghouses worked through the *Sociedad Rural Argentina,* whereas the breeders organized the *Confederación de Asociaciones Rurales de Buenos Aires y La Pampa* (CARBAP) as spokesperson for the interests of their sector. In the heated debates that ensued, what was discussed was not so much the terms of the agreement as the way in which the packinghouses were to handle domestic prices, the relative advantages of some producers over others, and the possibilities that producers might participate in the regulation of the business through a packinghouse cooperative, using the 15 percent quota that the treaty reserved for them. In 1933, the law was passed that established the National Meat Board, destined to intervene in a limited manner in the regulation of the market, with the composition of its directorship intensely disputed.

In 1935, the Santa Fe senator, Lisandro de la Torre, who already had expressed reservations about the London agreement, requested an investigation into the meat trade and the activities of the packinghouses. The pro-government senators acknowledged the existence of serious improprieties on the part of the packinghouses, of excessively low prices paid to the producers, of monopolistic practices, and of unwillingness to cooperate in the investigation. De la Torre went beyond such accusations and coupled the attack against the packinghouses with a strong campaign against the government. A landowner himself and leader in Santa Fe's *Sociedad Rural,* de la Torre had been a presidential candidate in the 1916 election won by Yrigoyen and again in 1932 against Justo. He was thus the outstanding figure among the opposition of Socialists and Progressive Democrats. De la Torre denounced the packinghouse companies, protected by the authorities, for not paying taxes, hiding their profits, and giving preferential treatment to some influential cattle ranchers, such as the minister of agriculture himself, Luis Duhau, who had been president of the *Sociedad Rural.* De la Torre's intervention in the congress was scintillating and lasted several days, attracting public attention and eliciting a violent response from the ministers Duhau and Pinedo. During the most acrimonious of these congressional sessions, the senator-elect, Enzo Bordabehere, de la Torre's fellow senator from Santa Fe, was assassinated by a shot intended for de la Torre, fired by a thug linked to Duhau. The debate ended abruptly and without resolution. The government lost a great deal of prestige in the public's eye, and the controversy demonstrated above all that the easy stage in governance was over. In following years, and with its eyes on the presidential elections, the opposition replenished its ranks.

Although he based his attack on the demands of a sector of cattle ranchers, de la Torre had been wise enough to give a broader political dimension to his demands, wielding an argument capable of galvanizing an opposition against "imperialism" and the "oligarchy" on the part of public opinion sensitive to the advance, in some ways heavy-handed, of British interests. This line of reasoning had roots in the socialist and leftist tradition of such figures as Manuel

Ugarte and Alfredo Palacios but also in the tradition of other intellectuals from more conservative sectors and stirred to action by the crisis. In 1934, the Irazusta brothers, Rodolfo and Julio, cattle ranchers from Entre Ríos and veterans of the anti-Radical nationalism, published a book that made a deep impact: *Argentina and British Imperialism* In this book, the Irazustas chronicled the history of a relationship that they judged baleful from its origins; beginning around 1810, they indicted this partnership of the British and the local ruling class, dazzled by liberalism and blind to true national interests. In contrast, the figure of the nineteenth-century caudillo, Juan Manuel de Rosas, was portrayed as an expression of authentically national interests and at the same time of a dictatorial form of government uncontaminated by a corrupting liberalism.

The vindication of Rosas had already begun in the previous decade and was intensely developed in the 1930s, by both historians and politicians. It was a touchstone as much for those motivated by a rejection of British influence as for those who saw liberalism as the principal enemy. To the cult of Rosas naturally flocked a fascist-inspired nationalism and especially the new currents in the Catholic Church, for whom Rosas represented not antiimperialism but the Hispanic tradition of a hierarchical, Catholic, and authoritarian society that was contrasted with the contemporary one corrupted by liberalism, Protestantism, Judaism, and Marxism. The rapprochement between the ruling classes and the Catholic Church—demonstrated in the great proceedings of the Congress of the Eucharist in 1934—created the space for the spread of these ideas that were beginning to undermine the traditional liberalism of Argentine society.

A Frustrated Popular Front

Despite its successes in the economy, Justo's regime was seen—with increasing intensity—as illegitimate: fraudulent, corrupt, and alien to national interests. If until 1935 the government had proceeded without great setbacks, since that date the signs of growing social and political unrest had become apparent. In July, the prestigious general, Ramón Molina, had publicly praised Alvear's presidency and shortly thereafter gave a speech in defense of popular sovereignty and free elections, receiving in the process the enthusiastic support of the University Federation, the organization representing the country's university students. When in 1937 he was furloughed and given early retirement, there was a large demonstration in his support at which the Socialist political leader Alfredo Palacios and Alvear himself spoke.

In October 1935, the Buenos Aires construction workers, led by the union's Communist leaders, began a strike that lasted more than ninety days. In the city's working-class neighborhoods, there was widespread support for the strike, and in January of the following year the General Confederation of Labor (CGT) carried out a two-day-long general strike—the only one of the decade—at the end of which the strikers obtained some of their demands. The most important outcome was perhaps the establishment of the National Construction Workers' Federation, destined to be one of the most important and combative unions in the country. In 1936, a number of strikes were undertaken, just as in 1935 and 1937, coinciding with a recovery in the economy. In that year, the CGT, whose leadership had been reconstituted with a predominance of Socialists and Communists, celebrated May Day in a common demonstration with various opposition parties: Radicals, Progressive Democrats, Socialists, and Communists espoused the workers' demands, lambasted the "heirs of September sixth," and demanded liberty and democracy. For the first time in the history of the May first celebrations, the national anthem was sung, and Marcelo T. de Alvear was praised as "an authentic worker in the service of the nation's democracy."

In 1936, the UCR, which the previous year had lifted its policy of electoral abstention, triumphed in the elections for congressional deputies in several of the principal electoral districts—the federal capital, Santa Fe, Mendoza, and Córdoba—and thereby achieved a majority in the chamber of deputies. In Córdoba, moreover, the UCR's candidate for governor, Amadeo Sabattini, also triumphed. Perhaps to compensate, the government interdicted the province of Santa Fe, governed by the Progressive Democrat, Luciano Molinas, and endorsed the brazen fraud by which Manuel Fresco won the province of Buenos Aires. A Manifesto of the Right, which Pinedo drafted, warned against the resurgence of the "blind masses" and the shady democracy removed from power in 1930 and justified the "patriotic fraud" that the government had systematically used in favor of the pro-government parties, with the sole exception of the federal capital.

The government's reaction was directed against the new combative trade unionism as well. The Residency Law, which gave the state broad powers to deport union militants, was enforced against the principal leaders of the construction workers' union, Communists of Italian origin, who were deported to fascist Italy. At the same time, the senate passed a law, Repression of Communism, proposed by Sánchez Sorondo, which was blocked by the lower house. To counterbalance the unity of the forces demanding democracy, Justo raised the stakes a bit and enlisted the support of those whom he had heretofore relegated to a marginal position. Thus, Governor Fresco could openly profess his fascist sympathies, and nationalist officers, enthused by the Third Reich's early success, could proselytize freely among the troops of the army. Colonel Juan Bautista Molina, a disciple of Uriburu in the creation of the *Legión Cívica*, reputedly conspired against Justo, who nonetheless promoted him to the rank of general.

The various currents of the right convoked a "national front" against the "popular front" that was taking shape. Theses names were not accidental, as the new alignments and political divisions occurring in the world were influencing local politics, awakening dormant forces, supplying slogans and banners, causing the undecided to take a stand, and thereby helping delineate potential alliances. In the camp of those opposed to the government, the changed position of the Communist Party was important. In March 1935, the Communists, rapidly adopting the new orientations of the Comintern, had embraced the concept of the popular front. In previous years, with the motto, "Class War," the Communists had equally combated Nazis, fascists, and the social democratic parties, stigmatizing the last as the proletariat's most dangerous enemies. But in 1935, they threw themselves into promoting the unity of the "democratic sectors" to confront Nazi fascism, abandoning the slogans and practices that could irritate or frighten the progressive and democratic sectors of the bourgeoisie. With such a program in France and Spain, they formed, together with Socialist and Radical parties of the center, popular front experiments that won the 1936 elections. Although the local situation was not exactly the same, the government of the *Concordancia* was identified with the great evil, and the demand for a popular and democratic front served to close ranks among its opponents.

Later, the Spanish Civil War, whose impact on Argentina was enormous, served to divide the opposing camps even more clearly. Not only was the very large community of Spanish exiles split; so was Argentine society as a whole, with collections proliferating, along with solidarity committees, demonstrations, and fights wherever supporters and adversaries of the republic came together. Among the right, the Spanish Civil War brought together authoritarian conservatives, nationalists with fascist orientations, and Catholic integralists in a common campaign against democratic liberalism. In the opposing camp, a solidarity bloc eventually took shape stretching from the Radicals to the Communists, with the middle ground occupied by the Socialists, Progressive Democrats, students of the University Federation, trade-union leaders grouped in the CGT, and a vast sector of progressive independent public opinion, among whom were figures from conservative liberalism. Except for the last, all the groups were probably the same ones that had supported the Citizens' Alliance of de la Torre and Repetto. What is clear is that the Spanish Republic, and the conviction that democracies were preparing to wage the final battle against fascism, created a lightning rod for solidarity and an attractive and mobilizing identity.

An important part of this sector of public opinion was based in the intellectual world, whose politicization deepened in the second half of the decade. The University Reform—anti-imperialist, democratic, and popular—was beginning to penetrate politics. Some of the University Reform's principal leaders joined political parties: José Peco the Radicals, Alejandro Korn and Julio V. González the Socialists, Rodolfo Aráoz Alfaro the Communists. Others such as Deodora Roca and Saúl Taborda were also involved in politics as independents. A similar combination of politics and academics from a progressive perspective took place in the *Colegio Libre de Estudios Superiores,* a popular university founded in 1930 and oriented as much to issues of high culture as to the discussion of political, economic, and social questions. The same combination was found in the magazine *Claridad,* dedicated to essays, literary criticism, and political questions, the latter occupying increasing space in its pages. *Claridad,* besides publishing several literature and essay collections for the general public, brought together intellectuals and writers who had belonged to the so-called Boedo group and had embraced a position on an "engaged art"; among them, Leonidas Barletta created in 1931 the People's Theater, where for twenty cents one could see plays by Ibsen, Andreyev, or Arlt. That same year, the heirs of the "Florida" group, supporters of an esthetic renovation and of art for art's sake, came together in the review *Sur,* founded by Victoria Ocampo. It is significant that both groups aligned themselves—although with different degrees of enthusiasm—on the side of democracy's defenders.

The appearance of several publishing houses founded by Spanish émigrés—Losada, Emecé, and Sudamericana, among others—intensified the activities of the intellectual and artistic world and gave work to writers, translators, and critics. This activity naturally grew beyond intellectual circles and found expression in a plethora of popular publications and lectures, the work of a broad group of cultural activists, who frequently were also political activists, especially as the climate of polarization spread. These movements had a strong tendency to analyze society's problems, to criticize and propose alternative solutions for specific problems whether about education, public health, the agrarian question, or the status of women. Although there were many references to the Soviet Union, they always saw it as the model of a society rationally organized rather than as an incitement to take power by violent means. What predominated was a reformist spirit and an outreach to all those who sympathized with aspirations for progress, freedom, democracy, and a more just society.

Many of these concerns were present in the CGT. The highest spokesperson for the country's organized workers, the CGT was born in 1930 and united the syndicalist and socialist groups until then separate. Its early years were precarious. Strong government repression, although directed at anarchists and Communists, discouraged any action that was too militant. Such actions were far from the intentions of the leadership, which was made up predominantly of syndicalists. The high unemployment caused by the Depression also took away from the unions' mobilizing capacity, despite the fact that motives were not lacking as wages fell sharply and only in 1942 recovered their 1929 levels.

After 1933, economic recovery and industrial reorientation began to be apparent. Unemployed workers were gradually absorbed, and the movement of migrants from rural areas to the great urban centers, which attracted them because of new industrial jobs, slowly began. In Buenos Aires, this growth occurred until the middle of the decade in neighborhoods on the periphery of the city and proceeded to swell the suburban belt. Among the trade-union organizations, the great transport and service unions continued to predominate: in first place, the powerful *Unión Ferroviaria,* the railroad workers' union—a model of organization; *La Fraternidad,* the engine drivers' union; the *Unión Tranviaria,* the urban transport workers' union; as well as the municipal workers and commercial employees' unions. Bit by bit, the numbers of workers in the new manufacturing industries and in construction increased. There Communist leaders had success in organizing industrial unions that grouped the old trades in the metalworking, textile, wood, and food-processing industries—among which the meatpacking workers dominated—and above all in the construction industry. With more than 50,000 members, the construction workers' union was the country's second largest union by 1940, behind only the *Unión Ferroviaria* with a membership of some 100,000.

Dormant in the years following the outbreak of the Depression, trade-union activity resurfaced around 1934 and increased significantly until 1937, accompanying the economic cycle. The union leadership of that time—led by the railroad workers—continued the trend that first appeared in the previous decade: separating their trade-union demands from their general political positions. The same was true for many who belonged to the Socialist Party. The unions gradually obtained some improvements, albeit conceded in a partial manner and reluctantly offered by the owners. Railroad workers were able to save their jobs despite the crisis, but at the cost of a reduction in wages. Commercial employees benefited from a proposed law that established sick leave and severance pay for dismissal; President Justo vetoed it in 1932, but it was later passed. The workday was progressively reduced, thanks especially to the gradual spread of the so-called English Saturday, and in certain industries retirement programs were implemented, though there were no paid vacations for anyone.

The state did not ignore the demands of this social actor. President Roberto M. Ortiz, who had succeeded Justo in 1938, not only maintained close contacts with the railroad workers but also sought to establish a base of support among them by vigorously intervening in their internal conflicts. Governor Fresco went even further. Following the practices of the Italian fascist state, he declared that his objective was to harmonize the relations between capital and labor. At the same time that he harshly repressed the Communists, he legalized unions and used the state's powers as arbiter to protect the workers. More discreetly, the national department of labor—which accomplished the notable task of collecting information on all labor-related problems—gradually extended the practice of collective bargaining and state arbitration. The fruits of these practices were revealed in the number of strikes resolved by such compromise.

Reaching a direct understanding with one of society's principal actors formed part of the interventionist and *dirigiste* state's general strategy and, at the same time, coincided with its leaders' tendency to reduce the space for party politics and representative institutions such as the congress. Recognizing the importance of the state and making it the principal interlocutor also constituted a very strong tendency among the union leadership. This tendency—labeled "syndicalist"—was criticized by those in the opposition parties, who began to give priority to demands for democracy and to political confrontation with the government and put pressure on the labor organizations to ally with them. An internal conflict in late 1935 in the *Unión Ferroviaria* led to—in the context of increasing labor agitation—a deep shakeup in CGT leadership and to greater influence for trade-union leaders firmly allied with the Socialist Party. At the same time, this conflict permitted the steady entry of the Communists—whose trade-union strength was increasing—to leadership positions. Together, the Socialists and Communists organized the 1936 May Day celebrations with the participation of the political parties that were supposed to make up the popular front. This cooperation was short lived, and in 1939 they celebrated separately, divided once Stalin signed his pact with Hitler. By then, trade-union unrest was declining, and difficulties for any potential popular front increasing.

The key player in the proposed popular front was the *Unión Cívica Radical.* The lifting of its electoral abstention in 1935 had been urged by most conciliatory sectors of the party, those that surrounded Marcelo T. de Alvear. With great influence in the chamber of deputies and the municipal government council of the federal capital, Radicalism helped to improve the image of the country's institutions whose legitimacy had been strongly tarnished. Radicalism also helped to support some of the government's most controversial decisions, such as the renewal of the concessions to foreign-owned electrical companies in the federal capital, a measure that, according to a subsequent investigation, provided the party with a handsome financial reward. But the return to political struggle also increased the possibilities for protest by the most progressive sectors of Radicalism and drew its strength from the young veterans of university activism and those who vindicated the party's *yrigoyenista* tradition. Governor Amadeo Sabattini in Córdoba implemented very innovative social programs, whereas in the federal capital the opponents of Alvear established a strong current that criticized the conciliatory electoral position of the Radical leadership. The *Fuerza de Orientación Radical de la Juventud Argentina* (FORJA), established in 1935, began to hammer out nationalistic positions. Alvear himself oscillated between both currents. He was the natural leader of the conciliatory faction, yet his platform in 1937, when he competed in the presidential election, adopted much of the progressive and leftist discourse and had affinities with the nascent popular front.

On that occasion only the Communist Party publicly supported him, because the Socialist Party found itself openly competing with the Radicals. Until 1936, the Socialists had had a strong parliamentary representation, which was drastically reduced with the Radicals' return to party competition. Simultaneously, the Socialists improved their situation among the unions with the new CGT leadership, but in 1937 suffered the loss of a group of union militants unhappy with the entrenched union leaders. Many of the defectors were members of the Socialist Workers' Party and went on to join the Communists. This conflict, which deepened in 1939 following the signing of the Nazi-Soviet pact, complicated a popular front alliance ever more problematic.

The cause of democratization, stripped of its more radical content, turned out to be tempting for groups in the government, concerned about the regime's legitimacy and wracked by growing internal disputes. In 1937, President Justo managed to impose on his partisans the presidential candidacy of Roberto M. Ortiz, of antiperonsonalist Radical background, but had to accept as vice presidential candidate Ramón S. Castillo from Catamarca, a representative of the most traditional conservative groups. To defeat Alvear's candidacy, the government resorted without dissimulation to fraudulent procedures that—according to Pinedo—made it "impossible to categorize these elections among the best, even among the most mediocre, that there have been in the country." For Ortiz, it turned out to be more difficult than it was for Justo to maintain the balancing act with the Conservative groups in his party, and even more so with the nationalists, strong in the street and in the army. At the same time, he was attracted to the idea of moving closer to the Radicals; with the support of Alvear, Ortiz proposed to clean up electoral practices and to remove the Conservative leaders from their principal bailiwicks. In February 1940, he interdicted the province of Catamarca—the vice president's home province—and the following month he did the same with Buenos Aires province just as Governor Fresco was preparing to transfer power to Alberto Barceló, the most conspicuous example of fraudulent and gangsterish *caudillismo.* That month, the Radicals triumphed in the congressional elections and consolidated their hold on the chamber of deputies.

Just as everything seemed to lead to the triumph of a version of the plan for democratization, condoned by the government and the right but initially supported by the Communist Party, President Ortiz's illness in July 1940 forced him to delegate power to the vice president Castillo. Although he tried to hold on, Ortiz finally had to resign, only to witness Castillo's undoing of all that had been accomplished in pursuit of democracy. At the end of 1940, in the provincial elections, the worst methods of electoral fraud were again employed. In October 1941, probably because of pressures by the military, Castillo abolished the municipal government council of the city of Buenos Aires without stirring important resistance by this measure. Thus, the attempt at democratization begun in 1936 was crumbling by late 1940. This failure undoubtedly had to do with changes in the international circumstances that had nourished the democracy campaign from the outset. The popular fronts had been defeated in Spain and France, Nazi Germany was piling up stunning military victories at the outset of the war, the Soviet Union was deserting the anti-Nazi camp, and the war was causing different political alignments.

Nonetheless, the current that had made democracy the point of convergence against the heirs of September 1930 had also been affirmed in a more specific social process. Democracy, granted in 1912, had slowly but steadily taken root in society. A network of associations of various kinds, intended to channel the demands of society's different sectors to the public authorities, also contributed to the formation of citizens, to the development of habits and practices of participation, and to the exercise of citizens' rights. The tutelary role that had been played by a broad intellectual and political movement of a progressive, somewhat leftist nature contributed to mold "educated citizens" characteristic of this decade. Unquestionably, the process was uneven, much more apparent in the great cities than in rural areas, but not for that reason any less real, and capable of becoming even more solid despite the restrictions the state had placed on party life and its bastardization by fraudulent practices. Perhaps the parties did not learn how to channel and give shape to that democratic mobilization, to find the points of agreement among them, and to adopt a true position of opposition. Those who could have confronted the government opted for cutting deals and contributed to an increasing public cynicism; the banners of democratic regeneration had been passed to members of the regime itself. In reality, the state had contributed much to discrediting the political parties and representative democracy itself. While politics remained associated with fraud, the state undertook government negotiations directly with society's different actors— unions, business, the military, the Catholic Church, and even civil associations—ignoring congress and the political parties.

The War and the "Nationalist Front"

The World War that erupted in September 1939 gradually changed the political landscape, caused a realignment of the different domestic groups— above all a rapprochement in the positions of the Radicals and some Conservative sectors—and established new options. But none of the political alternatives assumed power or even clearly delineated the political actors. Therefore, in the early years of the war, political alignments were confusing and contradictory.

The first impact occurred on economic and commercial relations with Great Britain and the United States. The gradual closing of European markets—caused by the German military victories—drastically reduced agricultural exports, but on the other hand greatly increased the sale of meat to the British, both frozen and chilled. Because imports from Britain simultaneously declined, Argentina began to have an important balance of trade in its favor with the United Kingdom. In 1939, an agreement between the Central Bank and the Bank of England established that whatever pounds Argentina earned would remain frozen in London for the duration of the war and that, once hostilities ceased, they would be used to pay off the debts for the purchase of British goods or to retire the bonds on the debt. In addition, taking advantage of difficulties in international trade as well as a regional "power vacuum," Argentina began to export industrial goods to neighboring countries. The sale of textiles, clothing, food and beverages, shoes, and chemical products deepened the industrial growth initiated with import substitution, and the country began to have favorable balances of trade, including with the United States.

The novel situation confirmed the expectations of many. The changes created by the crisis of the 1930s were becoming more pronounced, and the return to normalcy, that is to say the situation before the Depression, was becoming ever more remote. Among the business community, different alternatives were beginning to be discussed, without sectoral interests or fixed alignments being clearly defined. Traditional exports seemed to have few prospects in the long run, beyond the favorable circumstances provided by the war, which benefited the cattle ranchers. Industrial exports, on the other hand, and industry in general had a promising future. In either case, both sectors required increased state intervention and regulation of economic activity and also a greater autarchy for the local economy.

In November 1940, Pinedo, named minister of the economy by Castillo, gave a lucid assessment of this new setting and offered an audacious and reasoned solution. His Plan for Economy Recovery proposed as a solution to the difficulties occasioned by the war that the state purchase the harvests to maintain price levels while stimulating construction projects, both public and private, capable of encouraging many other economic sectors. Above all, he stressed the importance of fomenting industry; if foreign trade continued to be the "big wheel" of the economy, these other "smaller wheel" activities would contribute to the general equilibrium. Pinedo warned of an economy excessively turned inward and proposed stimulating the "natural" industries that used local primary materials and could export to neighboring countries and the United States. Along this road, in the long run, Argentina would find a solution to its trade deficit with the northern country, a deficit that unquestionably would become more burdensome to the degree that the industrial sector was growing and the demand for machinery, parts, and fuels increased.

All this involved a complex operation, one that modified the terms of the triangular relationship, proposing a close connection to the United States and even aiming for a fundamentally different role for Argentina in the world economy. It required a firm direction by the state and greater development of its instruments of intervention in the economy. The state would have to mobilize private credit, directing it toward long-term investments, among them industrial investments. The export of manufactured goods would have to have the benefit of a system of subsidies, antidumping laws, and intense promotion of industrial trade.

The bill was approved by the senate, with its government majority, but the chamber of deputies did not consider it. As Juan José Llach noted, the bill was a political rather than an economic failure. The Radicals, who were a

majority of the deputies and had no fundamental objections to the proposal—and indeed later adopted parts of it—had decided to block whatever
bill the government proposed as a way of repudiating the renewal of fraudulent practices by Castillo. Pinedo attempted to solve the problem by meeting
with Alvear, but did not manage to convince the Radical leader and in fact
had to resign his cabinet post for that very reason. The "democratic bloc" that
demanded closer diplomatic ties to the United States did not take note of the
advantages of this plan, which presupposed the end of the ironclad bilateral-
ism with Great Britain. Such a situation reveals how complicated political
alignments then were.

The other dimension of the triangle—the diplomatic one—advanced
along other paths. Since 1932, under Roosevelt, the United States had substantially modified its foreign policy, at least in appearance. The classic "big
stick" policy had been replaced by that of the "good neighbor." The United
States aspired to tighten bilateral relations and in the framework of
Pan Americanism to align the hemisphere behind it. This was a particularly
difficult proposition for Argentina. A commercial bilateral relationship—
a longtime aspiration of Argentina's rural producers—was faced with the obstacle of the U.S. farm block, that is to say, the interests of Argentina's agricultural competitors. Subordination to the United States was equally difficult
to accept for a country that still aspired to an independent and even hege-
monic position in the Southern Cone and that traditionally had opposed
North American leadership, offering in opposition to President Monroe's slogan of America for the Americans that of America for humanity, a Latin
America closely tied to Europe.

The government leadership of the 1930s continued that tradition in international affairs and in successive Pan American conferences did everything
possible to check an alignment with the United States. In the 1936 conference
held in Buenos Aires—which Roosevelt attended, transported in a warship—
a last-minute amendment inserted by the foreign minister Saavedra Lamas
weakened a declaration about consultation in case of foreign aggression, a declaration in which the North Americans had invested much effort. In 1938,
the foreign minister José María Cantilo snubbed his North American colleagues, unexpectedly abandoning the Lima meeting before the signing of the
conference's final declaration.

Neutrality in the event of a European war was also an Argentine tradition.
The adoption of this position in 1939—a logical decision because it allowed

the country to continue trading with its traditional clients—was not objected to by the United States, which proposed neutrality precisely as a common hemispheric policy at the 1939 meeting of the hemisphere's foreign ministers in Panama. By then, the Ortiz government was seeking to move closer to the United States in the context of its program to reestablish democracy, and the same policy was intended by Castillo's foreign minister, Julio A. Roca.

But the war increasingly dominated internal party debates and began to consolidate a sector of public opinion that associated support for the Allies with the vindication of democracy and attacking the government. In June 1940, the group *Acción Argentina* (Argentine Action) was established, dedicated to denouncing Nazi activities and interference by the German embassy in the country's internal affairs. Radicals, Socialists, many intellectuals without party affiliation, and a number of conspicuous members of the Conservative oligarchy participated in it. *Acción Argentina* was distinguished from the abortive popular front by the presence of these latter, recent converts to the virtues of democracy, which reflected the confusion and divisions among those who until then had supported the government of the *Concordancia*. It was also noteworthy for two conspicuous absences: the Communist Party, which, as a result of the Hitler-Stalin pact, had opted to denounce both imperialisms, and also the group of Radicals opposed to Alvear's leadership, among whom stood out the militants of the FORJA, who, like the Communists, were active in denouncing the interimperialist character of the war.

The panorama changed substantially in the second half of 1941. In June, Hitler invaded the Soviet Union, and in December the Japanese attacked the United States at Pearl Harbor. The United States entered the war and sought to force the countries of the Americas to accompany it. In January 1942, the hemisphere's foreign ministers met in Rio de Janeiro, and once again Argentina's opposition frustrated U.S. plans. The appeal for all the hemisphere's countries to enter the war was changed to a simple "recommendation" because of the staunch opposition of the Argentine foreign minister Enrique Ruíz Guiñazú, who had replaced Roca. For the United States, specific interests were at stake, especially national prestige, and it responded with harsh reprisals. Argentina was excluded from the rearmament program bestowed on U.S. allies in the war, with Brazil particularly benefited, and the pro-democracy opposition groups to the government began to receive strong support from the U.S. embassy.

The political front that came together around democratic and antigovernment slogans began to grow, now enlarged with the addition of the Communists—once again partisans of combating Nazi fascism—and with leading conservatives such as Pinedo and General Justo, for whom the choice between fascism and democracy encouraged an alliance with their former adversaries. The Investigating Committee on Anti-Argentine Activities, established by the chamber of deputies, devoted itself to denouncing Nazi infiltration and in a series of public demonstrations simultaneously proclaimed solidarity with the United States and opposition to political fraud. In that undoubtedly simplistic characterization of friends and enemies, the necessities of rhetoric and politics predominated. Castillo's government did not have to sympathize with the Nazis to cling to neutrality. It was enough to maintain the continuance of the country's traditional position—formerly upheld by Yrigoyen—and add to it loyalty to the traditional British partners, who viewed with alarm the U.S. advance, with the war as a motive, into Britain's traditional preserves. There were also clear political motivations. Those who supported rupture with the government and simultaneously took up the democratic banner were condemning the fraudulent government, whereas those who remained faithful to the government—and resisted the bargain that others such as Pinedo and Justo proposed—found in neutrality an effective cause with which to close ranks and confront their enemies. These enemies were ever more numerous among the politicians, causing Castillo to look for support in the military.

In this, Castillo was continuing the tradition of his predecessors. Justo had courted the military, increasing the number of troops under its command, constructing sumptuous buildings such as the war ministry—which eclipsed even the presidential residence—but at the same time proposing to depoliticize the institution, to silence internal debate, and to maintain a balance between its various factions. What he achieved was to maintain control over the high command, which forced his successors to rely on Justo's people. Ortiz found a faithful minister in General Carlos Márquez, who fell because of a scandal involving the purchase of land at the El Palomar military base, which ultimately benefited the president himself. Castillo in turn designated as war minister General Juan M. Tonazzi, another officer loyal to Justo, but dedicated himself to courting the commanders and gradually to placing among them enemies of the former president. During his presidency, the Department of Military Factories (a government agency run by the military, to over-see the administration of the country's military-industrial complex) and the Military Geographic Institute were created, thereby encouraging the advance of the armed forces into areas other than strictly military. During Castillo's government, the presence of the military was ever more apparent, as was the president's sensitivity to the opinions of and pressures from the military chiefs. The armed forces rapidly became a political actor.

A central element of the military's new profile was the development of a nationalist consciousness. The ground had been prepared by Uriburu's nationalism, and the idea was disseminated by a small but active group of na-tionalists, both in and outside the armed forces. Theirs was a conservative, antiliberal, xenophobic, and authoritarian nationalism. The war changed their concerns. The army, traditionally influenced by pro-German senti-ments, was predominantly neutral, but realized that the traditional balance of power in the region was being altered by U.S. support for Brazil and by Ar-gentina's exclusion from the rearmament programs. The solution had to be found in the country itself, and the war thus stirred economic concerns, be-cause military defense required industrial technology, which in turn required capital goods. Since the middle of the decade, the military had set up arma-ments factories. After 1941, through the establishment of the Directorate of Military Factories, it dedicated itself to support such industries as the steel in-dustry, which it judged as "natural" as food processing and indispensable to guarantee autarchy.

The military linked strategic concerns with those involving institutions and policies. The war demanded industrial development, and this, in turn, required an active and efficient state, capable of unifying the nation. The ex-amples of Italy and Germany faithfully demonstrated the success of such poli-cies, and publications supported by the German embassy such as *El Pampero* and *Crisol* promoted these policies. Also important was the role of the state in a society that would be torn after the war by bitter conflicts. Talk again of a popular front, the spectacle of red banners at workers' meetings, and the pres-ence of the Communist Party in the streets seemed to be ominous signs for the future. To confront such a future, order and social peace were required. The ideal of a strong state that enjoyed legitimacy and was capable of weath-ering the storms of war and its aftermath little resembled the shaky and pro-foundly illegitimate Castillo government. As early as 1941, some military officers had begun to conspire; others pushed Castillo down the path of authoritarianism. After December 1942, when the war minister Tonazzi resigned, the conspiratorial mood spread throughout the army.

This diffuse but potent nationalist sensibility was not limited to the army. Rather than a definite and precise idea, it was an ensemble of feelings, attitudes, and barely outlined ideas, present in vast sectors of society. If one could not discern an ideology in the strict sense of the word—because in it were divergent and even antagonistic positions—these ideas revealed a great capacity, partly attributable to the efforts of some of the more coherent, smaller political tendencies, to break down old polarizations and create others. Thus, when all seemed to lead to the triumph of a popular front, a "nationalist front" began to take shape as an alternative.

The roots of this nationalist sentiment were old, but in recent times they had been made more complex by European antiliberal currents, from Maurras to Mussolini, to which were added a Catholic Church strengthened by integralism. The new anti-British nationalism had flourished in this context. The first book of the Irazusta brothers was followed by that of Raúl Scalabrini Ortiz on the British railroads and in general by all the preachings of the FORJA group. In this new crucible, the enemies of the nation were no longer immigrants, "democratic rabble," or "reds"; they were the British and the "sell-out" oligarchy. This anti-imperialism turned out to be a rhetorical weapon and a formidable political position, capable of gathering support from the right and the left, as Lisandro de la Torre demonstrated in 1935. Anti-imperialist slogans began to appear frequently in the speeches of Radical or Socialist politicians, such as Alfredo Palacios, as well as of trade-union leaders; intellectuals began to analyze national problems, especially economic ones, from this perspective.

In this regard, the new nationalism shared the terrain already tilled by the left's progressive reformism, and both found some common ground. With the right's traditional nationalism, such agreement occurred in another area: the revisionist history in which condemnation of Great Britain and its local agents developed into a vindication of the figure of the nineteenth-century dictator Juan Manuel de Rosas, in the name of diverse and even antithetical values, from national emancipation to Catholic integralism. It was precisely its plasticity that explains the ability of this nationalist current to take root in a society whose concern for national issues was demonstrated in many other ways. In literature—especially that disseminated through newspapers and

magazines with a wide circulation—the themes of rural society and the countryside tended to stress the clash between the national interior and the immigrant littoral or between the rural creole world and the urban foreign one.
Characters drawn from history, in which Rosas's presence was frequent,
abounded in pulp literature and also in successful radio programs such as
Snapshots of Tradition, which were avidly listened to.

The concern for national questions was manifested, finally, among intellectuals and writers. Three important essays expressed profound intuitions
about the "national soul" and set the tone for a broad collective reflection.
In 1931, Scalabrini Ortiz published *The Man Who Is Alone and Waits:* Scalabrini Ortiz's man of "Corrientes and Esmeralda" streets, who embodied the
different traditions of an immigrant country and who was defined by his impulses, intuitions, and feelings. This "man" preferred his impulses to any
ruminations or rational calculations and—reminiscent of Ortega y Gasset—
constructed with them an image of himself and what he could become,
which he judged more valuable than the social reality surrounding him. For
Eduardo Mallea, any amalgam was of doubtful worth. Mallea observed the
crisis in the feeling of being Argentine, particularly among the elites, won
over to comfortable living, idleness, and appearances, renouncing spirituality
and more profound concerns about the nation's destiny. In his *History of an
Argentine Passion,* published in 1935, Mallea contrasted that "visible Argentina" with another "invisible" one in which the new elites, at first hidden,
were creating "an extreme exaltation of life." Ezequiel Martínez Estrada was
more radically pessimistic and saw the Argentine community as prisoner of
a fatal destiny, with its origins in the Spanish conquest. In *X-Ray of the
Pampa,* published in 1933, he noted the rift between the unruly masses, heirs
to the resentment stemming from their status as mixed bloods, and certain
Europhile elites incapable of understanding this society or of inculcating in it
a system of norms and principles upheld by collective beliefs. These efforts to
unmask the nature of "the Argentine soul," inquiring in ontological fashion
into essential and singular qualities of Argentine society and culture, though
reflecting common concerns throughout the Western world, were undoubtedly the intellectual expression of this new common restlessness to understand, defend, or construct "the national."

The strength of this nationalist current, which in the case of the war
leaned toward neutrality, was slow to manifest itself. At first, supporters of the
rupture with the Axis won new followers, especially among Conservative

groups. Nevertheless, in a few months, the principal leaders of the democratic bloc all died: Alvear in March 1942, followed by the ex-president Ortiz—whose hypothetical return to power had until then been the source of speculation—then the ex-vice president Roca, and in January 1943, Agustín P. Justo, who had been emerging as the strongest candidate to head a common ticket with the Radicals. Finding new candidates was not easy, and the possible electoral victory seemed more in doubt to the extent that the government was unconcernedly returning to fraudulent practices. At the end of 1941, the Conservative Rodolfo Moreno won the election for governor of the province of Buenos Aires, and the following year the *Concordancia* triumphed in the elections for the legislature. Shortly before, Castillo had shut down the Buenos Aires municipal council and declared a state of siege, for all practical purposes ignoring the congress. Castillo finally opted for Rubustiano Patrón Costas as his successor, a powerful sugar magnate from Salta and a leading figure in the National Democratic Party. Opinions were divided about Castillo's choice; many interpreted it as a change of course in future foreign policy, dividing his supporters even further.

Both political alliances, feeling themselves weak, began to court the military leaders, hoping that the armed forces would assist in restoring the balance in a deadlocked situation and in strengthening an increasingly weak institutional regime. The Radicals, for their part, joined the new game and gambled on the candidacy of the new minister of war, General Pedro Pablo Ramírez. The military leadership almost openly discussed all the options, and groups of a diverse nature appeared in favor of a coup d'état, prominent among whom was the military lodge, the Group of United Officers (GOU), which included some colonels and other lower-rank officers. Many wagered on the collapse of the institutional order, without any clear instigator of such a collapse yet emerging. This collapse was finally precipitated when Castillo asked for the resignation of Minister Ramírez. On June 4, 1943, the army overthrew the president and for the second time interrupted the constitutional order, before having defined the coup's agenda or even naming the head of the new government.

four

The Perón Government, 1943–1955

The military government that assumed power on June 4, 1943, was headed in succession by General Pedro Pablo Ramírez and General Edelmiro J. Farrell. But Colonel Juan Domingo Perón, one of the government's leading members, was successful in rallying a vast political movement around his persona, permitting him to win the February 1946 elections shortly after his popular support was demonstrated in a watershed day, October 17, 1945. Perón completed his first six-year administration and was reelected in 1951, only to be overthrown by a military coup in September 1955. In these twelve years when he was the country's central political figure, to the point of giving his name to the movement that supported him, Perón and Peronism left their imprimatur on Argentine society and gave substantial and lasting new direction to the country's public life.

Crisis

The June 4, 1943, revolution was initially headed by General Rawson, who resigned before being sworn in and was replaced by General Pedro Pablo Ramírez, a cabinet minister in the previous constitutional government. The episode is revealing of the multiple tendencies existing in the revolutionary group and of the uncertainty of the road they would follow, beyond the shared conviction that the constitutional order was finished and that the proclaimed candidacy of Patrón Costas would not fill the void in power. The new government raised diverse expectations outside the armed forces, but many agreed with the government's diagnosis and hoped to gain something from the coup, among them the Radicals. Nevertheless, the government was made up almost exclusively of military men, and the center of debate and decision was in the war ministry, controlled by the group of officers who were members of the GOU lodge and who surrounded the minister of war, General Farrell.

The military members of the government agreed on the necessity of silencing political unrest and social protest; the Communists were outlawed, the unions persecuted, and the CGT—then divided into two factions—was interdicted. In addition, they disbanded Acción Argentina, which included those who supported breaking off relations with the Axis. The government later did the same with the political parties, as well interdicting the universities, dismissing a vast number of professors who were members of the opposition, and eventually establishing obligatory religious instruction in the public schools. In these actions, the country's new military leaders counted on the collaboration of a cast of nationalists and Catholic integralists, some of them with a long-standing political involvement that went back to the Uriburu years, who set the tone for the military regime: authoritarian, antiliberal, messianic, obsessed with establishing a new social order, and avoiding the chaos of Communism that, they thought, was an inevitable consequence of the war. It was not difficult for the democratic opposition to identify the military government with Nazism.

Nonetheless, in the government, together with some who sympathized with Germany, there were others who supported the Allies and many who were supporters of maintaining the neutrality that Castillo's government had followed, one that was benevolent toward Great Britain. Moreover, in 1943, the war was progressing in such a way that an alignment with the Axis was unthinkable. Indeed, the trade agreement with Great Britain was maintained. The United States, on the other hand, attacked with increasing fury one of the only governments in the hemisphere reluctant to accompany its the war effort against the Axis, one suspected of harboring Nazis. The State

Department launched a crusade against the military government, unconcerned about the political consequences of its actions and ignoring conciliatory gestures on the part of Argentina. This campaign allowed the staunchest supporters of neutrality to gain ground, and the conflict thus unfolded at an escalating pace.

For the United States, as Carlos Escudé emphasized, it was a matter of prestige and a moral imperative to put an end to the military government, and for Argentina it was a matter of principle not to accept the *diktat* of the State Department. At the beginning of 1944, after Ramírez decided to break off relations with the Axis, he was removed by the more staunchly anti-U.S. officers. Isolated domestically and internationally, the government found itself in an impossible situation. The solution was ultimately provided by one of the officers who had by then risen notably in the government: Colonel Juan Domingo Perón. Perón was one of the most influential members of the GOU, an undersecretary to the minister of war Farrell and then minister himself once Farrell replaced Ramírez as president in February 1944. Shortly later, in June of the same year, after having removed several possible competitors, Perón became vice president and the very soul of the government.

Perón stood out among his colleagues for his professional abilities and for the eclecticism of his political ideas. A stay in Europe in the years before the war had allowed him to witness the accomplishments of the Italian fascist regime as well as to see the terrible results of the Spanish Civil War. Foresight and concern caused Perón to pay attention to a social actor little taken into account until then: the workers' movement. In charge of the National Directorate of Labor—which soon was converted into a secretariat—Perón devoted himself to establishing ties with labor leaders. All were summoned, save the Communists who, after a frustrated initial courtship, were systematically persecuted and whose position in the labor movement was eradicated. Perón compelled the rest to organize themselves and to press their demands, which were beginning to be met. Besides settling specific conflicts via collective bargaining agreements—supervised by the secretariat—Perón extended the retirement system, paid vacations, and accident insurance. In addition, adjustments were made in job classifications, and relations between management and labor in general became more equal, even at the factory level. Often it was simply a case of implementing long-ignored legal measures.

Other actions were more innovative, such as Perón's sanction of the Statute of the Peon, which extended these policies to the rural world, introducing a public dimension to relations until then handled in a paternalistic and private manner.

From the secretariat of labor, Perón expanded the machinery of the state's powers of arbitration, first outlined during Yrigoyen's government and hardly used during the 1930s, with the exception of Governor Fresco in Buenos Aires province. At the same time, Perón promoted union organization, encouraged the workers in their demands, and exercised pressure that such demands be satisfied. The union leadership's reaction was initially hesitant and disconcerted. Since early in the century, they had gradually come to recognize the central role of the state in labor-capital relations and had become accustomed to negotiating with it. But more recently, confronted with governments hardly interested in playing a role as mediator, they had reached an agreement with the opposition political parties in which trade-union demands merged with demands for a restoration of democracy, along the lines of a popular front. The original syndicalist tendency, however, had not disappeared. In 1942, the CGT split between one sector headed by the Communists and including many Socialist leaders with greater affinity for the opposition parties, and another that identified more with the old syndicalist line, among them the railroad workers. Perón's overtures intensified an already existing debate among the union leadership. The idea of a popular front was losing its appeal, but at the same time the polarization occasioned by the war had revived it. Perón's improvements were too significant to reject, and the unions could not confront the government without the risk of losing the workers' support. The syndicalists adopted what Juan Carlos Torre called an opportunistic strategy; they accepted the government's invitation without closing the doors to the "democratic opposition."

Nor did Perón close them, disposed as he was to speak with all sectors of society and politics. Perón was capable of fashioning his discourse to suit everyone, from the Radicals to the leaders of neighborhood organization, though with a constant appeal to "all Argentines." To his military colleagues, he signaled the dangers that the postwar era posed: the threat of social disturbances and the need for a strong state able to intervene in society and the economy and at the same time ensure economic autarchy. In the National Postwar Council that Perón established, he insisted on the importance of deepening social welfare policies, as well as ensuring full employment and labor stability to face the eventual crisis that the industries that had grown during the war might suffer. To business, he noted the threat represented by the unorganized working masses and the danger of Communism, then advancing in Europe. To all he presented himself as the one who could harness this commotion if he acquired the necessary power for that purpose. But businesspeople were increasingly distrustful of the "pyromaniac fireman," in Alain Rouqié's felicitous description—of the one who threw fuel on the fire at the same time that he claimed he could put the fire out. Gradually, the employers' organizations distanced themselves from Perón and from the policies of the secretariat of labor, while Perón stressed his support for the workers, increasing his anticapitalist harangues and fully developing the concern for social justice in his discourse. At the same time, the suspicions of the union leaders lessened; they found less of a reception in the democratic parties and less interest than that demonstrated by Colonel Perón.

The democratic opposition, which to define its own identity had discovered in the military government a much more convenient enemy than the former oligarchic regime, began to reconstitute itself just as the imminent end to the war was making the government's intransigence increasingly difficult to maintain. The liberation of Paris in August 1944 gave rise to a noteworthy and unmistakable anti government protest, and from that point onward a vigorous social movement took to the streets and revitalized the political parties. The government itself was in retreat. In March 1945, with the end of the war at hand, Argentina accepted the U.S. demand—where a new leadership in the State Department promised better relations—and declared war against the Axis, the condition for being admitted to the United Nations, then in the process of being established. At the same time and for the same reasons, it eased its domestic politics.

The opposition parties demanded the withdrawal pure and simple of those in power and the transfer of power to the supreme court, the last vestige of republican legality, and sealed their agreement for the elections they saw as imminent. Their *Unión Democrática* (Democratic Union) represented the repudiation of civil society for the military and total adhesion to the principles of the victors in the war. This political front, which included Communists, Socialists, and Progressive Democrats and counted on the implicit support of conservative groups, was given life by the Radicals, although an important sector of the party, led by Amadeo Sabattini, rejected the "unionist" strategy and demanded an intransigent and "national" position that banked on the existence of some army interlocutors who were not in Perón's camp. Sabattini's position did not fare well, and the Democratic Union continued to define its positions and alliances. In June 1945, a Manifesto of Industry and Commerce repudiated the government's social legislation. In September 1945, a massive March for Freedom and the Constitution finally sealed the political alliance, and also a social one, which excluded the majority of the workers, a sector of society that formerly had been vocal supporters of the popular front.

The army, pressured by public opinion and distrustful of the workers' colonel, forced Perón to resign on October 8, 1945, but without finding a replacement. Perón was shortly thereafter arrested. General Avalos, the new war minister, and the democratic opposition contemplated several possibilities, but could reach no agreement. In the middle of these vacillations, a novel event transpired to change the balance of forces. On October 17, 1945, thousands of protesters gathered in the Plaza de Mayo and demanded Perón's freedom and the restitution of the offices he had held. Perón's partisans in the army got their way. Perón was released, spoke to the crowd, and returned to the center of power, now as an official candidate for the presidency.

What was decisive about the October events was not so much in the numbers of the crowd—perhaps less than those who had participated in the March for Freedom and the Constitution—as in its composition, markedly working class. The workers' emergence crowned a process that until then had been one of quiet growth, organization, and politicization of the working class. Industrialization had substantially increased during the war, both for purposes of exporting to neighboring countries and for substituting imports made scarce by the difficulties of trade as well as the U. S. boycott. Industrial employment had grown, and the mass of industrial workers had begun to swell with rural migrants, expelled from the countryside by the agricultural crisis. It was not a visible growth because it often occurred in the periphery of big cities such as Rosario, La Plata, or Buenos Aires. Nor was it a social actor whose increased presence was expected, not even by as astute an observer as Ezequiel Martínez Estrada, who ignored the workers in his 1940 edition of his cultural-sociological essay on Buenos Aires, *La cabeza de Goliat.*

Yet there they were, ever more united in a few unions of heightened power, ever more enthusiastic about Perón's policies, and then increasingly concerned about his resignation. Flanked by their unions and led by their leaders, many of whom still harbored suspicions about Colonel Perón, on October 17th, the workers marched to the Plaza de Mayo, the country's symbolic center of power, thereby appropriating a public space and making a demand that was immediately political but that also had profound social consequences. They decided the crisis in Perón's favor, inaugurated a new way of participating in politics through social mobilization, defined an identity, and won their political citizenship, sealing at the same time an enduring alliance with Perón. Some of these outcomes were probably not apparent at the time—many saw in the protesters marginal sectors of the working class, the rabble, or the lumpenproletariat—but slowly they revealed themselves, at the same time that a mythic and legitimizing image was enshrouding the events of the real October.

With the elections in sight, Perón and those who supported him devoted themselves to organizing their electoral support. Trade-union leaders, strengthened by the October protests, decided to create their own political party, the Partido Laborista (Labor Party), inspired by the eponymous party that had just triumphed in Britain. The new party's organization ensured the predominance of trade-union leaders, and its program drew on diverse sources, from the more strictly socialist ones to those advocating state intervention in the economy and the welfare state. In the new party, Perón was nothing more and nothing less than the number one member and presidential candidate, a status still far from the unfettered control that he later assumed. Perhaps to look for alternative bases of support or to garner broader support outside the working class, Perón instigated the division of Radicalism, with a breakaway faction supporting his candidacy—the *UCR-Junta Renovadora*—a group that few Radical leaders of any standing joined and from among whom Perón chose an old and colorful figure from Corrientes, Jazmín Hortensio Quijano, to be his running mate. Relations between members of the Labor Party and those of the *UCR-Junta Renovadora* were poor. The former sought to have Colonel Domingo Mercante, Perón's second-in-command in the secretariat of labor, as Perón's running mate, but had to be satisfied with making him the candidate for governor in Buenos Aires province. Also supporting Perón were many minor conservative leaders from the provinces, but above all the army and the Catholic Church. In a pastoral letter, the Church straightforwardly recommended that Catholics vote for the government's candidate who had fought Communism and established religious instruction in the schools.

The *Unión Democrática* included the leftist parties but—because of the insistence of the Radicals—excluded the Conservatives, who had to resign themselves to support the electoral coalition from the sidelines or pass over quietly to Perón's camp, as many did, motivated by their long-standing rivalry with Radicalism. The Radicals' candidates—José P. Tamborini and Enrique Mosca—came from the heart of the Alvear faction of Radicalism's leadership. The Radical program was socially progressive—perhaps just as much as Perón's—but its impact was attenuated by the enthusiastic support the Democratic Union received from the employers' organizations. For its leaders and for the masses whom the coalition was mobilizing, however, the essential idea was the defense of democracy and the defeat of totalitarianism, which had succeeded, and to a certain extent perpetuated, fraudulent government. Thus were the politics of the previous ten years interpreted, with the conviction that, in free elections, the champions of democracy would triumph.

But the country had changed, in a slow and gradual fashion, although the discovery of this transformation was sudden and dramatic. Perón fully embraced the discourse of "social justice," of the necessary and possible reform opposed, he insisted, only by the selfishness of a few privileged people. Such a discourse deeply rooted in concrete social practices had been elaborated over the course of the previous ten to twenty years, a fact that explains the resonance of Perón's words, when he contrasted the formal democracy of his adversaries with the real democracy of social justice and divided society between the "people" and the "oligarchy." A second component of these changes, nationalist sentiment, emerged suddenly as a response to the untimely intervention of the U.S. ambassador, Spruille Braden, who renewed the State Department's virulent attack against Perón, accusing him of being a Nazi agent and publicly backing the Democratic Union. Perón's response was dramatic and forceful. His slogan "Braden or Perón" added a second antinomy to the campaign and capped the process of fashioning the bloc of popular nationalism capable of confronting what remained of the popular front.

On February 24, 1946, Perón triumphed by some 300,000 votes, equivalent to at least 10 percent of the electorate. It was a clear victory but not a landslide. In the big cities, the division between the working class and the middle and upper classes was evident. Elsewhere in the country, the divisions had a more traditional character, linked to the influence of certain caudillos, the Church's support, or the decision of conservative sectors to support Perón. Perón had won, but Peronism was yet to be constructed.

Internal Market and Full Employment

The new government continued the anti-U.S. rhetoric, which it expressed as a doctrine in the so-called third position, distancing itself both from Communism and capitalism, although it established diplomatic relations with the Soviet Union and did everything possible to improve its relations with Washington. Through pressures from Perón and despite the reservations of many of the old nationalists who had supported him, in 1946 the congress approved the Act of Chapultepec, which permitted the country to rejoin the international community; the following year it did likewise with the Treaty of Reciprocal Inter-American Assistance, signed in Rio de Janeiro. In the same place where, five years previously, Argentina had fully demonstrated its diplomatic independence, the foreign minister Juan Antonio Bramuglia confined himself on this occasion to pointing out minor differences.

But U.S. hostility did not diminish, fed by long-standing economic disputes—especially competition with U.S. farmers—and more recent political frictions. The United States continued to be disposed to make Argentina pay for its neutrality during the war. The boycott was systematic. The blockade of armaments and vital inputs could not be maintained during the postwar period, except for a few cases, but foreign trade was vulnerable. Industrial exports to neighboring countries, which had grown greatly during the war, began to retreat in the face of North American competition. Agricultural exports to Europe—which entered peace literally hungry for them—were hindered by the United States' restricting transport or selling its own exports at subsidized prices. The hunger of the countries ravaged by the war was too great for this maneuver to prevent sales, but none of these countries possessed either the goods to exchange or the convertible currencies that Argentina could use to balance its trade deficits with the United States. As a result, Argentina harvested few benefits during these exceptional years. In 1948, the Marshall Plan was launched, but the United States prohibited the dollars provided to Europe from being used for imports from Argentina. Then from 1949 onward as the European economies began to recover, the United States flooded markets with subsidized grains, and Argentina's participation declined drastically. For the government, the hope remained that a third world war would reestablish the exceptional circumstances that had existed at the beginning of the decade, and in truth there were signs of just such an outcome, such as the Berlin crisis or the Korean War, which broke out in 1950. The containment of such conflicts, and the rapid U.S. response to prevent any change in the global market, ended the last hope.

Great Britain, however, did not accept U.S. pressures to restrict its purchases from Argentina. Besides the meat trade, Argentina's sterling pounds frozen in London during the war and British investments that were in the country were at stake. The size of Britain's debts—Argentina was only a minor creditor—made the payment of pounds unthinkable. The dreadful situation of the railroad companies, their decapitalization and obsolete nature, and their general loss of profitability made it convenient for the British to get rid of them. After a long and complicated negotiation, their purchase was arranged at a price similar to the value of Argentina's pounds frozen in London banks. In addition, an agreement was reached on meat sales that henceforth would be paid in convertible pounds. Behind the nationalist rhetoric that surrounded this operation—presented as part of the program of economic independence and celebrated with a great demonstration in the Plaza de Mayo—the agreement was undoubtedly a victory for the British who were dealing with a country that had no options. The British financial crisis of 1947 and the abandonment of the pound's convertibility put an end to the only tangible benefit that Argentina had obtained.

Selling grains was increasingly difficult, and selling meat was increasingly less profitable. The result was a decline in agricultural production—caused also by other aspects of Perón's economic policy—accompanied by a substantial growth of the share destined for the domestic market. Argentina's traditional place in the world as a privileged producer of agricultural commodities was becoming ever less advantageous, and this contributed to define the options—economic and political—that the war had posed.

The World War, the crisis in the markets, and isolation, accentuated by the U.S. boycott, had contributed to deepen the process of import substitution industrialization begun in the previous decade, extending beyond what were considered the "natural" limits—the elaboration of local primary materials—and extending to the metalworking sector and others. A typical firm was SIAM-Di Tella, the country's largest metalworking company, which began as a manufacturer of bread-kneading machines and gasoline pumps for YPF, the state-owned oil company. SIAM-Di Tella grew notably during the war, moving into the manufacture of refrigerators, fans, electric irons, and washing machines. In some cases, industrial goods were exported to neighboring countries, which also suffered from import restrictions. In others, needed imported products were manufactured locally for the domestic market, with models and productive processes adapted with ingenuity although perhaps in an improvised and inefficient manner. Industry was labor intensive, which, added to the difficulties in incorporating machinery, meant increases in production translated into declining labor productivity. Thus grew, together with the established industrial firms, a broad array of small- and medium-sized establishments that significantly augmented the size of the labor force nourished by increasingly large waves of internal migrants.

The termination of the war and the end of this "power vacuum" in the world, which had permitted the growth of industries in the periphery as in Argentina's case, posed various options. With the idea of returning to the "normalcy" existing before 1930 or 1914 definitively abandoned, those who were most tied to the traditional business groups—both in the export sector and in industry—adopted the ideas presented by Pinedo in 1940: to encourage "natural" industries, those capable of producing efficiently and of competing in foreign markets; to associate with the United States to sustain growth and at the same time maintain a balance between the industrial sector and agriculture, which provided the foreign exchange needed by industry. The option was difficult to attain, not only because it meant rebuilding a very deteriorated relationship with the United States as well as firmly seeking to recover agricultural markets, but also because it implied a strong shakedown of the industrial sector, eliminating less efficient sectors that had grown during the war under the natural protection that the conflict provided and confronting the costs of a difficult absorption of the labor force that would be left unemployed. A second alternative, posed by military groups during the war, expressed both the strategic concerns of the armed forces and the ideas firmly rooted in the nationalist tradition: to deepen import substitution industrialization, to extend it to the production of basic inputs such as steel or oil through vigorous state intervention, and thereby to ensure economic autarchy. The shadow of the Soviet Union—which beyond its Communism had constructed a powerful state—was present in this proposal and in the subsequent rhetoric of Perón's two Five-Year Plans. But as in the case of the Soviet Union, such undertakings implied an enormous effort in capital accumulation, restrictions on consumption, and probably a "sacrificed generation."

Perón had participated in these debates, which he himself had promoted in the National Postwar Council established in 1944. His solutions were eclectic and novel and took into account principally the immediate interests of the workers, who constituted his most solid base of support. The military's aspirations for economic autarchy were revealed in the first Five-Year Plan, which was supposed to serve to plan the economy but was limited to a series of vague declarations and the creation of a state steel company, SOMISA, which would remain in the blueprint stage for the next ten years. The presence of the industrial sector that had grown during the war was seen in Perón's first economic team, headed by Miguel Miranda, a manufacturer of tinplate containers, seconded by Raúl Lagomarsino, a textile industrialist, and advised by José Figuerola, a prominent Spanish technocrat. Miranda, named president of the Central Bank, of the powerful Argentine Institute for the Promotion of Trade (IAPI), and of the Socio-Economic Council, was for three years the regime's economic tsar. The state's policies—a state endowed with, as will be seen, much more powerful instruments to intervene in the economy—were geared to the defense of the established industrial sector and to its expansion under the prevailing standards of government protection and support. Industry received ample credits from the *Banco Industrial* (Industrial Bank) established by the military government in 1944 as well as tariff protection to prevent foreign competition, and foreign exchange acquired at preferential rates to acquire foreign technology and inputs. Moreover, the policies of redistributing income to the working-class sectors contributed to the steady expansion of consumption. In this singular period, high employment and rising wages were accompanied by an expansion in demand and a rising inflation but also by handsome profits for business.

In sum, Perón opted for the internal market and for the defense of full employment. These years witnessed a veritable "chain effect of happiness," which could be financed primarily because the existence of an abundant reserve of foreign exchange accumulated during the prosperous war years permitted an accelerated, unbridled, and frequently inefficient industrialization in the postwar period. Defying the laws of fiscal restraint, in the hope of another world war, Argentina spent much more abroad in these years than came in. Furthermore, IAPI monopolized foreign trade and transferred to the industrial and urban sectors the income generated in the countryside through the difference paid rural producers and the amounts obtained for the sale of harvests in foreign markets. This was a strong blow to the agricultural sector, no longer regarded as the "linchpin" of the national economy or perhaps as a sector capable of withstanding anything. Rural producers also suffered from the lack of inputs and agricultural machinery—for which there were no preferential exchange rates—the freezing of tenant leases, which affected the natural cycle of recovering the land's fertility, and rising labor costs because of the application of the Peon Statute. All these factors exacerbated the decline in cultivated land, at the same time that the increase in domestic consumption—reflected in wheat and above all in meat consumption—reduced even more the amount available for export.

Peronist policies were characterized by a strong stimulus to state participation in the management and regulation of the economy. They continued tendencies begun in the previous decade under conservative administrations, but extended and deepened them, inspired by Keynesian ideas in vogue in many parts of the world after the war. At the same time, there was a general nationalization of foreign investments, particularly of companies controlled by British capital, which experienced a full process of repatriation. All this was invested with great symbolism, expressed in the slogan of Economic Independence solemnly proclaimed in Tucumán on July 9, 1947. To the railroads were added the telephones, the gas company, and some electric utility firms in the interior, without affecting the legendary *Compañía Argentina de Electricidad* (CADE), which supplied electricity to the federal capital. A strong impetus was given to the newly created public company Gas del Estado, constructing a gas pipeline from Comodoro Rivadavia, as well as to a merchant marine—in which were incorporated the ships of the powerful Dodero shipping firm—and to the fledgling state-owned airlines, *Aerolíneas Argentinas*. The state even moved into industrial activities, not only via its armaments factories but also with a group of nationalized German companies that were added to the state holding company, DINIE. The most important reform was the nationalization of the Central Bank. Through it were managed monetary and credit policies and also foreign trade, because all bank deposits were nationalized, and the Central Bank was assigned control of the IAPI.

Nationalization of the economy and state control were keys to the new economic policy. The other—and perhaps the most important—had to do with the workers, with maintaining full employment and improving their standard of living, probably more in response to political considerations than to economic ones. The fear of the possible social consequences of unemployment, the memory of the crisis of the first postwar period—in which Perón himself had a firsthand experience when he participated in suppressing the rioters during the 1919 *semana trágica,* as well as Europe's own inter- and postwar experiences must have influenced not only general economic policy but the priority assigned first to industrial employment and second to redistribution of income. Social justice thus served at the same time to uphold the domestic market. Between 1946 and 1949, the social welfare measures launched before 1945 were expanded and extended to the general population. Through collective bargaining negotiations, guaranteed by law, wages began to increase notably. To this were added paid vacations, sick leave, social programs covering health care, and tourism, all activities in which the unions played an important role. Along other paths, the welfare state contributed decisively to raising the standard of living: freezing rents, establishing minimum wages and price ceilings, improving public health, financing public housing projects, building elementary and secondary schools, organizing a national retirement plan, and undertaking initiatives in all things related to the realm of social welfare.

The Peronist State

This combination of what was attained through struggle and what was simply granted from above is revealing of the complex relationship established between the workers and the state. The terms under which the state operated until the 1946 elections changed radically immediately after Perón's victory.

Using as a justification the countless number of conflicts between the members of the Labor and Radical Parties who made up his electoral coalition, Perón ordered the dissolution of the organizations that had supported him. Among those organizations was the Labor Party, through which the old trade-union leaders had hoped to conduct an autonomous politics, supportive of Perón yet independent of him. The decision—which culminated in the creation of the Peronist Party—was at first resisted; but in truth only Cipriano Reyes, the leader of the Berisso meatpackers' union, confronted Perón, earning him bitter persecution. Shortly thereafter, Perón stripped the leadership of the CGT from Luis Gay, a veteran trade-union leader, mastermind of the Labor Party and one of the promoters of the idea of an autonomous workers' project. Perón replaced him with a trade-union leader of little account, thus indicating his willingness to subordinate the trade-union leadership to the state. Once again, there was no resistance. Probably for the majority of the workers, solidarity with the one who had made a reality of so many benefits mattered more than a political autonomy whose intentions, in this context, were unclear.

But, at the same time, the workers' organization was firmly consolidated. As Louise Doyon demonstrated, union affiliation, low until 1943, spread rapidly, first to the industrial unions and then to the public employees, reaching its high point around 1950. The Law of Professional Associations ensured the existence of large and powerful organizations—one union per industry and a single labor confederation—with the strength to negotiate as equals with business but at the same time dependent on the legal recognition (*personería gremial*) granted by the state. Perón preferred that the orientation and demands of the unions be guided from above rather than from below, and the CGT, led by mediocre figures, was responsible for transmitting the state's orders to the unions and controlling the unruly among the union leadership. The unions had a similar function with respect to rank-and-file organizations: to control, to lessen the space for autonomous action, to intervene in any locals that were too bumptious. At the same time, the unions assumed increasingly complex duties, both in collective bargaining negotiations and in social welfare activities, and had to develop a specialized administration. As a result, the character of the union leaders, transformed into a stable bureaucracy, differed notably from that of the old militants. Among the rank and file, union activity retained a great deal of vitality, thanks to the shop stewards committees that looked after a wide variety of immediate problems related to working conditions. Such committees negotiated directly with owners and managers and established a fairly high degree of shop floor democracy in the factory. In the early years, until 1949, strikes were numerous and were undertaken in behest of the reforms launched from the government, either to have such reforms implemented or to extend them, with the workers convinced that they were complying with Perón's deepest desires.

Perón, however, worried about this ceaseless agitation and sought to strengthen his control over the trade-union movement. The union leaders who had initially accompanied him gradually drifted away, replaced by others chosen by the government and more inclined to obey its instructions. Strikes were considered inadvisable in the beginning and simply unwanted later. The government sought to resolve conflicts through arbitration procedures and, that failing, chose to repress them, whether at the hands of the union itself or of the public security forces. From 1947 onward, Eva Perón, the president's wife, devoted herself from the secretariat of labor—a post left vacant by Perón—to carrying out the duties of mediating between the union leaders and the government, expediting the negotiation of conflicts with a very personal style that combined persuasion with coercion.

The relationship between Perón and the labor movement—a crucial facet of the Peronist state—was undoubtedly complex, in a constant state of negotiation, and difficult to reduce to a simple formula. Despite the strong government pressure on the unions and the decision to control their actions, the latter never ceased to be the social and political expression of the workers. From the workers' perspective, the state not only facilitated and promoted their organization and showered them with benefits; it also created a situation of communication and fluid participation, almost of a family nature, and thus the workers were far from considering it as something foreign. The Peronist state, in turn, had a great legitimizing force in the workers and recognized them as such. This was not a simply rhetorical or abstract recognition, but a concrete view of its organizations and its leaders, to whom it granted a prominent place in the movement.

But at the same time, the Peronist state sought to extend its support to a broad stratum of unorganized popular sectors, with which it established a deep relationship, although of a different nature, through Eva Perón and the foundation that carried her name. Financed with public monies and more or less voluntary private contributions, the Eva Perón Foundation realized works of notable importance. It founded schools, old folks' homes and orphanages, and hospitals; it distributed food and presents at Christmas; it encouraged tourism and sports activities, through juvenile championships at the national level, baptized with the names of the governing couple. Above all, it practiced direct action. Its neighborhood committees—the building blocks of the Peronist Party—detected individual cases of need and transmitted requests to the foundation, where Eva Perón tirelessly received a permanent procession of petitioners who might obtain a sewing machine, be assigned a hospital bed, or receive a bicycle, a job, or perhaps a retirement pension, and certainly unfailing solace.

Eva Perón thus turned out to be the very incarnation of the welfare state, which through the Lady of Hope acquired a personal and emotive dimension. Her beneficiaries were not exactly the workers; many lacked union protection and owed everything to the state and to the woman who intervened in their behalf. The media harped incessantly on this image, a combination of benefactor and caretaker, an image then propagated in the schools where children first learned to read with the slogan "Eva loves me." The experience of direct social action, combined with the state's incessant discourse, ended up creating a new social identity, that of the "downtrodden," thus completing the constellation of the government's popular support.

According to an idea that became more widespread as the years transpired, the state should establish ties with each one of society's sectors, a society conceived as a community and not as mere collection of individuals. The state, in turn, wanted each of these sectors to organize itself and to establish its corporatist representation. More or less successfully, the state sought to organize business, uniting in the *Confederación General Económica* (CGE) all business sectors, as it did the university students and professionals. It also attempted, cautiously, to redefine the relationship with the country's great traditional institutional powers. With the Catholic Church there was a basic agreement, which translated into the Church's open support in the 1946 election. The Peronist government maintained religious instruction in the schools and granted control of the universities to personalities linked to Hispanophile clericalism. It reserved an important place in public ceremony for high prelates such as Monsignor Copello and incorporated into its governing team some prelates, such as Father Hernán Benítez, Eva Perón's private confessor, or Father Virgilio Filippo, the fiery parish priest from Belgrano who exchanged the pulpit for a seat in congress. The government's relationship with the Church was nonetheless somewhat distant. An important group of ec-clesiastics—among them Monsignor Miguel D'Andrea—concerned about the growing authoritarianism, firmly aligned with the opposition. Others lamented Perón's later abandonment of nationalist positions, and many more looked on some aspects of the democratizing effects of the new social rela-tions with reservations, for example, creating equal rights for "natural" and "legitimate" offspring.

With respect to the armed forces, though Perón routinely turned to offi-cers to carry out important duties during his administration, he took care ini-tially to refrain from meddling in their internal affairs and also gave them an institutional presence in his government. Above all, he sought to preserve the identification established in 1943 between the armed forces and a government that he wanted to be the continuation of June 4, 1943: the "Olympic episode in history," which continued to be a dramatic foundational moment. Central planks of the government, such as economic independence, national unity, order, and above all the image of a world at war where neutrality translated into the "third position," served to consolidate a field of common solidarities, disturbed however by what the military saw as the excessively populist style of the government, above all by the presence, in words and in action, of the president's wife.

According to Perón's ideas, the state, besides directing the economy and looking after the people's welfare, should be the forum where the different sectors of society, previously unorganized, negotiated and resolved their con-flicts. This line of thinking—already taking shape in the 1930s—was inspired by models widespread at the time, ones that could find past affinities both in Mussolini and the Mexican Lázaro Cárdenas and that broke with liberalism's conception of the state. These ideas implied a restructuring of democratic institutions and a subordination of constitutional powers to the executive branch, where the leader resided, whose legitimacy was derived less from these institutions than from the popular plebiscite.

Paradoxically, a government that had emerged from one of the few clean elections in the country's history resolutely embarked on the road to authori-tarianism. Thus in 1947 it purged the supreme court via a rather unconvinc-ing political trial. It also made liberal use of its powers of interdiction in the provinces. In many cases—in Santa Fe, Catamarca, and Córdoba among oth-ers—and in traditional Argentine fashion, it did so to resolve issues among sectors of its heterogeneous collection of supporters. But in one case, Corrientes, without any such conflict serving as a pretext, it used its power to depose the only non-Peronist governor elected in 1946. A 1947 law ended university autonomy, requiring that any professorial appointment obtain presidential approval.

Legislative power was formally respected—the corpus of legislative acts elaborated in these years was extensive—but it was stripped of any real content. Legislative bills were prepared in the president's office and were passed without amendments. Opposition members were accused of contempt, barred from the chamber of deputies, or stripped of their congressional immunity, as happened with the Radical leader Ricardo Balbín. Parliamentary discussion was avoided, members frequently resorting to a preemptory motion to "close the debate," the specialty of the Peronist congressman Astorgano. In 1948, a change in the system of electoral districts—gerrymandered by the minister of political affairs, Román Subiza—reduced to a minimum the representation of the opposition in the chamber of deputies. The encroachment of executive power occurred also with the undeclared "fourth branch" of government, the press. With resources of a diverse nature, the government established an important chain of newspapers and another of radio stations, which it controlled through the secretary of press, administered by Raúl Alejandro Apold, whom the opposition liked to compare to the Nazi minister of propaganda Josef Goebbels. Independent newspapers were harried in a thousand ways. They were faced with newsprint quotas, circulation restrictions, temporary closures, attacks, and in two extreme cases—*La Prensa* and *La Nueva Provincia* in 1951—they were expropriated outright. The reform of the Constitution, realized in 1949, ended the last great institutional safeguard and established the possibility of presidential reelection. Two years later, in November 1951, Juan Domingo Perón and J. Hortensio Quijano were reelected, garnering on that occasion—when women voted for the first time—around two-thirds of the electorate.

For Perón, as important as affirming the preeminence of the executive branch over the other political institutions was giving shape to the heterogeneous ensemble of forces that supported him, from different sectors, with diverse traditions, and often led by cadres and activists without experience or political training. All these people had to be given a discipline and organization according to Peronism's most general principles, to avoid both internal conflicts and the possibility that they could animate and transmit tensions and demands from society as a whole. To achieve these ends, Perón resorted to a traditional method previously employed by Roca, Yrigoyen, and Justo— the use of state's authority to discipline his own followers—as well as a novel method—the use of his personal and inalienable leadership, shared with his wife, lawfully created and carefully nurtured by the government's propaganda machinery.

In congress, Perón demanded of every Peronist deputy and senator a pledge to resign at his discretion as guarantee of their loyalty. The Peronist Party, created in 1947, adopted a totally vertical organization in which every level was subordinate to the one above it, reaching its apex with the leader, president of the country and the party, who had the right to modify any party decision. This organization was the local version of the celebrated German *Führerprinzip,* albeit with a less drastic implementation: The Peronist Party, run by Admiral Teisaire, limited itself to organizing the party tickets, and Perón arbitrated in difficult cases or simply mentioned who should be selected. The party's organization was modified several times and, as Alberto Ciria showed, the increasingly complex structure accentuated its verticality. Finally, the party was incorporated in the movement, together with the Women's Peronist Party—which Eva Perón organized—and the CGT, all at the orders of the Supreme Leader, to whom were subordinate the party's "Strategic Command" and "Battle Commandos".

Besides this military terminology, Peronism's organization included another revealing characteristic: At every level of government, all power was concentrated in the hands of the executive—whether mayor, governor, or president—making it clear that the movement and the nation were considered one. What was initially the Peronist Doctrine was converted into the National Doctrine, enshrined in those terms by the 1949 Constitution, which included an article equating the state with the "organized community." State and movement, movement and community came together in the leader, who formulated the doctrine and put it into practice in a flexible and practical way, with his leadership skills that, although personal and inalienable, could be taught to those who assumed subordinate commands. Here was combined the army's traditions, in which leadership was a fundamental aspect of authority, and those of modern totalitarian regimes that undoubtedly had made an impression on Perón in their fascist versions.

This rhetoric was unquestionably foreign to the country's dominant political tradition, liberal and democratic, although its emergence should not be seen as something entirely surprising if it is remembered what had previously been the country's concrete political practices. Neither the identification of the party with the nation, nor the marginalization of the congress, nor the combination of the chief of state and the party leader was an absolute novelty. On the other hand, if Peronism systematically eliminated the areas of autonomous participation, whether of a party, trade-union or societal nature, tended to penetrate and "Peronize" all facets of civil society, it is no the less true that it incarnated and constructed a highly vigorous democratizing movement that guaranteed political and social rights to vast sectors that had previously been neglected, culminating with the establishment of the vote for women and other concrete measures guaranteeing women a place in the country's institutions. The more traditional concepts of democracy cannot be applied to this very modern form of mass democracy.

This singular form of democracy was constituted from the state. The diverse actors that made up its base of support were regarded as "masses," that is to say, an undifferentiated conglomeration whose political autonomy was dismissed. The masses had to be molded, inculcated with the "doctrine." A massive propaganda effort was directed to them, a campaign that saturated the media—used for the first time in a systematic way—and also the schools. The regime showed a marked tendency to "Peronize" all institutions and to transform them into instruments of indoctrination. It would be difficult to overestimate the effectiveness of this propaganda, which translated into massive electoral support for Perón or Perón's chosen candidates.

But the most characteristic and singular facet of this mass politics was the mobilizations and rallies. Realized on certain day such as May 1st, October 17th—and on special occasions, when something had to be celebrated or a political decision ratified—such mobilizations preserved, albeit more in the popular memory and in their potential than in the demonstrations themselves, much of the defiant, spontaneous, and revolutionary pathos of the October 17, 1945, protests, Peronism's founding mobilization, now a ritualized and restrained public holiday. The masses were no longer spontaneous but summoned, with the means of transportation provided by the government. Orderly and with the workers aligned in squares, they even included attendance rolls. Above all, they were festive occasions, stripped of any overtones of political confrontation, except the diatribes against the metaphorical "oligarchy" or "antipatria," which expressed a sense of national unity more than they did the nation's conflicts. In the May 1st "festival of work," the workers—according to the inspired words of Oscar Ivanissevich, the minister of education, government bard, and lyricist of the "Peronist March"—"united in the love of God," met "at the foot of the sacred flag." In reality, this process was not new; the slow transition from the combative to the festive event had begun in the 1920s, but Perón gave it a new impetus. The revolutionary tradition was also remembered and maintained by Perón above all in inflammatory rhetoric, full of populist fervor, and in the class-charged defiance of Eva Perón.

As a renewal of the foundational pact between the leader and the people, the great rallies fulfilled a fundamental role in the government's legitimacy via the plebiscite, considered much more important than elections. Such rallies were the ideal moment for the construction of an identity that turned out to be that of a worker, the people, and the Peronist combined in one. Everything was prepared for the sublime moment and the reception of the leader's speech; by making his appeal to the "comrades," from the balcony of the presidential palace, he granted them a place, beyond passions and conflicts, among those who supported him and accepted his leadership—the fatherland, the people, and the workers. The speech also defined the position of enemies, described as enemies of the fatherland, and therefore excluded from the ideal of peaceful coexistence. Perón urged "for our enemies not even justice." Silvia Sigal and Eliseo Verón noted in all this the definitive incorporation into the popular political culture of two elements barely compatible with the country's previous democratic tradition: a vertical structure and factional nature, both transformed since then into political virtues.

To what extent was all this the exclusive responsibility of Peronism? The opposition ended up occupying an assigned role in this system. The 1946 electoral defeat totally tore asunder the project of the Democratic Union—the final incarnation of the popular front—and confronted the opposition parties with a difficult question: how to deal with Perón. The Socialists, removed from all meaningful political representation, stood fast to the "Nazi-Fascism" characterization of Peronism, denouncing the steps taken toward authoritarianism and judging that the priority was to put an end to the regime. The Socialist groups that took a more conciliatory position with regard to the workers who had adhered to Peronism were unable to break the Socialists' solid and now sclerotic party structure. Something similar occurred in the Communist Party. A brief period of rapprochement and sympathetic understanding, expressed via the labor movement, culminated in the expulsion from the party of those leaders who had favored such a position. The conservatives were rattled by the number of their leaders who "passed over" to the government, but they eventually recovered and formed an open opposition based on the defense of democratic principles and the rule of law.

In Radicalism the process was more sweeping. The 1946 defeat opened the road to party renewal. A coalition of unyielding reformers and *sabattinistas* (followers of the Radical leader from Córdoba, Amadeo Sabattini), critics of the strategy of the Democratic Union, dislodged the so-called unionists who came from the *alvearista* wing that controlled the party. In 1947, in the Avellaneda Convention, the Movement of Intransigence and Renovation (MIR) formulated its principles, substantially changing the Radical program, which heretofore had been ambiguous and unclear. The MIR, without abandoning democracy and the defense of the Constitution as guiding principles, combated Peronism from a position that was presented as more progressive, both socially and economically, and did so with greater ease to the degree that the regime, because of the demands of governing, abandoned its initial, more progressive positions. While the Unionist branch of the party opted for a frontal challenge and contemplated the possibilities of a military coup, the Intransigents debated in the congress each one of the government's bills, at times supporting them and at others raising well-founded objections that in many cases were attended to. In the Radical bloc of forty-four deputies presided over by Ricardo Balbín and Arturo Frondizi, the entire post-Peronist Radical leadership cut its teeth. But they did not succeed in constituting a true democratic opposition, in part because of their factionalism was also very strong. Above all, they failed because the Peronist majority was not disposed to convert the congress into a place of debate or even to tolerate its being a tribune for dissidents of the National Doctrine. Every means was used to silence their voices and finally to place them in the position that had previously been assigned them, that of a formal opposition.

A Cultural Conflict

The virulence of political discourse and the inflamed attacks against the "oligarchy" did not reflect a genuine state of social conflict, much less a class war, as might be inferred. The Peronist regime did not attack any fundamental interest of the traditional upper classes, although some segments of the latter may have been adversely affected by Perón's agricultural policies. The institutions that expressed the interests of the propertied classes—the *Sociedad Rural* and the *Unión Industrial Argentina* among others—did not publicly oppose the government, and even accepted discrete cooptations. There were indeed new incorporations of successful businesspeople, particularly those who learned how to take advantage of the access to power and the sinecures it offered for making handsome profits. In the social imagination, the "new rich man," the parvenu who merged with other new members of an elite leadership, occupied a prominent place. Such a leadership was certainly more varied than before 1945. Trade-union leaders occupied visible positions in the government, together with a new a coterie of politicians, professional athletes, and artists. The traditional middle class perhaps had more reason to complain, especially those living on fixed incomes reduced by inflation or those who lost their state jobs. But on the other hand, the government received its sustenance from new and vigorous contingents who ascended socially via the most traditional route of Argentine society: the modest economic prosperity of workers, and the education of their children, because one of the outstanding characteristics of these years was the formidable expansion in enrollments in secondary schools and the equally significant expansion of university enrollments.

Internal migrations had been deeply transforming the physiognomy of the popular sectors. Among these popular sectors, the crisis in the pampa's agriculture exercised as strong an influence as did the enticement of industrial employment; and once the latter reached a stable level of growth, it was simply the allure of life in the cities, which reflected the processes of modernization and the appearance of new expectations and aspirations made widespread by movies and the radio. During the final years of the 1930s and the war years, migrants were primarily from the neighboring provinces of the pampa zone. Later they were joined by migrants from the traditional interior, who contributed to the social image of the *cabecita negra,* the racial slur employed to describe this new wave of migrants with *mestizo* or indigenous features. With such migrants, the boundaries of the country's big cities— Buenos Aires, Rosario, and Córdoba—grew, repeating a familiar social history: the small lot, the somewhat precarious dwelling (constructed in a piecemeal fashion)—with the novelty of the support of government housing programs—and finally the cooperative effort to create an urban community.

What was new about this process, which continued the century-old expansion of Argentine society, was the sudden incorporation of the popular sectors into public spaces that had previously been prohibited. Beyond their political significance, the October 17, 1945, events had been symbolic precisely for that reason. Encouraged and protected by the Peronist state, taking advantage of a new degree of economic comfort, the popular sectors joined the world of consumption, urban life, and politics. They bought clothing and shoes, radios and refrigerators, and sometimes the new domestically-manufactured motorbikes that Perón took it on himself to promote. They traveled throughout the country, thanks to the programs of social tourism, and gained access to places of relaxation and entertainment, taking advantage of the generalization of the English Saturday law, some even taking the entire Saturday off. People filled the soccer fields, plazas and parks, and dance halls such as La Enramada, where folk music brought back memories of the old identity and helped facilitate the assumption of the new one. Above all, they went to the movies, the great pastime of those years. In a word, they invaded the city, including the downtown, and made use of everything. They exercised fully a social citizenship that was born intimately tied to politics.

Recognition of the existence of working people and the exercise of new rights were associated with state action; and social justice was a key and constitutive idea of both state discourse—from which was derived the so-called Justicialist doctrine of Peronism—and the new social identity being established. The essentials of this idea had been taking shape over the two previous decades, because of the experiences of the popular sectors as of diverse discursive sources, from the Socialists to Catholic doctrine. This idea had been distilled in a perception, rational and emotional at the same time, of society's injustices—a sensibility manifested in everything from the speeches of the Socialist leader Alfredo Palacios to the movies of Tita Merello—of a society united in a purposeful undertaking to solve its most pressing problems, to achieve improvements, perhaps modest but realistic and immediate, in which the welfare state had the primary responsibility and the political organization of those it benefited was relegated to a secondary plane.

What was singular—as José Luis Romero justly emphasized—was the combination of this new conception with that other one, less a product of official discourse and more truly constitutive of modern Argentine society: the idea of social mobility. State action did not replace the classic individual adventure of social ascent, but rather provided an initial head start, the elimination of the most formidable obstacles so that the traditional mechanisms of social mobility might begin to function. "Social justice" was thus culminating a century-old process in the integration of Argentine society and the identity that was constituted around that concept simultaneously strengthened class identity and integration with the state. Unlike previous decades, everything having to do with the world of work and its inherent dignity, held center stage, strengthened by the role of that working class institution par excellence—the union—which had inserted itself in many facets of national life, both those related to the world of labor and elsewhere, because the union's hand was found in everything from its members' health care to tourism and sports activities. The state oversaw the workers' integration into the nation and into established society, whose accumulated resources the workers aspired to enjoy through practices already developed by those who, in previous periods, had followed the same process of integration.

To the strong impetus given to education—particularly at the secondary level—was added the sponsorship and promotion of diverse cultural activities: concerts and plays at reduced prices; opening the *Teatro Colón,* the great opera house of Buenos Aires, to a wide variety of activities; strong protection for the national film industry; and finally the natural spread of the radio. The state distributed and the public received, together with tangible goods, a massive dose of propaganda. A majority of the newspapers and all the radio stations were controlled, directly or indirectly, by the secretariat of the press. The sardonic tango singer Enrique Santos Discépolo and the mediocre Américo Barrios were the spokespersons for government propaganda that spilled over into the sports announcing of Luis Elías Sojít, and that was finally established in the schools when Eva Perón's ghost-written autobiography, *La razón de mi vida,* was made a required text.

The state facilitated access to highbrow culture, but above all distributed the products of "popular" culture, which included much traditional folklore as expressed in the works of Antonio Tormo or Alberto Castill, and much of a purely commercial nature. Taken together, the state implanted in society's imagination the established social and cultural models as decades before, the magazine *El Hogar* had done. The so-called white telephone movies that transmitted the conventional image of the upper classes—seen in the movies of Zully Moreno—or the school textbooks where workers were portrayed in their home, seated in a chair, dressed in a coat and tie, reading the newspaper, were emblematic in that regard. The state also imparted a particular vision of national traditions, apparent in its efforts to unravel the mythic "national character" that was supposed to unify the nation. Curiously, for a movement with nationalist origins, though the primordial figure of the liberator, General San Martín—the centennial of whose death was lavishly celebrated and who was represented as the precursor of the second liberator (Perón)—the figure of Rosas was conspicuously absent. The names of representatives of the most classic liberal tradition—Urquiza, Mitre, Sarmiento, and Roca—baptized the lines of the nationalized railroads. This new beginning separated the present from a black and ominous past, to such an extent that Peronism—without losing its roots in tradition—could fully display its foundational and revolutionary dimension, legitimized by a future in the process of being built. A dark past and a rosy future, a before and now, were the central elements in the textbooks and speeches of Peronist Argentina.

That discursive construction, and the manner chosen to disseminate it, did not need bona fide intellectuals so much as it did propagandists, some of whom were convinced militants, and others who were simply obsequious. Unquestionably, despite the support available, government-sponsored intellectual and artistic creation was negligible with only a few noteworthy exceptions: the philosopher Carlos Astrada, the writers Leopoldo Marechal and María Granata, and the poet Horacio Rega Molina. The best intellectuals, critics and creative artists coexisted, together with representatives of the old and now somewhat-decrepit established culture, in institutions that emerged on the fringes of the state, animated by a certain sacred fire: *Ver y Estimar, Amigos de la Música, the Colegio Libre de Estudios Superiores,* the latter functioning as an alternative university, and finally the literary review, *Sur,* whose cosmopolitan and apolitical aestheticism converted it at times into an opposing ideology. Perhaps the most novel aspect in terms of cultural activity in these years was the rise of "independent" theater, cultivated by non-professional actors, which provided a suitable terrain for a renewal in national production—beginning with the play *The Bridge,* by Carlos Gorostiza—and contrasted with the repetitive mediocrity of the big commercial or state theaters.

Peronism had emerged during the war years and early postwar period in the context of strong social conflict fomented by the state itself. With the passing of time, such conflict was partly manifested in a pronounced political confrontation between the government and the opposition and also in a conflict that was cultural in nature, rather than strictly social. The state had worked hard to fit social conflicts into a more general conception of class harmony, the community of interests and negotiation, a negotiation in which the state arbitrated while shifting such conflict to the domain of the social imagination.

This cultural conflict was infinitely more violent than the one between the basic social classes, that which pitted the "oligarchy" against the "people." The popular culture combined working-class and integrative dimensions but lacked the strictly class-based components that, in other societies, manifested themselves in a closed culture turned inward. Such a popular culture did not promote a different cultural model from the established one but rather sought in its own way to appropriate it, to participate in something it viewed as valuable but also heretofore forbidden. From that perspective, the oligarchy—portrayed as cold and selfish—sought to restrict access to the nation's resources and to exclude the people. In a certain sense, such feelings represented a precise definition, above all in its ethical dimensions, though socially it was vague, and allowed for a coexistence of violent discursive attacks—particularly in the plebeian voice of Eva Perón—with few concrete actions against the targets of the discourse, against "the oligarchy enclosed in its dens." Conversely, from the opposition, the resistance to Peronism's political practices was combined with irritation over the Peronist brand of social democratization. In much of this there was a horrified reaction by polite society to the popular invasion of the spaces that previously were its own and a great deal of anger over the loss of respect and deference which were judged a product of the regime's demagogic excesses. The opposition's response was, together with attacks on the regime, to ridicule the parvenu, both the new rich and the humble urban resident, awkward in their handling of the instruments of culture and often dazzled by the city's more superficial manifestations.

These two antagonistic and incompatible cultural configurations mutually rejected each other but competed for meaning in a common area. Around the figure of Eva Perón, a battle of this sort was fought. Two antagonistic and equally stylized versions confronted each other, and the true historical personality vanished into thin air. As Julie Taylor showed, the "Lady of Hope" stood in contrast to the "Lady with the Whip," two versions of women's images and roles, elaborated by the middle classes as they sought to appropriate the figure of Evita. Even more apparent was the dispute surrounding the image of the *descamisados* (the "shirtless ones"), which in practice alluded to the union leaders' ritual act of taking off their jackets in official ceremonies (perhaps to show off their silk shirts). Originally the term, like the French *sansculotte,* captured polite society's contempt for an unexpected dinner guest. Yet for the workers, the idea of the *descamisado* was positive; it was an appropriation of and a reified meaning for the pejorative term, which became an integral part of Peronist working-class identity.

Crisis and a New Economic Policy

The favorable international conjuncture in which the Peronist state emerged began to change around 1949 when the prices of grains and meat returned to normal and the markets shrank, while the accumulated reserves, spent with little foresight, were exhausted. The situation was serious, because the development of industry, perhaps paradoxically, made the country more dependent on imports: fuels, intermediate goods such as steel and paper, parts and machinery whose scarcity hindered industry's growth and ultimately provoked inflation, unemployment, and strikes. The first signs of the crisis consequently brought the fall of the minister of the economy, Miguel Miranda, who was replaced by a team of professional economists—headed by Alfredo Gómez Morales—which took charge of implementing austerity measures. Three years later, the measures did not prevent the reappearance of the crisis in foreign trade, aggravated by two successive droughts. In the harsh winter of 1952, people were forced to eat black bread, made with millet, while there was a shortage of meat, and electric power failures were frequent. In that winter, Eva Perón, one of the symbols of the lost prosperity, died.

Precisely in 1952 the government firmly adopted a new economic course, subsequently ratified in the Second Five-Year Plan—a plan much more specific than the previous one—which was to be implemented between 1953 and 1957. To reduce inflation, internal consumption was restricted; subsidies for goods of various popular uses were eliminated; a partial ban on meat consumption was established; and rent control was curtailed. Moreover, Perón appealed for a voluntary and deliberate reduction of consumption, with surprising effect. On the other hand, a "return to the countryside" was proclaimed. IAPI, overseen by a "liquidating minister," reversed its practices and began to encourage agricultural producers with competitive prices, at the same time that it gave priority to the importation of agricultural machinery. This policy, whose results would be unremarkable, was intended to increase the availability of foreign exchange to continue fomenting the development of the industrial sector and was essential for the entire Peronist system.

By now industrial stagnation was evident. In previous years, shielded by a broad protectionist policy, an extensive sector of small-and medium-sized generally inefficient industrial establishments had proliferated; these survived through the protection and high prices paid to them by the large factories. Nonetheless, the food-processing and textile sectors, the leading branches of industry, had reached their limits of growth. Other branches, such as the metal-working industry, or domestic appliances, rubber, paper and petrochemicals, still had interesting possibilities in the domestic market but found themselves hindered by obstacles of a diverse nature. The principal problem of the industrial sector was its limited efficiency, hidden by protection and by the subsidies it received from the state through various means. The causes of this inefficiency were multiple: To obsolete machinery were added the deterioration of the service sector, especially the shortage of electricity, and deficient transportation, particularly the railroads whose modernization the state had abandoned. In the factories, without the incentives that competition would have provided, inefficient and costly productive practices had survived. Finally, industry employed a high proportion of workers, and the burden of wages for labor was particularly heavy and difficult to reduce because of low unemployment and the trade unions' strong powers of negotiation. The growth of demand, which initially compensated for high labor costs, had lost its dynamic effect, and therefore the labor problem began to become onerous for business.

The new economic policy was aimed at those problems. Industrial credit and the use of foreign exchange were restricted, and new priority was given to big industry, and especially to the capital goods industries. The SOMISA project to build a national steel mill was revived and the government sought to initiate the manufacturing of tractors and automobiles. Collective bargaining agreements—the cornerstone of the trade-union policy—were frozen for two years. At the beginning of 1955, business and labor were convoked to discuss productivity questions; on the agenda were the issues that concerned business: the inefficiency of the labor force, the excessive power of the factory shop stewards, and high absenteeism. Union concern also quietly appeared, partly expressed in the demands for the return to the government's early economic policies and partly in strikes such as those of the metallurgical workers in 1954, carefully ignored by the captive pro government press.

The government placed its greatest hopes on something that from that point on was a central theme in economic policies: the attraction of foreign capital, which some began to imagine as the economy's panacea and others as its Trojan horse. In 1953, the government sanctioned the Law of Capital Investment which, despite establishing important safeguards regarding profit remittances, assumed a fundamental modification with respect to the postulates of economic independence and Peronism's "third position." The law occurred in the context of a visible reconciliation with the United States, culminating in the support given U.S. policies in Korea and Guatemala—where the Central Intelligence Agency had just overthrown the reformist President Jacobo Arbenz Guzmán—and the enthusiastic reception offered the brother of President Eisenhower on his visit to Argentina.

In the context of this reorientation in economic policy, several projects, ones that would come to fruition after 1955 began to be realized. The Italian company, Fiat, became interested in investing in the production of tractors, automobiles, and motors; another Italian conglomerate established a steel plant in Campana; Mercedes-Benz established a factory to build trucks; and the North American firm Kaiser established a car plant, moving its already obsolete operations from Detroit to Córdoba. The most important foreign investment was in oil. In 1954, the government signed a contract with an affiliate of Standard Oil of California to search for oil over 40,000 hectares in Santa Cruz province, a contract that gave the company broad rights. This measure challenged deeply rooted convictions—and even a provision in the

1949 Constitution—and sparked widespread public debate, prompting Perón to choose to send it to the congress for its ratification. There it was debated both by the opposition—with the Radical leader Arturo Frondizi publishing a scathing attack against it entitled *Petróleo y política*—as well as by sectors of Peronism itself, whose most outspoken spokesperson was the young congressman John William Cooke. The bill was never passed.

The new direction in economic policy accomplished little. Inflation was reduced, and the balance of payments problems alleviated, but more substantial reforms in agriculture and industry were not forthcoming. The regime's policies had certainly established a new course for the economy, anticipating in their fundamentals the policies of post-Peronist governments. But their application was tentative and took into account the necessity of safeguarding the situation of the popular sectors, making such policies a bit incompatible with the economic orthodoxy that inspired them. Neither did the government resort to a devaluation—the powerful instrument that was subsequently employed to make swift and substantial income redistribution among sectors—nor did it reduce public spending, which in good measure subsidized wage-earning sectors. In that sense, the new economic policy sremained within the Peronist tradition on economic matters.

The beginnings of the economic crisis were accompanied by important signs of disagreement among two principal supporters of the government, the unions and the army, whose resolution entailed a step further along the path of authoritarianism. Around 1948 the state had managed to stabilize and establish control on the trade-union front, but from the following year, strikes, although fewer en number, were tougher and of an increasingly opposition nature. In 1949, on two occasions, the *Federación de Obreros de Tucumán de la Industria de Azúcar* (FOTIA), the union that represented the Tucumán sugar workers, undertook such strikes, with the result that the union was finally outlawed and interdicted. Subsequently, the bank workers, print workers, and railroad workers all carried out strikes in late 1950 and early 1951. The railroad workers' strike constituted a strong challenge to the regime because of its widespread visibility and because it occurred independently of the compliant and ineffective leadership of the union. The strikers, hard hit by government policies intended to reduce railroad costs, followed the old anti-Peronist union leadership in the strike. Their will could not be bent even by Eva Perón, who put her prestige on the line by rather pathetically making the rounds among the railroad workshops and demanding from "her" workers solidarity with Perón. Perón opted finally to implement a harsh repression: prison for the rebel leaders and military mobilization to control the workers.

Problems with the military followed the initial inroads made by the regime in that institution, which at first had maintained a certain compliant attitude toward the government. General Franklin Lucero, the new minister of the army, took pains to win support among the officer corps: Military pay was increased, promotions were expedited, and various benefits were offered to commanders and officers, including the junior officers benefited by the newly established right to vote. Until then, junior officers had been nonentities with little influence, but they were now granted the right to wear uniforms similar to those of the higher officers as well as having access to a scholarship program to educate their children. Such changes offered the possibility of "opening up the ranks" and allowing these officers to rise in the institution. All these benefits, which also implied also an increase in rivalries and internal jealousies, were intended to achieve a deeper commitment on the part of those who were supposed to be a central component in the organized community.

The sought-for commitment exposed all the misgivings and doubts that the regime—no longer just Perón himself—aroused in the military. The army wondered about the solidity of a proclaimed order based on permanent agitation of the masses. The military was indignant about the flagrant move toward authoritarianism, such as the expropriation of the newspaper *La Prensa* and were irritated with Eva Perón's interference in the affairs of state and with her peculiar personal style. The proclaiming of her candidacy for the vice presidency in the Open Assembly of Justicialism on August 22, 1951, a candidacy that she declined days later, was undoubtedly difficult to swallow.

These and perhaps other motives provided the minimal grounds for action on the part of officers determined to overthrow Perón; linked with these officers were those opposition politicians who were already embarked on a similar path. On September 28, 1951, General Benjamín Menéndez headed an uprising, glaringly improvised and easily put down. Although this episode revealed most of the army's firm support of and respect for constitutional authority, it also constituted a warning sign for a regime that until then had not run into any consistent opposition. Perón took advantage of the attempted putsch to declare a state of siege, which he maintained until 1955. With these powers, he devoted himself to purging the military commands of all adversaries, including those who were suspect, or merely unenthusiastic and vacillating. At the same time, at the height of the electoral campaign, he restricted even further the actions of the political opposition and won an overwhelming victory in November 1951, in the first election that allowed women to vote. Perón garnered 64 percent of the vote, and the Peronist won all the Senate seats, and 90 percent of the chamber of deputy seats, thanks to the advantages of the gerrymandered system implemented by the government years before.

Consolidation of Authoritarianism

Perón began his second administration visibly strengthened by the new economic plan, which appeared initially successful, the victory over rebel military and union leaders and the spectacular electoral triumph. Even the death of Evita, without question a heavy blow for the regime, was the occasion for funerals converted into singular public demonstrations of support. The end of the Peronist government's revolutionary stage—visible in the new economic policy and in the normalization of relations with the United States, and symbolized by the tragic silencing of the regime's shrillest voice—gave the impression of progress toward political peace and a more normal relationship with those who dissented, in the setting of a certain political pluralism. But other forces pushed in the direction of maintaining and deepening the authoritarian course: the natural expansion of the political machinery, which inexorably advanced into those areas not under its control, and the scant predisposition to rebuild democratic spaces on the part of much of the opposition, which was concerned to eliminate Perón by whatever means necessary.

In the final three years of his government, Perón displayed erratic behavior. The difficulty in filling the void left by the death of Eva Perón was evident. Both in the Foundation Eva Perón and in the Women's Peronist Party and the CGT itself a bureaucratic spirit and a loss of initiative could be seen. Perón appeared to lose his drive, demonstrating a certain weariness and less concentration in his work and political leadership. He spent much more time in the private presidential residence in Olivos and surrounded himself with the adolescents of the Union of Secondary Students (UES), whose headquarters were in the presidential residence itself, or he devoted himself to leading student parades on a motor scooter—the latest novelty in import substitution industrialization—revealingly sporting a baseball cap.

The Union of Secondary Students was precisely one of the new signs of this authoritarian system that sought to enlist all sectors of society in organizations that were controlled and "Peronized." The populist political machinery, superbly organized, produced regular if predictable summonses to the Plaza de Mayo. The Peronization of public administration and education advanced with demands for affiliation to the party, wearing of the Peronist "badge," obligatory mourning for Eva Perón, pressures to make contributions to the latter's foundation, and demonstrations in support of Perón and his wife, whose names emblazoned railroad stations, hospitals, streets, plazas, cities, and entire provinces. The Peronization even affected the armed forces. There were courses in Justicialist doctrine, and the promotion and selection of officers openly responded to political considerations. The space for political opposition was reduced to a minimum, both in the press and in congress where Hector Cámpora, Peronist president of the chamber of deputies, proclaimed the superiority of obedience over debate and legislation.

While the regime moved toward totalitarianism, it sought—although with fewer results—to rebuild a space for peaceful coexistence with the opposition. This basic objective met with some reception in the parties, whose situation on the edge of legality created tensions difficult to bear. Some leaders got up the courage to approach the government and initiate a dialogue. The response they received was as warm as it was harsh for their more reluctant comrades. First there was, in 1951, a secret negotiation with the conservative leader, Reynaldo Pastor; then a public offer by a group of leaders of the Communist Party, headed by Juan José Real, who proposed the formation of a United Popular Front, but ran into solid Peronist anti-Communism. Finally, at the end of 1952, a veteran Socialist leader, Enrique Dickmann, negotiated with Perón the release of imprisoned Socialist politicians and the reopening of their newspaper, *La Vanguardia*, a move that brought him immediate expulsion from the party. With government support, Dickmann founded the *Partido Socialista de la Revolución Nacional*, which gathered various dissidents from the left, and through which Perón unsuccessfully planned to divide the Socialists.

This tenuous beginning of a political opening up—undeclared by both sides—came to an abrupt end in April 1953. During a demonstration in the Plaza de Mayo, while Perón was speaking, bombs placed by opposition groups engaged in terrorism exploded, killing several people. The response was similarly violent. Peronist groups set fire to the *Casa Radical,* the Socialist *Casa del Pueblo,* and the Jockey Club, symbol of the shadowy and ubiquitous "oligarchy." The police, tellingly passive, moved into action only to prevent the burning of the offices of the newspaper *La Nación.* This wave of government terror was followed by the widespread and indiscriminate arrest of leaders and figures from the opposition, including everyone from the Radical Party leader Ricardo Balbín to the writer Victoria Ocampo. But in the second half of the year, the government eased up and agreed to free those imprisoned, provided that the parties themselves made the request and thus gave proof of their recognition of the regime, a policy that the smaller parties followed discreetly. In December, finally, an amnesty law allowed the release of the majority of prisoners. The following year, in 1954, the call for elections to choose a vice president—Quijano had died shortly after reelection—led once again to putting in motion the electoral machinery. Admiral Teisaire—who administered the party—defeated by the traditional wide margin Crisólogo Larralde, one of the most prominent leaders of the Intransigent Radicals.

By then Radicalism had defined its positions, finding an issue for possible opposition to a regime that wavered simultaneously between conservatism and authoritarianism. Just as with the other opposition parties, the Radicals had to contend with a strong internal division after 1946. The "unionists," heirs to Alvear's tendency in Radicalism and to the Unión Democrática, gambled everything on electoral abstention, total rupture, and a military coup, and Córdoba's Sabattini current in Radicalism also adhered to that position. The group Intransigence and Renewal, on the other hand, insisted since the outset on a political and ideological struggle and continued to do so despite the almost total elimination of outlets for such an opposition. In 1954, this latter tendency won definitive control of the party, when Arturo Frondizi reached the presidency of the national committee. Accused of being a "red" by his enemies in Radicalism, Frondizi sharpened his original image of an intellectual politician, strengthened by the publication of his book *Petróleo y política.* With that book, Frondizi stumbled on an issue with which to combat Peronism from what was most progressive in the latter: its popular nationalism. Without abandoning his criticisms of Peronism, Frondizi championed agrarian reform and anti-imperialism, issues that had become urgent with the signing of the oil contracts.

One might speculate about the sincerity of this proposal and the possible emergence of a renewed political opposition. But certainly, in 1954 it fit squarely with—as Félix Luna noted—a certain reopening of public debate, which coincided with an aging of the regime and of its leader. At this time, the magazine *Esto es* practiced an independent journalism that distinguished it from the monotonous encomiums of the government press. The newspaper *De Frente*, edited by John Willian Cooke, seemed to introduce into Peronism an unexpected internal debate, which had virtually no precedents in this hierarchical movement. The magazines *Imago Mundi* and *Contorno* opened a cultural alternative and demonstrated a renewed interest in the modernization of intellectual life. That same year, the founding of the Christian Democratic Party seemed to indicate—as Tulio Halperín Donghi said—that the Catholic Church was adhering to in somewhat belated fashion this image of a decrepit regime.

The Fall

The founding of the Christian Democratic Party marked the beginning of the conflict between Perón and the Church which rapidly led to his downfall. Despite the multiple sources of friction, it was not an inevitable conflict; and allowing himself to be dragged into the confrontation was unquestionably a serious mistake on Perón's part, as well as a sign that this skillful politician—as capable in unifying his own camp as in exploiting the weaknesses of his adversaries—had lost many of his abilities.

The organized community—or less modestly the Peronization of society's institutions—was a project with its own dynamic, implemented by a coterie of government functionaries who marched independently of the will or leadership of the president. The army, at first shielded in its independence and professionalism, succumbed along the way, and voices raised in disagreement in its ranks against the regime were increasingly strident. But the Church, with whom there had initially been established a mutually beneficial agreement, was especially impenetrable to Perón, and therefore a potential enemy, even more so to the degree that there were old enemies of the regime in the Church—identified with the opposition—and new dissidents, unhappy with different facets of the government's new direction, such as the abandonment of nationalist shibboleths. The Peronist state and the Church began to bump heads in a number of specific areas. The Church was sensitive to Perón's inroads in charitable activities, through the Eva Perón Foundation, and also in education; here, combined with its displeasure with the growing personality cult of Perón and his wife, there was concern about the progress made by the state in organizing of the country's secondary students, concerns heightened by dark suspicions of immoral behavior on Perón's part. The government, in turn, was disturbed by the conspicuous intrusion of the Church into politics with the Christian Democrats, and more underhandedly into the trade-union field, an action that, from the regime's point of view, verged on the treasonous.

The conflict erupted in September 1954, when two demonstrations celebrating the Day of the Student in Córdoba, one organized by Catholics and another by the Union of Secondary Students (UES), competed. In November, Perón launched his attack against the Church. The confrontation seemed to cool down immediately, but worsened in December, following a huge religious procession in Buenos Aires to celebrate the day of the Immaculate Conception. The attack demonstrated that the vertical nature of the Peronist movement had reached the government's political machinery: Everyone in the Peronist movement, with few exceptions, suddenly discovered the great vices of the Church. Although there was an attempt to limit it to "a few priests," the attack was ferocious, surprisingly so in a society that since 1930 had retreated so far in its appreciation for the values of secularism. Religious processions were prohibited; religious education in the schools was abolished; there was introduced—in a law in the process of being passed as a rider to another bill—a surprising clause that permitted marital divorce, authorized the reopening of brothels, and proposed a constitutional reform separating church and state. Many priests were arrested, and newspapers were filled with public condemnations and salacious commentaries about the conduct and morality of prelates and priests.

The defense of the Church was no less effective and demonstrated its power as an institution in a society that nonetheless was not characterized by its religious devotion. Attacked in the government-controlled media, the

Church inundated Buenos Aires with all sorts of pamphlets, while its lay organizations, particularly Catholic Action, mobilized its cadres, augmented by other members of the opposition who finally found a breach in the regime and were not dissuaded by the clerical, nationalist, and integralist tone that predominated in the ecclesiastical mobilization. On June 8th, the day of Corpus Christi was celebrated with a massive procession. The chief of police—it was later shown—burned an Argentine flag during the procession and accused the Catholic opposition of having done it.

On June 16, 1955, the navy rebelled against Perón. It would be difficult to trace the genesis of the uprising to the conflict with the Church because the navy was the most secular and liberal branch of the armed forces. But supporters of the coup—officers and opposition politicians—found their opportunity. The navy's plan—truly insane—consisted of bombarding the presidential palace to kill Perón; the execution of the plan was totally bungled and culminated in the bombardment and machine-gunning of a crowd of civilians who were in the Plaza de Mayo to support Perón, causing some three hundred deaths. The uprising quickly failed, and the army demonstrated once again its loyalty to legal institutions. As in 1953, the government's first reaction was managed terror: Groups that were visibly left unmolested set fire to the metropolitan cathedral and various churches in the capital city.

Also as on previous occasions, this paroxysm of fury was followed by a conciliatory attitude on the part of Perón, who, although the winner this time, had lost much of his freedom to maneuver and to a certain extent was the prisoner of his military saviors. Suddenly, the attacks against the churches stopped, attacks that had deeply disturbed the majority of the military commanders. There was an attempt to overhaul Peronism's leadership cadres, to exclude the more controversial personalities and incorporate others with greater aptitude for dialogue, as well as to call the opposition to negotiate. Perón solemnly declared that he was ceasing to be the leader of a revolution and was henceforth the president of all Argentines. The opposition leaders were invited to initiate a public debate, using the state-controlled press as a medium, including the national radio network, where Arturo Frondizi could be heard exhorting the government to return to the democratic path and to formulate, with soberness, a true program of alternative government. Other political leaders could also speak, though the Socialist Alfredo Palacios—who called for the president's resignation—was forbidden to do so. Perón quickly concluded that the possibility of opening a space for a democratic debate that included him was slight. On August 31st, after rhetorically offering his resignation, he convoked—for the final time—the Peronists in the Plaza de Mayo, where he denounced the failure of conciliation and launched the strongest of his attacks against the opposition, proclaiming that "for every one of ours who falls, five of theirs will."

It was to be Perón's swan song. Soon thereafter, on September 16, 1955, a military revolt broke out in Córdoba, led by General Eduardo Lonardi, a prestigious officer and conspirator in the 1951 uprising. Although there was considerable civilian support, especially among Catholic groups, few army troops joined the revolt. Yet among the "loyal" forces there was little enthusiasm for combating the rebels. The navy on the other hand fully supported them, and its flotilla threatened to bombard the coastal cities. Perón had completely lost the initiative and did not demonstrate the will to defend his government by mobilizing all the resources at his disposal; his vacillation coincided with the decision of those who until that moment had been his supporters in the army, who somberly decided to accept a resignation half-heartedly offered. On September 22d, Perón took refuge in the Paraguayan embassy, and on September 23d, Lonardi proclaimed himself in Buenos Aires the provisional president of the nation, before a crowd as large as those once assembled by the fallen regime, though undoubtedly different in its composition.

five

The Stalemate, 1955–1966

The day after the coup—if not before—the heterogeneity of the front that had conspired to overthrow Perón could be seen. General Eduardo Lonardi headed the new government and declared himself provisional president, thereby indicating his resolve to restore constitutional order. Surrounded by Catholic groups—the most active but also newcomers to the opposition— and by nationalist military figures, the leader of the *Revolución Libertadora* (Liberating Revolution) proclaimed that there would be "neither victors nor vanquished" and sought to find common ground among the principal forces that had backed Perón, particularly the unions. In his opinion, the nationalist and populist movement that Perón had founded continued to have merit, provided it was appropriately purged of its corrupt and undesirable elements. The unions showed themselves to be conciliatory with the new government, though in many working-class quarters—in Avellaneda, Berisso, and Rosario—there were spontaneous demonstrations against the military. But Lonardi's partisans shared the government with representatives of more traditional anti-Peronist groups, backed by the navy, the most monolithic of the three armed service branches, whose spokesperson was the vice president,

Vice Admiral Isaac F. Rojas. In the army, after an internal struggle, the supporters of an open rupture with the fallen regime prevailed. On November 13, 1955, barely two months after having been designated president, Lonardi was forced to resign and was replaced by General Pedro Eugenio Aramburu, a man closer to liberal and anti-Peronist sectors, while Rojas remained in the vice presidency.

The episode quickly revealed the complexity of Peronism's legacy. The formula with which that movement had been concocted—authoritarianism, nationalism, and populism, born of the exceptional wartime and immediate postwar conditions—had already reached a crisis point around 1950, when the world began to enter a more normal situation. Perón himself undertook a significant reorientation in his policies to bring them into harmony with the new circumstances. The characteristics of his movement, the social forces that supported him and that he himself had mobilized and created, prevented him from moving decisively in that new direction. With Perón fallen from power, those same social forces constituted an insurmountable obstacle to his successors' efforts to realize their declared objective of rebuilding a democratic coexistence lost years ago and also—albeit less clearly—to reorder substantially society and the economy.

In 1955, that reordering was encouraged and even demanded by a world in which new challenges loomed, after a stage in postwar reconstruction had concluded and amid the Cold War. The slogans of the Liberating Revolution in favor of democracy coincided with political tendencies in the West, where liberal democracy—both in practice and as a cause—clearly marked off the boundaries with the totalitarian East. As in Peronist Argentina, in the United States and Europe the state decisively intervened, presiding over economic reconstruction and mediating complex agreements between business and labor. But this increasing power of the state—of the interventionist and welfare state—was accompanied by an integration and liberalization of economic relations in the capitalist world. In 1947, the Bretton Woods monetary agreements established the dollar as the global currency, and capital began to move freely again in the world. Those countries shut off from the outside world grew fewer in number, and multinationals began to establish themselves in markets that had previously been prohibited. For the countries whose economies had grown based on the internal market and in carefully protected fashion, as in the case of the Latin American, particularly Argentine, economy, the International Monetary Fund (IMF)—a financial entity that had enormous power in the new context—proposed so-called orthodox policies: stabilizing the currency by abandoning unrestrained monetary emission, ceasing to subsidize "artificial" sectors, opening markets, and stimulating traditional export activities.

Nevertheless, an alternative policy gradually began to be formulated, elaborated especially by the United Nations' Economic Commission for Latin America (ECLA). ECLA proposed that the "developed" countries help the "underdeveloped" ones to eliminate the factors responsible for their backwardness through appropriate investments in key sectors, accompanied by "structural" reforms, such as agrarian reform. From that point on, the "monetary" and "structuralist" remedies competed in public opinion and as government policies. It might be thought that both strategies were in the end complementary, but for the time being they had different political representations; whereas the first led to revitalizing the old foreign economic partners, oligarchic sectors, and perhaps dictatorship, the second compelled deep changes: modernization of society that would be crowned by the establishment of stable democracies, similar to those of the developed countries.

To adapt itself to this world of reconstituted capitalism, liberalism, and democracy, it was not enough to restore constitutional order to Argentina and put an end to the vestiges of a regime inspired by the authoritarian governments of the interwar years. It was necessary to modernize and make adjustments in the economy, to transform the productive apparatus. After 1955, proposals to open up the economy and to modernize were shared values in Argentina. But the methods to be used for this transformation generated deep disputes between those who trusted foreign capital and those, from the nationalist tradition that had nourished Peronism or from the anti-imperialist left, who were distrustful of it. The debates, which dominated two subsequent decades, revolved around how either to attract or to control foreign capital. Some local business sectors discovered the advantages of an association with foreign capital, but others that had grown and consolidated themselves under state protection felt they were certain victims, either from competition or from the ending of protection. These firms sought to hinder the growth of foreign capital, and they found a welcome reception not only among nationalists and the left, but also among the majority of political parties.

Businesspeople, domestic or foreign, agreed that any modernization needed to alter the status achieved by the workers under Peronism. As it already had indicated at the end of the Peronist regime, business sought to reduce the workers' share of national income and also to increase productivity, rationalizing jobs and reducing the size of the labor force. These aims entailed curtailing the power of the unions and also the power that the workers, protected by legislation, had achieved on the shop floor. Cutting back wages and recovering management's authority in the workplace were the principal objectives in a general sentiment running against the status of greater equality achieved by the workers and the peculiar practice of citizenship on which Peronism had been based. Demands for a certain business rationalization combined with resentments that were difficult to admit but were undoubtedly strong among those who had made common cause against Perón.

Here was the greatest obstacle. As Juan Carlos Torre noted, at issue was a now-mature working class, well defended in a labor market, approaching near full employment, homogeneous, and with a clear social and political identity. The political identity turned out to be decisive, because of the unbreakable bond between the workers and Peronism, strong before 1955 but definitively consolidated after Perón's fall. In a general way, Peronism's political exclusion—which was extended until 1973—was, for the victors of 1955, the necessary requirement for bringing about the desired transformation of the country and at the same time the source of its greatest difficulties. Between the social forces embarked on such a transformation, which had not finished defining their objectives, priorities, and alliances, and those loyal to the fallen regime, which preserved a significant capacity for resistance, there ensued a situation that Juan Carlos Portantiero described as a "stalemate" that lasted until 1966.

A conflict ultimately loomed between modernization and democracy, a difficulty in reconciling the two principal demands of the postwar world. But in the short term, no such conflict was perceived. The proposal to proscribe Peronism, a sentiment that swiftly prevailed in the government of the Liberating Revolution, was decided not so much in the name of capitalist restructuring as in that of a democratic regeneration such as the world was encouraging. In the denunciation of Peronist totalitarianism, a vast and heterogeneous collection of groups joined together; at least initially they concurred in the diagnosis that Peronism as such was unacceptable, but that former Peronists, after a period of rehabilitation, could be redeemed and might be able to be admitted to the citizenry. The proscription of Peronism, and with it that of the working class, defined a political setting that was fictitious, illegitimate, and inherently unstable, one that opened the way for a struggle—unresolved—between the country's great corporative powers.

Liberators and "Developmentalists"

General Aramburu, who headed the provisional government until 1958, fully assumed responsibility to dismantle Peronism. The Peronist Party was dissolved, and the General Confederation of Labor (CGT) and the unions interdicted, placed under the control of officers of the armed forces. A large number of political and trade-union leaders were arrested, subjected to close scrutiny by investigative committees, and finally stripped of their political rights. Public administration and the universities were purged of Peronists, and the largely state-owned media tightly controlled. Propaganda of any kind favorable to Peronism was prohibited, as was the mere mention of Perón's name; henceforth he was referred to as the "fugitive tyrant" or the "deposed dictator." Through executive decree, the 1949 Constitution was abolished.

This policy was staunchly supported by the navy, transformed into a bastion of anti-Peronism, but it raised doubts and divisions in the army, where many officers had supported Perón until almost the final moments. The disagreements among the anti-Peronists from the outset and those who had joined the coalition against Perón late in the game worsened because of a professional problem—the reincorporation of officers who had been relieved of command in the regime's final years because of political motives—and the factional rifts became bitter. On June 9, 1956, a group of Peronist officers organized an uprising that counted on the support of many civilian groups and sought to exploit a climate of discontent and trade-union mobilization. The government suppressed it with unusual violence, ordering the execution of the principal military leaders, including the ringleader General Juan José Valle. This act of unusually cold-blooded violence revealed the depth of the sharp division between Peronists and anti-Peronists. After that, the purging of officers was frequent, and little by little the most decidedly anti-Peronist group—the so-called *gorilas*—won control of the army. Those who survived quickly adapted themselves to the new circumstances and embraced the by-then dominant liberal and democratic creed, to which they added a new anti-Communism, in tune with the country's closer links to the West.

The military proposed sharing the government with civilians and completely transferring it to them as soon as possible. With Peronism proscribed, military leaders fantasized about the idea of a democracy limited to proven democrats and presented themselves as the heirs of the tradition of the May 1810 independence movement and the battle of Caseros, when the forces of liberal Argentina defeated the dictator Rosas, whom Perón was systematically likened to. The military also convoked the political parties to share in the "proscription pact" and to join the *Junta Consultiva,* a kind of parliament without powers, presided over by the vice president Rojas. The agreement included all factions of the civilian forces, with the exception of the Communists, from the Conservatives to the most progressive parties. The latter were dominant in the universities, despite the fact that the minister of education was a traditional Catholic, but they were soon in conflict with the government when it proposed the legalization of private universities in response to the demands of the Church.

There was a similar ambiguity with regard to economic policy. Raúl Prebisch, the ECLA mentor, developed a program combining some ideas of the new doctrine that ECLA was promoting with a more orthodox stabilization and liberalization program. Economic policy followed the orthodox program, albeit with vacillations and doubts. The instruments that the state possessed to intervene in the economy—the Institute for the Promotion of Trade (IAPI) or control over bank deposits—began to be dismantled. The peso was devalued, and the agrarian sector thereby received an important stimulus, with which it hoped to balance the trade deficit. The government authorized the entry of Argentina into the IMF and the World Bank; assistance was obtained from those organizations to resolve the most immediate problems, which allowed them to offer the country their drastic recommendations. There was not, on the other hand, clear legislation about foreign capital whose effects on local business—a process already begun by Perón—continued to raise doubts. Social policy was more clearly defined. With a combination of efficiency and repression, owners and managers began to recover their authority in the factories. Collective bargaining was suspended, and, in the context of a strong downturn in the business cycle in 1956, real salaries fell sharply in 1957.

One of the sources of the workers' firm resistance is clear. Some workers confined their acts of resistance to singing the Peronist March at soccer matches or to writing "Perón Will Return" on the city walls. But strikes were also numerous and violent, above all in 1956, and sabotage and acts of terrorism were frequent, with primitive homemade artifacts employed for the latter. Both trade-union leaders and terrorists adhered at heart to different and even antithetical strategies; but in the climate of common repression that all suffered, these differences did not hold center stage. The policy of the victors of the 1955 coup, successful with other sectors of society that abandoned their Peronist militancy, served on the other hand to solidify definitively the identification of the workers with a Peronism that momentarily was more of a sentiment than an organic movement.

The basic elements of Peronism's ideology had not changed: the popular nationalism, the idea of an arbitrating and welfare role for the state. As in the previous decade, it was not a revolutionary or subversive doctrine, but it did become a more markedly proletarian one. The nostalgia for the lost paradise implied at the same time a utopia that was given a tangible expression in the widespread expectation of Perón's return, envisioned in the local political folklore as taking place in a mysterious "black airplane." Yet as Daniel James noted, workers simply aspired to the normal and correct functioning of capitalist institutions that included the welfare state and social justice. Confronted with a context so fundamentally at odds with this aspiration, the workers developed a strong reaction that was difficult to accommodate. This was Peronism's first novelty in the era of anti-Peronism. The other was the emergence of a cadre of new union leaders, formed not under the comfortable tutelage of the state but in the bitter struggles of those years, and therefore more battle hardened. The new government did everything possible to dislodge these leaders, but failed completely and had to resign itself to living with those who gradually won the elections in unions that were slowly being normalized. In September 1957, the "Normalizing Congress of the CGT" met, and the Peronists, grouped together in the so-called 62 Organizations, gained control of the labor confederation, though sharing power with some independent groups.

With Peronism proscribed, these union organizations simultaneously assumed the trade-union and political representation of the working class and were henceforth the "backbone" of the Peronist movement. From his exile—successively in Asunción, Caracas, Santo Domingo, and finally Madrid—Perón retained all his symbolic power, but in reality he had to allow his followers to act with considerable independence and to tolerate dissent in his movement in order not to be disobeyed outright, though reserving himself a power of veto. Perón devoted himself to mobilizing all those who invoked his name, encouraging and giving a nod to some against others to thereby reserve the final word in any negotiation. He had learned a new technique in the art of leadership and employed it skillfully.

For the government and the political forces that supported it, the "pact on proscription" posed a problem for the future, whether immediate or in the long run: what to do with Peronism. Some accepted the idea of exclusion indefinitely, ingenuously trusting that the "democratic education"—the name of a subject now required in the public schools—would have its intended effect. Others sought to understand and redeem the Peronists, and some, more practically, simply wished to garner their electoral supporters and thereby "integrate" them into society. The various options divided all political tendencies. On the right, some old nationalists and "popular Conservatives" chose to align with Peronism. On the left, the government's repressive policies forced people to abandon the anti-Peronist bloc in which they had until then coexisted alongside their natural enemies. The left's mission was to lead a working class that was and remained Peronist, and that program posed a serious dilemma for those who continued to believe in the bourgeois and even fascist nature of the movement. The Socialist Party split in 1956, divided between those who remained loyal to the anti-Peronist line and increasingly associated themselves with rightist groups, and those who believed that the party should build a leftist alternative for workers more attractive than Peronism. Some intellectuals, of either leftist or popular nationalist orientation, identified with Peronism; for many others, Arturo Frondizi began to represent an attractive alternative.

Frondizi's rise in the *Unión Cívica Radical* (UCR) caused a rupture in the party. Even before 1955, the so-called Intransigents coexisted with difficulty with the unionists and *sabattinistas,* both of whom were closer to the conspiratorial groups and those who supported the 1955 coup. After Perón's fall, Radicalism was divided in half: Those who followed Ricardo Balbín identified with the government of the Liberating Revolution, whereas Arturo Frondizi chose a position of reconciling with Peronism, based on Radicalism's traditional nationalist and populist principles, as well as on his visceral opposition to so-called democratic alliances of the kind that had first opposed Perón in the 1946 elections. To attract the Peronists, Frondizi's group demanded that the government lift the proscription and restore the legal status of the unions. In November 1956—at a time when the possibility of a presidential election was still remote—the UCR proclaimed the candidacy of Frondizi for president, which accelerated the rupture and caused the old party to divide in two: the *UCR Intransigente* and the *UCR del Pueblo.*

In 1957, harried by economic difficulties and growing trade-union and political opposition, the provisional government began to organize its retreat and to carry out the promise of reestablishing democracy. A constituent convention was convoked, in part to legalize the repeal of the 1949 Constitution and to bring up-to-date the Constitution of 1853 and in part to influence the results of the next presidential election. Perón ordered his followers to cast blank votes, and those votes—about 24 percent of the total—were the most numerous group, though certainly much fewer than those that Peronism had garnered in power and almost the same number as those cast for the *UCR del Pueblo,* the party backed by the outgoing government. In third place, not far behind, was the *UCR Intransigente.* The convention turned out to be a failure and was adjourned after introducing some minor amendments—among them, expanding article 14, which included the right to strike. But the lessons of the electoral results were clear: Whoever attracted the Peronist voters were assured victory, as long as Peronism continued to be proscribed, a situation guaranteed by the government of the Liberating Revolution.

Arturo Frondizi threw himself into this undoubtedly risky game. Employing a modern discourse, making clear references to the country's structural problems, and offering novel solutions—filled with concrete proposals based on long-standing principles of Radicalism, populism, and nationalism—he easily became the best option for the progressive forces and for a broad spectrum of the left. Frondizi's ties with the businessman Rogelio Frigerio introduced a novel twist to his discourse by emphasizing the importance of the development of the country's productive forces and the role that business should play in it. Frondizi's most audacious maneuver consisted of negotiating directly with Perón to gain his electoral support in exchange for lifting the proscriptions weighing against Peronism. Perón's order to do so was respected—except for some 800,000 holdouts—and Frondizi triumphed in the elections of February 23, 1958, with something more than 4 million votes against the 2.5 million won by Ricardo Balbín.

Frondizi was in power from May 1958 until March 1962. In the revised version of his program—which disappointed his leftist followers—Frondizi sought to renew the social pacts, with Peronist antecedents, between business and labor. The workers were called on to abandon their hostile attitude and to join and share in the benefits of an economic development driven by foreign capital, albeit in an unspecified future. This rhetoric incorporated the novel concept of "development" associated with foreign investment and combined it with a condemnation of the old-style British imperialism. All the country's modernizing forces were called on to unite in common opposition to the interests, both local and foreign, forged in the agroexport era. Besides holding out the prospect of a country with a growing economy and without political conflicts, Frondizi's deliberately vague rhetoric served to justify the president's risky tactical maneuvers. Thus gained legitimacy the technical teams headed by the economist and soon-to-be éminence grise of the government, Rogelio Frigerio—supposedly a representative of the "national bourgeoisie"—as well as the pact with Perón and the agreement reached with the unions. The confidence in the effectiveness of this program justified the concessions made to the country's other "factors of power" on issues regarded as of secondary importance, such as those to the Church on matters of education and those to the military, among whom nonetheless, it was hoped, would develop a "national and developmentalist" current.

The president's political realism included a tendency to lean toward tactical negotiations with the country's great corporative powers and therefore to devalue the political arena that had just been formally reestablished. It is true that the political parties—in particular the *UCR del Pueblo*—demonstrated an a priori rejection of anything the president did, regarding his electoral victory as illegitimate and showing scant appreciation for democratic procedures and little faith in the value of institutional continuity, to the point of flirting with the possibility of a military coup. But the political style of Frondizi and his circle—convinced of the intrinsic rightness of their proposals—was itself little inclined to programmatic discussion, persuasion, or the search for political agreements.

The new government had a large majority in the congress and controlled all the provincial governments, but nonetheless its power was clearly precarious. Its votes were borrowed, and the possibility of a falling out with Perón and his followers was real. Nor did the armed forces sympathize with those who had broken the commitment to keep Peronism proscribed; indeed they had won the election with Peronist votes and the military distrusted Frondizi's leftist background as well as his recent conversion to a progressive capitalism. The political parties, little interested in constitutional legality, were also no safety net for the country's institutions, and the governing party itself, controlled by the president, was incapable of any independent initiative. Perhaps for that reason, Frondizi gambled on working swiftly, as long as he could do so freely, and introducing immediate changes that would create a more favorable setting. A 60 percent increase in wages, an amnesty and lifting of the proscriptions against the Peronists—which did not include that of Perón or the Peronist Party—as well as a sanctioning of a new Law of Professional Associations for the unions almost identical to the 1945 law that the Liberating Revolution had repealed were all part of the electoral debt. Frondizi personally assumed responsibility for what he called "the oil battle," that is, negotiations with foreign oil companies about exploration and production contracts, while he announced the authorization for private universities, which generated a deep debate between the defenders of a "lay" education and those who advocated "free choice," mostly Catholics. By the president's calculations, both debates—on the oil question and on education—would serve to neutralize each other.

At the core of the government's economic program were the laws on foreign investment and industrial promotion, passed before the end of 1958. Through these, foreign capital was assured the freedom to remit profits and even to repatriate its capital investment. A special set of rules was established for what were regarded as key investments in this new stage of economic development: steel industry, synthetic fibers, automobiles, energy, and of course oil, which all the experts signaled as the greatest bottleneck to industrial growth. There was also to be preferential treatment in matters of importation rights, credit, taxes, supply of electricity, and purchases from the state, as well as tariff protection in the domestic market. All this was handled with a high degree of personal discretion, notoriously demonstrated in the agreements with the oil companies, which Frondizi negotiated in a personal and secretive manner. The results of these policies were notable: Foreign investment, which amounted to some 20 million dollars in 1957, rose to 248 million dollars in 1959 and 100 million dollars more in the two following years. Production of steel and automobiles grew spectacularly, and self-sufficiency in oil was almost achieved.

The strong economic expansion probably made more intense the three-year cyclical crises—the previous ones had been in 1952 and 1956—and was foreshadowed at the end of 1958 by high inflation and serious difficulties in the balance of payments. In December 1958, the government asked for help from the IMF and launched its Stabilization Plan, whose recessive prescription was exacerbated in June 1959, when Frondizi named Alvaro Alsogaray his minister of the economy. Alsogaray was one of the principal spokespersons for the country's "liberal" forces, and he implemented an orthodox austerity program, devaluing the peso, freezing wages, and eliminating price controls and state regulations, which resulted in a strong drop in workers' incomes and widespread unemployment. Alsogaray's program, liberal and orthodox, was in contradiction with the government's early "developmentalist" policies, which were in line with the structuralist proposals then in vogue, but in a certain sense it complemented and reinforced their effects. Nonetheless, its adoption marked the end of the illusion of integrating the Peronists into the government and made clear the necessity of confronting the trade unions.

The Stabilization Plan put an end to the precarious coexistence of the government and the Peronist unions, which until then had been appreciative of government measures such as the ending of the proscriptions and above all the restitution of the Law of Professional Associations, which reestablished industrial unions and obligatory paycheck withholdings to pay union dues. But the effects of the stabilization program and the harshness with which the government repressed the protests, beginning with the January 1959 strike of the Lisandro de la Torre meatpacking plant, put the unions on a war footing. Strikes intensified in the following months, and sabotage broke out again. The government responded by interdicting the unions and enlisting the army to repress the protests—according to a plan adopted by Frondizi's government termed the Plan *Conmoción Interna del Estado* (CONINTES)—while business, taking advantage of the recession, fired the most combative cadres in every factory.

The year 1959 was a turning point. The intense wave of trade-union protest that began with Perón's fall ended in utter defeat. Shop floor rationalization could advance resolutely, and in the unions a new leadership was consolidated, less committed to the daily shop floor struggle and more concerned about controlling the complex trade-union structures, even resorting to corruption or thuggery to silence internal dissent. These new union leaders recognized that they could not sustain a frontal assault against their adversaries and devoted themselves, more pragmatically, to striking a blow, especially against the government, and then immediately negotiating. Augusto Vandor, head of the metalworkers' union, was the principal figure and archetype of this new trade-union bureaucracy, a specialist in administering rank-and-file demobilization through general strikes that were tough in words but hardly combative while engaging in permanent negotiations with all the factors of power. At a moment when union influence in collective bargaining negotiations was weakening, this new unionism (dubbed "vandorismo") was acquiring enormous influence on the political scene.

This influence stemmed from the persistence of a pending and insoluble political problem—the proscription of Peronism—but especially from the repeated harassment that the government suffered at the hands of the military. The military viewed with mistrust Frondizi's triumph and devoted itself to keeping an eye on him and in particular to monitoring his relationship with the Peronists. The military was divided about how much constitutional institutions should be respected and how much of its own institutional influence should be exerted, in the form of "proposals" to the president that he adopt specific measures. The navy was most united in its rejection of the president's policies, but in the army a growing factionalism that deepened previous divisions prevailed. The government attempted to encourage a pro-government current in the army, but when a conflict broke out between the factions, Frondizi proved incapable of defending his supporters. Throughout the almost four years of his presidency, Frondizi was subject to thirty-two military "proposals," some demanding changes in his policies and others intended to curry favor in the institution itself. Frondizi capitulated to every single one. In June 1959, General Carlos Severo Toranzo Montero, the most hardline of the anti-Peronist commanders, became army commander-in-chief. For two years, he exercised a praetorian tutelage of the president. This was also the period that Alsogaray was the minister of the economy and the days of the Plan CONINTES, without question the period of greatest social and political repression in Frondizi's government.

The armed forces' praetorian tendencies became crystallized with the Cuban Revolution. Fidel Castro's triumph in 1959 had been celebrated by democrats and liberals, but by 1960 his move toward the socialist bloc profoundly divided the waters. The various factions of the left, vacillating on the question of Peronism, found in the support for the distant Cuban experience a propitious area of agreement. Nonetheless, sectarianism persisted. In early 1961, the Socialist Alfredo Palacios won a senate seat representing the federal capital, revealingly polarizing the country's progressive and leftist forces. Anti-Communism, by contrast, caught fire strongly in the right, anti-Peronist liberalism, and the Catholic Church. Latin America and Argentina were entering the Cold War world, and the military, under the strong ideological influence of their U.S. colleagues, assumed with resolve an anti-Communist position that, under the pretext of internal security, served to legitimize their praetorian behavior. The military associated everything from Peronism to the group headed by Rogelio Frigero to university students with Communism. At a time when the United States was beginning to demand alignment and solidarity against Cuba, the military discovered another area in which to pressure the president.

Frondizi, who had adhered enthusiastically to the slogans of Kenndey's Alliance for Progress, was reluctant to condemn Cuba and to lose a certain freedom to maneuver afforded by the existence of a socialist alternative in the hemisphere. A few tepid gestures of independence horrified the military: a treaty signed with the suspect populist Brazilian president, Janio Quadros, in April 1961; Frondizi's private meeting with Che Guevara, at the time Cuba's minister of industry, in August of that same year; and, above all, Argentina's abstention at the foreign ministers' meeting in Punta del Este, which expelled Cuba from the Organization of American States. The fact that the foreign ministers who presided over these actions were well-known conservative leaders such as Adolfo Mugica and Miguel Ángel Cárcano did not persuade the military, who put strong pressure on the president until, a month following the abstention, Argentina broke off diplomatic relations with Cuba.

By then, the course of events in the political and electoral process was leading Frondizi's weak government to its final catastrophe. The 1960 elections, with Peronism proscribed, had demonstrated that the votes of Perón's followers continued to be decisive, beyond any minor changes in the balance of forces between the government and the principal opposition. The elections of early 1962 were destined to be riskier, because the provincial governors were scheduled to be elected. To contest the elections with greater possibility of success, Frondizi removed the minister of the economy Alsogaray and the army commander Toranzo Montero in early 1961, bringing to a conclusion the stabilization program. The president adopted more flexible social policies and threw himself into the arduous task of confronting the Peronists in the elections, whose proscription could not be maintained without risking their throwing their support behind any of the government's enemies.

As on other occasions, various scenarios took shape, all according to whether or not the Peronists were proscribed. One of them, the one that caused the greatest concern, was for the Peronists to support some of the leftist forces, among whom the Cuban Revolution had created a cause that encouraged solidarity and weakened partisan squabbling. The mere existence of this alternative, which the trade-union movement looked on with deep reserve, showed that Peronism was beginning to grapple with a profound ideological renovation. But the general desire of the Peronist leadership was to have the proscription lifted, to participate in the elections, and to recover lost ground in the congress and the provincial and city governments, a proposal Perón himself had to accept. Many provincial caudillos desired such an outcome, which assumed that the Peronists would not be vetoed by the military; the union leaders particularly wanted it, masters of the only formal structure existing in Peronism. Through the 62 Organizations, they dominated the Peronists' electoral machinery and put their candidates at the heads of the party tickets. Regardless of the election results, they had won the movement's internal power struggle: Peronism was now the trade unions, and these in turn belonged to the union leaderships, which Vandor headed and controlled.

At the national level, a Peronist victory continued to be unacceptable for those who had subscribed to the tacit pact on proscription, including Frondizi himself, who declared that if faced with a Peronist victory, he would not cede power to them. But no one wanted to assume the costs of the proscription, and the government, encouraged by some electoral successes, took the risk of running against Peronism in free elections. On March 18, 1962, the Peronist candidates won handily in the most important provinces, including the key Buenos Aires province. In the subsequent agitated days, Frondizi attempted the impossible: to ride out the situation. He interdicted provinces where the Peronists had won, completely revamped his cabinet, and entrusted General Aramburu with negotiating with the political parties, which refused to support him and demonstrated themselves totally indifferent to the president's fate and the fate of democracy itself. This was the signal that the military had been waiting for, and on March 28, 1962, they deposed Frondizi, who retained enough calm to oversee his replacement by the president of the senate, José María Guido, and thereby save a shred of institutional legitimacy.

Crisis and a New Attempt at Democracy

Many of those who had accompanied Frondizi during the final period also surrounded Guido and the fragile institutional legality that he represented, looking to negotiate a political alternative that in some way took the Peronists into account. But barely three months later, the military, which had completely assumed its tutelary role, imposed a decidedly anti-Peronist cabinet on the government. The political crisis and a crisis in the business cycle coincided, feeding each other, giving rise to erratic measures. In a ministry of fifteen days, Federico Pinedo implemented a drastic devaluation of the peso, which generally favored agrarian interests, particularly, it was said, those of his friends. He was immediately replaced by Alvaro Alsogaray who repeated his stabilization program, which also hit hard the domestic industry that had grown during the Frondizi period.

The political instability of those months in 1962 reflected above all the conflicting opinions of different sectors of the armed forces, the country's undeclared power brokers. While the most anti-Peronist officer groups dominated the government and continued to look for an exit based on an intransigent demand—the categorical proscription of Peronism—an alternative position began to take shape in the army. This position appeared among the officers of the army's cavalry division, made up of tank regiments and controlling the strategic Campo de Mayo military base, outside Buenos Aires. This development reflected in part internal professional rivalries but especially a different assessment of the costs and advantages of so direct a participation by the army in politics. The Campo de Mayo group discovered that the price paid for such involvement in politics—the exacerbation of factionalism, divisions in the army, its increasing weakness in regard to the other social actors—was too high. This group believed that a hands-off policy was in order, which in political terms meant among other things greater deference to constitutional authorities.

The legalism the army brandished was thus in reality an expression of strict professionalism, rather than a manifestation of democratic values. The army also believed that the association of Peronism with Communism was simplistic and exaggerated and that, in view of Peronism's nationalist character and emphasis on class harmony, it could even contribute something to the anti-Communist front. This position was taking shape through successive confrontations with the *gorila* faction, which reached a crisis point in September when the two groups—the "blues" and the "reds," to use the terminology then adopted—took their troops into the streets and threatened to come to blows. The "blues" triumphed in the military rivalry and in the struggle for public opinion, benefiting from the propaganda of the military's civilian advisers. In successive communiqués, the blue faction's concern for legality, respect for the country's institutions, and search for a democratic solution were all explained. A short time later, groups tied to this faction were behind the appearance of a noteworthy magazine, *Primera Plana,* devoted to defending their position.

The September triumph of the "blues" brought General Juan Carlos Onganía to command of the army and brought to the government those who, like Frondizi before, had attempted to build a political front that in some way included the Peronists. This group consisted of individuals with ties to Christian Democracy and nationalist organizations and some to Frondizi's *desarrollismo* itself, searching for a formula that would unite the military, business, and union leaders. They had at their disposal various vacant electoral organizations—among them the *Unión Popular,* a so-called neo-Peronist party—but lacked a candidate, with Onganía himself being rumored as a possibility. But conditions for this alternative were still not ripe. The majority of the business sector did not trust the Peronists and generally any policies not strictly in favor of minimal state intervention and the free play of market forces. The Peronists, in turn, mistrusted Frondizi and his followers, while the traditionally anti-Peronist forces such as the *UCR del Pueblo* indignantly denounced the new alternative as spurious. The navy was also opposed and, having been absent in the September confrontation, on April 2, 1963, undertook its own uprising. This time the confrontation with the army was violent, with bombardments and barracks destroyed. The navy was defeated, but its opposition was successful. At the termination of the episode, the final communiqué of the "blues" again adopted anti-Peronist positions and called for Peronism's proscription.

Those who supported the idea of a front nonetheless insisted on finding a magic formula, this time without the military, which would unite Frondizi's group, the Christian Democrats, and the nationalists. In the negotiations to construct such a front, union leaders made their voices heard, taking to its ultimate consequences the "double game" that did not definitively commit them to any one alternative while permitting them to take advantage of all possibilities. In January 1963, they managed to negotiate the "normalization" of the CGT, with which they fortified their trade-union structures, and immediately began to pressure the government by means of a so-called Week of Protest. But at the same time, they played the political card, negotiating their participation in a possible front that, it was increasingly apparent, would compete with Perón. The negotiations did not turn out well. When Perón threw his support behind the candidacy of Vicente Solana Lima, a veteran Conservative politician who since 1955 had moved closer to Peronism, the bulk of the *UCR Intransigente* distanced itself, as did other smaller parties. At the same time, the government vetoed the ticket, using the legislation proscribing Peronism in force since 1955.

Thus the situation in July 1963 was very similar to the 1957 elections. The Peronists decided to cast blank votes, but a portion of their votes emigrated to the candidate of the *UCR del Pueblo,* Arturo Illia, who, with 25 percent of the votes cast, obtained the largest plurality and election by the electoral college. The surprising support of the Peronists was probably influenced by the candidacy of General Aramburu, a perennial candidate for various electoral coalitions since his 1958 exit from power, who ran on a decidedly anti-Peronist platform.

Arturo Illia governed between October 1963 and June 1966. This second post-Peronist constitutional experience began with dimmer prospects than did Frondiz's government. The country's principal corporative powers—the military, business, and the unions—were for the moment incapable of elaborating an alternative to constitutional democracy. They had called a truce, but were still far from identifying themselves too deeply with the government. The winning party, the *UCR del Pueblo,* had won a meager part of the electorate, and, although it held a majority in the senate, it controlled only a bit more than half the provincial governments. Neither did it have a majority in the chamber of deputies, where, because of the system of proportional representation, a broad spectrum of political forces was represented.

In contrast to Frondizi, the new Radical government gave much more importance to the congress and the democratic political scene, as much from genuine conviction as because of its little willingness or ability to negotiate with the principal corporative powers. Parliamentary life had more action and brilliance, but Radicalism did not manage to build a stable alliance or to win an authentic commitment from the other political forces in defense of democratic institutions.

Arturo Illia, a Cordoban politician coming from the Sabattini faction of Radicalism, was not the most outstanding figure of his party, and it is probable that his candidacy was the result of the lack of faith in the ability of the party's principal leaders to gain a victory. Among the panoply of tendencies in Radicalism, Illia sympathized with the more progressive ones but had to negotiate with the other sectors, which occupied important positions in his government. His presidency was characterized by a respect for democratic procedures, a resolve not to abuse presidential powers, and a desire not to exacerbate conflicts, in the hope that these would be resolved in time. Criticisms centered on this way of operating, seen as unrealistic and inefficient, revealing the slight appreciation that existed in Argentine society for democratic procedures and institutions.

Illia's economic policies had a definite profile, given by a group of technocrats under the strong influence of the ECLA. The basic criteria of a reformist populism, which the *UCR del Pueblo* inherited from the original program of the Intransigent Radicals—emphasis on the internal market, redistribution policies, protection of national industry, were combined with Keynesian elements, namely, a state active in the regulation and planning of the economy. The government also benefited from the favorable conjuncture that followed the 1962–63 crisis: the industrial recovery that ensued, particularly two good years for exports. Workers' incomes increased, and the congress passed a minimum-wage law. The government established price controls and advanced resolutely in some controversial areas, such as government regulation in the sale of prescription drugs. Standing up to foreign capital without antagonizing it, Illia's government sought to reduce foreign capital's unrestricted freedom, granted as part of the post-Peronist economic development measures. The contracts with foreign oil companies were a special case. They had been a central issue in the opposition to Frondizi and were canceled and renegotiated.

Illia's economic and social policies were intended to reverse the course followed since 1955 and prompted bitter resistance on the part of business sectors, both by the spokespersons of *desarrollismo,* who complained of the lack of incentives for foreign investment, and especially by the "liberals," who reacted against what they saw as state interference and demagoguery and were concerned about the unions' increasing power and the government's passivity in dealing with them. The government had attempted to use the powers invested in the Law of Professional Associations to control the union leaders, especially their handling of union monies and union elections, in the hope that a dissident current of union leaders would emerge to break the Peronist monolith. The union leaders responded with a *Plan de Lucha* that consisted of a series of staggered factory occupations between May and June 1964. Some 11,000 factories were occupied, in an action that involved nearly 4 million workers, realized in accordance with a strict plan, without violence or threats to property, and demobilized as quickly and with the same care that it had been organized. Although both the right and the left tried to see in this the beginning of an attack against the system, it was only an expression, of rare perfection, of Vandor's tactics, one capable of obtaining the maximum benefits through a controlled and limited mobilization. Such a display was in part intended to win concessions from the government—particularly to end its pressure against the unions—but above all to demonstrate that the labor movement was undeniably a social actor with real power in any serious negotiations, a status shared only with the military, business, and Perón himself.

Vandorismo thus took advantage of its absolute dominion over the unions and also over Peronism's political organizations, to act simultaneously or alternately on two fronts and to practice Vandor's art of negotiation. During the first six months of 1964, encouraged by a possible lifting of the proscription against Peronism, the unions spearheaded a reorganization of the Justicialist Party—the new name of the Peronist Party—accomplished in a manner to their liking because a relatively low party affiliation allowed the union leaders absolute control. Such behavior led them to an escalating confrontation with Perón whose leadership was threatened. The dispute between both sides could not exceed certain limits; Perón could not dispense with the most powerful unions, and the unions could not renounce the symbolic leadership of Perón. The competition was characterized by a continuous tug-of-war, in which Vandor slowly gained ground. In late 1964, the union leadership organized Perón's return to the country, a challenge to the government and perhaps to Perón himself, with preparations on the scale of an electoral campaign. This maneuver brought to the forefront the issue of the tacit agreements on proscription. Operation Return aroused great expectations among the Peronists and revived nostalgia and fantasies. Perón took a flight to Argentina, but before the government was forced to decide what to do, Brazilian authorities detained him and sent him back to Spain. It is not clear who lost the most with this outcome: the government, Vandor, or Perón himself—subsequent events made the whole affair irrelevant—but what is certain is that Perón was prepared to play his cards to avoid any agreement that might exclude him. By then he had begun to shelter and encourage the incipient sectors critical of the union leadership and inclined to tougher tactics, even to follow the path of the Cuban Revolution.

Perón's principal concern was the electoral arena, where he could better compete with Vandor. In March 1965, congressional elections were held. The government proscribed the Justicialist Party but authorized the Peronists to run with less provocative names, such as that of the *Unión Popular,* controlled by *vandorista* union leaders and neo-Peronist provincial caudillos, all of whom interpreted Perón's leadership in a broad, flexible, and largely symbolic way. The results for Peronism were good but not spectacular. Adding together all their votes in the various parties, they obtained about 36 percent of the vote. The Peronists did manage to constitute a strong parliamentary group, headed by Paulino Niembro, one of Vandor's men, and began to prepare for the 1967 elections in which—as in 1962—they would compete for control of the provincial governments. Vandor placed his candidates in power in the principal provinces and managed to unite the neo-Peronist provincial groups. His goal was to achieve the institutionalization of "Peronism without Perón" and assemble a powerful dissident force. This implied that on some level Perón and the government had a common interest in confronting him.

In the final months of 1965, Perón sent to Argentina his wife, María Estela, known popularly as Isabel, as his personal representative. Isabel assembled all the trade-union groups opposed to or at odds with Vandor's leadership, from both the right and the left, and precipitated a division in the 62 Organizations. Although this rebellion was led by the CGT president himself, José Alonso, the attempt to take over the union leadership failed. But at the beginning of 1966, during elections held in Mendoza province, Isabel threw her support behind a Peronist candidate opposed to Vandor's candidate. Isabel's candidate handily defeated Vandor's. Thus, by mid-1966, the rivalry between Perón and Vandor ended in a stalemate: Perón was victorious in the electoral arena, while Vandor reigned supreme in the labor movement. Perhaps for that reason, Vandor for the moment abandoned electoral politics, directing his efforts at the great corporative actors.

The armed forces did not look with great sympathy on Illia's government—where the defeated "red" faction enjoyed influence—but they refrained from conspiring against him or exerting pressure on the government. In the army, the priority of its commander, General Onganía, and of the group of officers in the armored division around him, was rebuilding the institution, the establishment of order and discipline—long broken in the years following 1955—and the consolidation of the commander's authority. Rather than respect for democratic institutions, there was a conviction that, given the characteristics of the political scene, any intervention would provoke factious divisions.

Slowly but surely, the armed forces ceased to speak except through their commanders-in-chief, among whom Onganía was acquiring a national primacy. In 1965, in a meeting of hemispheric army commanders at West Point, Onganía stated his adherence to the so-called Doctrine of National Security: The armed forces, though prohibited from strictly political competition, were nonetheless the guarantor of the nation's supreme values and should act when these values were threatened, particularly by Communist subversion. Shortly later, he completed this statement, declaring—this time in Brazil where the military had just deposed President Goulart—the doctrine of "ideological borders," which in every country divided the supporters of Western and Christian values from those who wanted to subvert them. Democracy—the banner of the military after 1955—did not figure among those central values, a fact that revealed not only an internal change but an international one: The era inaugurated by President Kennedy had come to an end; the United States reassumed or at least intensified its classic interventionist policy; and the military began overthrowing democratically elected governments suspected of weak anti-Communist credentials. In this renovated discourse of the armed forces, which seemed unconcerned about its obvious implications, democracy began to appear as a liability for security. From this perspective, the armed forces were ultimately also in favor of economic modernization, which needed efficiency and order.

The Economy Between Modernization and Crisis

The economic program, which Frondizi convincingly embodied in 1958, expressed a collective sensibility and a set of beliefs and shared illusions about economic modernization. In part, this was supposed to follow from the state's planning and promotional policies and from a technical and scientific renewal on which great efforts were expended from 1955 onward. Thus emerged the National Institute of Agricultural Technology (INTA) with enormous influence in the agricultural sector and the less influential National Institute of Industrial Technology (INTI). Basic scientific and technological research was carried on by the National Council of Scientific and Technical Research (CONICET), created in 1957, and by the "National Atomic Energy Commission," both of which frequently acted in association with the universities. The Federal Investment Council was supposed to address the country's regional disparities, and the National Development Council, created in 1963, would assume responsibility for general economic planning and the elaboration of national plans of development. In sum, a collection of institutions was supposed to use, through economic planning, the leverage of public investment, science, and technology in pursuit of development.

The greatest faith was placed in foreign investment. This arrived in considerable amounts between 1959 and 1961, then dropped until 1967, when a second wave occurred, though this time with a heavy preference for short-term investments. But foreign capital's influence greatly exceeded its direct investments. Investors had a great capacity for taking advantage of the internal mechanisms of capitalization, whether public credit or private savings, which judged it advantageous to use foreign companies to channel their money. Foreign capital also established itself through the purchase of or association with existing national companies or simply through the concession of patents or brands. Its influence was seen in the transformation of the services or in marketing practices—supermarkets at first were the most characteristic—and in a general change in society's consumption habits, stimulated by what was seen and made desirable through television. The growing presence of the English language testifies to the degree that Argentine society adopted worldwide changes in economic life.

The effects in these first years were dramatic. In industry, the new sectors—oil, steel, synthetic fibers, petrochemicals, automobiles—grew rapidly, because of both the effects of advertising and the multinationals' ability to take advantage of an unsatisfied demand. Those sectors that had led the industrial growth in the previous stage—textiles, shoes, even consumer electronic goods—stagnated or declined. In part this stagnation occurred because the market had become saturated or had shrunk, in part because these sectors had to compete with new products, as was the case with cotton, which competed with synthetic fibers in the textile industry. In addition, industry became more concentrated, transforming the relatively dispersed structure inherited from the Peronist era. In the new branches where foreign capital predominated, this resulted from the heavy initial investments required as well as the very terms of state promotion that, with the exception of the automobile industry, guaranteed such concentration. In the older sectors, traditionally dispersed and in a context of market retraction, some firms with a greater ability to adapt managed to grow at the expense of others, thanks to an access to credit or to an advantageous association with a foreign company.

In summary, a gap was created between a modern and efficient sector of the economy in a process of steady expansion, tied to the investment or consumption of society's wealthiest sectors, and a traditional sector, more tied to the mass market, which was stagnating. The gap had to do with the presence of foreign firms or associations with them, with the experience thus being strongly negative for many local businesspeople and especially for many workers. Industrial employment tended to stagnate, and the increase in the number of firms in operation failed to compensate for the loss of jobs in traditional industries. The incomes of wage earners deteriorated both for economic and political reasons. To more breathing room for employers in the labor market, because of the results of rationalization and a reduced demand for labor, was added a decline in the unions' bargaining power, especially at the shop floor and factory levels. Thus the respective participation of capital and labor in the gross domestic product (GDP) changed significantly, revealing the coherence of the project for capital accumulation that had been set in motion: The participation of wage earners in the GDP fell from approximately 49 percent in 1954—the high point of the Peronist stage—to 40 percent by 1962.

This dramatic impact was supposed to be compensated for by another deeper and long-term economic restructuring, which nonetheless turned out to be relatively unimportant. Even in the modern sectors, the new investors had to operate in a context with singular and deep-rooted characteristics. The factories inherited from the Peronist era were characterized by small scale, a high degree of vertical integration, high costs, and lack of concern for competitiveness. They were more like large workshops than genuinely modern factories. The new establishments—particularly in automobiles—had to adapt their technology and organizational structures to this new reality, which they could not ignore. As a result, as Jorge Katz showed, their efficiency was much less than in their country of origin. Many companies ended up profiting from the unsatisfied demand of a small, privileged group of buyers rather than making riskier long-term investments. Such was the case with the twenty-one auto terminals existing in 1965. Even the few with broader investment plans were not prepared to sacrifice the awarded protection that guaranteed them control of the local market, even though it condemned them to be limited to that same market.

In those years, Argentine society, dominated by the problems of development, dependency, and imperialism, debated much more the size and final destination of the profits of these companies than their contribution—undoubtedly relative—to the economy's modernization and competitiveness, particularly those of the industrial sector. What is clear is that foreign capital contributed to maintaining some of the economy's established practices, which had been fashioned in the 1930s and buttressed during the war and the postwar period. The foreign companies' world continued to be that of the internal market, just as it had been for their Argentine predecessors, and it was not a priority to achieve an efficiency—except with specific enticements—which would permit them to compete in foreign markets that were supplied by their other subsidiaries. Attracted by the promotional schemes of the national governments, they fought to maintain their original privileges and even to broaden them. In this way, together with the national companies that followed their lead, foreign companies contributed to the state intervention that guaranteed them special treatment.

Despite the fact that the government had created a number of planning agencies, its industrial promotion policies did not take into account key questions, such as when to cease promotional policies to encourage competitiveness or how to balance fiscal needs with such policies, which generally consisted of tax exemptions. Such economic policies were highly erratic. There were wild policy swings, determined in part by the ability of each interested sector to exert pressure on the government—such as when the minister of economy Pinedo was removed in 1962—and in part by general political conditions—such as when Illia's government rescinded the oil company contracts, an act that strengthened the companies' resolve to protect their established privileges.

In the ten years after the fall of Peronism, the economy was not only substantially transformed, but it also, in its totality, grew, although probably less than hoped for. In the industrial sector, this growth was the result of the cumulative effect of the growth of the new sectors—many of which had a long maturation cycle—and the retraction of the traditional ones. The agricultural sector began to experience some positive effects resulting from the occasional incentives in exchange policies or of technological improvements promoted by the INTA or by groups of enterprising businesspeople, as well as from the greater diffusion of tractors manufactured in recently established plants. Though not spectacular, the results allowed production to reach on average the levels of 1940, before the onset of the great decline in production. There were also some relative improvements in foreign trade. All this laid the foundation for a period of generally moderate but steady growth, based principally on the domestic market, a process begun during Illia's government and continuing until the middle of the following decade. In hindsight, it can be seen that this relative bonanza remained hidden because people's perspective was dominated by the cycles of economic expansion and contraction and the violent crises between.

These crises erupted with regularity every three years—1952, 1956, 1959, 1962, 1966—and were punctually followed by so-called stabilization policies. From the strictly economic point of view, they expressed the limitations that the country experienced for sustained economic growth from 1955 onward. The expansion of the industrial sector, of commerce, and of the services linked to the internal market depended ultimately on the availability of foreign exchange with which to pay for the capital goods and inputs necessary to keep the system operating. These were provided by an agricultural sector with few possibilities for growth, facing difficult conditions in world markets, and routinely used, through foreign exchange and price manipulations, to cover government expenses in the domestic economy. Thus, all growth of industry implied an increase in imports and led to a serious deficit in the balance of payments. The foreign debt, increasing in these years, and the need to remain current on the service payments, added another element to the crisis and was a cause for concern among creditors and their local agents. The stabilization plans, modeled on the guidelines of the IMF—which the country resorted to in emergencies—consisted of a sharp devaluation, and then of deflationary policies (freezing credit, suspending public works projects, and so on), which reduced industrial employment, wages, and imports, until the lost equilibrium was recovered, thereby creating conditions for a renewed growth.

Each one of these stop-go cycles—effective in justifying the widespread pessimism about the future of the economy—was inscribed in the context of the struggle between different sectors over resources, which also formed part of the more general political struggle, because the political stalemate was linked to an economic stalemate. In the negotiations between the various parties, winners and losers were constantly changing, as were alliances and conflicts. During an expansionary phase of the economy, the interests of business and labor might coincide, at the expense of exporters. Such a coincidence of interests, which was one of the foundations of the Peronist alliance, explains the negotiating space achieved by the unions after 1955. At other moments— and in these years more frequently—business took advantage of the conjuncture to accumulate capital intensely. In turn, with the crisis and devaluation phase, there was a transfer of income from the urban sector to the rural sector, and also from the workers to business, because real wages declined under strong inflation. Small firms also tended to be losers to big companies, and in these conjunctures industrial concentration increased greatly.

In summary, economic crisis fueled the struggle over resources among those sectors with the ability to negotiate and created the possibility of a new conjuncture, of a change in the rules of the game, instrumented from the halls of power, and taking another's share. It was a game without logical and predictable rules; no sector could impose rules on the rest. Although the state's actions were of paramount influence, the state did not design policies autonomously but was at the mercy of those who could capture the state for the moment and use it to take as much advantage as possible. Among the propertied sectors, there were those who perceived the possibilities that such an abnormal capitalist system offered and who discovered the advantages of such instability. There were others, however, whose best prospects were in the establishment of order and a more logical system. They began to demand the presence in political power of anyone who could fulfill that task.

The Middle-Class Masses

Economic modernization introduced some deep changes in society, but also gave a new impetus to transformations that had been at work for some time. As a result, the potentially disruptive effects of the recent changes did not immediately manifest themselves. The pronounced migration from the countryside to the city that characterized this period in reality formed part of a trend begun in the 1940s. The point of origin changed somewhat. The traditional pampa zone, where agricultural crisis had already completed its work of expelling country folk and sending them to the city, had been replaced by the traditionally poor regions of the Northeast and Northwest, hit hard by crises in their regional economies of cotton and sugar, respectively. Immigration from bordering countries also began. Migrants continued arriving in greater Buenos Aires, making up some 36 percent of its population, and the city reached the apex of its relative growth. Other great urban centers also attracted migrants, among which Córdoba began to stand out.

Perhaps the greatest novelty was the ways these migrants were integrated into the cities. Except in Córdoba, industrial employment, which had been the great enticement during the Peronist decade, stagnated and even declined. Construction—public works undertaken by big companies and also private construction dominated by small firms—replaced industry and together with petty commerce and some service activities absorbed internal migrants as well as the contingents of Bolivians, Paraguayans, or Chileans whose immigration contributed to enlarging the number of workers.

It was not only the possibility of employment, generally precarious, that enticed the migrants but also the desire to enjoy the attractions of urban life. In that sense, the migrations formed part of the social process of Argentina's era of expansion, of constant incorporation of new contingents of humanity into the benefits of progress, strengthened by the spread of mass communications and particularly television. But the result was now a phenomenon, common in all of Latin America, of the new marginality: a belt of *villas miserais* ("misery towns") in the great cities and their outskirts, which combined, in a startling manner for outside observers, shacks made of corrugated tin and television antennas.

The world of urban workers experienced profound change. The number of wage-earning workers remained stable, which implied that they lost relative importance. Workers were in general victims of the regressive social policies that dominated those years, except for the Illia period, although economic changes caused a great disparity in income and clear advantages in favor of workers in modern companies. The unions organized an effective resistance and performed sufficiently well in the struggles for their share of national income, so that the leadership was not removed by the rank and file. Their actions contributed to maintaining the homogeneity of the working class, which was unionized and Peronist. The greatest growth occurred among construction workers, and especially those who were self-employed, tied to the service sector or to petty commerce. The growth of this sector was still a result of the economy's needs, not yet disguised unemployment, and it frequently offered moonlighting jobs with decent pay. Nonetheless, poor people, who grew in numbers precisely as the welfare state relinquished some of its responsibilities, slowly began to constitute one source of tension in society.

New contingents swelled the amorphous but nonetheless real ranks of the middle class, prolonging and indeed climaxing a century-long process of expansion, diversification, and social mobility of that sector of the population. But this overall assessment must take into account important internal changes that strongly complicate its meaning. According to the analysis of the sociologist Susana Torrado, the number of small manufacturers was drastically reduced as a result of industrial concentration, and although the number of businesspeople engaged in commerce increased, all together fewer owned their own businesses. What did grow, in contrast, was the number of middle-class wage earners present in all sectors of the economy and especially in industry, where new firms demanded technical specialists and professionals of all kinds.

Their presence pointed out the decisive role that education continued to play as the road to success par excellence for the middle class. With primary education well established, secondary education was expanded, and enrollments had grown spectacularly during the Peronist decade. In the universities, problems of overenrollment versus limited resources began to appear for the first time. Old and new expectations came together in this growth: the traditional search for social prestige associated with a university degree, the desire to participate—through new professions—in the modernization process of the economy and science, but also the desire to become part of intellectual and political circles. The traditional mechanism to achieve this began to reveal flaws: The number of university graduates began to increase much more rapidly than did available jobs—one of the signs of the weaknesses of the proclaimed modernization—while, gradually, university degrees declined in worth. For example, certain positions for which a high school degree had been sufficient were now taken by college graduates. This foreshadowed another source of tension in the new society.

Among the upper classes, the changes that were occurring completed those presaged in the Peronist decade. Despite the fall of the hated regime, the traditional upper classes did not regain their former prestige. Possession of an aristocratic surname or frequenting the society pages of *La Prensa* or *La Nación* did not guarantee wealth or power. The elites continued to become more diversified and added to their ranks new businesspeople, military officers—who frequently also became company presidents—and even some particularly successful trade-union leaders.

Most characteristic of these years was the emergence and visibility of a stratum of so-called executives, who according to their degree of importance fell somewhere between the upper and middle classes. They were on the one hand an expression of economic modernization, a sign that companies were ceasing to be run by offspring of the founding families and were passing into the hands of expert managers, masters of efficiency and of an international business culture. As such, they were glorified as heroes of civilization. But they were also the latest version of the parvenu, a bit too nouveaux riches in the showy display of their wealth and what was judged as their usurpation of status symbols. They embodied the grandeur and misery of modernization.

Changes in lifestyle were noteworthy, above all in the big cities. Birth-control pills and a generally more open attitude toward sexual behavior and the family modified the relations between men and women, though such changes only modestly reflected—in a still prudish and traditional society—those taking place in the industrialized countries. The use of the familiar *vos* in addressing others began to become established in daily dealings, and common conversation began to employ terms borrowed from sociology and psychoanalysis, one of the passions of the middle class. Indeed, Buenos Aires had one of the largest communities of psychoanalysts in the world. As in the rest of the world, changes in consumption began to serve as signposts in social differentiation. It was significant that the new popular sectors, unlike their predecessors in the first half of the century, did not place their hopes in owning a home—a symbol at the time of social mobility—but in owning a television, in part because it was beyond the means of most, and in part because of the immediate pleasure it offered and the prestige afforded by owning one, followed by an electric domestic appliance or a motor bike. Among the middle class, the automobile especially filled their dreams and illusions; books also entered the circle of mass consumption, and best-sellers began to serve as a common point of reference.

Powerful forces drove the expansion and homogenization of consumption—mass production, advertising, marketing techniques—and also deeper tendencies in the democratization of social relations and generalized access to goods traditionally considered the preserve of the upper classes. Everyone consumed many more new products. In every city, the old downtown lost importance, and new commercial centers became scattered throughout all the neighborhoods. A pair of jeans became the universal article of clothing, and at least on the surface, the cities appeared inhabited by vast contingents of the middle class. But if blue jeans homogenized everyone and prevented social differences from becoming crystallized in fixed appearances, an opposite tendency immediately appeared in response: the recourse to exclusive and expensive brands, flaunted with readily visible labels, which were quickly copied by bootlegging and popularization of those labels. Thus, faced with the homogenization in appearances, the comfortable middle and upper classes, encouraged by a growing concentration of income, sought original ways to demonstrate class distinctions through an exclusivity that was supposed to change constantly in taste, rather than becoming trapped in a popularization of styles. To know in every circumstance what marked off that difference, to be aware of the precise moment when what was "in" became "out," and to know what was classy and what was commonplace became a respected science and the subject of the most popular magazines.

One such magazine, *Primera Plana,* fulfilled an essential function in the education of the new middle and upper sectors. The magazine appeared for the first time in 1962, serving as the spokesperson for those groups beginning to congregate around General Onganía and supporting the elusive idea of a political "front." In addition—perhaps precisely for that reason—the magazine assumed with enthusiasm and a certain ingenuousness the task of disseminating modernity among its readership, who, thanks to the profusion of codes and standards that the reading public demanded, were supposed to be a minority, recruited from the new strata of professionals and efficient executives. To them were revealed the secrets of what should be known about "modern life," the latest scientific breakthrough, or the new Latin American literature, which experienced a decisive boom in those years, as well as all those things whose consumption set those in the know apart. Elsewhere, a cartoon character who went on to immortality—Quino's "Mafalda"— expressed a whole other range of the middle-class imagination, combining dreams of owning a car—even if just a modest Citröen—and of taking short yearly vacations with concerns about pacifism, ecology, and democracy, common themes in the wave of dissent and reform spreading throughout the world. Perhaps for that very reason, Mafalda achieved international notoriety and, despite expressing a very different sensibility, shared a role with *Primera Plana* in demonstrating just how close to the rest of the world Argentina was in those years.

The University and Cultural Renewal

Anti-Peronist intellectuals—among them, those who had managed to identify themselves with both scientific rigor and vanguard aesthetic and intellectual currents—went on to permeate government institutions and the entire cultural field, dominated by the concern to open up and bring up-to-date the national culture. Old groups, such as the *Colegio Libre de Estudios Superiores* or *Sur,* lost influence, replaced by new institutions that were nonetheless often weakened by internal divisions. The artistic vanguard was concentrated in the *Instituto Di Tella,* thriving under the patronage of what was then a prosperous and modern company, and combining experimentation and the avant garde. Those who gave life to this experiment—in particular, Jorge Romero Brest—were convinced that they were turning Buenos Aires into an international artistic center. If their prediction was perhaps excessively optimistic, it is true that, as in few other times, local artistic creativity was linked to that of the world. Located in the very heart of the city, in the so-called crazy block near the University of Buenos Aires' School of Arts and Sciences, the Di Tella became a point of reference for other emerging and moderately but provocatively radical currents, such as the hippie counterculture.

The principal focal point of cultural renewal however was the university. The 1955 designation of José Luis Romero as rector of the National University of Buenos Aires, with the support of the powerful student movement, set the course for the next ten years. Students and progressive intellectuals sought first a "de-Peronization" of the university—that is, the removal of the clerical and nationalist groups, of very little academic merit, which had dominated it in the previous decade—and then a modernization of its activities, in line with the transformation that the entire society was experiencing.

According to the utopia of the predominant *desarrollista* ideology, science was supposed to become the economy's linchpin, an idea that elicited a long debate about priorities: whether to give emphasis to the hard sciences, holding them up to international standards, or to applied technology, looking at specific problems of the Argentine economy and attending to the training of skilled personnel that the economy might require. Alongside the old professional-training university emerged a new one, geared to biology, biochemistry, physics, agronomy, and computer science. The science departments were nourished by laboratories and scientists devoted full time to teaching and research, and graduates left in massive numbers to complete their studies abroad. Even the old majors changed. Economics and business administration—a training ground for executives—began to replace the old public accounting major.

In the social sciences—an idea new in itself—modernization was associated with two new disciplines: psychology and sociology. The school of sociology founded by Gino Germani, which adhered to modernization theory and was easily compatible with ideas of economic development and even Marxism, constituted at once a diagnosis and a program, mutually reinforcing: All societies were marching along a similar path, from the traditional to the modern, and science showed the way for Argentina to pass through those stages and in that way incorporate itself into the world. Sociology supplied at the same time a philosophy of history as well as a vocabulary—frequently badly translated from English—and other signs of modernity. Similarly, there emerged a vast group of new professionals engaged in everything from marketing or companies' industrial relations departments to work in the various planning and research agencies supported by the state. Before the unemployed or underemployed predominated among them, sociologists constituted—along with psychologists, economists, scientists, and industrial technicians—an entire cohort of new middle sectors, champions of modernity and privileged consumers of its products.

Since 1955, the university had been governed according to the principles of the 1918 University Reform, whose legacy constituted a true ideology for students and progressive intellectuals: university autonomy and a tripartite government of students, graduates, and professors. From the beginning, the university's relationship with the government was conflictive, and the final rupture occurred when President Frondizi decided to legalize private universities—a measure euphemistically justified in the name of "educational freedom"—on an equal footing with the country's public universities. The 1958 public debate between partisans of "educational freedom"—which meant basically universities with ties to the Catholic Church—and those who supported "secular education"—supporters of which encompassed a vast arch, stretching from liberals to progressives—was noteworthy, though the great outpouring of support for the "secular" position did not dissuade Frondizi from handing over this prize to one of the recognized factors of power in the country, the Catholic Church. The confrontation—erupting again subsequently in the demands for a larger budget for public education—demonstrated that the university was becoming a focus of criticisms not only of the government but also of ever-more-pronounced tendencies in society and politics. At the same time, it showed how questioning was internally processed, questioning that was political but not partisan and was concerned with maintaining—beyond any changes in national politics—the entire platform of the progressives' alliance: in the first place, faith in science and then confidence in humanity's progress, exemplified in the broad solidarity awakened by the Cuban Revolution. In that sense, thanks to its autonomy, the university became a "democratic island" in a country that was ever less so and—what was worse—that increasingly believed less in democracy, so that the very defense of the "island" contributed to strengthen internal alliances.

It was not a question, however, of an island with a desire to shut itself off from society. Although a multitude of political proposals that would soon be transferred to the public debate germinated in it, the university concerned itself intensely, though with mixed success, in extending its activities to society as a whole. The most successful example of that was Eudeba, the publishing house established by the University of Buenos Aires and founded by Arnaldo Orfila Reynal, whose alma maters were two Mexican publishers with a deep influence in the intellectual world, the *Fondo de Cultura Económica* and *Siglo XXI*, and then by Boris Spivacow, who recreated in the decade of the 1960s the great popular publishing projects of the 1930s and 1940s. What was singular about the Eudeba was its combination of a policy of aggressive marketing and innovation—cheap books sold at newsstands in the city streets—placed in the service of the dissemination of the latest advances in the sciences. Its editions—it sold some 3 million copies between 1959 and 1962—as much reveal the reality of the growth of the reading public as they do the decisive role of the university and its academic press in fashioning that reading public.

In this pole of modernity concentrated in the university, certain growing tensions began to manifest themselves. The absolute value of universal science—already present in the debates over hard science or applied science—was questioned in light of national necessities. First was discussed the financing of many scientific groups by international foundations—which were customarily linked to large companies, such as the Ford Foundation, or with foreign governments themselves—which assumed that such financing influenced research either in irrelevant directions or directly contrary to the people's and the nation's interests. From there, discussion turned to questioning scientific paradigms themselves, posing a "national" way of doing science, different from that identified by international centers of domination. Ultimately, the very need for science would be questioned. The call to look to the country, or to Latin America, was connected with the question of the commitment of intellectuals; commitment to their reality, an old debate—one that the partisans of the *Boedo* and *Florida* groups had given life to in the 1920s—but with new motives. Although commitment was a value shared by all progressive intellectuals—who did not hesitate to show themselves massively in favor of besieged Cuba—some questioned the supposed neutrality of science defended by the "scientists"—and insisted on its always value-laden character. A similar debate was posed in the artistic field where there were those who questioned the frivolity and lack of commitment of the *Di Tella* and contrasted it, for example, with the realist theater of Roberto Cossa and Germán Rozenmacher—which dramatized the bewilderment of the middle class confronting Peronism—or with the theater of the absurd of the "crazy block."

By then, despite the determination of the modernizing groups, the national reality did no more than demonstrate the superficial nature of the changes that the country had experienced, as well as the strength of the resistance such changes awoke in conservative circles. A turn to the left by a good part of the progressive sectors especially revealed the impossibility of maintaining the consensus on which the modernization experience had been based.

Politics and the Limits of Modernization

The radicalization of the progressive sectors and the formation of a new left—whose trajectory Oscar Terán and Silvia Sigal reconstructed—had a favored environment in the university before departing, after 1966, for wider destinations. Until that date, its penetration in other circles was slight. The unions were zealously watched over by an always-hostile labor leadership, and it was in the university and its debates that intellectuals presented and revised their interpretations and discourses, which were subsequently channeled into a broad range of political options.

The rupture between the most progressive sector of the intellectuals and their more conservative allies in the anti-Peronist front, foreshadowed since before 1955, became manifest almost immediately after Perón's overthrow, by virtue of the antipopular and repressive policies of "Liberating Revolution," above all because of intellectuals' self-guilt about the lack of understanding for the popular masses whose continued identification with Peronism, regardless of the manipulation of the state apparatus under Perón, was revealed in the 1957 elections. From the literary review *Sur* to the Socialist Party, groups and parties that had sheltered anti-Peronist opposition suffered all kinds of schisms. The attraction that Frondizi exercised among progressive independents and even among militants of the traditional left-wing parties responded to the overtures to Peronism without having to renounce their identity. This was due to the energetic anti-imperialist tone—a sentiment then on the rise—and above all to the modern character and efficiency that informed Frondizi's political style, which combined the illusions of the period with the private temptations for intellectuals of being able to exert political power without passing through the party apparatuses. The disillusion that quickly followed initiated a stage of reflection, criticism, and debate that culminated in the formation of the "new left."

The new left was formed looking first to Peronism for inspiration and then to the Cuban Revolution. It was characterized by the spectacular growth of Marxism in the society, the source of all beliefs: One either was or was not a Marxist. In Marxism, the varieties were endless. Orthodox Stalinism retreated in the face of new doctrinal sources: Lenin, whose central place was maintained because of his thesis on imperialism, Sartre, Gramsci, Trotsky, Mao, from whom were derived every imaginable interpretation—leading to everything from condemning Peronism to embracing it—legitimized by a Marx who lent himself to all points of view. Simultaneously, anti-imperialist sentiment grew, harvesting a wave of worldwide effervescence that started with the anticolonial movements of the postwar period—soon to become the Third World—continued with the Algerian war, and culminating in the incipient struggle in Vietnam, all of which seemed to foreshadow the coming crisis of imperialism. The disillusionment with Frondizi and with his Brazilian equivalent, Juscelino Kubitschek, the assassination of Kennedy, and the 1965 U.S. invasion of the Dominican Republic weakened faith in the Alliance for Progress. Theories of development gave way to those of dependency, which restated the previous interpretation of underdevelopment but subordinated the roots of economic backwardness to political factors. To confront the latter, the solution was a national alliance for liberation.

This populism built a bridge to Catholic groups, which, rereading the scriptures and giving them a more political interpretation, became interested in a dialogue with Marxism, whereas the anti-imperialism of the leftist currents allowed them to establish links with nationalist sectors, also undertaking a deep process of revisionism. From José Hernández Arregu—whose book *The Formation of the National Conscience* was a touchstone in this amalgamation process—to José María Rosas, nationalist intellectuals incorporated Marxism—in its most crudely economic form—retracing a path that Rodolfo Puiggrós and Jorge Abelardo Ramos had traveled from an opposite direction. Puiggrós and Ramos were authors of two books with enormous influence: *A Critical History of the Political Parties* and *Revolution and Counterrevolution in Argentina,* respectively. In turn, the various factions of the left revised their "liberal" interpretation of history—in which Rosas incarnated feudalism and Rivadavia capitalism—and began to reread it in light of revisionism, a path that permitted them, ultimately, to assign Peronism a legitimate place in humanity's progress.

The combination was difficult and the polemic intense. The Cuban Revolution—which all agreed in supporting—had the virtue of synthesizing the majority of these sentiments. It revealed a Latin America that had risen up against imperialism, especially after the spread of guerrilla movements in Venezuela, Colombia, and Peru, and it led to a cultural renewal that stretched from the partisans of the "teluric forces" to the new Latin American novel. The close connection between Marxism and revolution, which was fading among the great European parties and in the Soviet Union itself, was revealed with all its force in Cuba. Even before attempts were made to extract specific political lessons from its experience, Cuba enshrined the very idea of revolution, the conviction that, despite enormous obstacles, reality was malleable and collective human action could shape it. That transformation, whose possibility was strengthened by its historical necessity, was a political question, one that postponed or subordinated other questions such as economic growth, scientific development, or cultural modernization. For nationalists, the author of this transformation continued to be, in a romantic spirit, the "people"; for the left, it was the working class, behind whom, as Oscar Terán wittily said, did not yet lurk the shadow of the guerrilla.

Indeed, the new left still did not have a clear idea of what to do. It looked longingly at Peronism, encouraging its very hard-line tendencies—some trade-union militants, or the intellectual leader of the Peronist left, John William Cooke, returning from a prolonged residency in Cuba—and speculating about Peronism's turn to the left while toying with different alternatives: Leninism—which gave priority to mass action; *foquismo*—which sought to establish a pole of power through guerrilla warfare; or *entrismo*—devoted to winning over Peronism from within. Nothing was definite in 1966, except for the increasingly categorical rejection of the liberal and democratic tradition. For the new left—which did not distinguish between more general principles and the immediate Argentine context—democracy was a mere formality, civil liberties a farce. To place one's faith in them was to merely condone oppression.

In reality, no one had much faith in democracy, not even the political parties who were supposed to defend it. Democracy was certainly a somewhat fictitious concept in Argentina and one with scant legitimacy, but those with the greatest stakes in its survival and improvement gave it up for dead without a struggle, until the predicted end actually arrived. If the various factions of the left believed it to be a bourgeois opiate, Frondizi's followers preferred to place their bets on technocratic efficiency. The UCR and its allies did not hesitate, on occasion, to prefer a military coup to any government that would open up the electoral game too much to the Peronists. The latter—less responsible for this situation, given their proscription—wavered between betting on elections and direct negotiations with the factors of power. The right did not manage to organize a party capable of making its interests attractive to the whole of society, in part because of the chronic problems of the rightist forces—who were successful in implementing their agenda only when already ensconced in power—and in part because, in the very heart of the propertied sectors, there endured the conflicts that had prevented the establishment of a program that was valid for all of them, much less for the majority of society.

The most concentrated sectors of the economy, in which foreign capital had a decisive presence, moved with greater ease in the corporatist setting, where their interests were formulated with precision and clarity by a group of well-trained economists and technocrats. Through them, business maintained a dialogue with the real factors of power—the unions, the armed forces, and to a lesser extent the Church—which for different reasons also had little interest in strengthening democratic institutions. The union leaders, led by Vandor, had tested the electoral waters without luck, and Perón had bested them. The military was ever more attached to its tutelary role with the state and its role as defender of western and Christian values. Dialogue, however, was increasingly bogged down midway between democracy and authoritarianism, where none of the actors had the strength to turn the situation in their favor but where they could effectively veto any option that excluded them.

Voices of those in favor of breaking the stalemate began to multiply. For the military, democracy became an obstacle in the fight against an imagined Communist enemy, which it saw as increasingly menacing. If the military had come to admit that the bulk of Peronist trade unionism was for the moment salvageable, it saw the left in possession of the university, where it was attempting to attract Peronism. The military was also alarmed at the attraction that the Cuban Revolution exercised and was horrified by the questioning of society's traditional values posed by such ideas as the new sexual freedom, whereas revolution and avant garde art seemed merely different aspects of the same assault on western and Christian values.

This reaction, which touched everything from politics to culture and from there to the most private spheres, struck a deep chord in society, revealing that the advances made in the direction of modernization had not been great. Such fears were encouraged by the most traditional sectors of the Church, which enjoyed great prestige among the military and much of the business class. For integralist Catholicism, questioning the basic values of society—family, tradition, property—had its roots as far back as the French Revolution, if not the Reformation—and the Church's defense of such values was implicitly a condemnation of the modern world, in particular, liberal democracy, as well as a vindication of an organic conception of society in which authentic social interests were directly represented through corporativist organizations. This ultramontane position turned out to be well received by those who, for other reasons, found in the democratic scene and its pratfalls the roots of the country's economic disorders. Such people demanded a strong state, capable of putting in order the economy, disciplining its actors, and overcoming obstacles in pursuit of an effective alternative. All demanded more authority and order, some in combination with tradition, others with the desire that government simply be more efficient.

Around this idea, disseminated by many different groups, there began a rapid coalescing of forces that, as was noted, had taken constitutional restoration as an interlude permitting a return to the options that had begun to take shape in 1962. Illia's government was condemned as inefficient by *Primera Plana,* spokesperson for this group, in September 1963, a month before the new president assumed office. From that point on, Illia was mercilessly pilloried by the opposition press. Different but not contradictory objectives—efficiency, order, modernization, and even a "destiny of greatness"—came together in the criticisms of the government, as did a proposal, somewhat vaguely defined as political proposals generally are, for a "change in structures," which was understood to mean a change in policies. This idea was systematically refined by a cast of propagandists, many of them specifically hired for that purpose, devoted to discrediting the government and the political system in general, and exalting the figure of Onganía—who retired from the military in late 1965—as a model of efficiency, but above all as "the last chance for order and authority," as Mariano Grondona wrote in *Primera Plana.*

During the final six months of Illia's government, one had the impression that a good part of the country that was "with the coup" believed, without any dissimulation and with patience and confidence, that it was undertaking, a road that would lead to redemption. Those who did not share that faith, on the other hand, did share the diagnosis of the problem, to judge by their minimal attempts to defend the institutional system that was collapsing, On June 28, 1966, the military commanders-in-chief deposed Illia and turned over the presidency to General Onganía. With the fall of limited democracy, the stalemate came to an end. The options were defined, and society's conflicts, until then hidden, were able to fully unfold.

six

Dependency or Liberation, 1966–1976

A Rehearsal in Authoritarianism

A broad consensus surrounded the coup d'état of June 28, 1966. Both big and small business, the majority of the political parties—with the exception of the Radicals, Socialists, and Communists—and even many groups on the far left were content with the end of "bourgeois" democracy. Perón gave it qualified support, though he recommended a wait-and-see attitude to his followers, "to get off the saddle until the weather clears," as he put it. The Peronist politicians were less equivocal and the union leaders downright elated, attending the new president's inauguration while contemplating the continuance of the traditional space for negotiating and pressuring the government, perhaps finding possible points of agreement with a military man who—like Perón—emphasized order, unity, a certain paternalism, and a definite anti-Communism.

This broad and varied support had to do with the initial vagueness in the positions of the various currents that coexisted in the government. The "general staff" of the big companies—the economic establishment—had direct interlocutors in many military commanders. However, other military men—above all those who surrounded General Onganía—were inspired by a more traditional vision, derived in part from the old nationalism but especially from the corporatist-organic doctrines that were making headway in the new right. The deep contradictions between corporatists and so-called liberals—who did not believe in either civil liberties or orthodox economic liberalism—were camouflaged in a web of social contacts and a hodgepodge of ideas, elaborated in the economics department of the Catholic University, the Institute of Political Science at the University of San Salvador, or the catechism courses that the Catholic Church—the latter embarking on a campaign to win over leadership groups and skilled in glossing over their differences—organized for the military, young businesspeople, or "technocrats of the sacristy."

Thus, for the moment, the points of agreement held sway. It was necessary to reorganize the state, to make it strong, to invest it with authority and resources, and to have it controlled from above. For some, it was the necessary precondition for an economic restructuring that would employ the traditional Keynesian recipes to break the bottlenecks to economic growth. For others, it was the necessary step for a restructuring of society itself, of its ways of organization and representation, which would eliminate the political institutions judged as harmful and create the foundation for others that were natural, corporatist, and hierarchical.

The first phase of the new government was characterized by an "authoritarian shock treatment." The beginning of a revolutionary stage was proclaimed, and to the Constitution was added a Statute of the Argentine Revolution sworn to by General Juan Carlos Onganía, designated president by the military chiefs of staff and remaining in power until June 1970. Congress was dissolved—the president concentrating both executive and legislative powers in his own hands—as were the political parties, whose assets were confiscated and sold to demonstrate that the ban on politics was irreversible. The military itself was carefully distanced from political decisions, although on matters of national security its representation was institutionalized through its commanders. The number of government ministries was reduced to five, and a military general staff of the state was created, made up of the Security Council, the Councils of Economic Development, and the Council of Science and Technology, because in the new order, economic planning and scientific research were considered part of national security.

With political power concentrated in the executive's hands, the regime began to stifle society. The suppression of Communism, one of the issues that most united all those in favor of the coup, was extended to all aspects of critical thought, of dissidence, even simply of difference. The principal target was the university, which was seen as the center of infiltration, the cradle of Communism, the place from which was propagated all kinds of corrupting doctrines, and the focal point of disorder, because its demonstrations demanding a greater share of the national budget were regarded as subversive behavior. The universities were interdicted, and they were stripped of their academic autonomy. On June 29, 1966, the so-called night of the billy clubs, the police burst into the departments of the University of Buenos Aires and roughed up students and professors. This grave, symbolic, and cautionary episode was followed by a notable wave of resignations by professors. Many continued their work abroad, and others sought to painstakingly reconstruct, in underground fashion, intellectual and academic networks, generally in recondite spaces, which some compared to the catacombs. In the universities, the rightist, clerical, and authoritarian groups that had predominated before 1955 began to reappear.

Censorship was extended to all manifestations of new fashions, from the miniskirt to long hair, all expressions of the evils that according to the Catholic Church were a prelude to Communism: free love, pornography, and divorce. As in the university's case, it was discovered that a deep stratum of society agreed with the diagnosis of the military or the Church about the dangers of intellectual modernization and the necessity of using authority to extirpate the evils.

The gestures of authority were repeated in arbitrarily chosen areas, where what was most revealed was the state's excesses or its weakness in dealing with the pressure of powerful interest groups. Before an economic policy was defined, the government proceeded to reduce drastically the personnel in public administration and in some state companies such as the railroads, whereas it undertook a substantial modification in the work rules in the ports to reduce costs. Another dramatic measure was the closing of the majority of the sugar mills in Tucumán province—which had been heavily subsidized by the state—for purposes of rationalizing production. In all these cases, trade-union protest, which was intense, was violently repressed, and although the Law of Professional Associations was not repealed—its existence was a point of disagreement between the corporatists and liberals in the government—an obligatory arbitration was sanctioned that restricted the possibility of strikes. Little remained of the union leaders' initial hopes, rudely shattered by the authoritarian policy. In February 1967, they launched a *Plan de Acción* reminiscent of the *Plan de Lucha* organized against Illia. But on this occasion, the unions ran into a strong response: mass firings, stripping them of their legal standing (*personería gremial*), interdiction, and use of all the means the law provided the state to control a rebellious labor movement. The strike moreover had little impact, and the General Confederation of Labor (CGT) was forced to admit total defeat and to suspend the measures.

The government had found the suitable political formula for bringing about the great restructuring of society and the economy. With the suppression of politics, the government put an end to the struggle for resources by sectors and interest groups, leaving Vandor's unions displaced from political influence, as was Perón himself, who took a momentary vacation from politics. With all avenues that might express society's tensions shut off, indeed with even personal opinions silenced, the government could design its policies undisturbed, without urgency—a revolution such as the government's did not have time limits, it was said—and with powerful state instruments in its possession.

But in the first six months, beyond these dramatic acts, a clear course had not been adopted for the economy because the designated economic team—with a faintly Social Christian orientation—was far from bringing into line the economic establishment. The conflict was resolved in December 1966 in favor of the so-called liberals. The general most associated with them, Julio Alsogaray—brother of Alvaro—was designated commander-in-chief of the army, and Adalberto Krieger Vasena became minister of the economy and labor. Krieger Vasena was an economist who came from the heart of the big business groups, with excellent connections to the international financial community and with a recognized professional ability. He commanded the government's central machinery—his influence extended to the ministries of public works and foreign affairs—but he had to continue to combat the corporatists concentrated in the ministry of the interior, where education was controlled—a key issue for the Church—and in the general secretariat of the presidency.

Krieger Vasena's economic program, launched in March 1967, was intended first to overcome the crisis in the business cycle—less acute than that of 1962–63—and then to achieve a prolonged stability that would eliminate one of the causes of the intersectoral struggle in the economy. But in the long run, the program proposed a rationalization in the entire economy to enhance the performance of the most efficient companies whose domination over the rest would definitively put an end to the stalemates and obstructions of the recent past in the economic sphere.

For that purpose, the program could count on the powerful instruments of a state that had perfected its interventionist orientations. In the case of inflation, the state was resorted to for purposes of regulating the big economic variables, to ensure a prolonged period of stability and to discourage inflationary pressures. With the unions defeated, wages were frozen for two years following a modest increase and collective bargaining negotiations suspended. Also frozen were the rates for public utility services and for fuels, and an agreement on prices was reached with the leading firms. The fiscal deficit was reduced with the rationalizations of personnel in the public sector and tighter tax collection, above all because the government sharply devalued the peso by some 40 percent, withholding a similar amount from the profits on agricultural exports. With the latter measure, the most immediately significant one, the government's accounts were balanced, avoiding a price rise in foodstuffs, but also preventing the rural sectors from benefiting from the devaluation. The devaluation thus ensured a prolonged period of monetary stability, buttressed by loans from the International Monetary Fund (IMF) and an important influx of foreign investment. In the short term, the successes of this stabilization policy were significant. By the middle of 1969, inflation had been drastically reduced—although it continued to be high by the standards of the industrialized countries—and the state's accounts were balanced, as was the balance of payments.

Other powerful instruments of state intervention were used to maintain the level of economic activity and stimulate those sectors judged to be the most efficient. There were neither monetary nor credit restrictions. The state undertook considerable investments, particularly in public works: the *El Chocón* hydroelectric dam, which was supposed to solve the severe energy shortage, bridges over the Paraná River, roads, and other means of access to the federal capital. To all this was added a strong similar impetus to private construction, and nontraditional exports benefited from tax rebates on imported inputs. The general efficiency of the economy was stimulated through a reduction, undoubtedly selectively applied, in tariff protection and elimination of the subsidies to regional economies, such as Tucumán's sugar or the Chaco's cotton. This effort and the overall success of the government were notable. The gross domestic product (GDP) grew, continuing the trend of previous years; unemployment was generally low—although the restructuring of the economy created pockets of unemployment—wages did not fall significantly; and investment was generally high, though concentrated in public works. Nonetheless there was no sustained private investment, so that around 1969 the growth seemed to reach its limits.

The most concentrated sectors—predominantly foreign—turned out to be the greatest beneficiaries of these policies, which besides establishing stability, were intended to profoundly transform the country's business culture and to consolidate definitively the changes underway since 1955. Many of the firms established during the Frondizi period had now begun to produce at full capacity, but foreign companies also bought out national companies—especially noteworthy in the banking and tobacco industries—thereby making the denationalization of the economy more apparent. Without relinquishing the advantages offered by industrial promotion programs that had first attracted them to the country, these companies took full advantage of the new stability that allowed them to exploit their advantages in organization, research and development, planning, and economies of scale. The great public works realized in this period generally solved their problems in transportation and energy and at the same time provided attractive opportunities for those companies that were in a position to gain state contracts for such jobs, a sector destined to grow considerably.

On the other hand, the list of those adversely affected was long. At the head of the list were the rural sectors. Although their modernization and technological level improved—the purpose of the government's feared tax on "potential income"—they felt themselves to be harmed by what they regarded as a spoliation: the large state appropriation of export profits. The national business sectors—which made their voices heard through the *Confederación General Económica* (CGE)—complained of the lack of protection and bemoaned the denationalization of the economy. Entire provincial economies —such as that of Tucumán, the Chaco, and Misiones—had been truly battered by the elimination of their traditional protection. The list of those who had been injured also included broad sectors of the middle class, negatively affected in various ways, from the ending of rent control to the spread of supermarkets and the effects on small, family-owned stores. The working class was the final group on the list of those hurt by the policies.

The new policies profoundly changed the balance of power—always changing but stable in their essentials—that had existed during the stalemate stage, tipping the scales in favor of large firms. The utilization of the most traditional instrument of economic policy—the transfer of income from the rural to the urban sector—operated in a different manner. Instead of encouraging the urban sector by means of state-supported increased consumption on the part of the workers and the expansion of the internal market—the classic distributionist alliance between business and the working class—it was now encouraged through the expansion of private demand: investments, nontraditional exports, an increase in import substitution industrialization. As Adolfo Canitrot noted, this program belonged and responded to the interests of the big bourgeoisie and could be proposed only in these social and political circumstances.

Supported by those who liked to call themselves liberals, the program in reality preserved and even expanded the powers of the interventionist state, although it diminished the powers of the welfare state. Business did not want to relinquish this powerful instrument, and the military would not have accepted weakening those very parts of the state it most deeply identified with: the military factories oriented in one way or another to defense and the various state companies it was often called on to administer. In these years, the expansion of the state seemed perfectly functional for capitalist restructuring, but probably did not hide from its beneficiaries the potential dangers of keeping alive such powerful practices.

Throughout 1968 began to be seen the first signs of the end of this *pax romana*. In March, a group of militant union leaders, headed by Raimundo Ongaro, leader of the print workers' unions, whose ideological orientations were those of Social Christianity, won the leadership of the CGT, although the old guard leadership immediately distanced itself from Ongaro's supporters. Throughout 1968, the *CGT de los Argentinos*—around which rallied political activists of all stripes—headed a protest movement that the government could control only by combining threats with enticements. This crisis united two groups until then in conflict: the *vandorista* current, which lacked the political space to carry out its traditional tactics, and the so-called *participacionistas,* disposed to accept the rules of the game imposed by the regime and assume its functions as a corporatist representative—orderly and apolitical—of the laboring sector of the nation.

It was in this group that those who surrounded Onganía placed their hopes. Once the phase of economic restructuring was complete, they thought, it would be possible to initiate the "social phase" with the support of a united and domesticated CGT. In addition to this line of thinking in the military, with supporters in the army and especially strong because of the proximity to the presidency, there was another fed by the increasingly more widespread social protests. The rural sectors had open lines of communication to the military commanders, as did the "national bourgeoisie," still able to strike a resonant chord among some of the military. Faced with the prevailing economic policy, there was, this faction of the military said, an alternative: a more national model of development, with a deeper social agenda and more equitable distribution of wealth.

All these voices of protest, not yet in unison, made the relations between the president and his minister of the economy tense. In mid-1968, Onganía relieved the three commanders of the armed forces and replaced Julio Alsogaray—an outspoken liberal—with Alejandro Lanusse, whose ideological-political sympathies at that moment were unclear. The voices of the establishment were raised in defense of Krieger Vasena and also complained of Onganía's excessive authoritarianism and his corporatist flirtations, and they began to think about a political exit, for which General Aramburu and Perón's personal emissary, Jorge Daniel Paladino, both offered their services. When in May 1969 a brief but powerful social protest—the *Cordobazo*—erupted, Onganía's only remaining source of legitimacy, the myth of order, vanished.

The People's Spring

The explosion that took place in Córdoba in May 1969 was preceded by a wave of student protests in various provincial universities—in Córdoba itself, one such protest had led to the death of a student, Santiago Pampillón—and of a strong union protest in Córdoba, an important industrial center devoted to automobile production. Student and worker activism—principal components of the wave of agitation just beginning—came together on May 29, 1969. The local CGT undertook a general strike, and groups of students and workers—with a massive participation of auto workers among the latter—took control of the city center, where common citizens soon joined them. The strong police repression sparked a violent confrontation. Barricades were erected, bonfires were started to combat the effects of the tear gas, and businesses were attacked, though little looting occurred. The multitude that controlled the downtown neighborhoods for various hours had neither slogans nor organizers—unions, parties, and student organizations were all overwhelmed by the magnitude of the protest—yet acted with unusual effectiveness, repeatedly being dispersed only to regroup again. The army finally intervened, with a curious delay, and retook control, except for a few redoubts such as the student neighborhood, Barrio Clínicas, where snipers held the army in check for another day while protesters appeared in the outlying neighborhoods, building barricades and assaulting police stations. Slowly, on May 31st, order was reestablished. Between twenty and thirty persons had been killed, some five hundred were wounded, and another three hundred arrested. War tribunals condemned the principal union leaders such as Agustín Tosco to prison sentences, thereby assigning them responsibility for the uprising.

As a mass protest, only the 1919 *Semana Trágica* or the events of October 17, 1945, can be compared to the *Cordobazo,* with the difference that in the 1945 protest the police supported and protected the workers. But like the October 17th events, the *Cordobazo* was a seminal episode in the wave of social protests that followed. Therefore, its symbolic significance was enormous, although it was given different interpretations by those in power and by the union leadership, or from the perspective of those who, in one way or other, identified with the popular mobilization and drew lessons from the events. Whatever the interpretation, one thing was clear: The enemy of those people who massively went out into the streets to protest was the dictatorship, behind which lurked the manifold presence of capital.

The wave of social mobilizations that the *Cordobazo* inaugurated was expressed in diverse ways. One of them was a new trade-union militancy, manifested first in Rosario and its environs and above all in Córdoba, particularly in the factories of the big firms established after 1955, especially the automobile plants. With workers who enjoyed job stability, a high number of skilled workers, and a relatively well-paid labor force, conflicts were not limited to wages—the area that traditional union activity confined itself to—but extended to working conditions, production rhythms, incentive schemes, and job classifications. These questions, of vital importance to the big firms, were especially so to the automobile industry, which, following the massive and improvised installation of its plants, faced after 1965 a harsh process of rationalization, thereby making the conflicts a permanent state of affairs. These same firms—determined to weaken labor's power—had acquired permission from the government to negotiate their collective bargaining agreements privately, thereby avoiding national contracts, and even to establish plant unions, such as happened with Fiat. Initially, this weakened the union organizations, but in the long run it permitted the emergence of new union leaderships with markedly different orientations from those of the national labor movement, in both their objectives and their methods. While the old guard union leadership restricted itself to negotiating over wages and secured its control through demobilization, cooptation, and thuggery, the new union leaders emphasized honesty, internal democracy, and attention to shop floor problems.

Mobilizations that went beyond the boundaries and control of the union bureaucracies and new demands fashioned a singular union activity, confined at first to the new industrial centers but by 1972 spreading to the more traditional zones of greater Buenos Aires, until then more effectively controlled by the trade-union bureaucracy. In this atmosphere, it was possible to move from concrete demands to broad questioning of social relations and even private property. The union activists of SITRAC-SITRAM—Fiat's plant unions—or of the Cordoban local of the SMATA, the national auto workers' union, were spontaneously *clasista*, even before the bands of left-wing militants of the most varied tendencies congregated around this activity to give it a fuller definition. Moreover, this union activity strongly flouted conventional boundaries and bordered on violence. Such tactics included plant occupations and the taking of hostages. The new unionism had a great ability to mobilize the rest of society, especially in the cities, where the factory occupied a very visible place and where in an active strike the workers went out into the streets and called for citizen solidarity.

By then, many had already taken to the streets. Shortly after the *Cordobazo*, there were similar episodes in Rosario—the *Rosariazo*—and in Cipoletti, in the fruit-growing zone of the Río Negro valley. These episodes were repeated in 1971 in Córdoba, in Neuquén, in General Roca, and with unusual intensity in Mendoza in July 1972. The same agitation could be seen in the rural regions, especially those outside the pampa zone, in the Chaco, Misiones, and Formosa where sharecroppers and small farmers, under assault by evictions and low cotton and yerba maté prices, organized themselves in the so-called *Ligas Agrarias*. Urban protests continued in the streets, adhered to by university students in a permanent state of ferment, and there were daily conflicts in neighborhoods or slums over immediate problems.

These original forms of protest—which evoked preindustrial revolts—were unleashed by some chance event: a new tax, an increase in public utility rates, a particularly impolitic government functionary. Yet they all expressed a deep discontent and a welter of demands that, because the dictatorship had cut off the established channels of free speech, manifested themselves in recondite social spaces, ghettos, neighborhoods, or small towns. As they emerged, they ignited extensive networks of solidarity. Having emerged over questions that affected daily existence rather than work issues—housing, running water, and health—they mobilized much larger sectors than unionized workers. Their participants ranged from members of the informal economy who did not belong to unions and were otherwise defenseless to middle-class sectors whose participation was one of the most novel aspects of these protests, manifested as well in the strikes of schoolteachers and professors, public employees, and judicial functionaries, or in the lockouts of small store owners and industrialists.

All this represented a chorus of protest of great diversity, heterogeneous but in unison, ruled by an inclusionary logic, to which were added the voices of other sectors that had been damaged, such as the great rural producers or sectors of the national bourgeoisie. They gave legitimacy to one another and gave shape to a social imaginary, a true "people's spring," growing and gaining strength—until it reached its full maturation in 1973—as it was discovering its adversary's weaknesses, which was by then incapable of finding a suitable response. According to a common vision gradually gaining currency just as it simplified the complexity of the situation, all of society's afflictions were concentrated in a single problem: the dictatorship and the small groups that supported it, the direct and willing culprits of each and every form of oppression, exploitation, and violence in society. Confronting them were the people, rising up in fraternal solidarity and without divisions, mobilizing to defeat the oppressors and resolve all of society's evils, even the most intractable ones, because everything seemed propitious for a transformation through the common efforts of men and women compelled to travel the path between immediate demands and the desire for a better world. Just what such a better world would look like and how to get there were questions that were beginning to be discussed.

Argentina's awakening was part of a global phenomenon, and there were signs of this "people's spring" all over the world. The broad social pacts that had presided over the long cycle of prosperity following the Second World War were unraveling, as could be seen in the wave of discontent that ran throughout diverse societies, above all in its most impressionable group, the students. Such unrest had its expression in such places as Prague, Mexico City, and Berkeley and reached its culmination in the events of May 1968 in Paris, with its protest against authoritarianism and call for the power of imagination. The most notorious expression of authoritarianism—imperialism—was visibly faltering, faced with the wave of protest movements. The Vietnamese people's surprising capacity for resistance created the image of the defeated giant that had to grapple with its own internal front of students, minorities, women, and indeed of an entire society that demanded its rights. If the Soviet Union—repressor of the Prague spring—had long ceased to embody utopia, China and its Cultural Revolution proclaimed the possibility of a different kind of Communism, at once national and antiauthoritarian. The images of Chairman Mao, as well as of Fidel Castro, were ubiquitous in the socialist world and the Third World. The Third World's representatives met in 1965 in the Tricontinental Congress in Havana and were increasingly sympathetic to the left. It appeared that different national expressions of socialism could find common ground for mutual coexistence and common action.

In Latin America, where the prospects of the Alliance for Progress and support for democracy had been confined to the dustbin of history, the sides were clearly drawn. If development was the fruit of national security for the dictatorship, for those who combated authoritarianism the only alternative to dependency was revolution, which would lead to liberation. Cuba stood as a touchstone, not so much for its own experience—about which little was known—as for its leading role in what its enemies called exporting revolution. The actions of Che Guevara in Bolivia demonstrated the possibilities and limits of revolutionary *foquismo,* but above all his death—dramatically represented in an image that traversed the world of his dead body—created the most potent symbol for those struggling, in one way or another, for liberation. On the same front, united against a common enemy, were aligned the urban guerrillas of Brazil and Uruguay—the romantic Tupamaros—the Chilean Marxist parties that brought Salvador Allende to the presidency through the electoral route, and military nationalists and populists such as the Bolivian Juan José Torres, the Panamanian Omar Torrijos, or the Peruvian Juan Velasco Alvarado.

Even the Catholic Church, traditional bastion of the oligarchic sectors, joined, at least in part, this people's spring. In the fervor of the institutional changes introduced first by Pope John XXIII and later by the Vatican Council II, part of the Latin American Church gave a singular interpretation to its doctrine. In 1967, the Third World bishops, headed by the Brazilian Dom Helder Camara, proclaimed their overriding concern for poor people—for their material, not just spiritual, problems—as well as for the necessity of becoming actively involved in social reform and of assuming the consequences of that commitment. This position gained partial legitimacy when in 1968, with the Pope present, the Latin American Bishops' Council met in Medellín, Colombia. A "liberation theology" adapted the Church's traditional message to the conflicts of the hour, affirming that the "violence from below" was a consequence of the "violence from above" and condoning crossing the boundary, increasingly narrow, between denunciation and action. It was a road that had already been followed by the Colombian priest and guerrilla Camilo Torres, killed in 1966, a figure as emblematic as Che Guevara.

This tendency in the Church had swift repercussions in Argentina. After 1968, the clergy who met in the Movement of Third World Priests and the laypeople who accompanied them worked in the poorest areas, particularly in the urban slums, promoted the establishment of neighborhood solidarity organizations, and were the driving force behind demands and protest actions, including hunger strikes. Their evangelical language quickly became political. The violence from below, they claimed, was legitimized by social injustice, which was also a kind of violence. Solidarity with the people—whose face, in contrast with the *clasistas,* they saw in the defenseless poor rather than in the unionized industrial workers—led inevitably to identification with poor people's basic ideology: Peronism. The Third World priests facilitated the incorporation into politics and activism of vast contingents of young people educated in religious schools and initially influenced by Catholic nationalism. They assumed a solidarity with and a commitment to poor people and also to Peronism, and though they became familiar with ideas coming from the left, continuing the tendency for a "dialogue between Christians and Marxists," they retained the strong imprint of their ideological origins.

Through this and other routes, sizable numbers of young people rapidly adopted a political activism whose character turned out to be unrecognizable to many. Traditional university politics changed in form and meaning after the dictatorship destroyed the "democratic island" that was the university, which had been built since 1955, in which it had been possible to combine academic excellence with political activism and a commitment to some degree of critical distance about concrete options. Since 1966, both missions of the university had been in a state of strong tension, but the repression cut short the best of that critical thought and launched it into activities totally subordinated to politics—a science that militants believed would precisely expose "dependency" and contribute in a direct way to "liberation." Students dove directly into dissident action, to such a point that the universities, whose academic standards increasingly declined, were becoming converted into centers of agitation and political recruitment.

For many, and especially for the youth without previous political experience, Peronism, proscribed but powerful, exercised a strong attraction as the movement where they could find the best outlet for their dissidence. From Peronism past and present—and from Perón himself—could be derived many images, and the new militants also created one of their own. In his exile in Madrid, somewhat removed from the country's daily problems, the leader had been modernizing his discourse, incorporating into it various strands that ranged from De Gaulle's Europeanism to the Third World struggle—which Perón associated with his so-called third way—and such causes as dependency, liberation, and issues of the environment and world hunger, which concerned the Club of Rome. While Perón was reconciling, from this welter of influences, those best suited to his role as the head of a veritable sect, forced to be the one for the many, those in Argentina who proclaimed him their leader selected those elements of his discourse that best coincided with their own perceptions of reality. Silvia Sigal and Eliseo Verón found in this ability for a "strategic reading" an explanation for the spectacular growth of those who identified with Peronism and also the roots of the profound drama that ensued.

Among its new disciples, in the absence of the one who could give legitimacy to a sole orthodoxy, Peronism turned out to be permeable to multiple discourses, those coming from Catholicism and nationalism, from historical revisionism and also from the left, especially to the extent that the latter was resolving its contradictory feelings about Peronism. Peronism was a phenomenon that had always disconcerted the left, regarded by both the left and the right, in the words of the revolutionary Peronist John William Cooke, as the "cursed thing," but for different reasons. Committed as the left was to the revolutionary path and to acknowledging that the workers—the essential component for the building of socialism—were irrevocably Peronists, a good part of the left agreed to profess the religion, some with sincerity and others with pangs of guilt, to become members of the "Peronist nation," hoping to be recognized as the people's vanguard. Not everyone was so attracted. The experienced of the *Cordobazo* energized those tendencies that, from a more classic leftist perspective, trusted in the possibilities of mass action and gave priority to "class" over the "people."

Those who opted for Peronism ended up taking to its logical conclusion their ideological reexamination and assigning the movement a central place in the great process of building socialism. Some of these individuals came from the Marxist tradition—such as Jorge Abelardo Ramos and Rodolfo Puiggrós—and others from nationalism—such as Juan José Hernández Arregui and Arturo Jauretche or José María Rosa. All finally created—at least in the eyes of those who read them—an intermediate route, in which the demands of socialism were complemented by those of national liberation, a subject to which the old nationalism had contributed as much as Marxism-Leninism. As with politics, history was read with a Manichean mindset that sought to decipher, behind the mask of "official history," the buried memory of the popular struggles to build the nation and to promote liberation, struggles in which Peronism was the heir to the federalist *montoneras*, Rosas, and Yrigoyen. In other interpretations, this tradition of popular struggles included such diverse figures as General Roca and the anarchists and socialists.

But all shared the conviction—expressed with force and fortune by historical revisionism—that there was a line separating history into two irreconcilable and eternally antagonistic sides, culminating in the confrontation between dictatorship and the Peronist masses.

In these interpretations, Peronism represented the first emergence of the people in the postwar period—characterized also by industrialization, the rise of the national bourgeoisie, the nationalist state—and would be so again as social forces gathered and a context was established that would lead Peronists to redefine Peronism's historic banners in favor of those of anti-imperialism and socialism. It could be debated—and indeed was—about who were the people's allies, the members of the proposed "national front," and even what this thing the "people" was. For some it was the organized and defiant working class, and for others the miserable and oppressed underclass, in need of paternal and firm guidance. In leftist circles, compelled to explain the present phenomenon of mass popular mobilization, these discussions were intense. But action prevailed over debate, which in the new context—so different in that sense from classic leftist political culture—assumed total priority over reflection.

The revolution was possible. Cuba, the *Cordobazo,* and social mobilization—as intense as it was lacking in leadership and a program—showed it to be so. To find such leadership and a program through action itself was what the new activism sought. The democratic alternative—discredited for the old militants and meaningless for the youth—was totally absent in the debates. The left offered a classic interpretation of the mobilizations and its possibilities by promoting *clasismo,* revolutionary trade unionism, in the labor movement, especially strong in Córdoba. In 1971, the Fiat unions SITRAC-SITRAM proposed a program that would unite the entire left, converting it into the vanguard of the most advanced sectors of the proletariat, but they discovered that the rank- and-file-workers were not disposed to accompany them in an undertaking that, in questioning social relations and private property, completely went beyond the limits of their union demands. As in the case of the anarchists and Radicals at the beginning of the century, Córdoba's workers followed the *clasistas'* leadership on work-related issues but not so on political issues and remained loyal to their Peronist identities.

On the other hand, the predominant political discourses, which combined elements of revolutionary Marxism with others coming from nationalism or Third World Catholicism, drew their inspiration from the people's spring, making it more potent in the popular imagination and strengthening and legitimizing it with theoretical principles. Though they interpreted reality and society in different ways, these discourses all sharply divided the world into two opposing camps: friends and enemies. The key to oppression, injustice, and the selling-out of the country was to be found among those who wielded power, the monopoly of a few (nationalists and Trotskyites both legitimized this conspiratorial vision). Thus, because everything stemmed from power, the sole purpose of political action was to capture it. The absence of suitable conditions and real possibilities for revolution could be overcome by the force of will, preeminently by violence, which was leavened with everything from Leninism, to Guevarism, to fascism. By one or another route, everything led to an interpretation of politics as an extension of war; naturally, those who best adapted themselves to that logic prevailed in the debate among activists and left their mark on popular mobilization.

The first guerrilla organizations had emerged—with little significance—in the early 1960s, under the influence of the Cuban experience. They were revived with Che Guevara's Bolivian campaign, but their real genesis was to be found in the country's experience with authoritarianism and the conviction that there was no alternative to defeating the dictatorship except armed struggle. Since 1967—in the ranks of both the left and Peronism—different groups were emerging: the *Fuerzas Armadas Peronistas, Descamisados, Fuerzas Armadas Revolucionarias* (FAR), *Fuerzas Armadas de Liberación,* and around 1970 the two that would have the greatest transcendence, the *Montoneros,* an organization with roots in Catholic integralism and nationalism but now Peronist, and the *Ejército Revolucionario del Pueblo,* tied to the Trotskyite group, the *Partido Revolucionario de los Trabajadores.*

The act that marked the guerrilla organizations' official birth in public life was the kidnapping and execution of the former president General Pedro Aramburu in May 1970 at the hands of the *Montoneros.* Shortly thereafter, the FAR occupied the small city of Garín, a few kilometers from the nation's capital, and the *Montoneros* occupied La Calera in Córdoba province. From that point on until 1973, the acts of violence escalated, both in number and in their spectacular nature. Although their purpose was not always clear, many of the actions were for purposes of supplying the organizations with money, arms, and medical supplies. Others, such as town occupations, were to demonstrate power, laying bare the state's impotence. There were also a number of "expropriating" actions that distributed the spoils among poor people in the manner of Robin Hood. In many cases, these actions sought to insert themselves in social conflicts and to deepen them, for example, kidnapping business executives and managers in the middle of a strike. The most spectacular actions were assassinations: Before Aramburu, Augusto Vandor had been killed—though the authors of his murder were never discovered—and then José Alonso, another prominent union leader. In 1972, almost simultaneously, an important Italian businessman and a high-ranking general were assassinated.

The case of Aramburu encapsulated all the explanations for the significance of this practice: vengeance—or justice—for the 1956 executions of a leader particularly hated by the Peronists, but also the elimination of a political alternative that the liberal groups had been preparing even before the erosion of Onganía's regime. Certain contacts between leaders of the *Montoneros* and members of Onganía's governing team suggested a conspiracy organized from above and caused some to reflect early on the manipulative character of the strategy of armed struggle.

Among all the leftist organizations, there were great strategic and political differences, but a common spirit prevailed. All aspired to transform the spontaneous mobilizations of society into a general uprising, and all found common ground in a reigning political culture that invigorated the leftist groups though in some ways drawing on that of their adversaries as well. The exclusionist logic—that constant in twentieth-century Argentine politics—was taken to its ultimate consequences: Enemies—lackeys of imperialism, the army of occupation—were to be annihilated. The leftist organizations were the vanguard of popular mobilization whose representation consisted of violent action. Unity, order, hierarchy, and discipline were—just as in the military and the societal organization imagined by the Church and the corporatists—the attributes of an armed organization. Violence was not only justified by the adversary's violence, it was glorified as the midwife of the new order. The signs of a true militant were heroism and sacrifice, being prepared to accept a glorious and redemptive death, the road of true transcendence, "among the heroes of the armed fatherland." As Juan José Sebreli noted, it was not the living Che Guevara but his cadaver that was the beacon for those who, from diverse origins and along different paths, agreed in cheering death.

As revealing of society's political culture was the fact that a broad sector of the youth made assassination a political weapon, as well as the way that the rest of society reacted to it, with a touch of sympathy for consummated justice. Many found satisfaction in a harsh blow dealt to the enemy or, in many cases, a titillation about the true reasons for crimes that were never fully understood but whose rightness, whether ethical or tactical, no one doubted. This widespread sympathy, superficial and lacking reflection, as would soon be seen, momentarily made any proposal aimed at repressing the perpetrators of this violence destined to fail.

Of the welter of guerrilla organizations, the *Montoneros* best adapted themselves to the political climate in the country and proceeded to virtually absorb all the others, with the exception of the *Ejército Revolucionario del Pueblo* (ERP). The *Montoneros* gave absolute priority to direct action and felt the least tied to previous political traditions or loyalties, which permitted them to operate with complete efficiency as a military organization. They also triumphed, within Peronism, in the difficult competition for Perón's "strategic reading," winning a space for their autonomous action and at the same time the recognition of a leader who had become a master in the art of, as he said, "using his two hands" (the left and right wings of his movement). They were in background and training the least oriented to the workers' movement and the most inclined to look for support and legitimization among the broad sectors of urban poor people cultivated by the Third World priests. From 1971 onward, taking advantage of the military's electoral exit and then Perón's return, they threw themselves into the organization and mobilization of these and other sectors in neighborhoods, slums, universities, and to a lesser extent, unions, through the *Juventud Peronista* (Peronist Youth), which grew notably.

The Military in Retreat

Popular mobilization was increasingly being identified with Peronism and with Perón, who by 1971 had come to occupy almost as central a place in Argentine politics as when he was president. In disarray and disconcerted, the military was warning that it had to find an electoral exit to the impasse it found itself in. In retreat, it was forced to negotiate the terms of such an exit with diverse social and political forces and finally with Perón himself. Although the ensuing disaster was perhaps inevitable, the paths to it were many.

In his own way, Onganía initiated the search. In May 1969, his authority had been damaged as much by his impotence in the face of social protest as by the army's vacillation in repressing it. Also felt was the impact on the economic arena, where there occurred a hurried flight of foreign capital and the reappearance of concerns over inflation. Onganía attempted to circumvent the difficulties with minor adjustments—he removed Krieger Vasena as the minister of the economy and replaced him with a lesser-known technocrat of a similar orientation—and with a more resolute political opening (*apertura*), especially with regard to the CGT and its *participacionista* leadership.

But the climate had changed. The trade-union leaders were less docile, and businesspeople openly demonstrated their distrust of populist posturing. A sector that until then had been sacrificed—rural producers—increased its protests and maintained a strong polemic with the foreign-owned packinghouses, apparently protected by the government. Onganía was increasingly isolated from the military, but benefited from its indecision and disarray. Some groups wanted to follow a nationalist course and perhaps a populist one, whereas the liberals wavered between a harsher dictatorship and negotiations for a political exit, an undertaking associated for their side with the name of General Aramburu. On May 29, 1970, exactly a year to the day after the *Cordobazo*, Aramburu was kidnapped, and a few days later his body was found. Many suspected, with some reason, that certain circles that surrounded the president were in some way involved. What is clear is that the episode removed any doubts for the military. In early June 1970, it removed Onganía from office and designated a president commander-in-chief, to whom was reserved the authority to intervene in matters of state. The one so designated was General Roberto Marcelo Levingston, a little-known figure at the time absent from the country.

Levingston, who governed until March 1971, revealed that he had his own ideas, very different from those of General Lanusse, the dominant figure in the military junta, and in tune with those of the small but influential group of nationalist officers. Levingston named an outstanding economist of the United Nations' Economic Commission for Latin America (ECLA) school, who had held posts in Frondizi's administration, Aldo Ferrer, as his minister of public works and then of the economy. Ferrer proposed reviving the nationalist-populist formula, at least in the modest terms possible following the changes of the previous ten years. A minister of labor sympathetic to Peronism negotiated with the CGT, and there was a wage increase to broaden income distribution. The national bourgeoisie was protected through credit and contracts with state companies. The "buy Argentine" and "Argentinization of credit" campaigns encapsulated a policy that was perhaps moderate in nature but original in the context of the times. Its proponents trusted that, in a period estimated from three to four years, the conditions would be created for a suitable political solution and an "authentic" democracy. Levingston confirmed the expiration of the "old" parties and encouraged the formation of "new" ones, perhaps even a National Movement that would assume responsibility for continuing the transformation project, for which he brandished various anti-imperialist slogans and attempted to attract lesser politicians from the traditional parties, together with leaders of smaller political forces. The aspiration by a military government to mobilize the "people" turned out to be ingenuous, but it was at any rate the first formal recognition of the necessity of a political solution.

Calling for negotiations, the government revived the down-and-out CGT. The union leaders, pressured by increasing rank-and-file demands and the inflation that had reappeared and encouraged by an opportunity to exercise their own pressures because of the government's weakness, launched in October 1970 a *Plan de Lucha* that included three general strikes, each uncontested by the government. The traditional political parties, for their part, with the general encouragement of Lanusse, also reappeared on the scene. The People's Turn (*La Hora del Pueblo*) campaign, whose architects were Jorge Daniel Paladino, Perón's personal emissary, and Arturo Mor Roig, a veteran Radical politician, served as the basis of their common actions until 1973. Then it was agreed to end electoral proscriptions and to ensure, in a future democratically elected government, respect for the opposition and constitutional norms. Radicals and Peronists had at their disposal the weapons that they had traditionally wielded, and they offered society the possibility of an acceptable political coexistence. The plan also included some positions on economic policy, moderately nationalist and distributionist, which permitted the subsequent support of both the CGT and the CGE, organizations representing the unions and national business sector, respectively, which for their part also agreed to a common pact that established basic priorities.

The resurgence of the labor movement and the political parties was due in part to the opening up of the political game by a government that was seeking an exit from power. But it was fundamentally the result of the crisis in society, which indirectly revitalized the unions and the parties and converted them into possible mediators. Levingston turned out to be incapable of handling the negotiating space that was opening up. He was received with hostility by the economic establishment—whom the government, cultivating a nationalist rhetoric, labeled as representatives of "unpatriotic capitalism"—and was at odds with the political parties, with whom he did not wish to negotiate, as well as with the unions and even with the "national bourgeoisie." The military leadership deemed Levingston as incapable as Onganía of finding a solution, and when in March 1971 there was another mass protest in Córdoba—the so-called *viborazo* in which armed organizations appeared—it decided on his removal and replacement by General Lanusse, who at that time seemed to be to be the only military leader with the political clout to oversee the difficult process of retreat.

In March 1971, Lanusse announced the lifting of the ban on political activity for the parties and the call for general elections, subordinate however to what he called the *Gran Acuerdo National* (Great National Agreement), whose terms he had been negotiating with the leaders of the People's Turn coalition. Finally, the military opted for giving priority to a political solution and through it hoped to reconstitute the authority and legitimacy of an increasingly ineffectual state. While the issue of economic development remained on the back burner, that of public security continued to be pressing, in large measure because the military could no longer guarantee it. Disagreements over how to confront the armed organizations and deal with social protest were increasing and foretold future dilemmas. While an emergency antisubversive law and special tribunals to try the guerrillas were being created, some government sectors and the armed forces initiated an illegal repression: kidnapping, torture, and the disappearance of activists, assassination without risk of punishment, the fate suffered by a group of guerrillas detained in the military base at Trelew in August 1972. There were similar confusions in economic policy, until it was decided to renounce any clear course of action and to dissolve the ministry of economy, dividing it up into sectoral secretariats that were entrusted to representatives of each of the corporative organizations. Thus, in the context of runaway inflation, capital flight, a fall in real wages, and unemployment, all worsened by a general wave of societal demands, the sectoral tug-of-war was institutionalized in the very heart of a government ready to concede what each one demanded.

For the government, the central question was the *Gran Acuerdo Nacional* (GAN), which began as an open negotiation and became a power struggle between Lanusse and Perón, with the rest of society passive spectators. The government's initial proposal offered a general condemnation of "subversion," guarantees on economic policy, and respect for democratic norms, while assuring the armed forces an institutional role in any future government in which they could play a tutelary role in matters of national security. But the chief component was to establish an agreement about a transitional presidential candidate, a role for which Lanusse offered his services. Some of the points, those dealing with economic policy and democratic norms, had already been hashed out in negotiations with the People's Turn movement. Ensuring an institutional role for the armed forces, however, was impossible, given the political climate. The other two points—condemnation of subversion and agreement on a presidential candidate—were largely at the mercy of Perón's tactics.

In November 1971, Perón removed his personal emissary, Jorge Paladino—who until then had negotiated the agreements with the Radicals and the military—and replaced him with Héctor J. Cámpora, whose principal virtue was his blind loyalty to the will of the exiled leader. Perón proposed to oversee the negotiations without showing any of his cards. Just as he was the master of the country's social and political climate, neither did he relinquish his role as the point of reference in the wave of social unrest nor reject the support proclaimed by a good part of the armed organizations. Indeed, he continuously encouraged them and bestowed legitimacy; when in 1972 the Peronist Youth was organized, he included its best-known leader, Rodolfo Galimberti, in his own strategic command. At the same time, he encouraged the People's Turn movement, the *Frente Cívica de Liberación Nacional* (Popular Front of National Liberation) with allied parties, and then the CGT-CGE pact. In truth, no one knew where Perón was headed.

Lanusse at first proposed the GAN as the precondition for elections, but gradually had to lower his demands, given the impossibility of making Perón negotiate. In July 1972, convinced that nothing could be hoped for from Perón, Lanusse opted to ensure a minimum guarantee: that Perón would not be a candidate, in return for Lanusse's own self-proscription. Perón tacitly accepted the conditions. In November 1972, Perón returned to the country for a few days. He had no dealings with the government but spoke with political leaders, particularly the Radical boss Ricardo Balbín, thereby sealing the agreement regarding the reestablishment of democracy. Perón cultivated his image as peacemaker, spoke about world issues such as the environment, and avoided any provocative statements. Finally, he organized his electoral front: the *Frente Justicialista de Liberación Nacional* (Justicialist Front of National Liberation or FREJULI). Perón thereby established an electoral front along with a number of small parties and imposed his presidential and vice presidential candidates: Héctor Cámpora, his personal emissary, and Vicente Solano Lima, a Conservative politician who since 1955 had faithfully supported the Peronists.

Perón continued his back and forth game, alternating provocation with pacification. The FREJULI constituted a challenge to the politicians of the People's Turn and above all to the union leaders, who had been excluded from the negotiations, and was an endorsement of the Peronist movement's revolutionary wing that surrounded Cámpora and gave his electoral campaign a defiant air. Its slogan, "Cámpora to the government, Perón to power," signaled the fictitious character of political discourse in what was a kind of deal struck between the partisans of the electoral solution and those who disdained it but who went along with it in pursuit of "national liberation." The Radicals, with Balbín's candidacy, accepted a Peronist victory and a future role as a minority opposition that bestowed legitimacy on the government, and from the left and right emerged tickets of scant importance. The Peronist Youth set the tone for the campaign, repeatedly stretching to the limit the terms of the agreement among the political parties and constituting a true culmination of society's alienation with military power.

The climate continued after the FREJULI's electoral triumph on March 11, 1973—when the Peronists triumphed with almost 50 percent of the votes—until the following May 25th, the date of Cámpora's inauguration. On that memorable day, there were in attendance such figures as the Chilean president Salvador Allende and the Cuban, Osvaldo Dorticós. In the name of the continent's two socialist experiments, a mobilized society and its leaders ridiculed the military, turning a retreat by the latter into a rout, and freed from jail political prisoners incarcerated for acts of subversion. Congress provided a democratic legitimacy to these acts by immediately passing a general amnesty law. For many, it appeared that the moment of the *Argentinazo,* of the great national insurrection, had arrived. Others more cautiously took note of the removal of Galimberti ordered by Perón, after the Peronist Youth leader had threatened to form "popular militias." These and other assessments—because virtually anything was possible that May 25th—all hinged on the designs, secret but undoubtedly brilliant, of Perón, regarded as the nation's savior.

This phenomenon, utterly unique, of Perón's being simultaneously many things for many people, was due to the heterogeneity of the Peronist movement and Perón's decision and skill in not dispensing with any of its many parts. Furthermore, as José Luis Romero wrote, Perón's symbolic figure, one and many at the same time, ended up replacing the real historical personality. For all, Perón expressed a general sentiment of a nationalist and popular kind, in reaction to the recent experience of denationalization and privilege. For some—die-hard Peronist trade-union leaders and politicians—these sentiments were incarnated in the historic leader who, as in 1945, would bring back the old prosperity, distributed by a munificent welfare state. For others—the younger ones of every political stripe—Perón was the Third World revolutionary leader who would eliminate the traitors in his own movement and would lead the country to liberation, national or social, animating his people's potential.

In contrast, others, heirs to the movement's venerable anti-Communism, saw in Perón someone who would cut off the head of the hydra of social subversion with all the energy necessary, all the more dangerous and deserving of extermination for having usurped Peronism's traditional banners. For many others—sectors of the middle or upper classes, those who were perhaps the most recent discoverers of his virtues—Perón was the pacifier, the leader bereft of personal ambitions, the "herbivorous lion," as he was called, who would put the interests of Argentina before those of Peronism and would be capable of harnessing society's conflicts, attaining a rebuilding process, and setting the country on the path of economic growth, in pursuit of Argentina's status as a "great power." The surprising phenomenon of 1973, the marvel of Perón's charisma, was its capacity to reconcile so many unsatisfied longings,

incompatible but all personified and legitimized in the old leader who was returning to the country. On March 1, 1973, the country voted massively
against the military and authoritarian power and believed that neither one
was ever coming back. It did not vote for any one of these options contained
in the winning ticket, but for a social, political, and also military space in
which conflicts were supposed to be settled.

1973: A Balance

For its protagonists, the roots of these violent conflicts were to be found in
a volatile economy, with its succession of fits and starts, unfulfilled promises,
and accumulated frustrations. Nevertheless, from a broader perspective—
undoubtedly an advantage of hindsight and enhanced by subsequent calami-
ties still not imagined in 1973—the economy performed adequately, a performance that lasted until 1975, and did not justify the apocalyptic prognosis,
though neither did it that of the "great power" Argentina.

What was most notable was the growth of the agricultural sector in the
pampa zone that, beginning in the early 1960s and lasting until the early
1980s, reversed the long stagnation and the previous slump. In these prosperous years, the world found itself in conditions to turn at least a part of its
needs for food into effective demand and new markets for Argentine grains
and oils, particularly in the socialist countries—compensating for the failure
of their own agriculture—which were either enjoying the benefits of high oil
prices or beginning their industrial growth.

The pampa's agricultural zone was substantially transformed, as were diverse modern economic islands in the traditional interior, such as the fruit-
growing Río Negro valley. The state promoted change in diverse ways—credit
and subsidies for investments and the systematic actions of the National Institute of Agricultural Technology (INTA)—although it did not change its
traditional policy of transferring resources to the urban economy, which continued with just a few modifications in its methods. What proved decisive
were the effects of the economy's general modernization. The local manufacturing of tractors and combine-harvesters, and also of silos and others storage
installations, completed the mechanization of agricultural tasks and the substantial changes in storage and transportation methods. Agribusiness—in

general, subsidiaries of large foreign firms—introduced hybrid seeds, and in the early 1970s spectacular results were achieved with corn production and then with sorghum, sunflowers, wheat, and soybeans. Later came pesticides and herbicides and finally chemical fertilizers. Modern business practices were also introduced into agriculture, facilitated by a flexibilization of the sharecropping system and the participation of businesspeople who were not themselves landowners. Around 1985, the final point in this wave of expansion, the amount of land under cultivation in the pampa region had increased around 30 percent with respect to 1960, above all because of the converting of livestock acreage to agriculture, but the productivity of the land had also increased twofold and that of the labor force four times.

This true revolution in productivity permitted the growth in grain and vegetable oil exports, although the markets for meat continued to stagnate or even decline. Industrial exports also increased. Agricultural machinery, machine tools, automobiles, metallurgical and chemical products were able to compete in neighboring countries, at times taking advantage of the opportunities offered by the Latin American Association of Free Trade. Thus, little by little, the strong limitation that the export sector represented for the whole of the economy declined, the impact of cyclical crises diminished, and the opportunities for industrial growth increased. The traumatic phase in the economy gave way to one of a mild but steady economic expansion that had taken off during the years of Illia's presidency and was sustained despite changes in government and economic policies.

As Pablo Gerchunoff and Juan José Llach demonstrated, industrial production grew steadily following the great 1963 crisis, without any slump until 1975. Some of that growth was due to the maturation of many of the investments made after 1958, but also contributing to it were a cluster of national companies, in both dynamic and traditional industries, large and small, that recovered after withstanding the first impact of the arrival of foreign firms. Some captured a share of the market in dynamic industries that had not been exploited; others grew at the expense of competitors, thanks to greater efficiency. Also beneficial was a sustained growth of the internal market, which gave new life to traditional industries such as textiles, food processing, and electrical appliances. The national companies, after suffering a strong shakedown, adapted themselves to the new conditions and accommodated their possibilities to that share of the market that the big foreign companies ceded them.

The nationally owned firms adopted what they could from the foreign companies or found ways of associating with them, as in the use of patents or licenses or the supply of parts for the great assembly plants. Simultaneously, they took advantage of an environment in which they moved with ease: the use of subsidized credit or of the state's promotional policies. In a process that Jorge Katz described as "maturation," they increased their economies of scale—factories replaced workshops—and then made an effort to make more efficient their organizations and productive processes. This push toward rationalization—which required many engineers, administrators, and executives in general, the heart of the new middle sectors—was common at that time among national firms and many of the foreign ones, as in the automobile industry, which after their establishment in the country had drifted away from the operational standards of their parent companies. The effects of these polices could be seen in the workers' reactions and their growing sensitivity to shop floor problems.

As in the case of agriculture, industry modernized and moved closer, as never before or since, to international standards. As previously noted, industrial growth was related in part to the process of concentration and shakedown, and also to the increase in state investment, the purchases of industrial products by the public companies and by the new public works projects, or simply the expansion of a sector of wealthy consumers, disposed to change their automobile every two years. Also reversing the tendency begun in 1955 was the growth of the internal market because of an increase in industrial employment and especially in construction, together with the recovery in wage earners' incomes. The tendency of the previous traumatic phase of economic development was reversed, and participation in the GDP rose—except for the agitated years of 1971–72—ultimately surpassing 45 percent of GDP. Despite the firms' rationalization policies, the unions retained their effectiveness in defending rank-and-file interests, although this did not aid the undoubtedly large mass of nonunionized workers, from whose ranks came many of the protagonists of the new forms of social protest.

Around 1973, this economic expansion was already approaching the limits of installed capacity, which because of the lack of significant private investment had not grown substantially. The high degree of social conflict sustained in a growth cycle and a rise in expectations could not be satisfied with a simple redistribution in income according to the historic prescription of

Peronism. Yet this formula contained other elements appreciated by those who placed their faith in Perón: greater state regulation of the relations between the various social actors and a larger space for those excluded from the negotiating table. In sum, the initiative for social peace belonged to the state.

Despite the proclaimed liberalism of the propertied classes, since 1955 there had been no decline either in the state's powers or in its ability to establish the rules of the game. Through it, the big decisions were made, such as the transfer of earnings from the export sector to industry, as well as other more specific ones such as the use of subsidized credit, promotional policies, purchases from state companies, or contracts for public works. For business, these represented possibilities for easier and safer profits than those derived from improving efficiency or competitiveness, but also equally easy and sudden losses, so that the control of the state's policies was a vital question.

But neither they nor anybody else completely controlled the totality of the state's structures, some having grown in a process of accretion and hardly subordinated to a single executive will. General Onganía's experience—the most systematic attempt to erect what Guillermo O'Donnell called the "bureaucratic authoritarian state"—demonstrated the difficulties even for the armed forces, prone to identify their own institutional interests with that of the state. The other special interests—the business lobbies, the unions, and the Church—the leading protagonists in the sectoral tug-of-war, tended to conclude their internal conflicts either in stalemates or by forming alliances, such as that achieved by the various union groups confronted with attempts to reduce the powers of the welfare state. The surprising degree of power retained by the labor movement after 1955 demonstrates another aspect of that uncontrollable state: the frequent alliances between two competitors—industrialists and union leaders, for example—to the disadvantage of a third party or of the nation as a whole.

Immediate benefits could bring with them future complications. Through the union leaders' repeated calls to participate in the sectoral tug-of-war, the organized working class had had access to the state since 1945 and had influenced its decisions. During Perón's government, the leader's power and desire to control all social and political forces ensured discipline. After 1955, the *vandorista* leadership of the unions was a guarantee for business of the demobilization of the workers and of a negotiation that was always possible. The rupture in this equilibrium after 1966, the strong social mobilization that opened the floodgates and undermined possibilities for negotiation, as well as the demonstrated incapacity of the military to hold onto power, revealed the danger that important parts of the state apparatus might fall into questionable hands. Those who in 1973 entrusted their fate to Perón were hoping that he would be able, as in 1945, to control social mobilization and at the same time discipline those who, like the sorcerer's apprentice, appealed in the tug-of-war to Perón's powers of persuasion. Each and everyone had to be organized and disciplined by the state itself. The agreement between the CGT and the CGE began to sketch out the outline of the *Pacto Social* (Social Pact) and the great negotiation between the principal corporative powers

In 1973, there was a glimpse of the future of this corporatist scene, one that Perón had demonstrated he knew how to handle very well. About the future of democracy, however, there were more doubts, despite the spectacular electoral experience of March. The political parties that were supposed to take charge of it were not overly enthusiastic. The Peronist Party barely existed in the ensemble of what was called, a bit euphemistically, the Movement, and Perón never considered it more than window dressing. The remaining parties, following a long period of inactivity or of only partial activity, were a collection of entrenched leaderships, veritable cliques, with few ideas and with scant ability to represent society's interests. The so-called People's Turn, which played an important role in the transition to elections, did not manage to become a recognized forum for debate and negotiation beyond the initial agreements. Perón used it only as a staging to persuade society of his vocation for establishing social peace or at most to guarantee respect for the Constitution.

The other parties, beginning with the *Unión Cívica Radical,* joined Perón in the general state of euphoria or felt overwhelmed with guilt for longtime support of Peronism's proscription. The Radicals limited themselves to accepting Peron's terms, relinquishing from the outset their role as watchdog and political alternative. The very idea of democracy, of the political representation of social interests, of negotiation first in the context of the party and then in shared political forums, had little prestige in a society long accustomed to a situation in which each of its parts negotiated separately with the state. Politics appeared a fiction that served to mask the real negotiations between the true factors of power. The propertied sectors felt much more comfortably expressed by their employers' organizations. The political parties, for their part, which might have been interested in the establishment of a specifically political environment, did not find for that purpose either a representation or spokespersons in society, much less among the corporative players.

This was crucial for the outcome of the experience that was beginning in 1973, with an election in which the popular will was expressed as freely and decisively as in 1946. The wave of mobilizations, leading to extreme social polarization, originated in a demand for participation, visible in each of the places in society where such mobilizations were gestated, from the neighborhood organizations, to the classroom, to the factory. But their potentially democratizing character collided with an entire political culture—forged in the long years of authoritarianism and fraudulent democracy—which encouraged Argentines to identify power with the enemy and with repression. Repression would result unless power were "taken," to be used then to repress in turn one's own enemies. Although the political parties lacked the strength or conviction to make themselves heard in such movements, the activists forged in the womb of Peronism, Catholicism, or the left tended to accentuate and give shape to this political culture and to incorporate into it—as was seen—a military logic. Thus, it was not difficult for the guerrilla organizations to insert themselves into the popular movements, whether in the neighborhood, the factories, or the student movement, filling a void that had to be filled. The *Montoneros* in particular had an enormous capacity to combine clandestine activities with political work through their surface organization, the *Juventud Peronista*. But by doing that, they introduced a direction in the development of such popular movements: They subordinated them, submitted them to a rigid organization whose strategy and tactics were elaborated from the outside, and eliminated all the spontaneity, popular participation, and pluralism of the mobilizations. Converted into part of a war machine, popular mobilization was removed from the democratic alternative and harnessed to undertake the final battle on new terrain.

The Return of Perón

On May 25, 1973, the government of President Héctor J. Cámpora assumed power, and on June 20th, Juan Domingo Perón returned to the country. That day, when an enormous crowd had congregated at Ezeiza airport on the outskirts of Buenos Aires to welcome him, a confrontation between armed groups from different factions of Peronism provoked a massacre. On July 13th, Cámpora and the vice president Solano Lima resigned; with the president of the senate absent, Raúl Lastiri, the son-in-law of Perón's private secretary and social welfare minister, José López Rega, assumed the presidency of the chamber of deputies. In September 1974, new elections were held, and the ticket Perón-Perón that the leader shared with his wife, Isabel (the former María Estela Martínez), obtained 67 percent of the votes. On July 1st of the following year, Perón died, and Isabel replaced him until she was deposed in a military coup on March 24, 1976. The three years of the second Peronist experience, truly dizzying in the accumulation of events of significance, brought to a close—in a tragic and ominous manner—an entire period in Argentine history.

It is difficult to know at what moment in his exile Perón ceased to see himself as the incorruptible leader of the resistance, prepared to foil all the temptations emanating from power, and to consider himself the one destined to pilot the vast project of national reconstruction that he assumed as his last mission in life. It might even be doubted whether it was a conscious decision or whether, despite his enormous political talents, he was simply swept along by events beyond his control. What is clear is that, once put in the game, Perón assembled his own project—similar but different from that of 1945—on three basic premises: a democratic agreement by the political forces, a social pact between business and labor, and a more centralized control of his movement, until then dispersed along various fronts and divided by heterogeneous strategies.

For his program to work, Perón needed the economy to perform moderately well—and expectations were high—and to strengthen the power of the state, just as the majority of society was demanding. The latter was a weak point: The mechanisms and instruments of state power were exhausted and proved to be ineffective. The control that Perón could exercise was therefore incomplete, because the military showed itself to be reluctant despite the mutual rapprochement it had experienced with Perón. Finally, the government turned out to be eroded by the formidable struggle unleashed in the Peronist movement. Thus, one of the premises of Perón's government failed at the outset. The Social Pact between business and labor worked badly almost from the beginning and ended in tatters; the democratic pact, though formally it worked well and the agreements were adhered to, finally turned out to be irrelevant because it served no purpose, either for establishing an effective opposition or for endowing itself, when other mechanisms failed, with the means necessary for the maintenance of the constitutional order.

The Program of Reconstruction and National Liberation presented in May 1973, despite the concession to the climate of the times in its title, consisted essentially of an attempt to surmount the limitations on growth in an economy with no thought of modifying its basic characteristics. Nothing in it indicated a move in the direction of a "national socialism" or an attempt to look for a new path for capitalist development. As in 1946, Perón turned to a successful businessman, in this case one from outside Peronism, to pilot it: José Ber Gelbard, the president of the *Confederación General Económica* (CGE), which represented the majority of companies of basically national capital. Its objectives, in agreement with the changes already consolidated in the country's economic structure, were strongly interventionist and to a lesser extent nationalist and distributionist, though they did not imply a direct attack on any of the established interests.

Repeating the pattern of the previous decade, the government sought to encourage the growth of the economy as much through the expansion of the internal market—in accordance with the tradition of this sector of the business community that supported both majority parties—as through the increase in exports. The prospects for the country's traditional exports were excellent: There were very good prices and the possibility of breaking into new markets, such as the Soviet Union. The nationalization of foreign trade was intended to ensure the transfer of part of the benefits of this trade to the industrial sector, although at the same time great care was taken to maintain the income of the rural sectors, whose productivity it was hoped to increase by combining incentives with sanctions. Among the latter, the possibility of the government's expropriating uncultivated land, including an agrarian reform law, ultimately unleashed a bitter conflict. But economic policy was above all geared to expanding industrial exports through special agreements, such as that signed with Cuba to sell that country trucks and automobiles.

The nationally owned companies, which were also supposed to share in the benefits of exporting, were supported by special lines of credit and by the practice among the public companies of buying from Argentine suppliers. To attain greater efficiency and control, the latter were combined in a *Corporación de Empresas Nacionales* (Corporation of National Companies). In addition, support was given, especially for some big industrial projects deemed to be of "national interest," through handsome subsidies. Many means were concentrated in the state's hands, such as the centralized handling of credit and price controls, essential for stabilization policies. Moreover, the state considerably increased its spending through public works projects and increased the number of public employees and state companies. In this way, it contributed to stimulating the internal economy, though at the cost of a rising deficit.

The key to the program was the Social Pact, through which the government sought to solve the perennial problem of the economy, one that successive governments since 1955 had failed to find a solution for: the ability of different sectors, engaged in the struggle over resources, to mutually paralyze one another. Whereas Onganía had failed to break the stalemate via pure authority, Perón made recourse to coordination, a common practice in the European social democracies but with deep affinities with his own conception of the "organized community." The state was to discipline society's actors, combining persuasion with authority. Agreements were reached with individual sectors, and a broad one that underpinned all of them was signed by the CGT and the CGE, establishing the price freeze and the suspension of collective bargaining for two years. This was a hard pill for the unions to swallow but was compensated for by an immediate across-the-board 20 percent increase in wages, which nonetheless fell short of the expectations generated by the advent of the Peronist government.

The early results of this stabilization program were spectacular. Inflation, unleashed with intensity in 1972, was suddenly halted, while the excellent conditions for foreign trade allowed the country to overcome the desperate situation in the balance of payments and to accumulate a handsome surplus. In addition, improvements in wages and the increase in state spending stimulated domestic economy activity. By these means, the country quickly managed to achieve nearly full utilization of installed capacity. But beginning in December 1973, problems began to accumulate. The increase in consumption caused inflation to reappear, while the rise in the world price of oil—which foretold the end of the cycle of postwar prosperity—made imports more expensive and began to complicate foreign markets and increase companies' costs. Finally, the European Common Market closed its doors to Argentine meat. All this represented a customary cyclical crisis, but its typical resolution was prohibited to a government that had made "zero inflation" its banner and knew that a devaluation would run into strong resistance. The Social Pact was supposed to find a fair and reasonable way to share the greatest burden, but the ever-increasing regulations that were resorted to, and were largely ignored, revealed not only the difficulties of persuasion but also the increasing inability of a state to assert its authority. Thus, before the Peronist government had been in power a year, the struggle by sectors again emerged, though the conditions for such a struggle had existed from the very beginning of this populist experiment.

The Social Pact's actors demonstrated scant ability and little will to carry out the pact. The CGE, conferred with the responsibility for representing all of business, represented it poorly, even business's most important institutions, which in many cases had been forced to join the CGE in accordance with Perón's organic conception of society. It is probable that for the same reasons many had reluctantly signed the agreements, hoping that better times were ahead. But above all, the CGE could not ensure that its members abided by what they signed. Business—especially the small- and medium-sized ones that were difficult to control—found many ways to violate the pact: stockpiling goods, price markups, a black market, clandestine exports. They also found a way to demonstrate their scant enthusiasm: Private investment was relatively slight.

The CGT was uncomfortable with a Peronist government in which its classic tactic of *golpear y negociar,* the only tactic it knew how to thoroughly handle, was of no use. Not only did Perón have to subordinate—as always—those who supported him, the union leaders lacked a tradition, instruments, and objectives for co-governing. Moreover, the mobilization of the rank and file, which held the union leaders in check, prevented them from freely negotiating. The electoral triumph revived society's expectations and gave a new impetus to the "people's spring." In the factories, this was translated into general increases in workers' demands and in a combative style that included factory occupations, which often overtook the union leaderships and even questioned the authority of managers and owners. Before the guerrilla organizations came to have an active role, the factories were, thanks to the rank-and-file mobilization, in a state of rebellion.

In the majority of cases, such mobilizations culminated in direct or camouflaged wage increases, which increased the pressures on the national union leadership that had been forced to tie itself to the Social Pact. Perón devoted himself to strengthening the union leaders' position. After his return to the country, he praised them in a thousand different ways, vindicating their public image under assault from the Peronist left and restored them symbolically to the very center of his movement. A change in the Law of Professional Associations reinforced the centralization of the labor movement, increasing the power of union leadership and lengthening terms in office, thereby enabling the leaders to confront the antibureaucratic challenge but not preventing them from calling for collective bargaining negotiations and demanding periodic wage adjustments. Having been violated from all sides, the Social Pact was unraveling because of the impotence of the national leadership. The government itself, which had frozen the prices for public services, was interested in renegotiating its terms, which occurred in March 1974, with a general round of price and wage increases that satisfied no one. The tug-of-war continued. On June 12, 1974, Perón convoked a massive demonstration in the historic Plaza de Mayo, making a dramatic appeal for discipline to the various parts of his movement and threatening otherwise to resign. It was Perón's last public appearance before his death.

In the second phase of the Peronist government, the actors changed strategy and the tug-of-war recovered its classic profile. In the CGT, the partisans of hard-line negotiations, in the best *vandorista* tradition, gained the upper hand, incarnated precisely by Vandor's successor in the metalworkers' union, Lorenzo Miguel. Isabel Perón—around whose symbolic figure all the political forces agreed to a tactical truce—threw herself into the task of building her own base of political power, surrounded by a group of stalwarts with little background in Peronism and headed by the strange and sinister figure of José López Rega, nicknamed the warlock because of his fondness for occult practices. Despite the fact that Isabel devoted herself to mimicking the slogans and gestures of her dead husband to capitalize on his symbolic legacy, her policies were totally at odds with those Perón had laid out during his final years. Isabel proposed to purge the government, place her friends and unconditional supporters in key positions, and break with the alliances that Perón had woven and which she hoped to replace with other new ones, with the military and business sectors. In some of these objectives, Isabel and the union leaders were in agreement. Thus they provoked the resignation of the minister of the economy Gelbard, and, taking advantage of the provisions of the new Law of Professional Associations and National Security Law, they systematically removed the heads of dissident unionism: Raimundo Ongaro, Agustín Tosco, and Renée Salamanca, all of whom lost control of their unions, leading to a notable decline in union agitation in 1975.

But Isabel and the union leadership were basically in conflict on the issue of what remained of the Social Pact. In 1975, the economic crisis called for drastic measures that would put an end to the Social Pact. Problems in the balance of payments were serious, inflation was spiraling, the tug-of-war over resources was ferocious, and the state was completely overwhelmed. In that context, the government had to accede to the CGT's traditional demand and call for collective bargaining negotiations. The imminent austerity measures thus had to be undertaken at the very moment that contract negotiations were going on, which created an unmanageable situation. By late March 1975, the majority of the unions had agreed to wage increases of 40 percent. On June 2d, the new minister of the economy, Celestino Rodrigo, a member of López Rega's team, caused an economic shock when he devalued the peso by 100 percent and decreed an increase in the price of fuel and public services by the same or even greater amount. The *rodrigazo* undermined the agreed-on wage increases, and the union leaders demanded contract negotiations while business accepted—with telling ease—wage increases that in some cases reached 200 percent. The president decided not to grant them, generating a massive resistance by the workers, which culminated in demonstrations in the Plaza de Mayo and a forty-eight-hour general strike. The strike was notable because, contrary to tradition, the CGT headed a general strike against a Peronist government. Isabel yielded, Rodrigo and López Rega resigned, the wage increases were approved and then devoured by inflation in a month. In the midst of a runaway economic crisis, the Peronist government entered its final stage.

The struggle surrounding the Social Pact ran parallel to that unleashed in the heart of Peronism, which drew in the government and the state itself and above all defined the fate of the popular movement. That struggle was already implicit in the ambiguous relations between Perón and those who, in the *Montoneros* and the Peronist Youth, constituted Peronism's so-called revolutionary tendency. Until 1973, united in a common struggle against the military, neither Perón nor the revolutionary wing had any interest in making their differences apparent. Perón solidified his leadership in his ability to include all those who invoked his name, from the revolutionary youth to the union leaders, conservative provincial politicians, or shock troops of the extreme right. His strategy of confrontation with those who expelled him from power consisted of using the youth, and the popular sectors that they mobilized, to harass his adversaries, and at the same time to present himself as the only one capable of restraining his followers. In that sense, he was repeating his 1945 strategy of the "pyromaniac fireman."

The *Montoneros* and Peronist Youth took advantage of their proclaimed adhesion to Perón to insert themselves more deeply into the popular movement and make use of their spectacular growth following 1973, when the entire society seemed to enter into a state of rebellion and effervescence. In the political culture of the popular sectors, massively incorporated into Peronism, two predominant ideas were apparent. The first found sustenance in the old Peronist tradition, national and distrubutionist, nourished during the long proscription by the illusion of the leader's return and, with him, magically, the return to the good times in which social justice crowned individual social mobility. Those who remained loyal to what was undoubtedly the deepest and most solid stratum of the country's popular political culture espoused the old political style, authoritarian, factional, *verticalista,* and viscerally anti-Communist. The other, more vague, took root in an important part of the popular sectors, but above all in those who belatedly joined Peronism's ranks, and added the radical critique of society, condensed in the slogan, "Liberation or dependency." Both ideas, in a country that was in a state of near civil war, defined themselves as battle slogans: the *patria peronista* versus *patria socialista.* The *Montoneros,* who aspired at the beginning to embody both, ended up identifying more with the second, whereas labor and the groups of the extreme right became the standard-bearers of the first.

The 1973 electoral triumph ended the ambiguities in Peronism and unleashed a struggle for both the real and symbolic directions of the movement and the people. Other revolutionary groups did not have the *Montoneros'* dilemma. The Trotskyite ERP, the other principal armed organization, believed neither in Peronism's revolutionary vocation nor in democracy itself, so that, following a brief truce in 1973, it easily took up again the struggle in the same terms as it had combated the military. Other revolutionary tendencies in Peronism had never counted on the possible support of Perón and were disposed to undertake a long war of attrition in which the 1973 electoral victory was just a stage and a circumstance. For the *Montoneros,* who fully identified themselves with Perón and Peronism, the March triumph unleashed a decisive struggle for control of the discourse and power structure of Peronism, both of them indivisible. The *Montoneros* concentrated all their efforts in monopolizing both, expelling the internal enemies, the "infiltrators and traitors"—a broad category applied to politicians, labor leaders, businesspeople, and Perón's inner circle—as well as winning Perón himself to their cause, pressuring him to ratify the revolutionary image that he had built and encouraged.

At the beginning of 1973, swept along by the electoral euphoria and the place that Perón himself had awarded them in Peronism—Perón having marginalized the trade-union leaders when drafting the party tickets—the militants of Peronism's revolutionary wing threw themselves into occupying positions of power in the state apparatus, perhaps believing that real power was within their grasp. Allies or sympathizers occupied various governorships—including the key provinces of Buenos Aires, Córdoba, and Mendoza—several government ministries, the universities that were the great mobilizing base of the Peronist Youth, and many other institutions and government departments. But the real hierarchy of political forces in Peronism was quickly reestablished. Following the resignation of Cámpora on July 13, 1973, one by one the Peronist left lost positions in the government. First were the ministries. Then, in January 1974, following an attack by the ERP on an important military garrison in Buenos Aires province, Perón took advantage of the situation to demand the resignation of the province's governor and shortly later to instigate a palace coup against the governor of Córdoba, who was closely identified with the Peronist left. The campaign continued after his death in July 1974, when the remaining governors fell, as well as many dissident union activists, while the universities were turned over to sectors of the ultra right to purge them.

Displaced from positions of power in the government, Peronism's revolutionary wing threw itself into the military struggle against the labor movement and the right-wing groups that surrounded Perón. It was a question of demonstrating, in diverse ways, who had the most power, who could mobilize the greatest number of people, and who could deal the harshest blows. In the Peronist tradition, street mobilizations and demonstrations in the Plaza de

Mayo, the place where power was symbolically represented, constituted the expression of popular power and the means by which the people's temper was transmitted to their leaders. In the climate of mobilization and factional confrontations, the former Sunday popular festival that previously characterized Peronist demonstrations was transformed into a display of strength where the various vanguards were supposed to display their ability to organize the people and convert them into a war machine embarked on a struggle against phalanxes that were equally well organized. The protesters proceeded in a disciplined fashion and competed for control of the most visible places or those closest to the leader, the placards, or the party banners. During each of these events, real battles were fought, as on June 20, 1973, at Ezeiza airport, when before some 2 million people gathered to receive Perón, there was a shoot-out for control of the space, or as on May 1, 1974, when Peronist left militants confronted their competitors and Perón himself and then abandoned the Plaza de Mayo, leaving it half-empty.

Simultaneously, the military struggle unfolded under the terrible guise of terrorism, particularly assassinations, which could be, to varying degrees, for strategic purposes, vendettas, or to set an example. The *Montoneros* devoted themselves to eliminating famous personalities, such as the CGT president and important figure in Perón's strategy with the union leaders, José Rucci, just a few days after Peron's plebiscite election in September 1974. Against them was unleashed another terrorism, with paramilitary groups drawn from union thugs, the ranks of Peronism's fascist groups, and paid gunmen of the ministry of social welfare—who operated under the name of the *Alianza Anticomunista Argentina* (Anti-Communist Argentine Alliance) or simply the Triple A. The assassinations multiplied and sometimes cost the lives of people relatively uninvolved in the conflict, but they served to demonstrate the power of both organizations.

Finally, the competition unfolded in the realm of discourse. The *Montoneros* had spoken in Perón's name, but as shown by Sigal and Verón, in Peronism there was room for only one spokesperson, though there were an infinite number of interpreters, each of whom regarded the others as virtual traitors to the movement. Laying claim to the status of Peronism's spokesperson when Perón was in Madrid, the *Montoneros* had to face the problem of a leader who had returned to the country and, abandoning his cultivated ambiguity, was beginning to speak unambiguously, reminding the orthodox wing of Peronism that his movement had little to do with "socialism" and denouncing the "hotheads" and "infiltrators." After June 20th, the conflict became public, but for a year the *Montoneros* managed to sidestep the definition. Although they aimed all their artillery at Peronism's "traitors," the *Montoneros* went to the greatest possible lengths to reinterpret Perón's words, contending that the leader was engaging in merely tactical deviations, demonstrations of Perón's brilliance, which did not explicitly repudiate them. In the process, they elaborated the "fenced-in" theory or that of the "clique" that prevented Perón from knowing the true will of the people while clinging to the image of an "Evita *montonera*" that served to legitimize their Peronist credentials in the very origins of Peronism. On May 1, 1974, the rupture occurred. On abandoning the Plaza de Mayo, where Perón himself expelled them, they relinquished their right to speak in the name of the movement. They reappeared one more time two months later, in Perón's spectacular funeral ceremonies, and then sought to assume his legacy, founding the abortive *Partido Peronista Autentico* (Authentic Peronist Party). But the magic had disappeared, and only the diehards followed them now.

They soon opted to return to their old tactics and clandestine activities. There were more assassinations, spectacular kidnappings to improve their finances—such as that of the businessman Jorge Born, which reputedly netted them 60 million dollars—meddling in union conflicts in which armed force was use to used to turn negotiations with management in favor of the workers, and ambitious but generally abortive military actions. Along this path, they were followed by the ERP, which in 1974 had established a rural *foco* (revolutionary cell) in the Tucumán mountains. A clandestine repression increased against both, one that was vented above all on those—intellectuals, students, workers, community organizers—who had participated in the mobilizations of recent years but had not been able to turn to clandestine activities. After February 1974, the army, called on by the president, assumed the task of repressing the Tucumán guerrillas. The genocide was underway.

By this time, the Peronist government was approaching its demise. The *rodrigazo* unleashed an economic crisis that until the end proved impossible to rein in: runaway inflation, a rush on the dollar, the appearance of indexing mechanisms, and generally few possibilities for the government to control the situation. The economic crisis prepared the ground for the political crisis. In July 1975, neither the armed forces nor the country's leading businesspeople—on whose support Isabel had placed her bets—lifted a hand to support the president, whom they viewed as already finished. Business yielded passively to the union leaders' demands, as if it took pleasure in fomenting the chaos in the economy. With the agreements that Perón had constructed now in shambles, big business withdrew from the CGE and attacked the government with resolve. Until then, the military had adapted itself to the changing climate without confronting the government: With Cámpora they were populist and fraternized with the Peronist Youth; with Perón they had at the helm an apolitical military professional; with Isabel another who sympathized with the regime's rightist groups. But after July, when López Rega fell in disgrace, they began to ready themselves for the coup. General Jorge Videla, the new commander-in-chief, refused to back politically a government in crisis and imposed deadlines—as the military had done so many times before—waiting until the economic and political crisis combined to reach a critical point and prepared to assume control.

Following the resignations of López Rega and Rodrigo, an alliance of politicians and union leaders tested a solution: Italo Luder, the president of the senate, briefly replaced Isabel, and some speculated that the change was permanent, with Isabel either resigning or being impeached. Antonio Cafiero, a respected economist with close ties to the unions, attempted to ride out the crisis as the new minister of the economy, but runaway inflation, along with severe recession and high unemployment, made it impossible to establish an agreement between business and the labor movement. The congress, which, it was hoped, would find the means to remove the president, was also unable to gather the necessary support. The return of Isabel to the presidency eliminated the possibility and at the same time worsened the political crisis, which, added to the economic one, created a state of unbearable tension and an anticipated acceptance of any solution. Many Peronists became convinced that the fall of Isabel was inevitable, but thinking about the future, they preferred to avoid divisions and supported her until the end came on March 24, 1976, when the military commanders deposed and arrested her. As on previous occasions, the majority of the population received the coup with immense relief and high expectations.

seven

The "Process," 1976–1983

The Genocide

On March 24, 1976, the Junta commanders-in-chief, General Jorge Rafael Videla, Admiral Emilio Eduardo Massera, and Air Force Brigadier Orlando Ramón Agosti, assumed power. They immediately issued the legal instruments of the so-called Process of National Reorganization and designated General Videla president of the nation; he also continued as army commander until 1978.

The economic crisis of 1975, the crisis in leadership, the factional struggles and the daily presence of death, the spectacular actions of the guerrilla organizations—which had failed in two major operations against military installations in the provinces of Buenos Aires and Formosa—the terror sown by the Triple A, all created the conditions for the acceptance of a military coup that promised to reestablish order and ensure the state's monopoly on violence. The program of the military—which had done little to prevent the chaos from reaching this extreme—went beyond these goals and consisted of eliminating the root of the problem, which according to its diagnosis was found in society itself and in the unresolved nature of society's conflicts. The nature of the proposed solution could be read in the metaphors employed by the new government to describe that society—sickness, tumor, surgical removal, major surgery—all summed up in one proposal that was unambiguous and conclusive: The military had come to cut the Gordian knot with a sword.

The cutting with the sword was in reality an integral operation of terror, carefully planned by the leadership of the three service branches, rehearsed first in Tucumán—where the army officially intervened in 1975—and then executed in a systematic fashion throughout the country. These were the 1984 findings of the *Comisión Nacional sobre la Desaparición de Personas* (National Commission of Disappeared Persons, or CONADEP) created by President Raúl Alfonsín in 1984 and then by the justice system that found the military guilty and condemned many of its members to prison. The military commanders concentrated in their hands all the activities of this operation; the various paramilitary groups that had been operating in the years before the coup were dissolved and incorporated into the government's state terrorist machinery. The three branches of the military assigned themselves different areas of responsibility and even maintained a certain degree of competition between one another to show who was the most effective, a competition that gave their operations an anarchic and factional character. Nonetheless, such anarchy did not mean that the terrorism unleashed was by chance and lacked supervision, a view that formed part of the general population's conception of the horrendous operation.

The general planning and tactical supervision were in the hands of the highest levels of military leadership, and the ranking officers did not refrain from personally participating in the acts, a fact that highlighted the institutional character of the policy and the military's collective commitment to it. Orders came down through the chain of command until reaching those entrusted with carrying out the actions, the so-called Task Groups—principally young military officers, along with some noncommissioned officers, civilians, and off-duty police—who also had their own organization. The execution of their acts required a complex administrative apparatus because they were supposed to follow the movement—the entries, moves, and departures—of a vast array of people. Anyone arrested, from the moment he or she entered the list of suspects, was assigned his or her own number and file, with a follow-up, an evaluation of the case, after which a final decision would be taken, which always was the preserve of the highest levels of the military. The repression was, in sum, a systematic action carried out by the state.

The acts of terror were divided into four principal moments: abduction, torture, arrest, and execution. For the abductions, each group organized for that purpose—commonly known as "the gang" (*la patota*)—preferred to operate at night, to arrive at the victims' homes, with the family as witnesses; in many cases, family members became victims themselves in the operation. But many arrests also occurred in factories or workplaces or in the street, and sometimes in neighboring countries, with the collaboration of local authorities. Such operations were realized in unmarked but well-recognized cars— the ominous green Ford Falcons were the favorite—a lavish display of men and arms, combining anonymity with ostentation, all of which heightened the desired terrorizing effect. The kidnapping was followed by ransacking the home, a practice that was subsequently refined so that the victims were forced to surrender their furniture and other possessions, which became the booty of the horrendous operation.

The fate of those who were abducted was, first, systematic and prolonged torture. The electric prod and the so-called submarine—a practice in which the tortured individual's head was submerged under water to the point of unconsciousness—and sexual abuse were the most common forms of torture. To these were added others that combined technology with the refined sadism of the specialized personnel in the service of an institutionalized operation, in which it was not unusual to have the highest-ranking officers participating. Physical torture, of indefinite duration, was combined with psychological torture. The victims might suffer mock executions or witness friends, children, or spouses pleading for mercy—all these were proof that all ties with the outside world were cut off, that there was no one to intercede between the victim and the torturer. In principle, torture served to extract information and reveal the names, places of residence, and planned operations of the guerrilla organizations, but more generally it served to break the resistance of the abducted persons, to annul their defenses, to destroy their dignity and personality.

Many died under torture, "staying on," in the vernacular of their executioners. The survivors began a more or less prolonged detention in one of some 340 clandestine centers of arrest—the so-called *chupaderos* (literally, places that "sucked" their victims out of thin air)—operating in those years, although the authorities repeatedly denied their existence. These detention centers were sometimes located on military installations—the navy mechanics' school, the Campo de Mayo, the bases of the various army corps—but were generally found on police grounds and were given macabre names: Olympus, Vesuvius, the Pearl, the Little School, the Reformatory, the Basque Post, the Banfield Pit. The administration and control of the activities of this vast group of detention centers give an idea of the complexity of the operation and the number of people involved, as well as the determination necessary to keep their existence a secret. In this final stage of torment of varying duration, the victims' degradation was completed. Often badly wounded and without medical care, they remained permanently hooded or in solitary confinement, badly fed and without sanitary services. Many pregnant detainees gave birth in those conditions, only to be immediately stripped of their babies, many of whom were confiscated by their captors. It is not surprising then that in this truly desperate situation, some of those arrested may have chosen to cooperate with their captors, doing odd jobs for them or even accompanying them to identify on the streets former comrades still free. But for the majority, the final destiny was the "move", that is, their execution.

The decision to execute was the most important step and was taken at the highest levels of operation, such as the commander of each of the army corps, after a careful analysis of the detainee's background, possible usefulness, or potential "rehabilitation." Despite the fact that the military junta established the death penalty, it never applied it, and all the executions were clandestine. At times, the bodies appeared on the streets, as if people had been killed in combat or in attempting to flee. In some cases, piles of dead bodies were dynamited in reprisal for some action by the guerrillas. But in the majority of cases, the bodies were hidden, buried in unmarked graves, burned in collective graves dug by the victims themselves before execution, or cast into the sea weighted with cement blocks, after the victim was sedated with an injection. In that way, there were no dead, only the "disappeared."

The disappearances occurred in massive numbers between 1976 and 1978, a somber three years, and then were drastically reduced. It was a true genocide. The CONADEP commission that investigated them documented 9,000 cases, but it indicated that many more could have been unreported. Human rights organizations claimed 30,000 disappeared persons, mainly young people, between fifteen and thirty-five years old. Some belonged to armed organizations: The *Ejército Revolucionario del Pueblo* (ERP) was decimated between 1975 and 1976, and after the death of its leader, Roberto Santucho, in July 1976, little remained of the organization. The *Montoneros* organization, which also suffered numerous casualties in its ranks, continued operating, though it had to limit itself to terrorist acts—with well-publicized assassinations such as the chief of the federal police—unrelated to political objectives, at the same time that the leadership and the principal members immigrated to Mexico. When the real threat from the guerrilla organizations ceased, the repression continued its course.

There were casualties from social and political organizations, union leaders in factory shop-stewards' commissions—some factory owners tended to co-operate with the military to eliminate "troublemakers"—together with poli-tical activists of various tendencies, priests, intellectuals, lawyers representing political prisoners, human rights activists, and many others detained solely because they were someone's relative, appeared in someone's address book, or were mentioned in a torture session. But beyond the accidents and mistakes, the victims were often those sought after. Using the argument of confronting and destroying the armed organizations on their own terrain, the operations sought to eliminate all political activism, including social protest—even a modest demand over school bus fares, as happened on one occasion—any ex-pression of critical thinking, and any possible political outlet for the popular movements that had been evolving since the middle of the previous decade. In that sense, the results were exactly those desired.

There were many victims, but the true objective was to reach the living, the whole of society that, before undertaking a total transformation, had to be controlled and dominated by terror and by language. The state became divided in two. One-half, practicing terrorism and operating clandestinely, unleashed an indiscriminate repression free from any accountability. The other, public and justifying its authority in laws that it had enacted, silenced all other voices. Not only did the country's political institutions disappear, but the dictatorship also shut off in authoritarian fashion the free play of ideas, indeed their very expression. The parties and all political activity were prohibited, as were the labor movement and trade-union activity. The press was subject to an explicit censorship that prevented any mention of state terrorism and its victims. Artists and intellectuals were watched over. Only the voice of the state remained, addressing itself to an atomized collection of inhabitants.

The military government's propaganda, massive and overwhelming, picked up traditional themes of Argentine political culture and took them to their final, terrible consequences. The adversary—demonized and referring to any possible dissident—was a nonperson, a "subversive without a country," without a right to express an opinion or even to exist, somebody who could and deserved to be exterminated. Against the violence no arguments were made in favor of a popularly supported rule of law, as would be appropriate in a republic and a democratic society, but only in favor of an order that was in reality another version of the same violent and authoritarian equation.

Terror ran through all of society. With outlets shut off for individuals to join broader collectivities, everyone became isolated and defenseless against a terrorist state; and in a paralyzed society incapable of reacting there was established what Juan Corradi called a "culture of fear." Some could not accept the situation and fled abroad—compelled by a combination of political and professional considerations—or took refuge in internal exile, in hidden spaces, blending into the surroundings while waiting for the breach that would allow a return to the surface. The majority of the population, however, justified the little of the repression that simply could not be ignored with the argument that "they must have done something" or took refuge in a deliberate ignorance of what was happening in sight of everyone. What was most notable, however, was an appropriation and internalization of the state's actions, translated into self-control, self-censorship, and spying on one's neighbors. Society patrolled itself and became full of informants, and through a collection of practices—from the family to the manner of dressing to its beliefs—revealed just how deeply rooted in it was the authoritarianism that the state discourse legitimized.

The military government never managed either to arouse enthusiasm or to garner explicit support among the whole of society. It attempted to do so in mid-1978, when Argentina hosted the World Cup soccer championship and the government's highest officials attended the matches, with Argentina winning. The military government attempted to exploit dark nationalistic sentiments in this event as it did in late 1978 when the country came close to going to war with Chile. It encountered only passivity in society, but that was enough to permit it to undertake the deep changes that, in its estimation, would definitively eliminate the conflicts in society and whose first consequences, the speculation fever, contributed to the atomization of society and the elimination of any possible response.

The Imaginary Economy: The Great Transformation

The transformation was overseen by José Alfredo Martínez de Hoz, the minister of the economy during the five years of Videla's presidency. When he assumed the office, Martínez de Hoz had to face a deep crisis in the business cycle—rampant inflation, recession, problems with the balance of payments—complicated by the political and social crisis and the strong challenge the guerrilla organizations posed to the state's authority. The first wave of repression, which quelled popular mobilization, added to a classic economic austerity program—more or less similar to all those implemented since 1952—allowed the government to surmount the situation. But this time, the armed forces and those sectors of the establishment that accompanied them had decided to go further. According to their diagnosis, the chronic political and social instability was born of the impotence of political power when faced with the great corporative groups—labor but also business—which continuously fought with one another, generating chaos and disorder, or which, united by a peculiar logic, allied to use to their mutual benefit the powerful tools of an interventionist and welfare state. A long-range solution was supposed to change the basic variables of the economy and thus modify a chronically unstable social and political situation. It was not just a question of finding a formula for economic growth—though it was judged that the chaos often arose there—but of establishing order and security. Reversing what until then—from Perón to Perón—had been the objectives of different political regimes, the government sought to solve the problems that the economy posed for political stability, at the cost of economic growth if necessary.

According to an assessment that gradually began to predominate among the governing forces, the interventionist and welfare state, such as it had been constituted since 1930, was the great culprit. The market, on the other hand, appeared to be the instrument capable of equally disciplining all the social actors, rewarding efficiency and discouraging unhealthy interest-group behavior. This argument, which as will be seen came to dominate discourse and the popular imagination of those years, obfuscated what was definitively the ultimate solution: At the end of the transformation presided over by Martínez de Hoz, economic power was concentrated in such a fashion among an ensemble of business groups, of transnational and national corporations, that the former corporative tug-of-war and negotiation were no longer possible. This transformation was not the product of impersonal and divine forces. It required a strong state intervention to repress and dismantle the actors in the corporative game, to impose rules facilitating the growth of the victors, and even to transfer to them, through the classic route of the state, the resources of all of society that made possible their consolidation.

The implementation of that transformation did pose a political problem: The economic team had to remain in power for a long enough time and then create a situation that was irreversible, whether or not it remained in power. The minister of the economy and his team stayed in the government for five years. The irreversibility of the system they created was manifested immediately after their exit from government, when their successors tried to change course and failed completely.

Martínez de Hoz initially counted on the strong support, almost of a personal nature, of the international financial organizations and foreign banks—which allowed him to circumvent several difficult situations—and of the most concentrated sector of the local economic establishment. The relationship with the military was more complex. In part this was because of deep divisions—between the services and among factions—expressed in statements of support, criticisms, or obstructions to his ministry. In part, it was also because of the strong feeling among the military that many of the ideas and proposals of the minister's economic plan ought to be changed to gain public support. It was a conflictive relationship, power confronting power. The military deemed that in suppressing popular mobilization, the elimination of society's great corporative organizations and the strong reduction of the income of the working sectors should be balanced, for reasons of public security, with the maintenance of full employment, which meant that a classic austerity recipe was discarded. The military also had a more traditional vision of the question of the state, at least that part of it that the military aspired to control for its personal or institutional benefit. Many of those who accepted the basic proposition of eliminating the state's role in the distribution of income demanded, on the other hand, the survival of state companies—generally run by upper-rank officers—and increased public spending, which also obstructed the adoption of an austerity program and ultimately torpedoed Martínez de Hoz's economic program.

Neither were the minister's relations with the business community easy, owing to the number of sectoral interests affected. He imposed his program thanks only to his single-mindedness, combined with his powers of persuasion in pointing to the promised land that lay at the end of the desert crossing, with all the more certainty as reality seemed to belie his predictions. But his most powerful weapon was having placed the economy for a number of years in a situation of such instability that it was possible only to continue on the same course, with the same pilot at the helm, under the threat of a catastrophe. By the time this logic ceased to work, economic concentration and foreign debt had already created the perfect mechanisms to discipline and control the economy and society.

The first measures of the ministerial team, which filled the first year in power, gave no inkling of a future course. After interdicting the General Confederation of Labor (CGT) and the principal unions, repressing political activists, militarily occupying many factories, eliminating collective bargaining negotiations, and prohibiting strikes, the government froze wages for three months, leading to a situation in which—given the high inflation—real wages fell around 40 percent. Nonetheless, the state surmounted the deficit, and private companies managed to generate profits with rapidly granted foreign credits, enabling the country to overcome the crisis in the business cycle without unemployment.

From the middle of 1977—as the economic team was strengthening its position—ambitious reforms began to be discussed, implying a deep change in the basic rules of the game that Argentina had lived by since 1930. Financial restructuring put an end to the state's classic devices to distribute income between sectors: the regulation of interest rates, the existence of credit with negative interest rates, and the distribution of this subsidy according to norms and priorities established by public authorities. Resorting with greater frequency to a practice that had been operating since 1975, interest rates were freed, a proliferation of new banks and financial institutions was authorized, and financial instruments were diversified—indexed government bonds and securities of all kinds, emitted by the state, were added to the high interest-paying savings plans (*plazos fijos*) preferred by small savers. As a result, in a highly speculative climate competition kept interest rates high, and with it a rate of inflation that the economic team could almost never reduce, nor was it interested such a reduction. One rule from the old system was maintained: The state not only guaranteed the bonds that it emitted but also the savings accounts with their free-floating interest rates. Thus, in the case of an eventual bankruptcy, the state would return the savings to savers. This combination of liberalization, elimination of controls, and the state's underwriting of the financial system by offering its guarantee created a mechanism that soon brought the entire system to ruin.

The next great change was the opening up of the economy and the gradual elimination of the classic mechanisms for protecting local industry in effect since 1930. Tariffs were reduced, albeit in a selective and uneven fashion, followed by the subsequent overvaluation of the peso, causing local industry to confront brutal competition from a flood of cheap imported goods. A speculative fever took hold of the entire population: To defend the value of their income, people had to deposit it in high interest-bearing savings accounts for a few days or try some even more risky trick. Together with the flood of cheap imported goods, these were the most important features of the deep and deeply destructive transformation of the Argentine economy.

The transformation was completed with the so-called pegged exchange rate, an important measure adopted in December 1978, shortly after the military junta confirmed Videla for an additional three years in the presidency, an act that fanned rumors about the job security of the minister of the economy. The government established a monthly devaluation scale that would slowly devalue the national currency to a final fixed rate. It was thought that in this way inflation would be reduced and greater predictability introduced in the economy. Because inflation persisted, however, the peso's value was considerably readjusted with regard to the dollar. The adoption of the pegged exchange rate coincided with a great influx of money from abroad, originating from foreign banks' recycling the petrodollars generated by the increase in oil prices, which rose again considerably in 1979. The influx of dollars—the origins of the country's huge foreign debt—was common throughout Latin America and in much of the Third World. Argentina encouraged this influx by allowing the money to be placed in the money markets. Such speculation earned huge returns with minimal risk because it took advantage of the high internal interest rates, whose stable return the state guaranteed as a reward. But the *tablita*—the popular name for the pegged exchange rate program—did not suffice to reduce interest or inflation, in good measure because of growing uncertainty aroused by the overvalued peso, which promised a future large and necessary devaluation. While the foundation of the large foreign debt was being established, the so-called financial bicycle, "easy money," and "Korean imports" spoken of in popular jargon created a substantial modification in the rules of the game of the economy.

The true heart of the national economy was now in the financial sector, where the greatest benefits could be had. Such a situation created a highly unstable economy, because most money was placed in short-term activities and capital could leave the country unhindered if conditions changed. Thus, rather than rewarding efficiency or entrepreneurial risk-taking, agility and speculation were rewarded. Many companies compensated for their big operating losses with earnings in the financial sector. Many banks also positioned themselves at the heart of a large network of enterprises, generally indebted to the bank and purchased at a low price. Many firms borrowed in dollars and used them to invest in plant modernization or in the financial markets; when the time came to pay back the loans, the firms were forced to resort to new loans, a vicious cycle that, as predicted, eventually collapsed.

That moment arrived at the beginning of 1980. While the imaginary economy of the financial markets drifted toward the precipice, the real economy was in its death throes. The high interest rates were incompatible with the rates of return on productive investment, so that no undertaking was profitable or could compete with the speculation. All firms had problems. Bankruptcies increased, and financial creditors, beginning to see unrecoverable loans pile up, solved their problems by getting more deposits under their control, thus raising interest rates even higher. This spiral revealed the consequences of the state's guaranteeing deposits and at the same time eliminating controls on financial institutions. In March 1980, the Central Bank finally permitted the bankruptcy of the country's largest private bank and three other important ones, all of them in turn the heads of three major holding companies. There was a dramatic run on the country's banks, which the government managed to halt at the cost of assuming responsibility for all the outstanding debts of the bankrupt banks, an amount that at one point ended up representing one-fifth of the entire financial system.

The financial problem worsened throughout 1980, and from then until the end of the military government there was a constant crisis. In March 1981, a new president assumed power, General Roberto Marcelo Viola. It was now apparent that Martínez de Hoz would leave the economics ministry, and with him the *tablita* would cease to be in effect, which massive capital flight in those months presaged. The government had to go into debt to cover its expenses—with public debt now beginning to be added to private debt—and finally had to abandon the exchange parity it had upheld. Throughout 1981, with a new economic team in charge, the peso was devalued some 400 percent, in the midst of an outbreak of inflation that reached 100 percent annually. The devaluation was catastrophic for companies whose debts were in dollars, and in 1982 the state, which had already absorbed the losses of the banking system, ending up nationalizing the private debt of the companies, many of whose owners had already covered their debts by sending undeclared dollars abroad.

The era of "easy money" was coming to an end. Many of its beneficiaries probably did not suffer the consequences of the catastrophic finale, but society as a whole had to shoulder the losses. Rising interest rates in the United States signaled the appearance of a strong competitor to capture financial resources. In 1982, Mexico announced that it could not pay its foreign debt and declared a moratorium. This act was the sign of change. The ample credit for Latin America was cut off, while interest rates rose in a spectacular fashion, and with them the amount of the debt. In 1979, the debt was some $8.5 billion. By 1981, it had climbed to more than $25 billion and by early 1984 to $45 billion. Foreign creditors began to impose conditions. With the financial sector in ruins, foreign debt occupied its place as the disciplining mechanism in the national economy.

The Real Economy: Destruction and Concentration

As for the "real" economy, there was a complete about-face with respect to the policies implemented in previous decades. The importance of the internal market was questioned, and priority was given to those activities in which the country had comparative advantages and could compete in the world market. The emphasis on protecting industry—a protection associated with its lack of competitiveness—was replaced by that of rewarding efficiency; the idea of economic growth and of society's welfare tied to industrialization was abandoned. A similar questioning was taking place throughout the world, but the local response was much more destructive than constructive.

The strategy adopted centered on strengthening the financial sector, opening up the economy, negotiating foreign loans; as will be seen, the growth of some groups established in diverse activities did not particularly benefit any of the leading sectors of the economy. On the contrary, Martínez de Hoz was in conflict with all of them, though he did not encounter any consistent resistance. In 1976, the agricultural sector found itself in an optimum situation: Its productive expansion was reaching a high point just as new markets were opening up, particularly in the Soviet Union, adversely affected by the U.S. grain embargo, at the same time that the government was eliminating export withholdings. But the overvalued peso led to a loss of income for rural producers and created a critical situation that came to a climax in 1980–81. The income of the agricultural sector in the pampa zone, which in previous stages had subsidized industry, now was transferred to the financial sector and through the latter to the purchase of dollars or imported consumer goods. Then, when the foreign exchange debacle placed agricultural producers once again in favorable conditions, the change in the conditions of international markets prolonged agriculture's crisis.

Through the loss of its traditional protection, industry suffered from the competition of imported goods, to which were added the rising cost of credit, the elimination of the majority of the policies of industrial promotion, and the reduction in the population's purchasing power. During the first five years of the military government, industrial production declined by some 20 percent, as did the employed labor force. Many factories shut down, and all together industry experienced an involution. The most serious result of this was that, rather than increasing efficiency as was the stated objective, industry went backward. The oldest and most inefficient sectors, such as textiles and clothing manufacturing, were swept away by the competition. But even the new ones that had grown notably, such as the metalworking and electronic industries, were badly hurt. At a time that significant technological advances were occurring globally in those industries, the breach that separated Argentina from the rest of the world, reduced during the previous twenty years, grew irreversibly wider again.

Those branches of industry that grew and benefited from economic restructuring were above all those that manufactured intermediate goods—synthetics, metals, aluminum, petrochemical products, petroleum, cement—and those that intensely used natural resources such as minerals (iron ore and coal) or wood. All of these industries had much less of a dynamic effect on the internal economy than the previously mentioned ones. The few industries devoted to these activities, together with the automobile industry, benefited from the promotional policies established before 1975, which the new government maintained, as well as from an ad hoc tariff protection in the case of newspaper print and automobiles. Planned at a time when it was assumed that this industrial growth was going to deepen, these companies found themselves limited by the size of the domestic market and in may cases converted themselves into exporting firms.

Although the size of the industrial labor force declined, in the economy as a whole there was little unemployment, just as the military leadership had demanded of the minister of the economy. There was a transfer of workers, in some cases from the big companies—which had better possibilities to reduce their labor costs—toward medium and small enterprises and from industry to services. Many workers changed from the status of wage earners to self-employment. The greatest expansion occurred in construction, especially in public works. The government embarked on a series of large projects, some related to the 1978 World Cup soccer championship and others to urban infrastructure improvements, such as highway construction around the federal capital. For both, the government took advantage of cheap foreign loans. In the first years, it made a systematic effort to keep wages low, despite low unemployment. Real income fell, as did the participation of personal income in the gross domestic product (GDP), declining from 45 percent in 1974 to 25 percent in 1976, only to climb to 39 percent in 1980. By then, the government permitted workers greater freedom to negotiate their demands, but without union intervention, which encouraged the increase in the differences between job categories and firms. Beginning in 1981, the inflationary crisis and the recession caused both employment and real wages to drop dramatically. On the eve of its exit from power, the military government could not show any significant accomplishments in economic policy.

When the financial bubble burst, it became evident that the principal consequence of the brutal transformation of the economy had been—together with the foreign debt—a high degree of economic concentration. In contrast to the previous period of concentration, which had occurred between 1958 and 1963, foreign companies did not play the principal role in this process. In these years, there were no new important investments by foreign multinationals; indeed, a number of them closed their operations in the country, and others sold their assets, though reserving to themselves the role of suppliers of parts and technology, in the case of several automobile plants. In contrast to twenty years before, the internal market, openly shrinking, turned out to be of little attraction. Moreover, for these foreign companies whose competitive advantage resided in the possibilities of medium-or long-range planning of their activities, it was not easy to conduct their affairs in an environment characterized by a high degree of financial speculation. In that atmosphere, daily decisions made the difference between big profits or huge losses, and local firms held the advantage. A number of locally controlled big economic groups grew spectacularly in these years: great conglomerates, directly tied to a businessperson or a successful family enterprise such as Macri, Pérez Companc, Bulgheroni, Fortabat, and domestically based multinationals such as Bunge y Born or Techint. Thus the economic establishment acquired a novel physiognomy.

In some cases, this was the result of concentration in one branch of industry, which coincided with the restructuring and rationalization of production and the closing of inefficient factories. Such was the case with the steel industry and with cigarettes, an activity in which three foreign firms accounted for all the production. The most spectacular cases were those of domestically owned holding companies, which combined industrial, service, commercial, and financial enterprises, as a strategy of long-range diversification and minimizing risk and—in a context of high financial speculation—as a way to find quick profit-making businesses. The groups that grew typically counted on the support of a bank or financial institution that allowed them to operate in a rapid and independent manner in the financial sector where, for some years, the greatest rewards were obtained. Many groups that made banking the center of their enterprises disappeared after 1980. Those that survived capitalized their resources, buying up companies in difficulty and building their conglomerates. What was decisive, however, was establishing an advantageous relationship with the state through some of the companies.

During the years when Martínez de Hoz directed the economy, the state undertook important public works projects—everything from highways to a new atomic nuclear reactor—for which it contracted with private construction and engineering firms. Moreover, the state adopted as a strategy privatizing parts of publicly owned companies, contracting the provisioning of material with third parties—as in the case of telephones—or jobbing out activities, as did the state-owned oil company, YPF, in petroleum extraction. Around all these undertakings some of the most important new companies were established. The companies awarded state contracts benefited first by the agreed-to terms and then by the policy of adjusting costs to the rate of inflation, which, given the high inflation rates and the government's inability to fulfill punctually its commitments, ended up signifying an even greater benefit than the jobs themselves. Other firms took advantage of the industrial promotional policies, which, though reduced, continued for specific projects. Those policies permitted important tax reductions, state backing for cheap credit, exchange rate guarantees for credits in dollars, monopolization of the internal market (decisive, for example, in the case of newsprint), or the supply of low-cost energy, a major concession for the steel and aluminum industries. In this way, many business groups, often without experience in an area, could accumulate capital with minimal contributions of their own.

These policies were at odds with respect to the more general economic policy, to the benefit of specific businesspeople. This turn of events was the result of business groups' specific abilities to negotiate with the state, to the additional promotional policies, and to the concessions in the agreements for "cost runovers," all of which resulted from new forms in the collusion of private and public interests. Thanks to all this, these business groups were able to grow without risks, under the protection of the state, and in a context of general economic stagnation. They accumulated such a degree of power that in the future it was difficult to reverse the conditions in which they operated. Together with the foreign creditors, they became the new guardians of the state.

Reducing the State and Silencing Society

The reduction of the state's powers, its conversion into an ancillary role, was one of the most loudly proclaimed goals of the minister Martínez de Hoz, echoing an argument that circulated with growing force throughout the capitalist world, where the ideas of an interventionist and welfare state of the kind established in Argentina between 1930 and 1949 were being deeply questioned. Economic liberalism, traditionally defended by the rural sector, had never been warmly received by either industrialists—generally beneficiaries of state support—or the military, on whom statist ideas and economic autarchy had left a strong mark. The minister won an important ideological victory when he managed to couple the antisubversive sermon with the antistate discourse, directed even against industrialization.

In the views of Martínez de Hoz, a strong and democratically run state became a dangerous instrument if even partially in the hands of the popular sectors, as the Peronist experience had shown. But even without being democratic, the argument went, the state inevitably created a spurious relationship between business groups and the unions, which by another route led to the same result. The history of the previous four decades offered abundant examples in support of this argument, which implicitly found the roots of the workers' powers—viewed as the great obstacle to what was regarded as society's normal functioning—in the country's industrial development, an artificial one subsidized by society through the state. The panacea consisted of replacing state intervention with the market—efficient, fair, and impersonal —which through the rational distribution of resources, in proportion to the efficiency of the economic actors, would eliminate any possibility of collusion between interest groups. Paradoxically, the minister proposed using all the powers of the state to impose the liberal solution by force and to restructure the state itself.

Thus, a major part of Martínez de Hoz's program between 1976 and 1981, the years when the military government operated with minimal resistance, had as an objective the dismantling of the instruments of state planning, regulation, and control of the economy that had been assembled since 1930. Exchange controls, regulation of credit and interest rates, and tariff protection were all to be dismantled. When the minister's influence declined and the government found itself mired in a crisis, it became the task of foreign creditors to watch over and pressure administrations to maintain the policy of opening up the economy and relaxing state controls. Given that a good number of the military were reluctant to see the state dispense with the public-service companies or with other state-owned companies such as steel, which were tied to their ideas of economic autarchy, the policy in this area was more direct. It combined a generic condemnation—it was held that the state administered these companies badly—with a deliberate sabotaging and destruction of them: The best administrative staffs left the companies because of the low salaries now being paid; all manner of collusion between the union leadership representing these public-sector workers and management was permitted; and the low rates charged customers caused a disastrous financial situation, subsequently worsened by the systematic resort to foreign credit.

The so-called privatization on the periphery, executed without any control or regulation, allowed private firms to grow at the expense of the public ones—with the private firms' executives placed at the head of public companies—thereby transferring the long experience from the public-sector companies to the private sector. Executives from private firms were given leaves of absence to oversee the administration of public firms in such sectors as oil and telephones. All this led to a situation in which the public-sector companies, until then relatively efficient, saw service deteriorate, fell into debt, and allowed the private contractors to grow in their place; on the other hand, the state took over a plethora of bankrupt banks that failed because of the workings of the state's own economic policy.

It was a paradoxical way to reduce the state. The free-market minister exercised a veritable dictatorship of the economy, directed with a singleness of purpose that contrasted with the anarchic fragmentation of military power. The free market was built through force, and violence was the *ultima ratio.* If economic modernization and competition were the true objectives, the results were not only meager but precisely the opposite of what was intended. Rather than encouraging efficiency, the state rewarded those who knew how to obtain different sinecures and favors from it, via practices not very different from the ones being criticized, though naturally without the trade-union participation of the old system. The state's efficiency was not improved even in those areas that were the state's natural and exclusive preserve: tax collection and the distribution of public revenue.

Despite the proclaimed desire to balance the budget, essential for controlling inflation, public spending grew steadily, fed first by monetary emission and then by foreign debt. The military was a direct beneficiary of an important part of this spending, rearming and modernizing itself in the event of a future war, seen as possible first with Chile and then with Great Britain over the Malvinas (Falklands). Considerable monies were also spent on lavish, so-called pharaonic public works projects. The opportunities for adulterated bids were endless, given the fact that the three branches of the armed services carefully divided public administration and the carrying out of public works projects among themselves, multiplying the demand over resources. Money was spent in a haphazard fashion without coordination between the branches —one more result of the lack of unity in the political leadership—which added to the inflation, making fiscal spending unpredictable, indeed making nebulous the very idea of a state budget.

The state found itself deeply affected in an even more dramatic fashion. The so-called Process of National Reorganization, or the Process as it was simply called, entailed the coexistence of a clandestine terrorist state in charge of repression and another visible one, subject to the norms established by the military government itself but submitting its actions to a certain legal scrutiny. In practice, this distinction was not maintained, and the illegal clandestine state was corroding, corrupting the state institutions in their entirety and the state's very juridical foundations.

The first ambiguity was found precisely where power resided. Despite the fact that a strong executive was an Argentine tradition and that the unity of command was always one of the principles of the armed forces, the authority of the president—who in the beginning was a first among equals and then not even that—turned out to be weak and subject to permanent scrutiny, with restraints imposed by the commanders of the three services. The Statute of the Process and the subsequent complementary government decrees— which shut down the congress, purged the judicial system, and prohibited political activity—created the Military Junta, with power to designate the president and control many of his actions. The problem was that no one's powers were clearly delineated but were rather the result of the changing balance of forces. A newly created Advisory Legislative Commission, made up of three representatives of each branch subordinate to the orders of their commanders, was another instance of alliances and confrontations. To top it off, every executive position, from governors to mayors, as well as the administration of state companies and other government agencies, was divided among the armed forces. Those who occupied these positions thus depended on a double chain of command: that of the state and that of their service branch. This amounted to a feudalized anarchy rather than a state made cohesive and constituted through executive power.

The same anarchy existed with respect to the legal norms that the government provided itself. There was confusion about the very nature of these norms—laws, decrees, and state regulations being jumbled together without criteria—as well as who had the power to declare them and what was the full extent of their powers. There was also a well-known reluctance to discuss the reason for such norms; even their very existence was on occasion a secret. The military government preferred omnibus laws and frequently granted itself broad discretionary powers, but also tolerated the repeated violation or only partial fulfillment of its own legislation. Contaminated by the clandestine terrorist state, the country's entire juridical structure was similarly affected, to the point that there were practically no legal limits on the exercise of power, which functioned as the discretionary power of the state. This corruption of purpose was extended to public administration, where the most able personnel were removed. Arbitrary decisions were made by minor bureaucrats, transformed into little dictators without control and lacking the ability to assert control themselves. In summary, the Process of National Reorganization did not limit itself to eliminating constitutional democratic procedures or to restructuring profoundly republican institutions, as had occurred under previous military regimes. From within, it carried out a veritable revolution against the state, affecting the possibility of exercising even those functions of regulation and control that according to liberal concepts were its rightful preserve.

Fragmentation of power, centrifugal tendencies, and anarchy were the product of the strict division of power among the three armed service branches, to the point that there was no means of requesting a final appeal to authority that might arbitrate in the event of conflicts between the branches. But such a state of affairs was also the result of the existence of clear factions in the army, where from the repression emerged true warlords, who recognized virtually no authority superior to their own. Around the generals Videla and Roberto Viola—Videla's second-in-command in the army—the most powerful factions were established, but even these were far from dominant. These commanders backed Martínez de Hoz—a figure criticized by the more nationalist military officers, who abounded in the ranks of younger officers—but they recognized the necessity of finding some political solution in the future. They maintained communication with the leadership of the political parties, who hoped that this group represented the most reasonable and even the most progressive sector of the military, perhaps because it was the faction that recognized the need to control the repression in some way.

Other groups, whose most prominent figures were the generals Lucaino Benjamín Menéndez and Carlos Suárez Mason, commanders of the army's Third Corps and First Corps with their headquarters in Córdoba and Buenos Aires, respectively, and the chief of police of Buenos Aires province, General Ramón J. Camps, a key figure in the repression, maintained that the dictatorship should continue sine die and that the repression—which these figures carried out with special savagery—should be taken to its final consequences. In permanent conflict with the military commander—first Videla and then Viola—Menéndez in fact committed insubordination several times: Once on the occasion of the conflict with Chile in 1978, he was on the verge of beginning a war on his own account and then explicitly in 1979, forcing his retirement.

The third group in the military was that of the navy, firmly led by its commander, Admiral Emilio Eduardo Massera, who, trusting in his own political talents, proposed to find a political agreement that would popularly legitimize the Process and at the same time carry him to power. Massera, who carried out a major part of the repression from the navy mechanics' school and gained distinction in that sinister competition, always played his own game. He harried Videla to limit his power and distanced himself from Martínez de Hoz. He took great pains to find issues and causes that would win some degree of popular support for the government, such as the World Cup soccer championships—played in the country in 1978 and hosted by Admiral Lacoste—and later the conflict with Chile, which served as a prelude to the Falklands-Malvinas War, also instigated by the navy. When he retired, Massera established a political think tank, his own newspaper, an international publicity agency based in Paris, a political party—Social Democracy—and a bizarre personal staff made up of former members of the guerrilla organizations kidnapped and imprisoned in the navy mechanic's school, who agreed to collaborate in the admiral's political projects.

The internal power struggle was undoubtedly much more complex than was apparent. The Videla-Viola group gradually advanced in its control of power, but in May 1978 Massera scored a triumph when he managed to have the powers of the president of the nation and commander-in-chief of the army separated, despite the fact that Videla had been confirmed as president until 1981 and Viola had succeeded him as army commander. The removal of Menéndez was an important victory for Videla, though shortly thereafter

Viola retired and was replaced as army commander by Leopoldo Fortunato Galtieri. In September 1980, Videla was successful in naming Viola as his successor in the *Junta de Comandantes,* but at the cost of a complex negotiation that portended the prolonged checkmate to which the second president of the Process would be subjected.

In summary, the politics of order began to fail among the armed forces themselves, because the military behaved in an undisciplined and factional manner and did little to maintain the order that it sought to impose on society. Nevertheless, for five years, the military managed to secure a relative peace, a peace of the tomb, owing to society's scant ability to respond, partly because it had been battered or threatened by the repression and partly because it was disposed to tolerate a great deal from a government that, after the preceding chaos, had promised a minimum order. Only toward the end of the Videla period—encouraged by the discontent that the economic crisis unleashed, as well as by the growing difficulties the military government encountered, and its strong internal dissension—did voices of protest, still weak and hesitant, begin to be raised.

This transition from silence to speaking out varied on a case-to-case basis. Business supported the Process from the outset, but from a distance. Despite the general points of agreement—above all those dealing with labor policies—there was mutual distrust. The military assigned business some of the responsibility for the social chaos that it had proposed to change, and business, divided in its interests, was incapable of establishing a direction or formulating clear and uniform demands. Those business sectors that had directly benefited from the regime's policies still did not constitute an institutionalized and organic group with its own voice. Business's organizational spokespersons—the *Sociedad Rural Argentina* and the *Unión Industrial Argentina*—criticized specific aspects of the economic policies that affected them, as well as general problems such as the high inflation. Beyond their immediate problems, these forces lacked the unity and strength to lobby as organizations and began to do so only when the military government began to give signs of simultaneous weakness and willingness to open up the system. General Viola, looking to distance himself from the policies of Martínez de Hoz, made overtures to the spokespersons of the leading business sectors and included them in his cabinet. But this participation ended with his fall, and from then on, business, seriously battered by the economic crisis, joined the opposition front with growing enthusiasm.

The labor movement was dealt strong blows. The repression affected rank-and-file militants and many top-ranking union leaders, a number of whom were imprisoned. The principal factories were militarily occupied, and there were blacklists to keep out activists and ideological screening for job applicants. The CGT and most of the big unions were interdicted, collective bargaining and the right to strike were eliminated, and the unions lost control over their *obras sociales,* the sundry social welfare activities they administered, funded by union dues. Virtually stripped of any role and with their memberships reduced as a result of changes in the labor market, which affected primarily industry, the unions' voices were little heard.

The government maintained limited contact with the union leadership, virtually restricted to the regime's selection of union representatives who attended annual meetings of the International Labor Organization in Geneva. Nonetheless, participation in these meetings allowed labor leaders some degree of activity and a certain space for denouncing abroad the harsh conditions existing for Argentine workers. Thus they could challenge the government on issues of wages, collective bargaining agreements, and strikes. The union leaders aligned, in a fluctuating manner, into two broad tendencies: those who supported dialogue with the government and those who maintained an intransigent position. In April 1979, by which point the repression had eased somewhat, the combative sector undertook a general protest strike that the faction in favor of dialogue with the government did not adhere to and that ended in violent repression and imprisonment for the majority of the leaders who headed the strike. In late 1980, the most-combative union leaders reestablished the CGT and elected as its secretary-general a little-known figure from the small brewery workers' union, Saúl Ubaldini. In 1981, taking advantage of the government's greater tolerance, the CGT launched another general strike, with consequences similar to those of 1979. In November of the same year, it led a march of workers to the cathedral of San Cayetano—the patron saint of the unemployed—demanding "bread, peace, and work." Around this time, their complaints merged with those of other sectors, such as the students and some regional business groups. Partial strikes were undertaken with greater frequency and intensity. On March 30, 1982, the CGT convoked, for the first time since 1975, a demonstration in the Plaza de Mayo, which the government violently repressed. Two thousand were arrested in Buenos Aires, and there was one death in Mendoza.

The Catholic Church also modified its behavior as the military regime showed signs of weakness. The Church initially adopted an obliging attitude to the military government, and the government established a close association with the bishops, awarding them important personal favors. The ecclesiastical hierarchy—with important exceptions such as the bishop of La Rioja, Enrique Angel Angelelli, later apparently murdered—condoned the association that the military made in its public statements between state terrorism and Christian virtues. The Church refrained from criticism and justified in a barely disguised manner the eradication of so-called atheist subversion; some clergy even participated directly in its eradication, as the CONADEP subsequently alleged and proved.

Gradually this initial reaction, which represented a triumph of the traditional sector of the Argentine Church, gave way to another more circumspect one, influenced by the conservative orientation stamped on the Catholic Church by Pôpe John Paul II. Revising its previous positions, which had encouraged the development of progressive sectors and particularly the Third World Priests movement, the Church proposed renouncing direct involvement in social and political questions while devoting itself to evangelizing and reestablishing lay participation in Church ritual in a society that had become excessively secular. In 1979, the archbishopric established a social pastoral team to rebuild the link between the Church and the workers, following the example of the Polish trade-union movement Solidarity, and instituted close relations with union leaders such as Ubaldini. It also concerned itself with the youth to capture and organize the signs of a new religious awakening in society, visible in the large pilgrimages on foot to the Luján cathedral, Argentina's most important shrine, and began to fill the positions left vacant by the disappearance of clergy activists who had so intensely occupied the Church hierarchy in previous years. Concerns over moral issues or over the family were extended to personal rights of all kinds, from the right to life to the right to work, extending even to political rights. The 1981 Church document "The Catholic Church and the National Community" reaffirmed republican principles and indicated the Church's preference for democracy, its distancing itself from the military regime, and its sympathies for society's rising demands.

The most notable of these demands was for human rights. In the midst of the worst moments of the repression, a group of mothers of *desaparecidos* ("the disappeared")—the word beginning to be used for the victims of state terrorism—started to meet every week in the Plaza de Mayo, marching with their heads covered with white handkerchiefs, demanding the return of their children. By demanding an explanation from the government, combining the painful personal display with an ethical claim on behalf of principles such as motherhood, they ensured that their motives were not questioned by the military, nor could they be linked to "subversion." The mothers attacked the very heart of the repression's patriarchal discourse and began to transform society's indifference. Soon, the Mothers of the Plaza de Mayo—themselves victims of the repression—became the point of reference for an increasingly broad movement and occupied the center of public debate, encouraged from abroad by the foreign press, governments, and human rights organizations. From late 1981, the military found itself obliged to provide some answers for a subject that it sought to bury without discussion. Though the military in general agreed that the issue should be regarded as closed, it revealed differences of opinion and contradictions that exacerbated previous disagreements and somewhat enlarged the space in which public opinion, long silenced, began to reappear.

This climate breathed some life into the political parties, which the military regime had prohibited from participating in public life. The political ban, imposed in 1976, put a freeze on party activity while prolonging the established party leadership's grip on power. The leadership, lacking compelling incentives, scarcely had a critical attitude toward the military government. The political proscription effectively ended in 1981. Essaying a political opening, the government itself called on scattered rightist parties to establish a pro-regime political party, while the Peronists and Radicals entered into conversations with smaller parties. In mid-1981, this situation culminated in the founding of the *Multipartidario,* made up of Radicalism, Peronism, and other parties (*Desarrollismo,* Christian Democracy, and the *Partido Intransigente,* a leftist offshoot of the Radical Party).

The *Multipartidario* had little more vitality than the desultory activity of the parties that made it up. The parties were sclerotic, hardly representative organizations whose leaders were the same as those of 1975. Ricardo Balbín, the veteran Radical politician who gave life to this undertaking, died in 1981—his burial summoned the first great street demonstration of those years—exposing even more the absence of leadership in the incipient movement. The parties committed themselves to shunning collaboration with the government in any restricted electoral exit from power and refused to accept a democracy subject to military tutelage. Theirs was an agreement of basic principles, revealing the difficulties of creating political alternatives that could mobilize public opinion. But the parties also slowly turned up the volume of their criticisms, demanding status for themselves as the only repositories of political legitimacy, incorporating the protests of businesspeople and union leaders into their platforms, but all the while leaving the door open for a negotiated transition to democracy. Together with other groups—union leaders, businesspeople, students, Church leaders, intellectuals, and above all human rights activists—they formed a chorus of opposition that by the beginning of 1982 was difficult for the government to ignore.

The Falklands-Malvinas War and the Crisis of the Military Regime

Since 1980 the leaders of the Process had discussed the question of an exit from power. They were concerned about the economic crisis, their isolation from society, adverse foreign opinion—in which demands for human rights weighed increasingly heavily, demands that the military government attempted to minimize, attributing them to an "anti-Argentine" campaign—and especially the intense internal confrontations that obstructed the consensus necessary for the exit being sought. Internal dissent had become public with the selection of Viola—opposed by the navy—to succeed Videla as president and had worsened during the long period intervening until his assumption of the presidency in March 1981. The internal conflicts came to a head when the new president's decision to change the course of economic policy became clear.

Viola sought to alleviate the situation of local business, battered by the financial crisis and the violent devaluation of the peso, and had the state assume responsibility for part of business's debts. At the same time, Viola tried to establish a consensus on economic policy, incorporating businesspeople into his cabinet. The military president also established contacts with sundry politicians—those who had been "friends" of the Process—and discussed with them the alternatives for an eventual, albeit distant, transition. Viola failed to organize any consistent support or to attenuate the eco-

nomic crisis unleashed by the devaluation of the peso and escalating inflation. The new president was harried by the sectors that had surrounded
Martínez de Hoz, and different military groups accused him of a lack of
firm leadership. In late 1981, Viola's ill health provided the opportunity for
his removal and replacement by General Leopoldo Fortunato Galtieri, who
also kept his position as army commander-in-chief, thereby disrupting the
precarious institutional stability that the military commanders themselves
had established.

Galtierei, a general who unlike Viola was little versed in politics, presented
himself as the savior of the Process, the vigorous leader capable of leading it to
a victory that by then seemed remote. In fashioning that image, his recent
stay in the United States as military attaché had been decisive. While in
Washington, he had been assiduously courted by members of the Reagan
administration, concerned to find allies for its complicated foreign policy.
Galtieri showed himself willing to align Argentina firmly with the United
States and support it in the covert war it was waging in Central America. By
then, Argentina was contributing advisers and armaments to the covert war
effort and received from the Reagan administration, together with warm personal support, the lifting of the sanctions that the previous Carter administration had imposed on the country for human rights violations. It was probably then that Galtieri conceived his destiny as Argentina's leader tied to the
world of the great powers, of the First World, where the country—protected
by its powerful ally—could play the big boys' game.

Once designated president, Galtieri threw himself into the political arena
and attempted, in a more energetic and personal way than had Viola, to assemble a coalition in which the "politician friends" of the Process supported
his leadership while he announced vague plans, without precise timetables,
for a future restoration of democracy. He entrusted the management of the
economy to Roberto Alemann, a distinguished economist of the establishment, who, surrounded by a good part of the team of Martínez de Hoz, returned to the initial path and, in agreement with the new circumstances created by economic crisis and the debt, established his priorities around a
program of "disinflation, deregulation, and destatization." In the interim, the
recession intensified, and with it the protests of the unions and business. For
the long term, Alemann announced a plan of privatizations, particularly
those related to subsoil rights, which provoked resistance even from sectors of

the government. Galtieri's efforts thus soon came into conflict with an increasingly bitter resistance, in ever more outspoken tones, with street demonstrations such as that unleashed by the CGT in March 1982.

In this context, the plan to occupy the Malvinas (Falklands) Islands was conceived as a solution to many of the government's problems. Argentina had been unsuccessfully demanding the return of these South Atlantic islands since 1833, the year the British occupied them. In 1965, the United Nations had ruled that the two countries should negotiate their differences, but the British had done little to make progress with respect to Argentina's claims, which were in accord with the global trend toward decolonization. In Argentina, there was a national consensus on the principle of Argentine sovereignty over the islands, though not on the means to achieve it. From the perspective of the Galtieri government, a military action leading to the recovery of the islands would also permit the unification of the armed forces behind a common objective and would achieve for the regime in a single blow the legitimacy that it now lacked.

A military action would have a another advantage: It would make it possible to find a way out of the morass created by the dispute with Chile over the Beagle Channel. In 1971, Presidents Lanusse and Salvador Allende had agreed to submit to arbitration the question of the ownership of the three small islands that guarded the passage through that channel uniting the Pacific with the Atlantic. In 1977, the islands were awarded to Chile, a decision that the Argentine government rejected. In 1978, both countries appeared to be on the brink of resolving the question by arms when, almost at the last moment, they decided to accept the mediation of the Pope, through his intermediary Cardinal Samoré. In late 1981, the Vatican quietly communicated its decision, which in essence upheld the arbitration decision favorable to Chile. The Argentine government, unable either to accept or reject the decision, chose to drag out its response and resumed its hostile activities toward Chile.

By that time, a bellicose current of opinion had arisen among the military and its friends, an attitude rooted in a strain of Argentine nationalism, which drew sustenance from strong chauvinist sentiments. Diverse ancient fantasies in society's historical imaginary—the *patria grande,* the "spoliation" that the country had suffered—were added to a new fantasy of "entering the First World" through a "strong" foreign policy. All this was combined with the traditional messianic military mentality and the ingenuousness of its strategies, which were ignorant of the most elemental facts of international politics. The aggression against Chile, stymied by papal mediation, was transferred to Great Britain, the traditional imperial power that the military assumed was old and ailing. Already in 1977, the navy had suggested occupying the Malvinas, but the plan was vetoed by Videla and Viola; Galtieri, however, took it up again as soon as he assumed the presidency. The idea was simple and attractive. After the initial seizure and occupation of the islands, an operation that would present few difficulties, the government could count on the support of the United States and a hesitant response by Great Britain, which would ultimately accept the occupation in return for all the necessary concessions and compensations. The possibility of war never entered into the calculations.

On April 2, 1982, the armed forces disembarked and occupied the Malvinas, after overcoming a weak resistance by the few British troops stationed there. The action caught almost everyone by surprise and sparked broad popular support. People spontaneously gathered in the Plaza de Mayo, and when called on a week later, they turned out again there and in other provincial capitals on the occasion of the visit of the U.S. Secretary of State, Alexander Haig. That day President Galtieri had the satisfaction of haranguing the crowd from the historic balcony of the presidential palace. All of society's institutions—ethnic societies, sports clubs, cultural associations, unions, political parties—offered unreserved support. Political leaders and military commanders traveled together to attend the swearing-in ceremonies of the islands' new military governor, General Mario Benjamín Menéndez, who declared a new name for the capital of the islands, formerly Port Stanley, rebaptized Puerto Argentino. The leaders of the CGT, which had been harshly repressed in a strike barely three days before, tried to differentiate their solidarity for the action from any possible support for the government, but this distinction was not easy to explain.

The military government had obtained a complete political victory on identifying itself with a deeply felt popular demand nourished by the country's nationalist and anti-imperialist political culture. The Process appeared to have consigned that nationalism to the archives, but it reappeared with a vengeance. The government also attracted the puerile and superficial expressions through which these sentiments were expressed, the crude chauvinism encapsulated in it, and the facile *triunfalismo* and unthinking war mongering.

Indeed, it was surprising that virtually no one questioned the legality of the takeover, which revealed the disintegration of political convictions that had once been deeper and more solid. The country that had celebrated the Argentine victory in the World Cup soccer tournament now rejoiced in having won a battle. With the same ingenuousness, it was preparing to proceed, if necessary, to war. If triumphant, the military believed it would have paid its debt to society, at the small price of allowing greater freedom for unfettered voices. Nonetheless, when dissenters departed from the official script and demanded such things as an abandonment of liberal economic policies or protested the declaration of a "war economy," they were easily ignored.

Great Britain adopted a surprisingly hard-line response. Those in favor of a pacific solution lost the debate to more conservative sectors, headed by Prime Minister Margaret Thatcher, who, as was the case with the Argentine military government, hoped to shore up her domestic political position. A large British naval force was immediately prepared, including aircraft carriers and invasion troops. On April 17, 1982, the Task Force rendezvoused at Ascencion Island in the Atlantic and began its journey to the Malvinas. At the same time, the Argentine government declared an exclusion zone around the islands and threatened to attack anyone who entered it.

Great Britain quickly obtained the solidarity of the European Community, which imposed economic sanctions, as well as the support of the United Nations Security Council, which passed a resolution declaring Argentina the aggressor nation and demanding an end to the hostilities and withdrawal of the Argentine troops. The powerful forces supporting the British were barely counterbalanced by Latin American solidarity with Argentina—broadly supportive with words but with little else—and some faint encouragement by the Soviet Union. The United States kept a relatively equidistant position and attempted to mediate between its two allies.

Without consistent support, even ignorant of the very rules of the game, the Argentine military government threw itself into the First World arena, believing, with the occupation a fait accompli, that the issue would be resolved through negotiation. The British reaction thus appeared not only unexpected, but rash. The United States, through Secretary of State General Haig's mediation, tried to find a negotiated solution and a compromise. Haig proposed a withdrawal of the Argentine troops and a tripartite administration of the islands that would include the Unite States, to allow negotiations to be reestablished. Both terms were acceptable to the Argentine government if a British commitment to a future recognition of Argentine sovereignty over the islands was added. Such a stipulation was unacceptable to the British. The military government was prepared to make concessions on any other matter, but could not appear to accept the very thing it had proclaimed to be its fundamental objective. Only in this way could the operation be presented as a victory to society and to the crowds in the Plaza de Mayo, whose magic the military government had now experienced. Thus, the government became a prisoner of the patriotic mobilization that it had unleashed, and more cautious individuals were forced to give way to more extreme voices.

Pursuing an impossible objective, the Argentine government became the victim of a growing diplomatic isolation that was worsened by the country's former sins, because those who had reproached it for human rights violations thought, with good reason, that if this military adventure succeeded, it would legitimize all previous behavior. The government's move of sending business representatives, trade-union leaders, and politicians abroad to explain the Argentine position did not serve to modify this perception, and in many cases it provided the government opposition a podium from which it could present its criticisms of the regime while defending Argentine sovereignty over the islands.

The military government attempted to pressure the United States, using the machinery of the Organization of American States and especially the Inter-American Reciprocal Assistance Treaty that the United States had formerly employed to align its southern neighbors behind it in its Cold War and Cuban conflicts. The Latin American countries held firm in their support of Argentina, but the resolution that they passed in late April was vague and did not imply any military commitment. After a month of unsuccessfully attempting to convince the military junta, as the British were beginning their attack on the islands, the United States abandoned its mediation. The U.S. Senate voted in favor of sanctions against Argentina and offered Great Britain logistic support. Ever more alone, the Argentine government looked for improbable allies—the countries of the Third World, the Soviet Union, and even Cuba—which definitively dispelled any illusion of entering the "First World." In the meantime, military conflict grew inexorably closer.

In the final days of April, the British Task Force, which had arrived in the Malvinas zone, recovered the South Georgias Islands. On May 1st, aerial bombardments against the Malvinas began, and on the following day a

British submarine sank the Argentine destroyer, the *General Belgrano,* far outside the declared exclusion zone. As a result of this action, the Argentine navy definitively removed itself from the line of fire. Prolonged air and naval combat followed. The Argentine air force bombarded the British fleet and caused considerable damage, including a direct hit against the destroyer, the Sheffield, with a guided missile, which made amends for the sinking of the Belgrano. Nonetheless, the British fleet was not stopped, nor could the air force prevent the British from cutting the islands off from the mainland. Argentine military commanders had stationed some 10,000 soldiers in the Malvinas; these were mostly raw recruits—for some reason, the commanders preferred keeping more experienced troops along the border with Chile—with scarce provisions, poorly equipped, without means of transport, and above all lacking any strategy, except to resist. In Buenos Aires, a fortress mentality set in and the possibility of a change in the global balance of forces fired the military's imagination. In the islands, subjected to a devastating attack of artillery and aircraft, on the other hand, doubts were becoming demoralization.

A similar change occurred in public opinion, delayed partly by a complete manipulation of information, which reached a public inclined to believe that Argentina was winning the war. In the midst of this triumphant climate, critical opinions began to appear. Some spoke in the name of the United States and argued against the war and its impossible alliances. Others, from the left, demanded that the anti-imperialist aspects of the conflict be given greater emphasis and suggested attacking the local representatives of imperialism. In the CGT's May Day celebrations, strident voices were again raised. Among the Radicals, whose official leadership had meekly accepted the terms of the debate over the war imposed by the government, Raúl Alfonsín, the leader of a dissident faction in the *Unión Cívica Radical* (UCR), proposed forming a civilian transition government headed by the ex-president Arturo Illia. Thus, among the growing protests over the lack of true information about the war, the subject of the country's future after the war emerged among the public and confirmed the military's initial conviction that there was no solution short of a military victory.

On May 24th, the British disembarked and established a beachhead at San Carlos. On May 29th, a decisive battle was fought at Goose Green, where several hundred Argentine troops surrendered. On June 19th, Galtieri for the last time addressed a crowd gathered in the Plaza de Mayo, and two days later

Pope John Paul II arrived, partly to compensate for his earlier visit to Great Britain and partly perhaps to prepare the Argentines for imminent defeat. Before the details were completed for the Pope's brief visit, the final attack began on Puerto Argentino, where the bulk of the troops had dug in. The rout was swift; surrender, virtually unconditional, occurred on June 14th, seventy-four days after the conflict first erupted. For Argentina, the war left more than 700 dead or "missing in action" and some 1,300 wounded. The government convoked the people in the Plaza de Mayo on the following day, only to repress in an extremely violent manner those who could neither understand nor accept the surrender because the media had convinced them that victory was near. It was then that the generals demanded Galtieri's resignation.

The Return of Democracy

The defeat heightened the crisis of the military regime, which had loomed since the 1981 financial debacle, and made public conflicts that until then had been hidden. The question of who was responsible for the defeat—which every group blamed on another—was temporarily resolved by assigning the blame to the military commanders in the Malvinas. More significant failures soon came to light, however, and these implicated the high command. The report of the investigating committee chaired by a prestigious general ultimately held responsible the military junta itself; this verdict led to a trial that subsequently found the commanders guilty. At the same time, the three branches of the armed forces could not to agree on a successor to Galtieri. Though the army was able to impose its candidate, General Reinaldo Bignone, the air force and the navy withdrew from the junta, thereby creating an unusual institutional situation with a president selected by the army commander-in-chief. The moment was perhaps ripe for a vigorous movement on the part of the civilian population to remove the armed forces from power. Because there was no such movement, however, the designated president managed to secure his position, thanks to the minimal consensus among the political parties on a plan to reestablish political institutions according to a definite timetable. Once the most severe moment of the crisis had passed, the military commanders of the navy and air force were replaced in an internal shake-up, and the junta reconstituted.

The electoral exit subsequently proposed by the government served to calm the demands of the political parties. But the government wished to negotiate the transition and to ensure that its retreat would not be in disarray. It attempted to procure an agreement with the parties on a series of past and future questions: economic policy, the institutional presence of the armed forces in the new government, and above all a guarantee of no investigation for acts of corruption or of unlawful enrichment and no holding anyone accountable for what the military was beginning to call the "dirty war," a euphemism comparable to the "disappeared." All these machinations were coming to light, portrayed in an almost sensationalist manner by a press that had decided to ignore censorship. The military's aspirations were included in a proposal presented on November 1982 and rejected by public opinion in general and by the political parties, the latter shortly later convoking a civilian march in defense of democracy. There was a massive turnout, and the government almost immediately set an election date for late 1983, although it continued to seek its fundamental objective: to head off any future inquiry of the military's past behavior. A final government document was supposed to bring to a conclusion the debate over the *desaparecidos,* with the affirmation that there were no survivors and that all the dead had died in combat. A law passed by the government established a self-amnesty, exempting those responsible from any future charges.

The leadership of the political parties might have come to an agreement that included drawing a curtain on the past and thereby ensuring a peaceful transition from a military regime to a civilian government. They were prevented from doing so as much by the increasingly intense mobilization of society as by the armed forces' own weakness, corroded by the growing awareness of their illegitimacy and by their internal conflicts. Those who headed the government and were negotiating the transition to civilian rule were incapable of controlling the repressive apparatus that they had erected, and the regime claimed some new victims that the society, now sensitized to such behavior, took note of with horror. The junta could not even ensure that they would not be overthrown by some group of officers—because the armed forces had begun a soul searching, about both the past and the future. The military had to face proof of its failure as administrator of a country in chaos and as instigator of an absurd war that had forced Argentina to fight against those people the military leaders wished to be their allies and to align with the countries of the Third World that they had always mistrusted. The government had to wonder why their former allies—the most powerful businesspeople, the United States, the Catholic Church—won over to a new faith in democracy—withdrew their former support, or why formerly abject judges now brought to trial officers accused of diverse acts of corruption. Above all, the regime had to confront a society that, after years of blindness, was learning about mass burial sites of unidentified people, undoubtedly victims of the military's repression, about hundreds of clandestine detention centers, about accusations of crimes by former government agents. All these facts revealed a sinister history, which few had any desire to learn about before this moment. In those conditions, it was highly unlikely that the alliances that had guided the final government of the armed forces could be mended.

After a long dormancy, society was awakening, and voices that had never been silent, such as the activists in the human rights organizations and especially the Mothers of the Plaza de Mayo, resonated with greater force. The Mothers' unparalleled manner of challenging military power was combined with a novel activism, one that was more tolerant, less factional than the traditional kinds, and did not preclude other loyalties. The Mothers' Thursday marches, sparsely attended during the years of harshest repression, were transformed after the war into large "marches for life," which effectively identified the government with death. The human rights organizations not only placed the question of the "disappeared" at the center stage of public debate, which thereby put the military on the defensive, but they also invested political activities with an ethical dimension, a sense of commitment, and a need to find basic points of agreement in society above and beyond party affiliations. In the context of previous experiences, these developments were truly original.

As the repression declined and the discourse of repression—so effective in the self-censorship of the period—lost legitimacy, various social actors, some new and others that had survived by going into hiding, began to mobilize. The economic crisis created legitimate reasons to mobilize. Taxes were onerous, the effects of the "indexization" were harmful, rents were high, and many debts had been caused by the bank failures. By protesting and mobilizing, society questioned both economic policy and the absence of political participation. In other cases, a small fragment of society—a neighborhood, a town—simply organized itself on the basis of common concerns, for purposes of making demands—at times violently, as happened in a series of neighborhood protests in greater Buenos Aires in late 1982—and for finding practical solutions to real problems in the form of cooperatives, development societies, or housewives' associations, without the help of public officials. Society's new activism was represented in the most diverse ways: cultural groups, such as those in the so-called Open Theater movement that, after 1980, organized the representation of cultural vitality separate from the regime's official culture, an undertaking transformed into a true political act; young people who gave life to community organizations at the parish level and who participated in the multitudinous pilgrimages to the shrine at Luján in those years as well as in massive concerts of "national rock," which also became political acts. Activism was reborn in the universities in the heat of protest against limitations on enrollment and the establishment of tuition in the country's public institutions. In the factories and workplaces, shop floor committees were reestablished and union activity resumed.

In some ways, society experienced a second "people's spring." A common enemy, now somewhat less dangerous but still fearsome, encouraged solidarity, fostered organization, and encouraged action in the hope of achieving concrete results. Once again, the terms of the conflict appeared clear, and solutions seemed possible if men and women of goodwill organized themselves as a coherent force. But in contrast to the previous "people's spring," people now not only totally repudiated violence or any veiled form of war, but they also had less confidence that a total, unique, and definitive solution would be found. There was also less certainty that the broad ensemble of demands defined one great protagonist, the sole actor of epic achievement, as the "Peronist people" had been for many years. The boundaries of this awakening of society lay precisely in the difficulty of gathering together the demands, integrating them, giving them coherency, and translating them into specifically political terms.

To a certain extent, this articulation of society's demands was also supposed to take place in union mobilization, which was intense. The unions called the people into the streets to protest the economic crisis and to demonstrate in favor of democracy. Throughout 1982 and 1983, a series of general strikes and numerous partial ones by the public-sector unions were distinctive for their novel and hardened militancy. But the union leaders put their efforts into recovering control of the interdicted unions and "normalizing" union activity, both of which they negotiated with the government by combining pressure and compromise. The two large factions into which the labor movement was then divided, largely for tactical reasons—the combative CGT Brasil headed by Saúl Ubaldini and the conciliatory CGT Azopardo—participated in this strategy. Their mobilizations lost their specific trade-union character and came together in a more general struggle in pursuit of a return of democracy.

Democracy was in many ways a panacea. It was the promised land that society could reach without struggle, although that same society had until recently adhered to the terms and agenda imposed by the military. After the double jolt of economic crisis and military defeat, democracy appeared to be the key to surmount frictions and frustrations, to create a formula for political coexistence, and to solve every concrete problem. Several decades without real democratic practice necessitated a new apprenticeship in the rules of the game and in democracy's values and general principles, including those that had to do with a republic. It was precisely this vague understanding of what constituted a democracy that permitted those who had never believed in it to climb on board the democratic bandwagon, especially those rapidly abandoning the sinking ship of the Process. The apprenticeship was an intense learning experience, and democracy was quickly put into practice. Party enrollments—once the government had lifted the ban on political parties—were so massive that one in every three people eligible to vote belonged to a party. The numbers of those mobilizing in defense of democracy were reminiscent of those ten years before, with the difference that the present mobilizations were neither celebrations nor exercises in the seizing of power but expressions of a collective will, demonstrating and recognizing the demonstrators as members of civil society. That difference was also expressed in the chosen gathering places: In addition to the traditional Plaza de Mayo, demonstrators gathered in the Plaza de la República, the Cabildo, and the Palace of Justice, the latter signaling the central role that, it was hoped, the judicial system would play in the new democracy.

The massive enrollment transformed the political parties. The widespread desire to participate breathed new life into the party and neighborhood committees to which society's new demands were directed. New party leaders were elected, incorporating many who had previously been active in student and youth organizations, such as the *Coordinadora Radical*. Many intellectuals who were recruited brought new ideas to politics, arising from their own society's concerns and from the experiences of more advanced democratic countries, along with modern ways of posing them. The old political leadership found itself challenged by others who had been voices of dissent from the sidelines, and the replacement of the old guard was broad and deep.

The changes in Peronism were notable. The old movement, always in a tense relationship with democracy, was transformed into an accepted party. The feature that had marked its existence, *verticalismo*—rigid hierarchy and unquestioning loyalty to one's superiors in the movement—was abandoned because of the notorious weakness at the top of the pyramid, where Perón's widow Isabel only symbolically occupied the presidency of the party. The party apparatus could now absorb sectors with strong corporative organizations, such as the unions. Participatory practices were adopted to moderate internal competition, while modern issues and democratic concerns, which had never been the movement's strong points, began to appear in its debates.

The renewal, nonetheless, was not complete. The old provincial political bosses continued to hold considerable power, as did the union leadership. The head of the powerful metalworkers' union, Lorenzo Miguel—Vandor's successor whom the military had reinstated in early 1983—again led the 62 Organizations, the trade-union wing of Peronism, and thanks to his control of the party inscriptions ended up occupying the real presidency of the party. Behind him, union bosses with suspect backgrounds, such as Herminio Iglesias, gained influence: Iglesias, for instance, became the Peronist candidate for governor in Buenos Aires province. The nomination for president fell to Italo Luder, a prestigious lawyer with little real power in the party. Luder was supposed to represent the balance between the old and new tendencies in Peronism, but could not dispel the mistrust that Peronism awoke in important sectors of society.

Radicalism also experienced a renewal thanks to the initiatives of Raúl Alfonsín, who had created the Movement for Renovation and Change in 1972 to contest the leadership of the stalwart Radical leader Ricardo Balbín. During the Process, Alfonsín had stood out from other politicians by energetically criticizing the military, assuming the legal defense of political prisoners, demanding explanations for the fate of the "disappeared," and standing aloof from the euphoria surrounding the Malvinas War. After the end of the war, his rise was meteoric, and he defeated Balbín's heirs in an internal power struggle for control of the Radical Party. Alfonsín made democracy his banner and combined it with a series of proposals to modernize the state and society. His demand for ethical standards in politics and his optimistic discourse, very different from Radicalism's traditional discourse, won the party numerous new members and sympathizers.

Radicals and Peronists reaped broad support and left little room for other parties. The right continued to have difficulty in unifying its diverse forces, many of which had compromised themselves too much with the Process to be attractive. The erstwhile conservative leader Alvaro Alsogaray established a new party, the *Unión del Centro Democrático* (Union of the Democratic Center, or UCD), which began to benefit from the worldwide upsurge in orthodox liberal ideas, though the party harvested its greatest rewards at a later date. The left suffered both from the harsh repression it had undergone during the Process years and from the anachronistic character of its proposals. Alfonsín's Radicals nevertheless adopted many of the left's proposals, though the *Partido Intransigente* (Intransigent Party) managed to gain a broad group of sympathizers, many of them nostalgic for the politics of 1973.

Strengthened by the mobilization of society and by this second and peaceful people's spring, the parties nonetheless had difficulties in fully accommodating society's multiple demands and desires for participation. Such concerns had a weak presence in the parties and found expression elsewhere, as in the human rights organizations, which grew increasingly intransigent about a question that the parties attempted to introduce into the political arena in politically acceptable terms. The same difficulty was apparent with respect to the organized social sectors, such as the trade unions or business, whose demands ran through corporative channels and which dispensed with the parties for their expression or negotiation. As a result, the growth of the political parties did not necessarily imply an effective mediation and negotiation of society's demands.

Such a situation did not cause undue concern. Society enthusiastically supported democracy, which was now seen as the priority of civil society. The ways of conducting politics in the recent past—the intransigence of the factions, the idea that the ends justified the means, the demonization of the adversary, political competition understood as an extension of war—were giving way to others affirming pluralism, compromise, and subordination of politics to ethical standards. Celebrating the novelty, because strictly speaking the give and take of democracy had been abandoned six decades previously, the efficacy of democracy was valued, even overvalued. To nurture and strengthen it, the accent was placed primarily on a consensus about the rules of the game and on common action in defense of the democratic system. Perhaps for that reason, an essential dimension of political practice was postponed for a later date: a civilized and pluralistic debate over programs and policies, which inherently entailed some degree of conflict of interests, of winners and losers. Instead, people trusted the power of the president and the ability of civil society to solve any problem. This combination of championing the idea of civil society along with a naive belief in the ease with which desires could be translated into reality was the result of a certain facile mentality, a "greenhorn democracy" that was bland and conformist.

The problems resulting from this situation became apparent only later. For the moment, the citizenry lived to the full its fantasy and supported the candidate who best captured that collective spirit. Peronism undertook its electoral campaign in much the old style, calling for liberation against dependency—in such an unconvincing manner that one of its candidates, in a revealing slip, inverted the equation in a public speech—while appealing to the worst in the movement's folklore to insult its adversary. Raúl Alfonsín, on the other hand, won the nomination of the UCR and then the presidential elections by appealing first to the Constitution, whose preamble—undoubtedly heard for the first time by many of his youthful supporters—was a "secular prayer." To this he added an appeal to transform society into something modern, just, and with a civic spirit. He excoriated the military regime, promised that justice would be done in the case of those responsible for human rights abuses, and denounced his adversaries as possibly in favor of the status quo through a military and trade-union pact. Above all, he assured everyone that democracy could resolve not only long-standing problems—fifty years of national decline—but could also satisfy the enormous accumulation of demands about to be unleashed. Society believed him, and the Radical Party, with more than 50 percent of the votes, handily defeated the Peronists, who for the first time in history lost a national election. A deep, pervasive, and somewhat ingenuous enthusiasm swept along Alfonsín's followers and to an extent all of civil society, which momentarily forgot how many problems remained and how little room for maneuver the new government had.

eight

Advance and Retreat, 1983–1989

The Democratic Illusion

The new president, Raúl Alfonsín, assumed the presidency on December 10, 1983, and a crowd gathered in the Plaza de Mayo for his inauguration. To signal both the continuities and the break with the country's previous political tradition, he jettisoned the practice of speaking from the "historic balconies" of the presidential palace. Instead, he chose to speak from the nearby *Cabildo,* the historic seat of municipal government and since independence a symbol of Argentine democracy. As in 1916, the multitude that spilled into the streets during the presidential inauguration believed that the citizenry had attained power. It was soon evident, however, that there was still resistance on the part of enemies thought to have been defeated, as well as difficulty in satisfying the welter of accumulated demands that society wanted to see immediately addressed. Perhaps such expectations were due to the fact that, in addition to a long-standing belief in a provident state, there was the conviction—encouraged by the triumphant presidential candidate—that the return of democracy implied the solution to all problems.

But the problems persisted, especially in the economy, though in the electoral campaign little mention was made of them. In addition to structural problems, the economy had been in a state of confusion, almost in chaos, since 1981. The country was plagued with runaway inflation, an escalating foreign debt with pressing repayment deadlines, and insufficient resources for attending to society's multiple demands, from education to public health to the salaries of state employees; finally, the government was markedly unable to manage the economic crisis.

The uncertainty surrounding the ability of the democratic government extended to other areas, where the country's corporative powers—business, the military, the unions, the Church—had demonstrated their still enormous strength, though almost all of these sectors were closely associated with the fallen regime and were tarnished by its demise. On the defensive, these powers found their old alliances were broken, and they lacked a political spokesperson to express their interests. Thus, they lay in waiting, joining the chorus in praise of the restored democracy and rendering homage to the new democratic power. The main political adversary of the Radical government, Peronism, had experienced a profound internal crisis, latent since before the election, but the crisis worsened following the first electoral defeat in its history. Whereas the Peronist labor movement distanced itself from the party leadership and attempted its own strategy to deal with the government's onslaughts, the political wing of Peronism sought unsuccessfully to establish an identity, attacking the government from the left, from the right, or even, like the Peronist senator Saadi, from both perspectives.

President Alfonsín's power was both great and slight. Radicalism had come to power with a percentage of the votes rivaled only by the great electoral triumphs of Yrigoyen and Perón, and it held a majority in the chamber of deputies. Nonetheless, it had lost in the traditional interior of the country and did not have a majority in the senate. Though Alfonsín's leadership in his party was strong, the *Unión Cívica Radical* (UCR), as a not-very-homogeneous force, debated and even obstructed many of the president's initiatives. Alfonsín preferred to surround himself with a group of intellectuals and technocrats only recently initiated into political life, along with the Radical university-student group, the *Coordinadora,* which resolved to establish control of the government and the party. Strong in the political realm, Radicalism lacked much consistent support among the country's corporative powers—beyond the initial support offered when the president triumphed in the elections. Radicalism's Peronist opponents moved with ease in this very area. The state, which was supposed to wage its battles against powers that the government did not completely control, lacked efficiency and even credibility with society.

But when he assumed power, President Alfonsín held an enormous degree of political capital, whose full potential was unknown. Civil society, beyond partisan loyalties, deeply identified with Alfonsín's project to establish the rule of law by which corporative powers would be subordinated to democratic institutions and in which practices capable of resolving conflicts in a peaceful, orderly, open, and equitable manner would be instituted. Such a goal entailed establishing a political identity founded on ethical principles that subsumed in a common undertaking the specific interests of the citizenry, in many cases represented by those same corporative organizations that had to be controlled. In the euphoria surrounding the recovery of democracy, this contradiction was at first not acknowledged. Even more than the politicians, society had lived the euphoria and illusion of the return of democracy, a sentiment that was profound and extremely naive at the same time. With support that had strengths and weaknesses, the government had to choose between actively governing, tightening to the maximum the string that was civil society, which implied confronting established interests and causing splits in their ranks, or giving priority to negotiated solutions, to agreements with the established powers, which implied postponing decisive solutions to problems. The government chose the first option but had to accept the second when it learned the limits of its power. Nevertheless, until 1987, the government held the initiative, searched for alternative paths, and presented new proposals at every setback. Many observers said that Alfonsín pulled solutions out of his hat like a magician.

In the diagnosis of the country's crisis, economic problems seemed less important than political ones. The fundamental objective was to eliminate authoritarianism and find authentic forms of political representation. The government gave great importance, symbolic and real, to cultural and educational policies and hoped to remove the authoritarianism that nested in the country's institutions, political practices, and consciousness, the "little fascist," it was once remarked, who lurked in the national soul. Coinciding with society's desires for participation and exercise of free speech, long repressed, the watchwords were cultural modernization, full participation, and above all pluralism and the rejection of all dogmatism.

In this terrain, progress was initially easy. The government established a program of mass literacy, attacked the authoritarian practices in the educational system, and opened channels to begin to debate the content and form —at times implemented with a dose of utopia and naiveté—culminating in the Pedagogical Congress that, as with the one a century previously, would determine what educational system society wanted. In the field of culture and state-controlled media, a broadly exercised freedom of expression allowed the pluralistic development of opinion and a certain *destape,* for some irritating, in form and substance. To the university and the state's scientific community returned the country's best intellectuals and scientists, whose marginalization had begun with the 1966 coup and Onganía's dictatorship. Though in many universities the changes were not great, in others, such as the public University of Buenos Aires, there was a profound transformation. These institutions, which had to resolve the problem posed by a massive desire on the part of the country's youth to attend university, were reconstructed on the basis of academic excellence and pluralism, sometimes attaining a quality comparable to that of their golden age at the beginning of the 1960s.

Besides returning to academic life, intellectuals entered the political arena, and politics became intellectualized. Intellectuals frequently appeared in the media. Alfonsín himself turned to them, as advisers or technocratic functionaries, and his discourse, which expressed in political terms the ideas that academics were elaborating, revealed itself to be modern, complex, and profound, in tune with what was expected of a world statesman. Alfonsín was not the only one—his best-known rival in this new political style was the Peronist, Antonio Cafiero—and political debate acquired a brilliance, and to lesser extent, a depth, it had not known for some time.

The high point of this cultural modernization was the passing of the law that authorized legal divorce—heretofore a taboo subject—and a subsequent law establishing joint shared custody of children and giving women equal rights in general with regard to their children. These laws completed the project to modernize family relations, an area in which Argentina was still visibly backward in relation to global trends. The divorce law was passed at the beginning of 1987, after a brief but intense debate. The most traditional sectors of the Catholic Church attempted to oppose it, not only with the customary methods of pressure, but even with demonstrations—complete with statue of the Virgin of Luján paraded in the streets. The opposition failed because of the high degree of existing consensus about the new law, even among Catholic sectors, who were perhaps concerned about the personal consequences of a practice that was already customary in their own circles. On the other hand, the Church mobilized with greater success on the issue of the Pedagogical Congress, paradoxically defending pluralism and freedom of choice against a supposed creeping state control over education.

The Church had stepped forward on behalf of democracy in 1981—albeit without undertaking a self-criticism of its intimate relationship with the military government—but was moving toward a growing hostility to the Radical government and a questioning of democracy itself. The Church was irritated by what it judged as Alfonsin's tepid support in the key area of private education, the sanctioning of the divorce law, and the general secular tone of the cultural discourse circulating in the public institutions and media. A change in the internal balance of power in the local episcopacy affected these developments, but most decisive was the general orientation stamped on the Catholic Church by the new pope, John Paul II, determined to battle for the unity of the Catholic community whose lifeblood was found precisely in cultural issues. This fight, taken up by the most conservative local bishops, led to rebuilding support among like-minded Catholic traditionalists who wished to join forces again. The Church's conflict with the Radical government gradually escalated, and in one particularly tense moment the president responded angrily in a synagogue to the political statements of a bishop who was also a military chaplain. The conservative sectors of the Church, which were gradually beginning to dominate it, assumed the role of social critic with a combative discourse: Democracy, they said, had turned out to be a compendium of all the century's evils—drugs, terrorism, abortion, and pornography.

The government's ethical discourse, based on the values of democracy, peace, human rights, international solidarity, and sovereignty of nations, was also placed in the service of reinserting the country into the international community that not long before had censured and even isolated the military regime. The black sheep became the prodigal son. The success obtained in this area, revealed by the great popularity the president achieved in different parts of the world, was used to secure and strengthen the still precarious local democratic institutions. From this perspective were addressed the principal pending questions in foreign policy, the dispute with Chile over the Beagle Channel, and the one with Great Britain over the Malvinas. In the first case, the papal arbitration decision that the military had considered unacceptable but had not dared to reject was accepted as the only possible solution by the government, which needed to reaffirm the values of peace and eliminate a source of tension that could keep militarism alive.

To overcome domestic opposition to approving the settlement—nourished by traditional nationalism and obstinate warmongering—a nonbinding plebiscite was called, and its outcome expressed a broad consensus for an immediate and pacific solution. Even so, the approval of the senate—where Peronism held the majority—was achieved by a small margin of votes. In the case of the Malvinas, ground was also recovered in an area where the military's blunders had lost the country a slowly won favorable international opinion on the questions of Argentine sovereignty over the islands and of constructive bilateral negotiations with the British. The United Nations votes urging both parties to negotiate were increasingly favorable to Argentina; they included the world's great powers and isolated the British government. Nevertheless, the expectation that this vote would persuade the British to negotiate on terms that in some way included the issue of sovereignty turned out to be totally unfounded.

In association with other countries that had just restored democracy—Uruguay, Brazil, and Peru—Argentina proposed to mediate in the conflict in Central America, especially in Nicaragua. Alfonsín sought to apply his government's ethical principles and general policies but also to avoid the domestic risks that might produce one of the final episodes of the Cold War. Disagreeing with the United States, but taking advantage of the latter's goodwill toward the recently restored democracies, the Alfonsín government finally managed to achieve a relatively reasonable solution. Acting with independence, maintaining a dialogue with the nonaligned countries, holding fast to principle but refraining from bitter confrontations—for example, the formation of a "debtors' club" to negotiate the foreign debt—the Argentine government maintained a good relationship with the United States, which resolutely supported democratic institutions. The United States cut ties with the nostalgic military leaders and supported various attempts to stabilize the economy.

Military and Trade-Union Clans

In the cultural realm and in foreign affairs, the Radical government made progress with relative ease. But the road became rockier when it had to face the two powerful corporative groups whose pact it had denounced in the electoral campaign: the military and the unions. On both fronts, it soon became clear that the government's power was insufficient to force both to accept the new rules of the game.

Most of society, which had begun by condemning the military for its failure in the war, learned in a stunning manner what it had preferred to ignore until then. The atrocities of the repression were revealed in an avalanche of lawsuits, in the media, and above all in the painstaking report compiled by the *Comisión Nacional sobre la Desaparición de Personas* (National Commission on the Disappeared, or CONADEP), established by the government and presided over by the writer Ernesto Sábato, whose final conclusions were widely distributed in the report titled *Nunca más* (Never again). The CONADEP report was absolutely incontrovertible, even for those who wished to defend the military. In society, there was some confusion, and certain ambiguities appeared. Was the military guilty of having gone to war over the Malvinas or simply of losing that war? Was it guilty for having tortured or simply for having tortured those who were innocent? But the overwhelming majority repudiated the military, mobilized, and demanded justice, a full and exhaustive inquiry, perhaps Argentina's own Nuremberg.

The defeat in the Malvinas War, the junta's resounding political failure, the division between the branches, internal dissent affecting the hierarchical organization of the armed forces—all these factors weakened the military, which nonetheless had not been expelled from power but had withdrawn on its own. As was often said at that time, in Argentina there had been no storming of the Bastille. The institutional solidarity of the military was soon reestablished around what it vindicated as its sole claim to success: the victory in the "war against subversion." The military rejected society's condemnation and reminded everyone that its actions had been undertaken with the country's general indulgence, including those politicians who now joined the chorus of detractors. At most, the military was willing to admit some "excesses" in what had been a "dirty war."

During the years of the Process, Alfonsín had been among the most active defenders of human rights and had made them one of his banners in the electoral campaign when he harshly criticized the military. He unquestionably shared the widespread desire for justice, but he was also concerned to find a way to subordinate the armed forces to civilian rule once and for all. For that purpose, he proposed some distinctions that were logical but difficult to accept for a now-mobilized society. Alfonsín thought it prudent to separate the trial of those guilty from a trial of the institution itself, which was and would continue to be part of the state. He wished to establish some limits to the trials, to distinguish between those who gave the orders that led to genocide, those who simply carried out orders, and those who exceeded them by committing aberrant crimes. Alfonsín attempted to concentrate punishment on the leadership and the most notorious perpetrators and to apply to the others the concept of "due obedience." Above all, the government trusted that the armed forces' leadership would commit itself to this proposition and would adopt an intermediate position between civilian demands and the predominant position among the military. Such trust assumed that the armed forces would criticize their own behavior and undertake their own purge, punishing the chief wrongdoers. For that purpose, the government proceeded to reform the Code of Military Justice, establishing a first military review to be followed by a civilian one, and ordered the prosecution of the first three military juntas, to which were added the leadership of the armed organizations, the *Ejército Revolucionario del Pueblo* (ERP, now defunct), and the *Montoneros*.

Alfonsín's first setback occurred when it became apparent that the military would not reexamine its actions and judge its commanders. At the end of 1984 when the first rumblings in the barracks were felt, the military tribunals proclaimed the actions of the juntas appropriate, at which point the president passed the cases to the civil courts. In April 1985, in an even tenser climate, the public trial of the commanders began. The trial, which lasted until the end of the year, ultimately revealed the atrocities committed by the military, but it also demonstrated a certain loss of enthusiasm on the part of the citizenry at large, at the same time that human rights organizations were making their increasingly critical and intransigent voices heard. Other voices also began to be heard as well, voices that had prudently kept quiet until then; these defended the military and demanded an amnesty. In late 1985, shortly after the government had won in the congressional elections, the court made its ruling known; it found the ex-commanders guilty and denied that there had been a war that justified their actions. The court also assigned individual responsibility to each commander and ordered that legal action continue against others responsible for crimes. The court condemned the aberrant behavior of the military commanders of the Process, dismissed any justification for such conduct, and subjected the military to civilian law—an absolutely exceptional circumstance—and in all these senses the ruling had been exemplary. Yet the ruling did not resolve the pending problem of the conflict between society and the military; it only brought it out into the open.

From this point on and increasingly so, the judicial system was active, dealing with multiple accusations against officers of different ranks, summoning them to court, and citing them for trial. The internal convulsion in the armed forces, especially in the army, had a new focal point. Now the focus was no longer so much on the institution but rather on the particular situation of those summoned to trial by the judges, lower-ranking officers who did not consider themselves responsible but simply carried out orders. The government, for its part, initiated a long and debilitating attempt to rein in and limit judicial action; it hoped thereby to contain the climate of unrest fermenting in the barracks, fed by an institutional solidarity that transcended its hierarchical structure. Alfonsín's was a political decision, based on neither ethical principles nor the law, but rather on a calculation about the balance of forces; his calculation turned out to be cautious as represented in the subsequent legislation, the so-called End Point and Due Obedience laws. The first, passed in late 1985, established a time limit of two months on suits against the military, after which a statute of limitations applied and no further judicial action was possible. No one outside Alfonsín's own party supported the government in passing this law. The right, both Peronist and liberal, supported a complete amnesty. The left, including Peronism's so-called renewal wing (*renovador*), refused to support the law to avoid its political costs as an apparent capitulation to the military. Such political costs were indeed high, and the law was counterproductive; it accomplished only a flood of subpoenas and lawsuits. Instead of alleviating the problem, it worsened it.

In this context, a military uprising took place during the 1987 Holy Week. A group of officers headed by Colonel Aldo Rico barricaded itself in the Campo de Mayo military base outside Buenos Aires and demanded a political solution to the question of the trials and a reconsideration of the army's conduct, in its opinion unfairly condemned. This uprising was not typical. The seditious officers did not question the constitutional order but rather asked the government to solve the problem of a group of select officers. Unlike all previous uprisings, the officers did not have the backing of sectors of civil society, normally the instigators of the coups d'état in the past. On the other hand, the mutineers questioned, with vehemence, the very leadership of the army. They excoriated the generals who discharged their responsibility in the dirty war on their subordinates, the leaders who were responsible for the defeat in the Malvinas, and the "sellout" of the country to foreign interests. The mutineers embraced the slogans of a fascistic nationalism and adopted tactics truly subversive of the military as an institution; they mobilized low-ranking officers and proclaimed themselves the leadership of the authentic "patriotic" army.

The response of civil society was unanimous and decisive. All the political parties and all of society's organizations—from those representing business to the unions to cultural associations and civilian organizations of all kinds—actively demonstrated their support of democracy. Everyone from business leaders to leftist political figures signed a Manifesto of Democratic Commitment and rallied around the government. The massive and immediate response made it possible to avoid desertions or ambiguity and cut off any possibility of civilian support for the mutineers. The citizenry mobilized, filled the country's public plazas, and maintained vigilance for the four days that the uprising lasted. Many were prepared to march on the Camp de Mayo itself. The enthusiasm in the civilian sector—which greatly supported the government—was enormous and prevented a direct attack on democratic institutions. Popular reaction was not, however, enough to force the military to submit to civil society. Though the rebellion won few adherents in the military, at heart they all agreed with their so-called *carapintada* comrades, the name given to this group because of the camouflage paint they smeared on their faces. None of the military was prepared to fire a shot to force the group to surrender.

Many negotiations occurred during four tense days, but none bore fruit until Alfonsín—who was presiding over a great civilian demonstration in the Plaza de Mayo—spoke with the mutineers in the Campo de Mayo. A strange agreement was reached. The government pledged that it would do what it had already decided to do—namely, support the Law of Dutiful Obedience, which exonerated en masse the subordinates in the dirty war—and the mutineers imposed no conditions and accepted responsibility for the uprising. But it appeared to everyone that the government had capitulated, in part because it was thus portrayed both by the mutinous *carapintadas* and the political opposition, which did not wish to assume any responsibility for the agreement. The most apparent reaction, however, was widespread disenchantment, evidence of the end of the democratic fantasy. Civilians could not force the military to yield. The failure of the attempt to resolve the army's confrontation with society in a dignified manner was the beginning of a long and debilitating series of disasters for the government.

In comparison, the battle with the unions, which had similar results, was much less dramatic. The power of the union leaders, partly restored when the military government ended, was weakened by the electoral defeat of the Peronists—among whose leadership the union leaders carried great weight. Society's repudiation of the old practices of the labor movement, which had come to the surface during the electoral campaign, also weakened the leaders' power. In addition, a deep division existed among the union leadership, and their position was institutionally precarious. Much legislation that established the rules of union behavior had been swept away by the military regime. Many unions had been interdicted, and in others the leaders had only provisional authority or had had terms extended since 1975 and so enjoyed little rank-and-file support. New union elections were supposed to be held immediately.

The government proposed to take advantage of this relative weakness, as well as the support of civil society that, so it believed, included sizable numbers of rank-and-file workers whose interest in participating in union affairs had been clearly demonstrated. The government thus threw itself into democratizing the unions, opening them up to a broad spectrum of political opinion. The labor minister, Antonio José Mucci—a veteran union leader with a Socialist background—drafted a law establishing "institutional normalization" for the unions, including secret, direct, and obligatory voting in union elections, representation for minority slates, term limits on union positions, and especially state overseeing of union elections. In this frontal assault against the Peronist trade-union leadership, all the currents of Peronism—trade union and political—united. In March 1984, the chamber of deputies passed a labor reform law, but the senate vetoed it by one decisive vote. The government immediately raised the white flag, appointed more flexible emissaries to represent it in negotiations with the union leaders, and reached an agreement on new procedures for union elections. By mid-1985, the legal status of the executive bodies of the unions had been normalized. Though opposition slates had won in a few places, by and large the established leaders were reelected.

The civilian and democratic advance had experienced an early and serious setback when confronting reconstituted trade-union power, supported by growing economic problems. Between 1984 and 1988, at which point labor decided to concentrate its efforts on the upcoming 1989 presidential elections, the General Confederation of Labor (CGT) organized thirteen general strikes against the government, a figure that contrasted with its few mobilizations during the previous military regime. Except for a brief period after June 1985 when Alfonsín obtained important support from society for his economic program, a support reaffirmed in the government's strong showing in the 1986 congressional elections, the CGT's pressure was intense. The undoubted social tensions generated by inflation—leading to a constant struggle to maintain real incomes—added to the union pressure, as did the first austerity measures in the state sector. These austerity measures especially mobilized public employees, though their mobilizations were predominantly of a political nature. The union leaders expressed their discontent with a united voice, integrated into their opposition the nonunionized sectors such as retired people, and also formed alliances with business, the Church, and some leftist groups. Their demands were hardly compatible—they ranged from the more liberal aspirations of the economic establishment to calls for a rupture with the International Monetary Fund (IMF)—but they were united in a common attack against the government, and in a moment of rashness, they demanded that the government "exit from power."

The CGT did not refuse to participate in the government's requests for coordination, but it participated in the style that it had displayed between 1955 and 1973: It hit hard and then negotiated, engaged in talks and then abandoned negotiations in a huff, thus galvanizing its own forces that in other ways showed deep divisions. Saúl Ubaldini, the leader of the small brewery workers' union and secretary general of the CGT, was the characteristic figure in these years, not only because of his peculiar style that allowed him to seal alliances between organized workers and poor people, but above all because the slight power of his own union made him a point of equilibrium between the different sectors into which the labor movement was divided.

The government, which was constantly undertaking initiatives to promote dialogue and agreement without opening up the basic outlines of its economic policy for discussion, was well able to resist the strong unions' attacks, despite the difficulties these presented for stabilizing the economy. The consistent support of civil society and the weak pressure of other corporative groups aided the government's position. The emergence of different opposition fronts, especially the military, compelled the government to adopt a more audacious stratagem: It established an agreement with an important group of unions—the so-called fifteen, which included the most powerful private- and public-sector unions—and named one of the group's leaders to the post of minister of labor.

From the unions' point of view, the reasons for participating in the government were obvious, almost insultingly so; they included passing the collection of laws that ruled trade-union activity—rights to legal status, collective bargaining procedures, rules about union control of social service programs—in terms similar to those established in 1975. In exchange for these important concessions, the government, which sacrificed long-standing objectives, obtained little in return—only a relative social truce, because the trade-union opposition remained totally divided, and a promise of future political support that never really materialized. More substantively, the labor movement's support of the government against the military uprising should be considered as part of the union agreement. After the Peronist victory in the 1987 election, the government dispensed with its minister-union leader, but adhered to the agreed-on terms. With the new legislation, union power was fully reestablished, and civil society's illusion of subordinating it to democratic rules vanished.

The Austral Plan

The strategy followed with regard to trade-union power had initially been one of confrontation, dismissing any possibility of finding a compromise with the labor movement for solutions to the economic crisis. In truth, although at first the economic problems seemed much less urgent than the political ones, they were extremely serious. Inflation, rampant since the middle of 1982, had become structural, and all of society's actors, even those who had to defend modest incomes, had incorporated into their practices the assumption of uncertainty and speculation. Together with the fiscal deficit and the continually growing foreign debt, this behavior constituted the most visible sign of the economic problems. These problems were particularly severe in an economy that had been stagnant since the beginning of the decade and that was protected, inefficient, and highly vulnerable to external factors. In such an atmosphere, few businesspeople were willing to take risks and bet on economic growth, and the most concentrated economic groups, which had absorbed all of society's resources through the state, could block any government attempts to modify their situation.

Despite the fact that capital flows to the country had ceased since 1981, the foreign debt continued to grow, partly because of accumulating interest, to the point that by the end of the decade the debt had more than doubled its 1981 value. In 1982, the state had assumed responsibility for the private debt and thus was burdened with paying the debt service that absorbed a good part of its revenue. Although the debt was constantly being refinanced, the government had to depend on the goodwill of the IMF, which demanded policies designed principally to institute immediate payment of the interest in return for loans. The state thus faced a growing deficit that could also be partly traced—as its liberal critics affirmed—to the expansion of social services in times of economic bonanza. Finally, the recent spectacular drop in tax collection added to the burden of foreign debt repayment, as did the multitude of subsidies received by business sectors tied to the state in a parasitic fashion. This welter of obligations had to be met with revenue that had declined, eaten away by inflation, tax evasion, and no external or internal credit—with people converting their savings into dollars—and without great pockets of accumulated reserves from which to finance the debt. In the past, foreign trade or the retirement pension program, periodically raided by governments to cover their expenses, had provided such reserves. The problem, which immediately resulted in a permanent inflation that distorted the workings of the economy, ultimately affected the state's ability to manage the economy and to govern society effectively.

If in hindsight the need to find deep solutions for the economy seems evident, at the time it seemed necessary to subordinate such concerns to the need of reconstructing a weak democratic system and an even weaker state. The new government, and many of those who supported it, believed it essential not to create divisions in civil society, the source of the state's greatest support, and to spare the population at large the costs of deep reform. The necessity for such reform, on the other hand, did not seem apparent, above all if one of the chosen paths to achieve it came into conflict with deeply rooted traditions about the state's obligations and functions. Moreover, if these reforms were to have a democratic, equitable, and fair character, they would be viable only with a strong and popularly supported state power.

During the first year of the Radical government, the economic policy, overseen by the minister of the economy Bernardo Grinspun, was in the tradition of a classic *dirgiste* state and was redistributive like the policies applied between 1963 and 1966, which in its basic outlines Radicalism had supported as much as Peronism. The improvement in workers' earnings, together with easy credit to small businesses, served to reactivate the domestic market and to mobilize idle capacity into production. These policies included close state control of credit, exchange rates, and prices; they were complemented by important social welfare initiatives such as the *Programa Alimentario Nacional* (National Nutritional Program or PAN), which provided basic food necessities to low-income groups. Not only did the government intend to improve the situation of the middle and working classes and poor people by means of all these programs, but it also hoped to satisfy the demands for justice and social equality that had been the banners of the electoral campaign. Such a policy incited the active opposition of diverse business sectors, which brandished the free-market slogans against what they called populism and state interventionism. It also elicited the opposition of the CGT, in its case largely for political reasons, which brought failure to the attempts at compromise that formed part of the government's strategy.

The government was forced to confront simultaneously a pincer move by powerful corporative groups—united for the attack—and a tug-of-war in society unleashed over the distribution of income, a struggle worsened by high inflation. It became apparent that government policy did not take into account the radical transformation in the economy after 1975: the decline in production, the economy's incapacity to react efficiently to increased demand, and the size of the deficit and the foreign debt. With respect to the debt, the government oscillated between two courses of action, both of which reflected the spirit of the moment's democratic fervor but each of which proved equally unworkable. On the one hand, the government sought to gain the good graces of creditors by arguing that young democracies should be protected; on the other hand, it threatened creditors with the formation of a Latin American "debtors club" that would repudiate the debt entirely.

At the beginning of 1985 as inflation threatened to become hyperinflation, social conflict worsened, and foreign creditors began energetically making their displeasure felt, Alfonsín replaced his minister of the economy Grinspun with Juan Sourrouille, a technocrat who had recently drawn near the Radical Party. Sourrouille remained Alfonsín's minister almost to the end of his government. Sourrouille spent nearly four months formulating his economic program, a difficult time for the government because in addition to the economic crisis, the CGT mobilized under its new *plan de lucha,* diverse business sectors protested through their political spokespersons, particularly Alsogaray and the ex-president Frondizi, and above all there was military unrest on the eve of the onset of the juntas trial. In late April when civilians were called to the Plaza de Mayo to defend the government and to thwart a possible coup d'état, they heard an announcement of the declaration of a "war economy" that nullified the recent attempts at compromise. Finally, on May 14, 1985, the new economic program was announced, baptized the Austral Plan.

The program's objective was to surmount the adverse circumstances of the moment and stabilize the economy in the short term, to create the conditions necessary to plan deeper structural changes, in pursuit of reform and growth. Some unannounced transformations included discouraging the speculative behavior stimulated by inflation and motivating the economic actors to engage in activities that encouraged productive investment and growth. Most urgent was the need to stop inflation. The government simultaneously froze prices, wages, and public utility rates; fixed foreign exchange and interest rates; eliminated the practice of monetary emission to balance the fiscal deficit—which implied assuming a rigid discipline about revenue and spending; and put an end to the policy of wage indexing developed during the previous bout of high inflation. This last practice had greatly contributed to perpetuating an inflationary culture. As a symbol of the beginning of a new era, the national currency was changed, and the peso was replaced by the austral.

The brainchild of a team of highly qualified economists without links to either the Radical Party or any big interest groups, the program hinged strictly on the government's backing, now of questionable worth, and on the plan's ability to win support in society at large. The Austral Plan quickly managed to halt inflation and thus win such support, largely because the program did not adversely affect any specific sector of society. There was no decline in economic activity and no increase in unemployment, traditionally hallmarks of stabilization plans, but neither did the plan affect the business sectors, including those that prospered in their relationship with the state and whose contracts were generally respected. Fiscal restraint had a perceptible but not dramatic effect. The wages of state employees were frozen more stringently than were the wages of those in the private sector, but there were no layoffs. Government revenue increased as a result of the sharp reduction in inflation, but there were no drastic cuts in state spending. The country's foreign creditors felt tranquil as much because of the government's demonstrated intention to fulfill its commitments as because of the prospect of an improvement in state finances and especially because of the program's firm support by the U.S. government and by the principal international economic institutions.

The Austral Plan, "the plan for everyone," was perhaps the purest expression of the democratic illusion. It was visible proof of the belief that the most complex problems could be solved in solidarity and without suffering, even problems entailing deep conflicts of interests. Alfonsín was rewarded in the November 1985 congressional elections. Barely six months after the country had been teetering on the brink of chaos, the government won a clear electoral victory that signaled the general support of civil society for the economic program. For the first time, however, economic issues had weighed heaviest in the population's concerns, and thus successes and failures would be judged according to accomplishments in the economy.

Tranquillity was short lived. By the end of 1985, the incipient return of inflation was apparent, and the government was forced to acknowledge this fact in April 1986 with public "recognition" of the problem and partial austerity measures. Growing problems abroad were partially responsible for this situation—the collapse of international grain prices caused by political decisions in the United States, which affected the incomes of both state and rural producers. In addition, there was none of the social discipline that the plan, sensitive to any attempt to modify relative prices, required. The old tug-of-war dynamic between the corporative groups over scarce resources was reborn, rekindling inflation. The CGT, decked out with its anti-wage-freeze banner—a wage freeze that especially affected state employees—and business, led by rural producers, mobilized against the price freeze. Curiously, their interests coincided in a common protest against the state.

This rapid reappearance of old problems indicated that when everything was said and done, nothing had changed much. Although the plan had been effective in achieving a quick stability, the government did not envision a thorough structural change but instead attempted to carry out the plan through measures that would be painless and conflict free. Rather than painful measures, it tried to revive foreign investment, especially in the oil industry—with President Alfonsín announcing his new energy plan in Houston, capital of the great international oil companies—and plans were also drawn for a deeper fiscal reform, privatization of state companies, and deregulation of the economy. All these plans clashed with ideas and attitudes that were firmly rooted in society, both in Peronism and in the governing party in which only certain factions accepted these initiatives. Unlike the Austral Plan, any of these initiatives would have meant coming into conflict with some of the strong established interest groups or burdening the bulk of society with the cost of the reforms. As the need to undertake more in-depth solutions became clearer, the Radical government was discovering that its base of support was more tenuous than was thought.

Perhaps for that reason at the beginning of 1987, when social tensions were rising, the government decided to turn to the big interest groups that it had at first criticized and attacked. At a time that a trade-union leader backed by a group of the most powerful unions took charge of the labor ministry, a group of managers from the major firms holding state contracts was called to direct the public companies, and a Radical politician with a long history of activism in agricultural lobbying associations was named minister of agriculture. The dream of getting control over the corporative groups began to be abandoned; the period of the illusion of the supremacy of the public interest was coming to an end; and private interests again predominated, among them, naturally, those of the most powerful. The benefits and liabilities of the new program offset each other. Although social peace was achieved, the various interest groups stonewalled policies that might affect them. Business and union leaders ceased to be in agreement, especially when the union heads gained the sanction of labor legislation that ended expectations of achieving flexible wage and collective bargaining procedures. On the other hand, when in April 1987 the military challenged the civilian government, it found no support in society for the first time since 1930. In a certain sense, democratic institutions had been saved at the cost of democratic economic reform.

In July 1987, the government began to implement a new reform program that counted on the endorsement of the principal international organizations—particularly the World Bank, whose policies began to distance themselves from those of the IMF—and sought to reconcile the need for state reform with the interests of big business. A deeper and harsher tax reform was supposed to be accompanied by a policy of privatizing state companies and a drastic reduction in state spending. But this attempt was stillborn, without the political strength capable of sustaining it, especially after the government's defeat in the September 1987 congressional elections. In November, the union leaders abandoned the cabinet. The business sector was divided among factions with incompatible interests and could not propose a common course of action, which added to the conflicts between labor and business. Above all, Peronism looked with renewed optimism at the 1989 presidential elections and refused to back reforms with such apparent social costs. Thus, the planned reconciliation with the corporative powers, which led to a sharp deterioration of the Radical government's image in civil society, failed to produce the anticipated results in the economy, where instability and the sensation of a lack of control were growing.

The Appeal to Civil Society

Initially, the Radical government had merely been tolerated by powerful corporative groups—strictly speaking, the Peronist candidate would have more thoroughly satisfied the interests of such institutions as the armed forces and the Church—and thus had to take refuge in its political power. Its support there was also limited, particularly in the congress. The Radical majority in the chamber of deputies until 1987 was counterbalanced by the Peronists' relative majority in the senate, where a group of representatives from small provincial parties played the advantageous role of occasional arbiters. Thus, the two biggest parties in the congress—the institutional heart of the democratic system—had the ability to veto each other. Because there were no prior agreements about how the political process would be conducted in the long term, it was difficult to reach such agreements when each party sought to play its role effectively as governing party and opposition.

This situation presented a problem for the government, which needed strong institutional support to resolve the economic crisis and to create those very democratic institutions. The government often faced the option of governing effectively, imposing its agenda but putting pressure on political institutions, or trying to reconcile different opinions and reach agreements that, at the cost of circumventing problems and discarding options, might strengthen democracy. Torn between two different political strategies, the Radical government adopted a middle-of-the-road approach between both alternatives for as long as possible.

The government's greatest support came from the ranks of Radicalism and the broad spectrum of civil society that had either directly or indirectly supported it. This sector was a much less stable political actor than the Radical Party, but it initially had a great deal of power because of the peculiar circumstances of the crisis of the previous military regime. The UCR had traditionally been the great civilian party with the longest history and the present capability to organize and galvanize the citizenry. It was a complex and fragmented party with diverse tendencies and multiple interests, often of a regional or local nature, making it a great mosaic that was difficult to unify.

Since 1983, Raúl Alfonsín had exercised strong leadership, able to capitalize in the party on the great support that he had won among the citizenry. Alfonsín's faction, the Movement of Renovation and Change—which he founded in 1972 when he first challenged the leadership of Ricardo Balbín—was little more than a network of personal alliances, simultaneously effective and inconsistent when it was no longer a matter of winning internal elections but of proposing to society a great new course of action. What was most noteworthy was the behavior of a group of young leaders, most of whom had backgrounds in student activism; this group made up the party's National Coordinating Committee, called simply the *Coordinadora*. This group appeared on the scene for the first time in 1968; its ideas and actions harked back to much of the experience that culminated in 1975: the confluence of socialist and anti-imperialist traditions, the sense of partisan militancy and party organization, and the faith in the mobilization of the masses.

In 1982, fully engaged in party life behind Alfonsín's leadership, the group contributed some ideological elements to his discourse, but stood out primarily in its organizational and mobilization abilities in relation to civil society. The group also contributed an effective cadre to Radicalism, both for electoral purposes and for the country's administration; in both areas, it distinguished itself for its discipline, efficiency, and pragmatism in the difficult art of weaving alliances and in implementing policies linked to the content of the original Radical program only in broad outlines. The *Coordinadora* won a great deal of power but provoked resistance in the UCR. Such resistance occurred in the context of party rivalry in which unity, difficult to achieve and always precarious, could be maintained only thanks to Alfonsín's strong and charismatic leadership of both the nation and the party.

The pact between Alfonsín and civil society was sealed in the historic 1983 electoral campaign, during great public rallies and in the common faith in democracy as a panacea. Conscious that his greatest political capital was to be found in society, Alfonsín continued using a mobilization strategy, convoking the people in the Plaza de Mayo or using referendums to resolve difficult situations, such as the senate's resistance to approving the Beagle Channel treaty or the welter of threats hovering over the government on the eve on the Austral Plan. But above all, he worked tirelessly to educate the public about fashioning civil society into a mature and responsible political actor. For street mobilizations—a political style whose origins could be traced to the dramatic period ten years previously—the *Coordinadora* was invaluable, but for the task of civic education, Alfonsín needed the support of an important group of intellectuals, called on to advise him in diverse situations. This group supplied him with ideas that were reworked and disseminated with singular skill by a leader who was convinced that the only legitimate government was one based on society's consent arrived at through reason.

Alfonsín laid out the big issues and established the great goals. The struggle against authoritarianism and for democratization occupied the first phase of the government. But from the Austral Plan onward, particularly following the electoral triumph of November 1985, Alfonsín's discourse dealt more with issues surrounding the democratic pact, participation, and consensus, and toward the new goal of modernization, a concept that included everything from modernizing institutional structures to the workings of the economy. Questions of reforming the state, market reforms, and deregulation were formulated in the context of democracy, equality, and the ethic of solidarity. Such issues manifested themselves in a series of concrete reforms that were successively presented: state reform, plans to move the capital from Buenos Aires to Viedma in the south, constitutional reform, none of which was accomplished but which kept public debate alive. Underlying all these issues was a common concern: the convergence of different political traditions behind a common democratic and modernizing project. There was also a shared temptation: the articulation of these traditions in a political movement that would synthesize such concerns and that, with Yrigoyenism and Peronism as its points of reference, would begin to constitute the third great popular movement.

This idea, which was never explicitly put forward, caused the structure of the governing party to creak, especially after four decades that Radicalism spent combating a political culture in which the popular will was expressed through social movements rather than through democratic institutions. This approach had characterized the behavior of everyone from Frondizi to Perón, from unions to business groups. The appeal to mobilization of the citizenry, combined with strong presidential action, especially raised doubts about this process's compatibility with the process of democratic institutionalization. Given the balance of forces in and outside the government, Radicalism was often forced to choose between strictly adhering to democratic norms—which in many cases would have led to compromises that implied renouncing pragmatic objectives—or combining support of a plebiscitary nature with the broad powers of presidential authority that the norms and precedents provided. In that way, the government could pressure congress from the streets, ignore it altogether, or perhaps influence the judicial system. In various cases, Alfonsín's government moved in that direction. But his solid ethical convictions quickly caused him to stop, and with it, Alfonsín exercised a moderating influence on a political power that, contravening Machiavelli's maxim, he refused to convert into a guiding maxim.

The government's fragile bases of support were found in the contradictions of the citizenry that had awarded him the presidency. The limitations of this support resided in the loyalty to the initial democratic pact, built around the principle of the common good, but soon undermined by a number of factors: the resurgence of sectoral interests, the priority of addressing new problems not initially contemplated, such as those in the economy; and the emergence of new political alternatives, which deprived the government of the discursive initiative. These alternatives emerged from both the left and the right but above all from a reformed Peronism.

A heterogeneous collection of forces coming from the left and the 1973 experience coalesced around the Intransigent Party (PI), with a program that occupied the same ground as Alfonsín's—the defense of human rights, the vindication of popular sovereignty and democracy—though it added nationalist and anti-imperialist slogans, invoked especially on the issue of the foreign debt. Initially, the forces compelling the PI aspired, in a manner already familiar among the left, to capitalize on the predicted disintegration of Peronism, but then it devoted itself to calling attention to the government's unfaithfulness to the original program. The PI also aimed to radicalize the human rights slogans at the same time that its anti-imperialism allowed it to find common ground with those sectors of the labor movement that raised the banners of repudiating the foreign debt. Nevertheless, the party did not manage to establish a viable alternative, and the PI disintegrated and was absorbed by a reformed Peronism.

On the right, also trying to take advantage of the two-party system that had emerged in 1983, was the Union of the Democratic Center (UCD), founded by Alvaro Alsogaray, the veteran mentor of free-market ideas. Those ideas, in the context of the crises in the Soviet bloc and the welfare state, enjoyed great prestige in the world and were translated in Argentina in a new and attractive way by a party that found in the context of democracy the formula for popularity, particularly among the young. Its electoral success was relative, and it never managed to gain a following outside the federal capital, though it did have legitimate aspirations of becoming the third party that would arbitrate between the Radicals and the Peronists. Its ideological success was much more decisive, especially to the degree that the economic crisis highlighted the need for profound solutions. Liberalism might not have had such solutions, but it did nonetheless possess simple and attractive recipes, along with a sharp ability for pointing out the ills of state interventionism. Liberalism thereby competed successfully with Alfonsin in the tutelage of civil society and even recruited followers in the governing party itself.

By attempting to compete with the government for support in public opinion, the parties and institutions, the left and the right—with the exception of some small extremist groups—all contributed to strengthening democratic institutions. Something similar occurred with Peronism after an initial period of vacillation. Immediately following the 1983 elections, in the midst of great consternation and deep divisions, those who predominated in Peronism—led by the archetypal political boss from Avellaneda, Herminio Iglesias—attempted to combat the government from the old right-wing nationalist positions and encouraged an alliance between Peronist politicians and trade-union leaders, the military, and those, such as the ex-president Frondizi, who had been converted into the military's spokespersons. In this context, the Peronists opposed the treaty with Chile and were thoroughly defeated in the plebiscite.

But an alternative tendency was gradually taking shape in Peronism—the so-called *renovador* (renewal) movement, which clashed bitterly with the established leadership. In fact, in 1985, the Peronist representatives in the chamber of deputies split into two opposing blocs, with the reformist faction gaining control of the party by the end of the year. This *renovador* Peronism—whose principal figures were Antonio Cafiero, Carlos Grosso, José Manuel de la Sota, and the governor of La Rioja province, Carlos Menem—proposed to adapt Peronism to the new democratic context, to insert into the movement the discourse of democracy while combining it with the traditional social demands championed by Peronism. The *renovadores* sought to compete from the left with the government, whom it supported even on such issues as the plebiscite on the Beagle Channel dispute. When the Holy Week military crisis of 1987 erupted, the behavior of the *renovador* leadership was exemplary. It demonstrated total solidarity with democratic institutions and offered the government unconditional support. The *renovadores* not only inserted Peronism into the democratic game, but they seemed to have finally created the conditions to make democracy viable: the possibility of alternating power between two competing parties.

The End of the Illusion

The year 1987 was decisive for Alfonsín's government. The Holy Week military uprising represented the culmination of civil society's participation in his government, the high point of tension, and at the same time proof of the government's limited ability to thwart a factor of power that was also in a state of tension. In Easter 1987, the illusion of democracy's limitless power came to a definitive end. Already embarked in negotiations with different corporative groups that had survived the democratic onslaught—the military, business, and the unions—Alfonsín lost his exclusive claim to leadership of civil society. Although competitors on both the right and the left reaped some benefits, the greatest gains went to the reformed Peronism. In a climate of increasing economic deterioration and growing inflation, the September 1987 elections gave a clearly important if not categorical victory to the Peronists. Radicalism lost its majority in the chamber of deputies and lost control of all the provincial governments, with the exception of Córdoba and Río Negro, the only places, along with the federal capital, where the Radicals prevailed.

The government was stung by the impact of a defeat that questioned its very legitimacy and ability to govern. From that point until it handed over the government in July 1989 to its successor, the administration's difficulties grew and culminated in disaster. The new economic program launched in July and completed in October gave the government a momentary respite, particularly because the Peronist opposition agreed to share responsibility in passing the new taxes necessary to balance state spending. But because the Peronists did not support any deep transformations, such as the privatization of public companies, the government's new orientation lacked credibility. The signs of the crisis—high inflation, inability to meet payments on the debt—soon reappeared. In the Radical Party itself, voices were raised in disagreement with the leadership of Alfonsín. Alfonsín quickly proposed as the candidate for the 1989 presidential elections the governor of Córdoba, Eduardo Angeloz, a figure closely associated with the Radicalism's more traditional sectors and someone scarcely identified with Alfonsín's current in the party.

The military, whose question was left unresolved with the April 1987 uprising, experienced two new rebellions, in part because the officers' situation was unresolved, but above all because hard-liners in the armed forces were prepared to take advantage of the government's weakness. In January 1988, Colonel Aldo Rico, the leader of the 1987 rebellion, escaped from prison and organized another military rebellion, this time by a distant regiment in the Northeast. In contrast to the previous year, civilian mobilization was minimal, though military support for the revolt also proved weak. Rico was pursued by the army, and after a brief combat, he surrendered and was imprisoned.

In late 1988, there was a new uprising, headed this time by Colonel Mohamed Seineldín who, like Rico, belonged to a select group, the so-called heroes of the Malvinas; people saw him as the chief of the *carapintadas.* Seineldín led a regiment in a revolt on the very outskirts of the federal capital and demanded a broad amnesty and exoneration of the military's actions in the dirty war. As in the Holy Week uprising, the bulk of the army and probably important sectors of the other service branches shared his ideas, refused to repress the mutineers, and even embraced their program. Also as in the Holy Week episode, despite the fact that the rebels were eventually imprisoned, the final result was ambiguous. From the government's point of view, it was clear that it had not succeeded in instilling solid democratic convictions in either the citizenry—which it found too willing to capitulate—or the officers, whose demands went beyond a "broad amnesty" to include a pardon for those already tried and found guilty as well as exoneration in the antisubversive campaign. The project of reconciling civil society and the armed forces had clearly failed. Society felt total aversion for the concerns of the *carapintadas,* and even those who had traditionally favored the military repudiated its seditious behavior and fascistic nationalism. The military, for its part, entrenched itself in its institutional claims and combined its demand for rehabilitation with new complaints over salaries, demonstrating how the crisis of the state had also reached the armed forces.

In January 1989, a left-wing terrorist group, small in numbers, poorly armed, isolated, and anachronistic, assaulted the *La Tablada* military barracks on the outskirts of Buenos Aires, and the army used this occasion to undertake a crushing demonstration of force that culminated in the deaths of the attackers. The recognition that the army was awarded for the action was the first indication of a change in the public's priorities and values. Some feared that the pending military question might now be solved with a vindication of the armed forces, that the crimes of the "dirty war" would be forgotten, and civil society's illusions buried. It fell to Alfonsín's successor in the government to take the fateful step of granting amnesty to those commanders who had already been sentenced.

Neither was the political question satisfactorily resolved in favor of a democratic citizenry. After the September 1987 congressional elections, Antonio Cafiero, governor of Buenos Aires province, president of the Justicialist Party, and leader of Peronism's *renovador* faction, gained stature and emerged as a possible presidential candidate for his party and therefore Alfonsín's likely successor. In many respects, Cafiero and the *renovadores* had refashioned Peronism in the same image as that of *alfonsinismo:* a scrupulous respect for republican institutions, modern and democratic initiatives elaborated by intellectuals independent of the great interest groups, and establishment of minimum guarantees with the government to ensure the orderly transition from one administration to another.

Perhaps this program hurt Cafiero when faced with the rival candidacy in Peronism of the governor of La Rioja, Carlos Menem, a figure drawn from the ranks of the *renovadores* but one who cultivated a more traditional political style. Menem demonstrated a notable capacity for gathering around him all of Peronism's many parts, from the trade-union leaders spurned by Cafiero to members of the extreme right to former 1970s leftist militants, together with local political bosses, the very ones who had been displaced by the *renovadores*. His was an "antielite" group that offended the sensibility of the democratic citizenry. With this heterogeneous support, and exploiting his image as a traditional caudillo, different from those of his modernizing rivals, and relying more on style than on programmatic positions, he won Peronism's party convention and in July 1988 became its presidential candidate. In private, he wove tight alliances with the influential sectors: important businessmen such as those of the Bunge y Born conglomerate, Church leaders, high-ranking military officers, including the *carapintadas*. Publicly, he appealed to the vast contingents of the "downtrodden," whom he addressed with an almost messianic discourse delivered with a theatrical display that made him appear like a holy savior. Menem promised a "productive revolution" and "great wage hikes" (*salariazo*) and foretold entry to the promised land. If this wishful thinking made him an heir to Alfonsín, everything else set him apart; he bore witness to the reality of a different society, dominated by misery and marginality, in which such a discourse proved effective. In short, no one knew exactly what the Peronist candidate would do if he were elected, but he would clearly be pragmatic and pay little heed to programmatic promises.

Angeloz, his competitor, criticized Menem, exploited the fear that Menem provoked in many, though Angeloz also tried to capture that part of the electorate that criticized the more progressive policies of Alfonsín. For that purpose, he emphasized aspects of his platform that were closer to liberal positions; whereas Menem promised to return to the paradise of the welfare state, Angeloz foresaw a reduction in state beneficence, represented symbolically by the red pencil that would cross all unnecessary spending out of the budget, which he brandished as part of his campaign imagery.

With such alternatives, the opposition candidate almost inevitably triumphed, in accordance with a dynamic characteristic of established democracies, in which the costs of society's difficulties are paid by the governing party. But a missing ingredient transformed a possibly orderly transition into chaos. In August 1988, the government launched a new economic plan named the Spring Plan, for purposes of arriving at the elections with inflation under control, but without causing hardships that might alienate the population and adversely affect the UCR's electoral prospects. To the freeze on prices, salaries, and public service rates—accepted begrudgingly by business's representatives—was added the declared intention to reduce drastically the government deficit, the necessary precondition for acquiring the indispensable support of foreign creditors, who were now much more reluctant to offer such support than before.

Launched in different political conditions compared with those of 1985, the new economic plan encountered difficulties from the start. There was little inclination on the part of the various sectors of society to uphold the price freeze; the cuts in public spending were resisted, and negotiation with the principal foreign creditors progressed very slowly, with the promised funds arriving in dribs and drabs. On the other hand, speculative capital did arrive, to take advantage of the differential between high interest rates and fixed exchange rates, but such capital was prepared to abandon the country once there was a threat of devaluation. In this explosive situation, safety rested exclusively on confidence in the government's ability to maintain the exchange rate parity. In September 1988, the Seineldín uprising occurred, to be followed by a severe crisis in the supply of electric power and, shortly later, by the attack on the *La Tablada* barracks. About this same time, Domingo Cavallo, an economist associated with the Peronists, recommended to the World Bank and the IMF that they limit their credit to Argentina. When both institutions announced that they would no longer continue to support the government's economic program, the entire edifice collapsed. On February 6, 1989, the government announced the peso's devaluation, devouring the fortunes and even the small savings of those who had not be able to exchange their pesos for dollars and initiating a period in which the value of the dollar and prices soared at a dizzying rate and the economy spun out of control. After long periods of high inflation, hyperinflation had arrived and simultaneously destroyed real wages and the value of the national currency, as well as affecting production and the circulation of goods.

It was in this climate that the May 14, 1989, presidential elections took place. The Peronists won a resounding victory, and Carlos Menem was elected president. The date for the transfer of power was scheduled for December 10th of that year, but it was soon apparent that the outgoing government was in no condition to govern until that date, all the more so when the winning candidate refused to collaborate with Alfonsín's besieged administration during the transition. In late May, hyperinflation had its first dramatic effects: the looting of supermarkets, which the public authorities harshly repressed. Shortly thereafter, Alfonsín resigned in order to move up the transfer of power; this took place on July 8, 1989, six months before the date prescribed by the Constitution. Alfonsín's 1983 image had been reversed, and the leader who had been received as the symbol of a desired regeneration left the scene accused of ineptness and betrayal.

nine

The Great Transformation, 1989–1999

Austerity and Reform

On July 9, 1989, President Alfonsín handed over power to the president-elect, Carlos Saúl Menem. This occasion was the first peaceful transfer by one democratically elected president to another since 1928 and the first since 1916 in which a president ceded power to the candidate of an opposition party. These facts spoke well of the consolidation of the democratic regime reestablished in 1983, but the significance of the transfer was clouded by a serious crisis. The hyperinflation unleashed in April continued until August. In July, inflation reached 200 percent, and in December it was still 40 percent. While some converted their *australes* to dollars, other groups of desperate people assaulted stores and supermarkets, and the repression of the protesters left a number of dead. A bankrupt state, the national currency in shambles, wages that did not meet basic necessities, and social violence exposed the government's inability to govern and ensure order. The first thing that the new president had to resolve was how to recover the government's credibility.

What was new was not the economic crisis, but the spectacular nature of the violence surrounding it. To deal with it, a general recipe had become common wisdom among economists and politicians throughout the world during the 1980s: Facilitate the opening up of the national economy to make possible an appropriate insertion into the global economy, and dismantle the powers of the welfare state, labeled as costly and inefficient. In Argentina's case and that of Latin America in general, these ideas had been distilled in the so-called Washington Consensus. U.S. government agencies and the great international financial organizations such as the International Monetary Fund (IMF) and the World Bank transformed these prescriptions into recommendations or requirements whenever they came to the aid of governments to solve their immediate problems with foreign debt. Economists, financial advisers, and journalists tirelessly devoted themselves to disseminating the new dogma and gradually managed to turn these simple principles into common wisdom. Their success coincided with the widespread conviction that democracy in itself was not enough to solve economic problems.

According to the prevailing diagnosis, the Argentine economy was inefficient because of the high degree of protection that the local market enjoyed and because of the subsidies that, under various guises, the state granted to different economic sectors that had managed to ensure their quota of state support throughout the tug-of-war over resources. In addition to low productivity that made any insertion into the global economy difficult, there were the chronic government deficits of an excessively spendthrift state that, to balance its accounts, customarily resorted to monetary emission with inevitable inflationary consequences. An entire way of conducting economic policy, which had been in place since 1930 and was consolidated under Peronism, began to be questioned. Some debated whether the crisis was intrinsic to that economic model or whether it was due to the excessive foreign indebtedness contracted during the Process, which put the state at the mercy of the whims of foreign creditors and bankers. But whatever the reasons for the problem, the conclusion was the same: Inflation and indebtedness, which for a long time served to postpone addressing economic problems, ultimately made them worse and finally culminated in the 1989 collapse.

The recipe disseminated by the IMF, the World Bank, and prestigious neoliberal economists was simple: Reduce state spending to the level of the state's real fiscal resources, eliminate state intervention in the economy, and open up the economy to foreign competition—in short, a program of austerity and capitalist restructuring. In its basics, such a program had already been implemented by Martínez de Hoz in 1976, though in its actual implementation this program departed significantly from those principles. But such a program was difficult to implement. It was resisted by all those who prospered behind state protection, including big business groups, in principle partisans of such measures but reluctant to accept them when their own interests were affected. The program was also opposed by those who, not without reason, associated these reforms with the recent military dictatorship. Nonetheless, already during the final phase of Alfonsín's government, the necessity of undertaking such a program had been acknowledged. There had been a certain degree of opening up of the economy and a plan to privatize some state companies, both of which collided in the congress with the opposition of a revitalized Peronism and the doubts of many Radicals. The 1989 crisis paved the way for the partisans of the reform recipe, creating a widespread consensus that the country had to choose between some transformation or the unraveling of the state and society.

The new president was one of the converts. Forged in populism, he had found hyperinflation a singular educational experience in two ways: as a danger and an opportunity. For Menem, the danger was that he would end up like Alfonsín, devoured by the maelstrom of a state in the process of disintegration. The opportunity resided in the fact that the social upheaval was so great and there was such a need for public order and stability that the bitter medicine until then rejected could be tolerated and could even become attractive. This prescription was also pleasing to the international financial institutions and to the select group of financial gurus who advised them, that is to say, the powers capable of stirring up or calming the waters of the economic crisis. To begin to establish possibilities for the exercise of effective power, Menem had to win the support of these figures. The new president's undeniable political abilities were a point in his favor, but his political background raised serious doubts. For a long time, he had served as the governor of La Rioja province in a sporadic fashion, almost like an absentee executive, and he was surrounded by a shady group of opportunists and social climbers. In the electoral campaign, he promised a huge salary increase (*salariazo*) and a "revolution in production" in the classic populist political style of the Peronists, which the *renovadores* had sought to modify. In sum, Menem seemed to represent a return to old-style Peronism.

Though he soon jettisoned a good part of Peronism's ideological and discursive baggage, Menem was at least faithful to perhaps the movement's most essential characteristic: its pragmatism. In a startling about-face he announced in apocalyptic fashion that "major surgery without anesthesia" was necessary; he declared himself a supporter of a "popular market economy" and at the same time forswore state intervention, praised the "opening up" of the economy, and proclaimed the necessity and virtue of the privatizations, while mocking those who "had remained in 1945." Businesspeople, bankers, and financial gurus had their doubts. Was his conversion sincere or just a stratagem to get around the crisis? Even if he was sincere, could he keep at bay those from each of the privileged bastions who might want to return to the old ways?

Pressed to win their confidence and widen his narrow maneuvering room, Menem resorted to almost outlandish gestures: publicly embracing the once rabid anti-Peronist Admiral Isaac Rojas, surrounding himself with the Alsogarays—father and daughter—and entrusting the ministry of the economy successively to two upper-level executives of the country's most important economic conglomerate—Bunge y Born—which was rumored to have a magical economic plan up its sleeve. To demonstrate his authority, Menem threw around Napoleonic phrases. Above all, he sought to persuade with decisive and irreversible actions. Such actions were supposed to demonstrate not only his beliefs but also his to ability to govern, a power that was not confined to exercising private pressure or fending off pressures from interest groups. Perhaps for that reason, from among the many possible ways of implementing the reformist prescriptions, such as overcoming obstacles, pacing the reforms, taking safeguards, and gauging the transition, Menem chose the most simple, crude, brutal, and destructive.

During the first two years of his administration, while he attempted to surmount the economic crisis, inflation, and instability, Menem and his closest collaborators were being tested by the "market." The first challenge was to gain freedom of action and overcome the obstacles that had plagued Alfonsín. Taking advantage of the disarray in Radicalism as his administration began, Menem had congress pass two major laws. The Law of Economic Emergency suspended all kinds of subsidies, special privileges, and promotional schemes and authorized laying off public employees. The Law of State Reform declared the necessity of privatizing a long list of state-owned companies and gave the president broad powers to choose the specific manner of achieving this. Shortly thereafter, congress authorized an increase in the number of supreme court justices. With four new justices added, the government was guaranteed a majority, which eliminated the possibility of an adverse ruling in any legal action that the reforms might occasion.

Looking for quick and spectacular results, the government concentrated on the rapid privatization of ENTEL, the state-owned telephone company, and *Aerolíneas Argentinas,* the country's principal airline carrier and also a public company. For Menem, it was necessary to demonstrate the will and ability to undertake reforms to obtain additional funds and to begin to solve the problem of the foreign debt. Everything was done rapidly, in a careless manner, at odds with other declared objectives, such as encouraging competition. María Julio Alsogaray, Alvaro Alsogaray's daughter and apparent heir to her father's leadership of the liberal forces, was instructed to conclude the privatization of the public telephone company before October 8, 1990, the date of Perón's birthday and her own. She convoked a heterogeneous group of buyers made up of local businesspeople, international financiers, and bankers who held the titles on the foreign debt. These titles were accepted as partial payment for the company at their nominal value, well above their market value. This action began to tranquilize the foreign creditors who exchanged bonds of doubtful worth for company shares. The former public telephone company was broken up into two private companies, which were guaranteed substantial rate increases and monopoly privileges for a number of years. Under similar terms, the government privatized the company's highway system, television networks, many railways, and important parts of the oil industry.

The government also proclaimed an economic opening up (*apertura*) as yet another fundamental plank in the new dogma. But the government reduced tariff barriers, quotas, and import duties without uniform criteria, because it was pulled in different directions by two overriding objectives: first, to reduce inflation, which was always difficult to control, by importing cheap goods, and, second, to improve fiscal collection by imposing high taxes. With regard to the fiscal deficit, the most urgent problem, there was no ambiguity. It was a question of quickly collecting more revenue by increasing the most basic taxes—taxes on sales and earnings—without considering questions that reformist proposals had always tended to address: how to improve savings and investment and how to apply some yardstick of social equality.

Despite the money that the state obtained with the privatizations and the improvement in tax collection, the government failed to attain stability during the administration's first two years. Inflation remained high, and the big business groups, despite offering the government nominal support and even participating in the decision-making process, continued to handle their investments in accordance with their particular self-interests. Perhaps for that reason, the government did not lament the exit of the Bunge y Born group from the government in late 1989, when a second bout of hyperinflation occurred. Once again, there were supermarket sackings and panic, though they were less noticed than in Alfonsín's final days in office. Ermán González, the new minister of the economy, warded off the crisis with a drastic measure: The government confiscated personal savings in the country's high interest-paying savings accounts (*plazo fijo*) and exchanged them for long-term redeemable bonds in dollars, dubbed the *Plan Bonex*. González, an obscure accountant from La Rioja who belonged to the president's inner circle, took the advice of the creditor banks and of Alvaro Alsogaray and applied a well-known prescription: He shut down the printing presses to curtail monetary emission and restricted the state's spending and the money supply as much as possible. In this way, he reduced inflation, but at the cost of a severe recession that, by the end of the year, had once more sharply curtailed government revenue. In late 1990, with the economy again in critical condition, a public scandal erupted—"Swiftgate"—a scandal involving a complaint by the U.S. meat-packing firm Swift to U.S. Ambassador Todman that the company been asked to pay a bribe to expedite resolution of a routine government regulation.

This was not the first and certainly not the last scandal of Menem's government. In the midst of the economic reforms, privatizations, and establishment of new rules of the game, those who surrounded the president had access to inside information and could influence policy decisions to their full advantage. Ministers Eduardo Bauzá, Roberto Dromi, and María Julia Alsogaray were accused of personally benefiting, in a big way, from the privatizations. The Peronist congressman José Luis Manzano and the president's brother-in-law Emir Yoma ruled over a center of influence-peddling dubbed the "little tent," it was said. Manzano's phrase—"I steal for the crown"—became infamous and demonstrated at the same time the extent of the corruption and the impunity enjoyed by those involved. "Swiftgate," which erupted in December 1990, was different from other scandals because this time the party damaged by bribery was a U.S. company. The injured party turned to the American ambassador in Buenos Aires, Clarence Todman—who operated as a veritable proconsul—and got the U.S. government involved. Menem had been successfully cultivating his relations with the U.S. president George Bush, and Argentina had firmly aligned itself with the United States, so that the U.S. government's intervention was effective. The entire cabinet resigned, and a series of ministry changes at the beginning of 1991 made the man who until then had been the foreign minister, Domingo Cavallo, minister of the economy.

Cavallo undertook a highly ambitious reform program, freer from the pressures of business and creditors than past programs. Shortly after assuming office, he got the important Convertibility Law passed. This law established a fixed exchange rate. By law, a dollar would henceforth be equivalent to the new peso, and the president was prohibited from not only modifying exchange rates but from printing money above the country's dollar reserves, thereby guaranteeing this parity. The state, which so many times in the past had practiced unrestrained monetary emission to cover its deficits—ultimately always ending in a devaluation—tied its own hands to convince the "financial operators" of its good intentions while it relinquished the principal instrument for intervening in the economy. The country's recent history of self-inflicted weakening of the state's ability to intervene in the economy, a process initiated under Martínez de Hoz and deepened by the foreign debt, culminated with this drastic measure. After it came another equally binding decision: the reduction of trade barriers—falling by a third of their former value—which made a reality of the often-announced economic *apertura* and gave credibility to the seriousness with which the reform program was being carried out. The immediate results were successful: The run on the dollar ended, there was a quick revitalization of the economy, and tax collection improved. In that context, because of the recovery of the titles on the foreign debt acquired with the privatizations, an agreement was reached the following year with the foreign creditors in the framework of the so-called Brady Plan. Argentina became trustworthy once again for foreign creditors.

This agreement was provisional. Despite the desire for reform, it was not certain that the state could balance its accounts. Some progress was made, thanks to improved tax collection, the work of the "bloodhounds" of the DGI, Argentina's internal revenue service, which hunted down even the "rich and famous"; everyone had to be prepared to show the CUIT card containing the person's tax number, and this became the new national identity card. But these measures would not have been enough without the influx of foreign loans and investments that were in search of "emerging markets" more profitable than those in their own countries. Between 1991 and 1994, a considerable amount of dollars came into the country, allowing the government to cover its deficit. Companies could modernize their technology, and the consumption of average Argentines increased. This influx created optimism and confidence and camouflaged the costs of the reform. "Structural reform" no longer seemed painful, the convertibility law achieved a broad consensus, and the government handily won its first electoral test at the end of 1991.

Now the government could put behind it concerns about instability and lack of credibility and undertake a new spate of reforms with greater peace of mind under the leadership of Minister Cavallo, an economist with a monetarist background and with strong political ambitions. Cavallo had first cut his teeth as a high-level functionary in 1982 when, as president of the Central Bank, he had rescued business by converting private foreign debt into public debt. Cavallo incorporated into the government a group of well-qualified economists and technocrats with little political experience. He led this team in a purposeful and disciplined manner, projecting it into diverse areas of the government, whose ministries and bureaucracies the group systematically colonized. He counted on the support of President Menem, who was at first perhaps reluctant but then offered decisive backing, especially at the moment when it became necessary to take on the old-style Peronists. For four years, both Menem and Cavallo drew strength from each other; Cavallo's resolve about the economic course to follow was combined with Menem's political intuition. Thus strengthened, the government team ceased to be at the mercy of the daily whims of financial operatives, representatives of the foreign creditors, or captains of industry. The government did not break off relations with these groups and closely listened to them but set a course independent of their momentary demands.

Cavallo resolutely advanced with the reforms, but he carried them out more carefully than the government had previously. The sale of state-owned companies continued, but the privatization of the electrical, gas, and water utilities included provisions guaranteeing competition, regulation, and even the sale of stock in the new companies to private shareholders. Indeed, the participation of the unions in the management of some new companies was foreseen, thereby winning the goodwill of the union leadership. YPF, the state-owned oil company and the most symbolic of the public firms, was privatized, but the state retained a considerable number of shares whose earnings were directed to balancing the deficit of the country's social security system and attenuating opposition from the country's retired population. As a corollary, the government attempted a reform of social security, which would have profoundly changed its purpose. Instead of being based on the solidarity of the working population with the retired sector, every worker would have his or her own savings account administered by private plans. It was hoped that this program would serve to mobilize an important amount of domestic savings and help reactivate the economy through such companies.

Resistance to such a plan was expressed in congress, and following a long negotiation it was decided to maintain in part the public system. A similar compromising spirit that moved away from the "surgery without anesthesia" prescription was demonstrated in labor reforms, an area in which the government barely advanced when confronted with union opposition, as was the case with the failure to deregulate of the *obras sociales,* labor-controlled union funds used to cover the expenses of union social services (drug prescriptions, vacation colonies, and so on) and another crucial issue for union leaders. With the provincial governments, a Fiscal Pact was signed as part of the policy to reduce state spending; those governments were given great leeway in handling local resources to palliate the effects of austerity and to practice political clientelism. The most notable example of such discretionary funds was a substantial Fund for Historic Preservation of Greater Buenos Aires in which the Peronist governor of the province of Buenos Aires had a million dollars per day at his disposal to spend as he saw fit.

Thanks to favorable international economic conditions, although the reform program advanced to the point of no return, its harshest effects were softened. In hindsight, these were three golden years. The gross national product (GNP) grew steadily, interest rates were more than respectable, and consumption increased, thanks to new credit plans with installment payments contracted in dollars. Inflation also fell drastically—with the memory still alive of the outrageous inflation rates of 1989 and 1990—economic activity increased, and the state improved tax collection and even enjoyed a few years of surplus, in large measure from the income provided by the privatizations.

This bonanza hid for a time the harsher and ultimately most abiding aspects of the great transformation. The most notable of these was unemployment. Each privatization was accompanied by a high number of layoffs. As a product of the long years of collusion of interests between administrators and union leaders, the state companies had accumulated many employees who were redundant from the standpoint of the new and strict management criteria. The effects of this process were at first hidden by generous severance payments, but they appeared with a vengeance beginning in 1995. With respect to private firms, the economic opening forced all those who competed with imported products to reduce their costs as an urgent necessity and to rationalize production or face the threat of bankruptcy. Their situation was made particularly difficult by the fact that the overvaluation of the peso meant that salaries, measured in dollar terms, were high. From the point of view of the workers and of the country's historic tradition of full employment, there was no reasonable alternative. If companies went bankrupt, everyone would be left in the street. If they improved efficiency, taking advantage of ample credit to install more sophisticated machinery or to rationalize production, the result would be the same: more workers than needed. In this respect a crucial objective was the flexibilization of working conditions. This indeed occurred and lessened the ability to resist on the part of trade-union organizations, which whenever they resorted to a strike were ominously defeated.

Unemployment, which in 1993 had surpassed the long-standing ceiling of 10 percent, was a serious matter. It occurred in a context of economic expansion and overall growth in production. What would be the consequences if the favorable economic conjuncture came to an end? Other sectors, such as state workers and the retired population, were battered by the freezing of their incomes; many others suffered from the rising prices of public services, the closing of their businesses—as happened with many small businesspeople—or the financial crises of various provincial governments, despite the federal government's rapid offer of assistance. In Santiago del Estero, Jujuy, and San Juan, the first public and violent demonstrations expressing discontent with the new order took place.

In these years, the government experimented with some palliative measures with limited effects, taking advantage of the fiscal resources at its disposal and increasing the foreign debt. The criteria for distributing its surpluses were hardly adequate. Not even in this stage of relative prosperity did the government have a genuine concern for attenuating the social costs of the great transformation in a consistent manner. The lower classes benefited a bit from the expansion of various social welfare programs whose effects however were diluted by bad administration and a clientilistic orientation. The economic *apertura,* in turn, was watered down to deal with the protests of the strongest groups. Thus the automobile industry recovered almost all of its traditional benefits. Export sectors, hurt by an overvalued peso (no one considered even a modification in the Convertibility Law), received subsidies, rebates, and various financial compensations. The firms that had been most adversely affected, those that had held state contracts, received the biggest prize: participation in the privatizations under advantageous conditions.

By this time, business had taken note of the limitations of the great transformation, which had been much more effective in destroying the old system than in building a new one. Some companies—the biggest, those with easy access to credit—managed to restructure their operations efficiently. Nonetheless, their possibilities for exporting and integrating themselves into the global market were restricted by an overvalued peso, chained to a dollar that was increasing in value, which raised their costs. They no longer could exert influence on the price of utilities or fuels, which before had been established according to political considerations. They could, however, attempt to reduce their labor costs, which in comparative terms were high, even though the beneficiaries, the workers, could not appreciate that fact. For the same reasons, the incentives to import were strong. The flood of foreign products wiped out a good part of local industry and created a swollen commercial deficit. The government deficit also grew, among other reasons because of a return to the practice of subsidizing exporters.

The solution was perhaps to be found in a devaluation that would make local industry more competitive, but such a devaluation was perforce impossible: The "confidence of the markets" resided in the Convertibility Law, which was fast becoming an albatross around the government's neck. To survive from day to day, eliminating the deficit and honoring the commitments to foreign creditors established in the Brady Plan were indispensable to renegotiate new loans. The final decision about capital flows no longer rested with the big banks, nor did it depend entirely on the backing of the IMF, institutions with some concern about the overall direction of economic policy. Rather, in the new economy, the bulk of highly volatile investments depended on the decisions of mutual fund or investment managers, on the lookout from day to day for the maximum return in any corner of the world and uninterested in any long-term economic policy. Factors totally foreign to the local situation—such as the oscillations of interest rates in the United States—caused them either to put in or to pull out their money, which gave them great ability to exercise pressure. Thanks to the Convertibility Law, the country's vulnerability to foreign economic interests, a characteristic of the economy a century ago, had now reappeared.

A Successful Leadership

After his election, while he had the confidence of the nation's powerful interests, Menem devoted himself to taking control of the government, altering and even subverting some of its institutions. Two initial omnibus laws, intended to deal with the economic crisis, gave him broad powers, which he used at his discretion; increasing the number of supreme court justices guaranteed him a sure majority in the nation's highest court. Indeed, the court ruled in the chief executive's favor in every controversial decision and even made encroachments on the authority of circuit judges and lower courts via the novel recourse of *per saltum,* a procedure whereby cases likely to be decided adversely for the president were remanded to the country's highest court. For the same purpose of eliminating possible controls and restrictions, the president removed almost all the members of the board of examiners of fiscal accounts, named by decree the attorney-general of the nation, reduced the institutional rank of the general secretariat of public companies, and replaced or reassigned judges and district attorneys whose initiatives were perceived as nettlesome. Later, when the congress began to question some of his initiatives, Menem combined a certain willingness to negotiate—as happened with social security and labor law reform—with a new affirmation of presidential authority. The president liberally used his veto powers and issued emergency decrees. He even went so far as to consider the possibility of closing the congress and governing by decree. This increase in presidential authority, which went beyond that established by republican principles inherent in the division of powers, had its background in Alfonsín's government under which the Austral Plan was passed in a similar manner. But in this case, Menem exercised power at his discretion, perhaps to demonstrate where power really resided.

Menem combined discretion with a style of governing more suited to a monarch than the chief of state of a republic. To judge by those who knew him intimately, Menem concentrated on politics but was not terribly interested in policy matters. He offered broad objectives and delegated to his collaborators the specific details, which bored him. Thus he is remembered as listening to the explanation for some important matter while he watched a soccer match or flipped through the channels of his television. Moreover, he continued to enjoy a playboy's lifestyle despite being married. For his nocturnal endeavors, he generally used a suite in the luxurious Alvear Palace, whose owner was one of the members of his intimate circle. Menem relished flouting convention and even the law; he drove a Ferrari sports car that he had received as a presidential gift, for reasons that were never made clear, at high speeds and traveled in two hours from Buenos Aires to the seaside resort of Pinamar and at similar speeds to other beach resorts for an occasional wild weekend. After his public separation from his wife, Zulema Yoma, whom he had evicted by force from the presidential retreat in Olivos, he became somewhat more sedentary and transformed the presidential residence into a veritable court, with its own golf course and private golf instructor, zoo, valet, physician, hair stylist, "court jester," and a select group of courtesans, comrades during his nights of insomnia and witnesses to his recurring bouts of depression. Like a medieval prince, he often trotted the globe with his retinue aboard a presidential airplane worthy of a monarch.

The behavior of this singular apex of the republic resembled that of fifth-century Germanic warriors, stationed in one of the provinces of the expiring Roman Empire. The "palace" was as much his private home as the seat of political power, and a similar confusion existed with respect to the public exchequer and its status as war booty. The entourage of warriors watching over the chief of state, ready to carry out any assignment, came from diverse backgrounds. Among the original *fideles,* there mingled provincial politicians, union leaders, former *Montoneros* now transformed into neoliberals, extreme right-wing groups, ex-collaborators of Admiral Massera, and other fauna that he had collected throughout his political career. Soon others joined him, recruited among his defeated rivals, the *renovadores.* Loyalty was rewarded with protection and impunity as far as possible.

In addition, the chief executive was the caretaker of the spoils of office, which he distributed generously. Such had always been the true sign of authority in political leadership in Argentina, and Menem refined the practice.

Corruption was widely employed to wear down resistance and coopt adversaries by sealing a pact among the members of the governing circle as powerful as the blood pact that united the military under the dictatorship. Corruption was practiced in an ostentatious fashion. "Nobody makes money by working," the trade-union official Luis Barrionuevo declared, before proposing as a solution to the country's troubles that "everyone stop stealing for two years." The right to steal was apparently a sign of membership in the highest circles of power. Just as a way to stabilize the economy was found, so also was it learned how to transfer public resources discreetly to private fortunes. Various important individuals, representatives of the country's most powerful lobbies or founders of new fortunes, had privileged access to government circles and sent some of the spoils to so-called black boxes, private accounts whose contents were generously distributed according to norms—not those of the state—but of rank and hierarchy. Technically speaking, the country was governed by a gang, by a coterie of corrupt and unscrupulous officials.

From early 1991, Menem's clique shared responsibilities with a professional group of technocrats headed by the minister of the economy Cavallo. There were two distinct but complimentary groups. Menem and Cavallo—so different from each other—complimented and strengthened the other. Their partnership was a combination of the arrogance of power and efficiency, which grew and evolved at the cost of democratic institutions. There were not a few conflicts. Those individuals with origins in a traditional Peronism, who saw looming a post-Menem world, began to demand greater concern for the social aspects of the transformation, as well as for a share of the resources that the government handled at its discretion and that the minister of the economy, always concerned about "balancing the books," wished to cut. There were opportunities to protest and even resist, partly because of Cavallo's concern to reduce the government's discretionary powers, safeguard conventions, and secure the rule of law.

That same concern made him sensitive to the bigger scandals that involved the president's men and women. On one occasion shortly after Swiftgate, Amira Yoma, Menem's sister-in-law and the presidential liaison, was caught carrying suitcases full of dollar bills. It was the beginning of the so-called narcogate scandal that ensued after the discovery of the close friendship between Amira and Monzer al Kassar, a well-known arms trafficker who held an Argentine passport. The issue only tangentially entered into Cavallo's orbit, but he harshly criticized the powerful businessman, Alfredo Yabrán, owner of private postal services and allegedly a member of the president's inner circle. By then, to the sudden attacks of the "Peronists" against the *menemistas* was added an increasingly visible rivalry among the putative fathers of the "model," Menem and Cavallo. Nonetheless, in late 1994, at the height of the congressional electoral campaign, Memen still declared emphatically that "Mingo was not leaving." By this he meant, of course, Domingo Cavallo.

Menem's political talents were demonstrated, above all, in his ability to have Peronism accept the reforms and in the Copernican revolution that he imposed with respect to its traditions. Certainly the Peronism of 1989 was not that of bygone days. Following the 1983 electoral defeat and accepting the new conditions that democracy established for the country's political life, Peronism had slowly abandoned its characteristics as a "movement" solidly anchored to the trade unions and became a more traditional party, with committees, district organizations, and national leadership elected by direct vote. The electoral triumphs and the control of provincial and city governments allowed the political cadres to become independent of union money, thereby diminishing the influence of the union leadership. In addition, the identification of Peronism with the "people"—deeply rooted in the party's political culture—weakened. The "enemies of the people," a category into which all non-Peronists fell, or the enemies of yesterday were today simply political rivals when not allies.

These changes did not alter the solidity of the Peronist identity or its traditional conception of leadership, though it is significant that Menem—the first to attain such status after Perón—had become Peronism's leader through internal elections. Menem used the combined resources of party leader and president in the tradition of Roca, Yrigoyen, and Perón to give orders to an ensemble of leaders and cadres accustomed to obey. Even if they expressed disagreement and went so far as to come into conflict, rarely were they prepared to break with the government or—in Perón's colorful phrase—"take their thumbs out of the pie." To this traditional Peronist principle that it is the leader who commands, Menem supplied some additional resources. He gathered support outside the movement, in Alsogaray's UCD or among notable social commentators tied to the establishment, such as the television news commentator Bernardo Neustadt, who organized one of Menem's few public demonstrations in the Plaza del sí, in April 1990, to proclaim support for the president's recent military pardons and free-market economic reforms.

In addition, Menem knew how to communicate effectively with people in general, regardless of their political affiliations and without the need to orchestrate the complex machinery of street protest. Instead of speaking in the Plaza de Mayo, he had only to give interviews on the radio or visit the most popular television programs, opine on the most diverse topics, and here and there make a presence. In that respect, under Menem the country fully entered the era of mass media politics. This also included the way specific social demands were received and processed through journalists and public-opinion surveys. In response to those demands, Menem tended to give a swift and unilateral response. Menem demonstrated that, when all was said and done, he could get along without Peronism and its cadres.

Under Menem, the *renovador* movement disintegrated, and many of its leaders joined Memen's bandwagon. On the other hand, Menem's most serious rival in the party, Antonio Cafiero, was ominously defeated when he sought to amend the constitution of Buenos Aires province to be reelected governor of the province. Cafiero was forced to surrender the presidency of the party to Memen and the governorship to the vice president Eduardo Duhalde, who built in the province a powerful bastion from which to keep an eye on who would succeed Memen. Among the union leaders, Saúl Ubaldini continued to stand for Peronism's historic positions, divided the CGT, and attempted to rally those hit hardest by the economic reforms, such as state or telephone workers. But Menem won the support of other union leaders and signaled the benefits of submitting to the reform program and above all of the costs of not complying. Many union leaders obtained personal benefits, and some unions, such as the Light and Power Workers' Union (*Luz y Fuerza*), were transformed into business organizations and participated in the privatization. Most union leaders, headed by Lorenzo Miguel, maintained a prudent distance, waited to test the solidity of Menem's leadership, and then attacked him.

At the beginning of 1991, Menem threw new leaders into the arena: the elected Peronist governors of Tucumán, Palito Ortega—a well-known popular singer—and Carlos "Lole" Reutemann, a famous race-car driver. The 1991 election was a success for the president and convinced the doubters that Peronism indeed had a new leader. The initial suspicions evaporated, with the exception of a small group of dissident congressmen, the so-called group of eight, headed by the congressman Carlos "Chacho" Alvarez, who abandoned the party. It was then that Menem began talking about Peronism's "ideological modernization," declared that he was moving away from the historic principles established by Perón—though he asserted that Perón would have done the same himself—and began to think about the possibility of his reelection.

Outside Peronism, there was little political opposition. The *Unión Cívica Radical* could not overcome the discredit it had suffered in 1989 and in the 1991 elections won only in the federal capital, Córdoba, Río Negro, Chubut, and Catamarca. In 1993, it lost even in the federal district, a traditional redoubt. Strictly speaking, the Radicals did not know how to challenge Menem, who carried forward in a brutal but successful manner the economic reform policy that Alfonsín began in 1987. Any differences that the Radicals demonstrated about how such a program should be implemented, though important, were insufficient to sustain a political opposition.

In 1990, Menem strengthened his military flank. From the days of his electoral campaign, when he gathered behind him all the groups that could weaken the government, he had maintained ongoing contacts with the *carapintadas* and especially with Colonel Mohamed Alí Seineldín. It is probable that Menem knew about and perhaps even encouraged the late 1988 military uprising. Menem certainly rewarded the *carapintada* mutineers by granting them a pardon in late 1989 as part of his general policy of reconciliation, which included pardons at the end of the following year for the incarcerated ex-junta members, sentenced in 1985, despite the strong public outcry against the pardon. But Menem did not introduce any substantial modification in the army's leadership of the sort the *carapintadas* demanded. In December 1990, following a number of provocations, Seineldín, with many of those who had been pardoned, headed an uprising that began in an unfortunate way, with the rebels killing two officers. The episode ended up separating the two camps: Menem ordered a full-scale repression and—in contrast to the 1987 uprising—the military commanders responded. There were thirteen deaths in all and more than two hundred wounded. Those responsible were tried, and Seineldín, who assumed complete responsibility, was sentenced to life imprisonment.

Shortly later, General Martín Balza, who played a prominent role in suppressing the rebellion, was named army commander, a position he held until the end of Menem's second administration. Menem found a prominent officer to uphold the army's discipline and subordination to civilian authority in the midst of difficult circumstances. The military budget had been drastically reduced in the context of the general cuts in state spending, and a number of military-administered companies had been privatized. In 1994, at the Zapala military base, a conscript, Omar Carrasco, died as a result of mistreatment during basic training. The scandal erupted just as Menem was making preparations for his reelection and led to the elimination of obligatory military service and its replacement by a voluntary professional military. In 1995, Balza surprisingly criticized the actions of the military in the "dirty war" and affirmed that "due obedience" did not justify the aberrant actions that had been committed. This was the military's first self-criticism, and even though Balza's declaration did not receive a warm reception among his comrades in arms, it contributed to the beginning of a reassessment of what had occurred during the Process.

Menem found similar support in the Church in the figure of Cardinal Antonio Quarracino, the archbishop of Buenos Aires. A group of bishops, which grew larger as the effects of austerity and reforms became more severe, emerged as the spokespersons for a broad sector of society adversely affected by economic reforms and demanded from the government policies with social content. Quarracino moderated this chorus of opposition and avoided the episcopal congress's making declarations condemning government policies. In return, Menem supported the Church in defense of the traditional positions backed by the Pope, such as rejecting abortion and defending the "right to life." Thus Menem managed to be accepted by most of the Church hierarchy, an acceptance based on an obviously pragmatic self-interest, all the more so taking into account Menem's status as a divorced man and his hardly circumspect behavior in areas usually closely watched by the Church's traditional sectors.

Menem obtained an additional support that was as important as those previously mentioned: the United States. Menem established excellent personal relations with George Bush and quickly created similar ties with Bill Clinton, enabling him to turn to them in search of support. Menem's foreign minister, Guido Di Tella, also established close relations with the United States, which he termed "carnal relations" as a complement to the agreement reached with foreign creditors. A consequence of this policy was that U.S. ambassadors expressed daily opinions on every domestic matter. In addition,

Argentina suspended initiatives that displeased the United States, such as membership in the Movement of Non-Aligned Countries and the missile defense program dubbed Project Condor. Menem's government also supported all the U.S. positions on international politics and symbolically supported the United States in its military adventures, sending troops to both the Persian Gulf War and Yugoslavia. Involving itself in Middle East questions had a high price. Two deadly attacks against the Israeli embassy in Buenos Aires and the AMIA, the principal Jewish community center in the federal capital, probably resulted from those actions.

Also in matters of foreign relations, Di Tella initiated negotiations with Great Britain, leaving in limbo the question of sovereignty over the Malvinas Islands to resolve new and more urgent questions about fishing rights. In the same spirit, in 1991, he hurried to find a solution to all the pending border questions with Chile, with two exceptions, both involving border disputes in the extreme southern part of the country. The first, the dispute over the *Laguna del Desierto,* was submitted to foreign arbitration with a ruling favorable to Argentina, which Chile accepted. On the other hand, the solution regarding the *Hielos Continentales* sparked a strong opposition, and the final agreement was signed only in 1999. Throughout the period, Menem often traveled abroad to flaunt his image as the leader and successful reformer who had vanquished inflation. He was a popular figure throughout the world.

Despite the harshness of the austerity measures, the government encountered little organized resistance. The more traditional outlets of discontent— the unions, political organizations, and citizen associations of a diverse nature—were strongly affected by the transformation of the economy and the political demobilization of society. The union leaders, intensely active during Alfonsín's government, mobilized only to protect their own privileges. In 1992, there was a tepid general strike during the negotiations to deregulate the *obras sociales* and to reform the labor laws. There were also some incipient grassroots resistance movements that failed to prosper. At first, the workers of privatized companies attempted, unsuccessfully, to resist. Then the public employees' unions protested, especially in the provincial government bureaucracies that had frequent problems in getting paid. The retired community and teachers also mobilized. The *Congreso de los Trabajadores Argentinos* (CTA), a trade-union faction that did not identify with Peronism, and then the *Movimiento de los Trabajadores Argentinos* (MTA), a dissident Peronist group at odds with the pro-government leadership of the CGT, managed to coordinate their protests with the "federal march" of July 1993 and with a subsequent general strike the CGT did not adhere to. In December 1993, there was a violent protest in Santiago del Estero. The state workers' demonstration there turned into a riot of the general populace, with attacks against and burnings of public buildings and residences of the province's most prominent politicians. The incident initiated a new kind of protest, to which the government was vulnerable, especially because President Menem was then embarked on his campaign for reelection.

Following the electoral success of 1991, Menem began to talk about the need for a constitutional reform that would permit him to be reelected. "Menem in '95" went the widely disseminated slogan. The idea of a reform intended above all to modernize the Constitution—though without discarding the question of reelection—had been put forth by Alfonsín in 1986 but failed to win Peronism's support. Menem worked diligently on the idea, overcoming innumerable difficulties, including serious personal health problems and then the death of his only son in an aviation accident. But he achieved his final objective: to be reelected.

It was not easy for him. He encountered reserve in his own party among those who wished to succeed him or those who sought to negotiate his support to their advantage. Neither were things easy among the economic establishment, concerned about the conflicts that such a project night cause. But the principal problem was the congress. The constitutional reform had to be sanctioned by a two-thirds vote by both houses. Immediately following the 1993 elections, Menem managed to obtain the senate's approval and convoked a nonbinding plebiscite with the intention of pressuring the *Unión Cívica Radical* (UCR) congressmen, because the Peronists and their allies were far from obtaining the needed two-thirds majority. He threatened to have passed a law that would reinterpret the constitutional provision on reelection and get around the restriction, a law that would then be upheld by the supreme court.

The UCR was on the defensive, without a clear strategy, and divided. The provincial Radical governors such as Eduardo Angeloz in Córdoba or Horacio Massaccesi in Río Negro, who depended on the support of the national treasury, were inclined to compromise and look for common ground, whereas Alfonsín was categorically opposed. It was in this context that, surprisingly, Menem and Alfonsín met in secret and agreed to the conditions to facilitate a constitutional reform. Such a reform was to include a reelection clause and a series of amendments promoted by the UCR in hopes of modernizing the Constitution and reducing the legal margin for presidential hegemony. These amendments included direct presidential elections with a second-round run-off in the event that a party failed to obtain a majority of the votes; reduction of the presidential term from six to four years—without excluding possible reelection; direct election of senators, with proportional representation of one-third in the senate for the minority party; direct election of the mayor of the city of Buenos Aires; creation of a magistrates' council to designate federal judges; and establishment of guidelines for the issuance of emergency decrees. With difficulty, Alfonsín succeed in having the UCR accept the agreement. He argued about the risk of a defeat in the plebiscite, about the possibility of divisions in the party and defections, and above all about the risks of a reform carried forward by the president without the support of the political parties. In sum, he resigned himself to the inevitable and took stock of the perils of a resistance at any cost and the benefits that could be obtained from an agreement to modernize the country's political institutions.

In the April 1994 congressional elections, the Peronists lost a moderate number of votes, while the UCR suffered a strong loss that benefited the *Frente Grande,* which garnered 12 percent of the votes and triumphed in the federal capital and Neuquén province. This new political party attracted those who criticized the so-called Olivos Pact, which had led to the constitutional reform and which was made up of Chacho Alvarez's dissident Peronists, Socialist and Christian Democrat groups, and human rights activists such as Graciela Fernández Meijide. In the constitutional convention that met in the neighboring cities of Paraná and Santa Fe, the majority parties voted to approve the agreement and passed en bloc its basic points of agreement. It was left to the congress to give concrete legal form to the initiatives and to decide to what extent the reform provisions did or did not weaken executive power.

Throughout 1994 while the Constitution was being reformed, international interest rates began to rise. Around this time, Cavallo launched his so-called Second Reform of the State, with new privatizations—among them the country's nuclear power plants and postal system—and a drastic cut in federal monies sent to the provinces. Confronted with such measures, the governors and other sectors of old-guard Peronists affirmed that the time had come for dividing the wealth, softening the impact of austerity, and acting with thoughts of the next elections in mind. Eduardo Duhalde, who had just reformed the constitution of Buenos Aires province to permit his own reelection, was one of the most outspoken voices in this campaign to Peronize the government and to adopt a social agenda. The president, however, completely supported his minister, particularly with the appearance in early 1995 of the crisis in the Mexican economy, which underwent a severe economic slump and financial panic that threatened to spread to the rest of Latin America. When the Mexican government devalued its currency in a highly tense climate, there was a massive withdrawal of foreign capital from Argentina. The economy's vulnerability was graphically revealed. The panic caused the government deficit to grow and triggered a recession as unemployment climbed to an alarming level of 18 percent. The government responded rapidly and efficiently. The budget was trimmed, and there was a reduction in the public-sector wages and a big tax increase, all of which the IMF and World Bank unswervingly supported. The economy thus did not collapse, but the recession was prolonged.

In the short term, the crisis gave a new impetus to the reelection campaign because Menem had come to represent order and stability. In the 1995 elections, he faced a divided UCR that lacked confidence and a new political actor, the FREPASO, the fruit of the alliance reached between the *Frente Grande* and a party hurriedly assembled by the maverick Mendozan Peronist leader, José O. Bordón. Menem, with Carlos Ruckauf as his running mate, defeated the Bordón-Alvarez ticket, with the Radicals Massaccesi and Federico Storani a distant third. Menem had achieved a clear victory, winning almost 50 percent of the votes. The chief of state's power reached its zenith.

A Leadership in Decline

At that very moment began the decline. Until then, Menem had dominated the fight and had held the center of the ring like a good boxer. But from the beginning of his second round, he lost the initiative. Harried on several flanks—above all on the Peronist one—he managed only to dodge the blows, take as best he could the hits he was dealt, and await the final round. Paradoxically, to stay on his feet, he had to gamble to prolong the fight and remain in office another term. The dilemma was perhaps not immediately apparent. The Mexican economic crisis, the first serious warning, was overcome. Despite the run on the banks, the banking system survived, albeit at a cost of greater concentration and greater foreign domination; a good part of the $600 million that had fled the country returned in the first weeks of the year. Companies surmounted the problems resulting from the overvalued peso, in part thanks to the strong drop in real wages and in part to the improvement in productivity achieved by the biggest firms, the same ones that, unlike the smaller firms, could easily obtain foreign credit. Good times appeared to be returning. The gross domestic product (GDP), which fell more than 4 percent in 1995, recovered in 1996 and grew vigorously in 1997, surpassing 8 percent. Unemployment, on the other hand, now a permanent feature of national life, did not decline one iota and remained slightly under 15 percent.

There was another disturbing figure. The foreign debt grew steadily, and the $60 billion owed in 1992 became $100 billion in 1996. Clearly, the Argentine economy was in need of intensive therapy, dependent on foreign capital flows and the mood of investors, which from this point on was generally sour and grew much worse during the years when various "emerging markets" collapsed. In 1995, the years of easy access to foreign capital came to an end and with it the government's fiscal strength. The predominant characteristic of Menem's economic policy was now financial restraint, which implied the familiar results: rising interest rates, recession, fiscal penury, and greater doses of austerity and reform. Along this path there was little room to maneuver in those things that Menem and his circle, with the blessing of the technocrats, had effectively done: to redistribute a little and to compensate those negatively effected in multiple ways, to silence complaints and to find allies. In the new conjuncture, zealous foreign creditors no longer permitted such actions, and their backing was indispensable to obtain new credit. The government became trapped between demands for greater austerity to "balance the books" and the growing demands of a society recovering its voice. Nonetheless, it had lost the possibility of influencing long-term policies and limited itself to riding out the situation on a day-to-day basis.

The one who first felt the impact of the new situation was Cavallo. The minister emerged successfully from the 1995 crisis. He then began a series of privatizations, got approval for a declaration of a state of emergency in the country's retirement system, and restricted the funds transferred to the provincial governments. The latter experienced moments of great anxiety because many could not pay the salaries of their employees and ultimately found themselves forced to implement their own austerity measures. In the process, they sacrificed some of their traditional sources of patronage and the bedrock of political clientilism by selling public companies and provincial banks, reducing the numbers of public employees, and transferring their retirement programs to the federal government. But Cavallo remained in the eye of the storm. Those politicians whose roots were in traditional Peronism echoed the strong social malaise that affected their own political bases. They criticized an economic program that they now judged to have little of the Peronist in it, one that was excessively attached to the formulas of the IMF, and they centered their broadsides on the minister of the economy. At the beginning of 1996, they only grudgingly gave their support to approval of the administration's budget and refused to pass another law that would have broadened the powers of the executive in economic matters. The government's wings had clearly been clipped.

The greatest conflict that Cavallo and his technical team had to face was with the governing "gang," that extensive contingent of hangers-on surrounding the president, weavers of suspicious business deals, and obligatory intermediaries for any private-interest group who wished to gain access to the president. On a controversy surrounding a proposed patent law on medicines, Cavallo supported the U.S. position in favor of such a law and locked horns with a number of senators, headed by Eduardo Menem, who defended local laboratories that formed a powerful and generous lobby with many friends. The privatization of the country's postal system produced another confrontation. According to Cavallo, who was a supporter of the private U.S. postal carriers, congress was preparing a law to suit the interests of Alfredo Yabrán, the postal magnate involved in highly lucrative but suspicious business undertakings. Backed by the U.S. ambassador and by the U.S. president himself, Cavallo accused Yabrán of tax evasion and of having underworld connections. He also accused two ministers close to the president, the interior minister, Carlos Corach, and the justice minister, Elías Jassan, of protecting Yabrán and influencing judges in his favor.

Cavallo was in a rage and lashed out against everyone. By doing so, he inserted into public debate the issue of government corruption that had grown at a dizzying pace. He received a forceful reply. His collaborators, and he himself, were charged with shady business deals of their own and forced to contest the accusations in court. Hounded, Cavallo went so far as to name the president, "who didn't dare to look me in the eyes," according to the minister, as a member of the conspiracy. It was the end of their relationship. In late July 1996, Menem removed him from office and replaced him with Roque Fernández, a conservative economist who until then had been president of the Central Bank. The markets accepted him and did not react.

Unlike Cavallo, Roque Fernández had no pretensions about becoming a political figure and had no long-range agendas. Trained as an orthodox monetarist, he was strictly concerned with balancing the government's fiscal accounts and did not waver one bit from that purpose, effectively resisting pressures coming from all sides. Thus, he increased without mercy the price of fuel, raised sales taxes—which reached an outlandish rate of 21 percent, reduced the number of public employees, and implemented significant cuts in the budget. In addition, he carried forward the pending privatizations: that of the postal system, the airports, and the National Mortgage Bank; he also sold the state's remaining stock in the national oil company, YPF, to the Spanish firm Repsol. Everything was done rapidly, with the primordial concern being to increase government revenue.

Fernández ran into growing resistance from the government's political wing, concerned about future elections. Every austerity measure requiring a law had to be arduously negotiated in the congress, where the minister failed to achieve legislation in favor of labor flexibility. The issue was a symbolic one for both business and the IMF and sparked strong opposition in and outside Peronism, above all by the union leadership. In late 1996, Menem sought to get around congress's opposition with one of his emergency decrees, which surprisingly—a sign of changing times—was contested by the courts. In 1997, in the midst of the electoral campaign, Menem abandoned the labor reform and focused on the voters and the upcoming congressional elections. Ermán González, his new minister of labor, reached an agreement with the labor leaders, guaranteeing the unions the exclusive right to represent the workers in collective bargaining negotiations. The law was rejected by business and by Fernández, who demanded that some of its provisions be vetoed. He also categorically opposed another law that guaranteed a fund intended to improve teachers' salaries and rejected an ambitious project to build some 10,000 kilometers of highways, which would have meant a rapid decline in unemployment and a significant increase in the deficit. In sum, Fernández defended the treasury like a good accountant against the spendthrift ways of an opposition that by then everyone believed would win the next elections. Fernández's task was limited to simply saying no.

He did not have many options because of the international financial circumstances. In July 1997, Thailand's devaluation of its currency unleashed a global crisis. When the Hong Kong stock market collapsed in October of that year, investors looked with distrust at the emerging markets, including Argentina. Other collapses followed: Korea, Japan, Russia, and finally Brazil, which devalued its currency in the first days of 1999. This was a harsh blow for Argentina, already affected by the increased cost of credit and the fall in prices for its exports, yet with a devaluation of its own impossible. During good times, Menem and Cavallo had encouraged an accelerated integration into the *Mercorsur,* the proposed South American common market that included Argentina, Brazil, Uruguay, and Paraguay, without concerning themselves about establishing agreements on monetary policy. In 1995, the opening up of the Brazilian market had been a godsend for Argentina, which exported food, oil, and automotive parts to its *Mercosur* partner. In 1997, some problems began to appear. Sugar producers criticized Brazil for dumping its sugar in the Argentine market and backed a law that would have established tariffs on its importation, which Menem, concerned about strengthening the *Mercorsur,* vetoed. But in 1999, the devaluation of the *real,* Brazil's national currency, shrank the market for Argentina's now more expensive exports and unleashed a wave of demands for protection, as the bigger firms, with more freedom of action, began to consider the possibility of moving to Brazil or at least of subcontracting there part of what they produced.

The crisis that began in 1998 was deeper and lasted longer than that triggered by the Mexican economy and had no clear end in sight. All manner of problems appeared at once: increased interest rates on the foreign debt, lack of credit or its high cost, fall in export prices, and domestic recession. That year, the GDP declined some 4 percent, and the production of automobiles decreased by almost half. All these factors contributed to deepening the transnationalization of the economy. Various banks and companies were bought out by multinational corporations or large investment funds such as Exxel, which acquired Yabrán's companies. Menem's government came to its end without enough economic breathing space even to finance postelection government patronage and had to work out its budget with a swollen deficit that it never dared to acknowledge. The foreign debt by then had climbed to $160 billion, double what it had been in 1994.

Hard pressed to deepen the austerity program, without room to negotiate, Menem began to suffer from an increasingly active social opposition. Those who until then had been silent began to speak, and their demands were expressed in novel and effective ways, stirred up further by an opposition from Peronism itself. The year 1995 was critical in that respect. Violent protests in various provinces were led by public employees who were being paid in government vouchers of doubtful worth. To these problems were added the closing of various sugar mills (*ingenios*) in Tucumán and in Tierra del Fuego and the withdrawal of some electronics firms just before some promotional investment-incentive programs in effect were about to expire. The following year, while union organizations such as the General Confederation of Labor (CGT), the CTA, and the MTA were finally coming together to undertake two general strikes against the proposed law of labor flexibility and the government's economic policies in general, the political opposition—the FREPASO and the UCR—organized a protest of the citizenry: a collective blackout and pot banging (*cacerolazo*) of five minutes' duration, a protest supported by organizations of all kinds, including those devoted to defending human rights. By then the leadership of the bishops' council had changed, with the more independent Monsignor Estansilao Karlic, replacing the progovernment bishop Quarracino, and the Church began to add its voice to the protests.

The following year the teachers' union—the CTERA—which for some time had been unsuccessfully undertaking protest marches and strikes, discovered a new tactic that turned out to be very effective. The union set up a "white tent" in front of the congress, where teachers from the entire country took turns in a hunger strike while they received visitors and gestures of support. At the same time, the unions organized demonstrations and made declarations on radio and television. The teachers became permanent news, without the cost in terms of public opinion of interrupting classes. Something similar, though of a different tenor, was the setting up of roadblocks in Cutral Có and Tartagal, towns in the oil-producing zones of Neuquén and Salta, respectively, both hard hit by the privatization of YPF, which caused mass firings. Pickets and so-called bonfirers—who also appeared in Jujuy, affected by the firings at the Ledesma sugar mill—interrupted traffic, set fire to tires, and organized soup kitchens. Behind the protesters rallied unemployed workers, young people who had never been able to find a job, and their families and friends, disposed to face an eventual police repression with often nothing more to defend themselves than stones and sticks. It was a mobilization of the unemployed, simultaneously violent yet reluctant to undertake any organized political action. The government resorted at times to the courts and to the police, which led to violence, injuries, and even occasional death. At other times, it negotiated with the good offices of the unfailing priest or bishop. There was not much to offer, but the protesters were generally satisfied with little: donations of food or clothing and above all with contracts for temporary work that might alleviate their dire situation.

This type of mobilization had imitators to the degree that the crisis deepened: Students who set up road blocks in city streets or farmers who arrived en masse in their tractors to tie up traffic, added to occasional violent episodes, attacks on, and sacking of public buildings. All these acts revealed a state of widespread unrest and the reappearance of the politics of street protest, as in the 1960s, but now before the eyes of the camera. Television was converted into the essential medium for such actions to assume importance and be effective, because the key to the new protests' success was to be dramatic and gain publicity. Simultaneously, the government was confronted with problems on the internal front: the resurrection of old-style Peronism, which now discovered the problems of the austerity and reform programs at the moment that the change of leadership was being debated in the selection of a Peronist presidential candidate for the 1999 election.

In 1995, with the presidential elections of that year having ended, the governor of Buenos Aires province, Edurado Duhalde, announced his candidacy for the next elections and began to campaign. Duhalde traveled to Europe and the United States, announced plans for his government, and expressed his desire to distance himself from the "model" and to recover Peronism's historic banners. Despite the fact that the Constitution was clear and categorical with regard to the impossibility of a third term, Menem's conception of power, so typically Peronist, was not to transfer it during his lifetime. The president tried to push the idea, partly because of his blind faith in what he called his destiny and partly not to be given up for dead before his second term ran out. At first, he tried the gambit through circuitous routes.

To neutralize Duhalde, he encouraged the rival candidacy of Palito Ortega—popular despite his disastrous term as governor of Tucumán province—while he kept the other governors' hands tied because they depended on the largesse of the national treasury. He then informally launched his own candidacy with millions of T-shirts, balloons, and posters reading simply "Menem 99."

The war between the veteran leader and the one who wished to succeed him went from gestures and threats to stunning acts. A formal display of the best democratic decorum barely camouflaged cruder methods that conjured up memories of the military. In part, the struggle was played out in the media. While the media widely diffused Cavallo's continued denunciations of illicit business deals, other sources provided journalists with information to damage Menem and his circle, which the media also widely disseminated. The widespread corruption in the governing team became public. The clandestine sale of arms to Croatia and Ecuador, which compromised various government ministers and even the president himself; the business deals of the so-called gold mafia, which realized fictitious exports; the underground customs house, much more lax than the official one; and finally the bribe paid by the U.S. firm IBM to the directors of the *Banco Nación* to win a bid for installing a new computer system were exposed in the media. There were also incidents of violence: the explosion of the armaments factory in Río Tercero, which may have erased without a trace the tracks of the arms contraband deal at the cost of a number of lives, and the suspicious suicide of the go-between in these sales and of the individual who had paid the IBM bribe, as well as the kidnapping and torture of the sister of the special prosecutor investigating the case of the gold mafia.

There was a true "uncovering" of the country's dirty laundry, compelled by investigative journalism and facilitated by Peronism's internal war. The police of Buenos Aires province, the so-called *Bonaerense,* described at one moment by Duhalde as "the best in the world," appeared implicated in various cases of corruption: auto theft, drug trafficking, and prostitution. It was even proved that the police were involved in the brutal bombing of the AMIA, the Jewish community center in Buenos Aires, with a high-ranking officer supplying the automobile used to blow up the building. While Duhalde was initiating a purge of the force, the so-called Cabezas affair erupted. Cabezas, a photographic journalist, was brutally murdered, and his body appeared on the outskirts of the governor's summer residence. "They threw a dead body at me,"

Duhalde declared, convinced that he had received a threat from the underworld. The journalists tenaciously kept the question alive, and Duhalde launched an investigation, convinced that his political future was at stake in the affair. The investigation rapidly arrived at the doorsteps of the *Bonaerense,* then the businessman Yabrán, the mysterious figure who Cabezas had photographed against his will, and finally the presidential circle and even the president himself, who at first defended Yabrán. Ultimately, an officer of the Buenos Aires police force, the author of the murder, and Yabrán's head of security, the direct instigator, were accused of the crime. When the justice system called for his arrest, Yabrán dramatically committed suicide. Many murky aspects of the affair lingered, but there were two clear results: The corruption was seen to have penetrated all public institutions, and no holds were barred in the dispute for power and money.

Before the dramatic outcome of the Yabrán affair, the Peronists suffered a big defeat in the congressional elections in October 1997, losing even in some of their traditional bastions: Santa Fe, Entre Ríos, and Buenos Aires provinces. In the last province, the governor's wife headed the list of a defeated slate of congressional candidates. The "heir apparent" to the presidency, Duhalde, had been damaged, and Menem dealt him another blow, asserting that only he, Menem, could win in 1999 and openly launching a new reelection campaign despite the fact that no one showed much enthusiasm. Menem played various cards at once. A fanciful interpretation by the supreme court of the Constitution, a plebiscite in favor of constitutional reform, pressure exercised on the governors to line up behind him and leave Duhalde defenseless, all these were possibilities. Menem even went so far as to introduce a fifth column in the governor's territory, buying the support of some of Duhalde's *fideles.* By then, the opposition, now united, began to see the possibility of electoral success in 1999, but Menem attended to nothing else but destroying Duhalde, risking all that Peronism had achieved in its party institutionalization. When Menem launched a plebiscite on reelection in La Rioja, Duhalde responded by calling another in Buenos Aires province, where the president would undoubtedly suffer a decisive defeat. Menem then desisted in his reelection campaign, "excluding himself," though apparently not completely convinced by his decision because months later he attempted to campaign again. But this time the courts declared that his plan was completely illegal.

Menem failed in his efforts, but he managed to keep the illusion alive almost until almost the end of his government, dragging out the issue of his successor. In addition, he profoundly affected Duhalde, who in the electoral campaign had to sharpen his profile and offer alternative proposals, some rather far-fetched, which convinced no one. In addition, the Peronist governors preferred to distance themselves from the conflict, and many moved up the elections in their provinces so as not to compromise themselves because Duhalde had been unable to align behind him a unified and galvanized party. As in 1983, Peronism came to the 1999 elections without a leader, and it lost.

Indeed, since 1995, the space had been growing for a potential opposition political force, whose outline had yet to be defined. Late that year and shortly after Menem's resounding reelection triumph, the government suffered three electoral defeats: in Tucumán, where an ex-military figure from the *Process,* General Bussi, was elected governor; in the Chaco, where the Radicals, with the support of the FREPASO, triumphed; and in the federal capital, where the human rights activist Graciela Fernández Meijide of the FREPASO was elected senator with 46 percent of the votes, handily defeating the UCR and the Peronists. The results indicated various possible future contenders. The most novel was the FREPASO, which experienced a notable increase in votes. In it came together dissidents of the Peronists and the UCR, the *Unidad Socialista,* and other small leftist or populist groups. The FREPASO never achieved a national following comparable to the great parties or a party organization or explicit procedural rules of debate and decision. It was a party of leaders. Shortly after the elections, the presidential candidate, José O. Bordón, abandoned the party. Chacho Alvarez, a politician with a gift for speaking to the press and articulating the party's daily positions, emerged as the principal leader, seconded by Graciela Fernández Meijide and Aníbal Ibarra. The FREPASO enthused many and was the expression of a new and miniature "people's spring." The party tapped into different desires of society, which were not always compatible: a revamping of politics and the political leadership and the establishment of a center-left party as an alternative to the two traditional parties. Without repudiating the economic transformation that had occurred, the accent was put on social problems that reform had occasioned and on ethical and political questions such as corruption and the degradation of the country's institutions.

The UCR recovered from the crisis that it had been passing through since the catastrophic finale of Alfonsín's presidency, managed to overcome internal divisions, and won some significant electoral victories, above all with Fernando de la Rúa—an unbeatable *porteño* candidate—triumphant in 1996 as the first elected mayor of the city of Buenos Aires. Since 1995, the UCR and the FREPASO had coordinated their parliamentary actions and then established a working arrangement in the city government of Buenos Aires while they began to discuss the terms of a more formal alliance. It was not an easy task, given the different natures of both parties. The UCR had a long history and a solid party apparatus that was difficult to discipline and align but also not inclined to sudden changes; its members did not easily accept the idea of making room for a party with no history or formal party organization. But there was a conviction that together the UCR and FREPASO could defeat the Peronists, whereas individually defeat was almost assured. In 1997, they created the *Alianza para la Justicia, el Trabajo, y la Educación* (Alliance for Justice, Work, and Education), a named that transmitted the crux of their platform. They rode on the same ticket in nineteen of the twenty-four electoral districts and won a notable victory in the congressional elections. In total, they surpassed the Peronists by some 10 percent, prevailing in key districts such as Entre Ríos and Santa Fe. Graciela Fernández Meijide, twice the victor in the federal capital, defeated Chiche Duhalde, wife of the governor, in Buenos Aires province.

While Peronism was torn apart by infighting, the *Alianza* steadfastly advanced toward its victory in the 1999 elections. It was not easy for it to agree on a common platform, given the alliance of strange bedfellows both between the two parties and in them, though its was finally agreed not to question Cavallo's Convertibility Law and to emphasize social equality, respect for democratic institutions, and the struggle against corruption. José Luis Machinea, a former member of Juan Sourrouille's economic team and a man with good relations with the business community, was put in charge of the economic program. The negotiations over who would run on the *Alianza's* tickets were successfully resolved. There was an open convention for the presidential candidate in which de la Rúa easily defeated Fernández Meijide, and agreement was reached on the distribution of the principal candidatures and positions in the new government. Alvarez ran on the ticket as de la Rua's vice president, while Palito Ortega was the running mate of Duhalde for the Peronists, and Domingo Cavallo created a new party, *Acción para la República,* to organize the vote of the center-right sector of the electorate.

In the presidential election, de la Rúa and Alvarez obtained a clear victory: 48.5 percent of the votes, almost 10 percent more than Duhalde. On assuming office, the *Alianza* governed in six provinces and had a majority in the chamber of deputies. Peronism enjoyed a wide majority in the senate and controlled fourteen provinces, among them the most important ones: Buenos Aires (where Graciela Fernández Meijide had been defeated for governor by the Peronist Carlos Ruckauf), Santa Fe, and Córdoba, where the Radicals had lost for the first time since 1983. De la Rúa inherited a presidency with limited political powers and constrained by the economic crisis. Soon there was added the difficulty of transforming the electoral alliance into a governing force.

Epilogue: The New Argentina

Ten years of Menem's government unequivocally revealed how much the country had been transformed in the last quarter-century. The year 1976 was a turning point in Argentine history. The changes that have taken place since then, whose significance in some ways remained hidden during the first years of the democratic transition, were demonstrated during the 1990s. The country of the year 2000 resembled very little the one that in 1916 established a democratic political system that crowned the expansion of its economy and society. Nor did it resemble the other one that in 1945 linked the growth of its internal market to the promotion of social justice directed by the state. With respect to its expectations, illusions, and utopias, neither did it resemble the country that in 1960 dreamed of modernization and caught a glimpse of a promising future. In 2000, the prospect that the new Argentina presented was one of uncertainty about a difficult future, the reappearance of some of the negative traits of the past, but also a democratic political system that has been working efficiently.

In a certain sense, those changes are part of general global trends. The end of the Cold War on the one hand and on the other the deep economic restructuring compelled by rapid technological change, as well as the neoliberal ideological hegemony and what has come to be called "globalization," are causing the old ways to disappear and new ones to replace them with great difficulty, in the transition causing uncertainty, unemployment, and misery. Everywhere the state is relinquishing its role in overseeing the economy and is reducing its social welfare functions. Everywhere the great social pacts forged in the postwar period are unraveling, and the strong prosper at the expense of the weak. In this general crisis are revealed the two elements that customarily create such a situation: the destruction of the old, experienced by those who live through it as a collapse, and the slow emergence of the new, more difficult to perceive.

How much is there of each in the Argentina of the last quarter-century? An assessment in midstream of a turbulent river—thus undoubtedly will the final decades of the twentieth century be judged in the future—must acknowledge the depth of the crisis, one that is different in every country, and above all the singular way this process of restructuring is being directed. Argentina's experience in the twentieth century is that of Sisyphus: successive attempts that take off vigorously and end in catastrophe, falling far short of the established objectives. At the beginning of the 1990s, many thought that there was a new opportunity, that the other side of the shore was near, certainly within range, provided that a great and determined effort was made. Ten years later, the question remained open, but the predictions were more pessimistic and less quixotic. Many believe that another opportunity has been lost.

What strikes the observer first are the economic changes. The questions being debated a quarter-century ago today seem like ancient history to us. The opening up of the economy, and the retreat of a state that once regulated, provided assistance, and directly participated in economic life, have changed all the rules of the game. Another decisive change was price stability. For ten years, the country has lived without violent tugs-of-war between corporative groups, which had accompanied the outbreaks of inflation and formed the background to the country's political history. The decisive variable has unquestionably been the foreign debt, steadily growing since 1977. Nowadays it causes less of stir than it did ten years ago because the debt will clearly never be paid. Most agree that the country will depend indefinitely on constant infusions of credit by fickle and distrustful creditors and that, in sum, Argentina is a dependent country. Paying the service on the debt requires an efficient export economy, which seems a remote possibility. Debt repayment also entails permanent cuts in state spending, the pound of flesh repeatedly demanded by foreign creditors, with whom the country cannot afford to have a falling out, except under pain of being declared insolvent and reaching pariah status.

In the meantime, the policies that Martínez de Hoz initiated and that Cavallo brought to a conclusion have strongly shaken the productive apparatus. Unemployment is one problem that stands out clearly and seems now to be a structural characteristic of the new economy, but other facets of the economy's general outlines are less clear. With the Convertibility Law—a corset that supports at the same time as it asphyxiates—the overvaluing of the peso conditioned integration into the world economy. Initially this was demonstrated in the boom in imports that hit hard numerous businesspeople unable to compete. More slowly, there was a surge in exports, principally in agricultural products, oil, natural gas, all areas in which the country had some comparative advantages. The principal contribution came from agriculture, in a full process of transformation via agrochemicals, hybrid seeds, and mechanization. To the notable growth in its productive capacity is added the *Mercorsur,* which opened up an important market. The industrial sectors with an export profile have also been efficiently restructured by means of a high degree of concentration and by taking advantage of state support, which did not cease despite the so-called liberalization of the economy. Both agriculture and industry together accounted for three-fourths of the exports and were highly dynamic, but they had minimal impact on the overall economy, because of their limited linkage effects in the internal economy and because their greater efficiency was often based on a drastic reduction of the labor force, as was the case with the mechanization of agriculture.

The blow was much greater for those businesspeople whose interests were geared to the domestic market and who were forced to undergo a process of a survival of the fittest. Some adapted and prospered, others survived with difficulty, and many went bankrupt. The changes affected both the rudimentary national industry that had emerged in the postwar period and the more modern sector that had emerged after 1958 with the heavy participation of multinationals. Both had grown thanks to a captive internal market and systematic state support. Nevertheless, in the years before 1976, this system's pernicious effects on efficiency and competitiveness had already been greatly reduced, and in many sectors there had already occurred a transition from a "mechanical world" to "an electronic world" and to an approximation to global standards. That development was stunted with the great economic opening initiated in 1976 and completed in 1991. Subjected suddenly to the blow of strong competition that was more efficient and that had lower labor costs, only those firms survived that could modernize their productive processes. Simultaneously, a growing presence of foreign capital expanded into banking and retail chains, both characterized by a high degree of concentration. Among local businesspeople, the big holding companies best passed the Darwinian test, those that had grown after 1976 and had actively participated in the privatization of the state companies, diversifying their activities and even becoming international in their operations.

It is not easy to foresee the final result of these transformations, whose proponents claimed they would serve to restore a dynamic capitalism, atrophied by decades of state intervention, and occasion the re-encounter between private interest and the commonweal. There is no doubt that the transformations have benefited a segment—small but significant—of the economic actors. The "winners" triumphed across the board. But these changes seem to have created a limited general benefit, as the high rate of unemployment demonstrates. Those who adhere to an optimistic diagnosis—a smaller and less enthusiastic number at the end of the decade compared with the beginning—must deal with two big question marks, one structural and the other with regard to the actors themselves.

On the one hand, it is evident that Argentina cannot return to the path of economic growth, or even survive the suffocating presence of the debt, without increasing exports. But it is not clear that there is room in the world for such a change. What can the country do better than others, for whom to do it, and in what ways so that these undertakings have a beneficial effect on the economy as a whole? Such questions are not new. They were posed for the first time in the years between the two World Wars, with the decision made to opt for the shortcut of the protected domestic market. With that option closed, the question reappears today with even greater urgency. On the other hand, business has been liberated from state tutelage, which it always condemned, even though it took full advantage of it. After the final feast that was the privatization of the state companies, some are still gorging themselves on the leftovers of the former system and enjoying all kinds of state support. Will they opt in the future for that business culture they have demanded for so long, with risk taking and the maximization of benefits through innovation and efficiency, or will they find more appealing some new variant of that behavior that in the past they characterized as "perverse"?

It is highly unlikely that this restructuring, of the economy and the business classes' behavior will be successful if it is not guided by vigorous public policies. This possibility has been discarded with the local version of reform of the state, a program that nearly all the countries in the world have embarked on but that was implemented in Argentina with a characteristic combination of haste, carelessness, and insensitivity. In the short term, the state has abandoned all the means to intervene in and regulate the economy, means that had been built since 1930. It relinquished its ability to control the great economic variables and abandoned the financial instruments that made possible redistributing income, discarded its policies of economic promotion, its subsidies and incentives, and sold off the public companies. The latter, following the dismantling process, were transferred to private owners with the argument that this would bring greater efficiency and lower fiscal costs. But the state simultaneously relinquished in good measure its powers to control the workings of public services. In general, it renounced the very possibility of disciplining the economic actors, without even a minimum conception of the public interest.

In sum, the state threw the baby out with the bathwater. This relinquishing cannot be explained simply in general ideological terms. The neoliberal consensus and the success of its local spokespersons lay above all in the recognition that the old system had come to an end, that it had nothing left to give. Until 1930 the state redistributed part of the extraordinary largesse generated by the agricultural export sector. After that date, despite having concluded a period of exceptional prosperity, it redistributed more than ever, handing out support and sinecures to those who successfully fought for them. The state also had recourse to various methods: withholding a share of export earnings, printing money, borrowing from social security funds, increasing foreign debt. Only the situation of extreme vulnerability occasioned by the foreign debt and the decision to "tie up oneself" with the Convertibility Law to satisfy creditors' demands brought these practices to a halt; nonetheless, they reappeared every time those in power found some leeway for distributing the largesse, now confined to an increasingly select group of beneficiaries.

The neoliberal critique that circulated throughout the world affected not only the *dirigiste* state but also the social welfare state pledged to society's well-being. In this second aspect, the reduction in spending was part and parcel of the tendency to show less interest in those other social concerns that under any conception of the state are its preserve. The state reduced its role as an agent of economic development but also its role in providing health care, education, social security, defense, public safety, and public works. It sought to transfer responsibility to the general public, according to their respective means, and assumed an obligation only for poor or destitute people. The principle that the state had a role to play in guaranteeing equality and social justice, one of the most important conquests of Argentine society in the twentieth century, was abandoned.

Moreover, the very instruments of government eroded. Over the course of several decades, a slow destruction of the state apparatus occurred, a destruction that took place from within. Without fanfare, there was a systematic effort to remove efficient government functionaries, dismantle departments, pervert established norms, and install corruption. In recent years, longtime practices in government administration have been graphically exposed, abuses in power that the reduction in the size of the bureaucracy, brought about by concentrating decision-making power in fewer hands, made even more visible. The gravity and depth of the crisis in government administration were demonstrated by the effort expended to neutralize it by the presidents Perón in 1973 and Alfonsín ten years later and by placing such reforms of the last ten years or so on the agenda.

The program of state reform currently underway has not made progress in improving the efficiency in those areas that are typically the preserve of the government. The state's ability to collect taxes continues to be weak. Little has been accomplished in the area of judicial reform or in public administration at the provincial level or in the political system in general, where the costs of licit activities are high and its illicit ones incalculable. Where reforms were undertaken, as in education, it was along the ill-advised path of destroying what there was—for example, in secondary education—with the illusion, aborted in midstream, of building something new on the ruins. In sum, before neoliberalism's antistate crusade, the state had already proved incapable of imposing on society rational and foreseeable norms to guide the actors, mediate their conflicts, or provide a minimum of vigilance for the public interest. Lacking power, the state left people to their own devices and even used its final resources to favor the strongest among them at the expense of the rest.

The vast transformation was simply given legitimacy by the so-called neoliberalism, a new collective belief that in Argentina succeeded as well in establishing itself in society's "commonsense" understanding. The local version is a poor imitation, drawing inspiration above all from the Manchester school of liberalism in its advocating a great deal of freedom for the market and little political freedom, ideas distant from the original liberalism. Neoliberalism has advanced like a steamroller since 1976. During the last quarter-century, it has taken advantage of the elimination of alternative discourses accomplished during the military dictatorship, which frequently also eliminated the very people who could provide such alternatives. During the early years of democratic restoration, neoliberalism had to compete with the discourse of ethics, justice, and social solidarity. But the subsequent disillusion, and especially the experience with hyperinflation, was decisive in establishing the conviction that there was no alternative to the neoliberal proposals. At the same time, the great social pacts of the last half-century were explicitly or implicitly broken. The concept of the welfare state fell before the neoliberal advance, and with it the values of equality and social justice, as did populism, which was linked to such principles, as well as the left, which had proposed its own alternative for a better world.

During the decisive years in the first half of the 1990s, neoliberalism won over public opinion to its proposals and its agenda for resolving the country's problems. All public debate was reduced to the economy, and all debate on the economy to the issue of "stability." The new belief was effective in the attack, in its criticisms, and in establishing ideological hegemony. Thus were such expensive illusions of society abandoned as that of a good salary and full employment, the right to health care, education, social security, and generally an equality of opportunity ensured by the state. After 1995, faced with the real consequences of reform and austerity, the state revived those aspirations, but in an almost nostalgic way, confined to the parameters of neoliberal thinking.

Society differs notably from that established at the end of the nineteenth century. Since then, the prolonged expansion cycle combined economic growth, full employment, and a steady ability to integrate new contingents into the benefits of civil, political, and social rights. There were successive waves of mobilization and integration that endured even as late as the final decades of the twentieth century, with immigration from neighboring countries. The tendency was maintained in the two decades after 1955, despite a high degree of turmoil, but changed course in a sudden and decisive manner after 1976.

The world of work, where full employment had always been one of its chief characteristics, found itself eroded by high unemployment in what was its backbone, industry. The public sector, whose growth had compensated for some time for the contraction of industry, was also drastically reduced with the privatization of the public companies. Only those workers who were self-employed grew in numbers. But what in other times indicated a step in social ascent today camouflages unemployment. The latter has already easily exceeded 10 percent and hovers around 15 percent, climbing during downswings in the business cycle to above 18 percent. To this figure must be added a perhaps similar figure for underemployment. Such figures are not the result of momentary crisis or conjunctural conditions but now are structural features of the economy. Even those who have jobs suffer different forms of deterioration or precarious situations or work in the "underground economy."

The end of full employment has shaken working-class identity. The idea of the right to work and the guarantees associated with it have given way to "labor flexibility" and state employment granted as a form of welfare. Workers' representation suffers from a similar transformation: The unions have fewer dues-paying members and their social programs fewer resources. Their possibilities to exercise pressure or to lobby, characteristics of the period after 1945, have been considerably reduced. Many union leaders opted to go along with the changes and to pursue personal benefits for themselves or for their unions, which in some cases have been transformed into business enterprises. A few union leaders of a more combative stripe energetically protest in the street but lack the ability to exert influence in the collective bargaining process.

A parallel development is the consolidation of a permanent stratum of poor people, whose ranks have been augmented with seasonal workers, as well as of those self-employed in small-time endeavors, retired people, the unemployed, and the youth who never had a job, all of them "marginals" in one way or another. Such people represent an increasingly "dangerous" sector that often lives with one foot inside the law and one foot outside it. They have a social identity that partially overlaps with that of the working class, though it is one that is more attributed to than recognized by them. It is now agreed that a very large sector of the population—between a quarter and a third of the population—is living below what society regards as the poverty line. A bona fide and emblematic product of the restructuring of the state and the economy, today these people are a subject of academic study, a constituency for many nongovernmental organizations, and a disquieting reality whenever there is news of supermarket sackings, blocking of highways, land squatting, an inexorably growing mendicity, and a proliferation of street children without homes. Faced with such problems, the state timidly experiments with some social programs that are little more than forms of charity or electoral clientilism. There is a public perception of an acute crisis, but ultimately it is accepted with a bit of Christian resignation, encapsulated in President Menem's offhand remark, "There will always be poor people."

The middle class, the most characteristic class in the former society of social mobility and integration, has experienced a strong internal differentiation, particularly in terms of income. The outlines of the middle class have become blurry. Today it is difficult to know who genuinely belongs to it. Unlike what occurred at the beginning of the century or in 1950, a professional or university degree does not say much about one's income, although it is clear that there are entire groups of professionals, such as teachers or the military, whose situation has deteriorated en bloc. There are myriad personal stories in this saga. Some managed to gain entry to the winners' ranks; others at great pains were able to keep their heads above water; still others sank into the world of poverty. But as a whole, the middle classes have lost status. The values that made them have changed. In a Darwinian and changing world, the middle class has lost the ability to plan for its future and that of its children. Foresight—one of its classic attributes—gave way to a "live for the day" attitude, to taking advantage of whatever opportunities might arise—a trip abroad or the purchase of some household appliance. On the other hand, the prospect of owning one's own home, the bourgeois ideal, disappeared from the horizons of many.

Seen in its totality, society has become more polarized. The instruments and channels of negotiation and redistribution have disappeared, and some have won while others have lost. A vast sector sinks into poverty or sees its standard of living deteriorate, while the "rich," a group that includes a not-negligible part of the middle class, prospers ostentatiously and shamelessly flaunts its wealth, in many cases of recent origin. As a result, social inequalities are not hidden but are more apparent and dramatic. The former society, stolid and relatively homogeneous, in many ways egalitarian, has given way to another, sharply hierarchical and disconnected, separated by different possibilities for consumption and access to basic services, even by political and legal inequalities. In the cities, there are what have been described as "machines of duality," a reflection of those changes that simultaneously express contrast and exclusion: the deterioration of the urban infrastructure and services, unregulated urban growth and the crisis in public security, the rupture of a homogeneous urban public space and the development of some isolated redoubts—the exclusive shopping mall, the country home, entire neighborhoods—where small groups live in a world that is orderly, safe, prosperous, and efficient.

Just as in the cities, in society as a whole the public interest is disappearing as a concept of common responsibility, one that is built and upheld by solidarity with one's fellow citizens. Equal education in the public schools, public health provided in the country's hospitals, a public security protected by the police, and even the very public spaces—the city squares and streets that had been the center of a highly integrated society—are disappearing. What is growing to replace them is private space—the school, the health plan, the private security, the exclusive neighborhood—which only those who can pay have a right to. With the idea of social citizenship in tatters and social equality increasingly impaired, the new society encourages few practices beyond electoral participation with which to sustain democracy.

In terms of said democracy, the balance sheet is complex, although there are a number of recent accomplishments. The tragic legacy of the Process helped to eliminate some negative elements in the country's political culture, such as the recurring tendency of the actors to regard themselves as the embodiment of the nation and their adversaries as its enemies. With its fall from power, the military regime opened the door to building a democratic order based on absolute respect for human rights and respect for pluralism, debate, and the rule of law. Since December 1983, the country has achieved all kinds of records, among them four consecutive elections, all won by opposition candidates. Another milestone was that Peronism has lost two presidential elections, one while it was in power.

The country has also entered into a state of electoral normalcy. In 1983, Argentina's destiny seemed to hinge on a single election. There was a great confidence in the regenerative capacity of the vote. In hindsight, this belief was perhaps somewhat naive, but it was fundamental for rebuilding democratic institutions whose legitimacy rested on those convictions. By the next elections, expectations had already declined, and from that point on elections and voting gradually generated even fewer expectations. Voters learned to weigh their votes, to cast them alternately as rewards or punishment, with the final outcome generally decided by a fluctuating sector of independent voters. Voting today is routine, uninspiring but safe, and no one doubts the strength of democracy, whereas other alternatives—a coup d'état or revolutionary mobilization—have been banished from the scene.

Undoubtedly the sacred fire of former political life has considerably diminished, and the basic contours of the country's democratic system seem solid, with little room for participation outside the institutional framework. Austerity and reform awoke only isolated resistance, which had no significant political expression. In part, this was due to the transformation that society had experienced, which affected established ways of articulating and realizing political desires. Today it is difficult to imagine the networks of participation from an earlier period that were represented in mutual aid societies or rural cooperatives, culminating in the founding of political parties, or the chain effects of social and political protest, as was unleashed with the *Cordobazo*. But in part this is also related to the way that political practice was institutionalized beginning in 1983.

Unlike the unions, the political parties enjoy excellent health. They are not the forums of debate and participation and the incubators of ideas imagined in 1983. More prosaically, they are organizations devoted to recruiting political personnel and winning elections. They nominate candidates, build an image, and elaborate a discourse, try to win a following for both, and persuade people to vote for them. In the case of the Radicals and Peronists, a strong political identity gives them an electoral base, significant but insufficient. To win, the parties must attract independent votes. They do so with the resources of current politics; street mobilizations, which were still effective during the transition period, matter much less now than does television. The network of political clients continues to fulfill an important role, above all in the maintenance of a voting constituency, but the candidate's image is the decisive factor, as well as the latter's ability to interpret with words or actions the electorate's mood of the moment. The parties have become professional, making use of public consultants and image makers, and the party activist who once plastered posters to walls is no longer necessary. Finally, after the elections, the winners do not feel particularly bound to what was said in the campaign.

The political class gained efficiency, but at the price of distancing itself from its constituencies, which encourages the demobilizing tendencies in society, as was demonstrated in the first phase of Menem's government. As in any process of building democracy, there are positive and negative aspects, the half-full or half-empty glass that differentiates the optimists from the pessimists. The politicians' efficiency, almost bereft of any passion, makes the exercise of government easier. The politicians all belong to the same profession; they have similar problems, such as the compensation they receive for their work, and they come to a common understanding easily, sometimes with scandalous outcomes. But this situation facilitates the political agreements that are indispensable for governing. In the previous experience with democracy, such agreements always had a bad reputation, were labeled as "spurious" or done "behind the people's back." But today it is understood that they are more useful and constructive than factional strife and the negation of the adversary.

In the same way, the relationship between the various branches of government has become more fluid. Since 1853, the political custom in Argentina was to adapt constitutional precepts to the government's necessities; and generally the executive's power was enhanced in the process. With the rebuilding of democracy, the care taken to protect the powers of each branch of the government often came into conflict with the demands of a swiftly changing world, in particular because of the crisis unleashed at the end of Alfonsín's government. The pressing needs to manage the crisis, added to Menem's peculiar style of leadership, brought to the breaking point the relationship between the various branches of the government. At the end of his first administration, with reelection a success, democracy seemed threatened with extinction, overwhelmed by the individual will of the "leader." Nevertheless, things did not get out of hand. At crucial moments, both the congress and the courts established limits on executive power, public opinion was expressed, and the "leader" was forced to back off. The constitutional reform, on the other hand, has left room for a modification in the relationship between the branches, one that balances the government's necessities in times of emergency with the requirements of democratic checks and balances. As has happened between the parties, between the branches of the government there seems to predominate a pragmatic spirit.

Recent years have witnessed an awakening in society and a recuperation of practices that were common during the early years of the democratic transition but that fell into misuse during the height of Menem's government. A new "people's spring" took place, more modest than previous ones but an indication that civil society remains alive. An emblematic development has been the strengthening of the collective memory of the Process. Twenty years later, remembering the 1976 coup has become an established rite in the public schools; human rights organizations remain vigorous, and a legal opening appeared for redressing one of the Process's most terrible legacies—

the abduction of children of the "disappeared"—which, beyond the End Point Law and the pardoning of the ex-military commanders, permitted resuming legal action against those guilty of genocide. Another development is the press's persistent actions to revive the debate over social injustice, corruption, the abuse of power, and impunity. For their own reasons, in part professional ones, journalists have assumed a task that the parties are poorly fulfilling. On the other hand, episodes of social protest have begun to occur. The contrast between the general condemnation of the economic model and the rudimentary nature of the concrete demands demonstrates the abysmal disorganization of social protest, but also the existence of forces that are trying to break free and act. Finally, the development of the FREPASO, a new political force that gave a voice to the climate of unrest, was significant. Its platform, flimsy both ideologically and in policy, nonetheless was sufficient briefly to stir enthusiasm and galvanize support.

Whoever compares this collective enthusiasm that culminated in the presidential election of Fernando de la Rúa in October 1999 with that of the 1970s or 1980s would undoubtedly notice its much more modest character and the enormous breach between aspirations for change and possibilities of achieving them even incompletely. This poses a dilemma to the democratic system. Confronting reality, aware of the scarce room for maneuver that any government today has, political parties have little ability to articulate the still-diffuse discontent that the economic model has occasioned. They have even more difficulty in channeling and giving direction to the outbreaks of social protest that, without political containment and guidance, have the potential to become simultaneously both more violent and uncontrollable. Today the political parties give priority to their governing responsibilities, more than to capturing votes, perhaps because they realize that with votes alone they cannot maintain themselves in the government. But with such realism, they sacrifice their responsibility to think about a different country.

This situation facilitates the normal functioning of democracy. There is no extraparliamentary opposition or those who want to "upset the apple cart." But at the same time, a problem of illegitimacy is taking shape because of the weakening of democratic convictions. It is probable that some of the basic variables of the social reality may endure and grow even worse: unemployment, polarization, marginality, in a word, inequality. Although democracy is based solely on the concept of political equality, it requires some degree of social equality, without which it ceases to be credible. As was said in the French Revolution, the republic cannot just proclaim equality; it must do something to achieve real equality. Today not only does the state not do so, it deepens the inequalities. That is the risky feature of our recent democratic experience, which paradoxically has been successful in institutional terms, whereas society, which was traditionally egalitarian, has ceased to be so.

Postscript: January 2002

Fernando de la Rúa assumed the presidency of Argentina in December 1999, in a climate of enthusiasm and expectation. Two years later, on the night of December 21, 2001, he was forced to abandon the presidential residence in a helicopter. Outside, in the *Plaza de Mayo*, the scene of so many decisive events in Argentine history, an enraged multitude destroyed everything in sight and attempted to storm the *Casa Rosada*. What then occurred was one of the most violent examples of police repression in memory; no one knows at whose orders. The commotion did not end that day. Since then, and as of the middle of January 2002 when I write these words, there have been four successive presidents while the protests and outbursts of popular fury have continued sporadically.

Historians attempt to explain the past. That is their privilege. But in circumstances such as these, the historian surrenders to the concerned citizen and observer of events, who struggles to understand what is happening without the advantage of knowing the outcome. What follows is thus necessarily provisionary but unavoidable in a book that tries to explain to those who do not live in Argentina what is happening in a country difficult to understand, even for us Argentines. I write this as both a justification and excuse for the following words.

Why Did the *Alianza* Want to Win the Elections?

The *Alianza*, an electoral alliance of the *Unión Cívica Radical* and the FREPASO (*Frente para el País Solidaraio*), began to take shape in 1995 and was formally established in 1997. It won in that year a first and notable electoral success, one that would be ratified two years later in the presidential elections won by the Fernando de la Rúa of the UCR and Carlos "Chacho" Álvarez, the founder of the FREPASO. The Alliance was founded with a platform that was both limited and attractive: to make improvements in the "great transformation" that had been wrought during Menem's ten years in power and to correct its deficiencies. A new direction in the economy, taken for granted as firmly consolidated, would be added to those changes that the progressive community longed for: a respect for democratic institution—instead of Menem's virtually monarchical regime—and a strong dose of social equality, in order to correct the sharp inequalities occasioned by the economic "model."

The Alliance platform implied accepting said model, that is, the rules of the game imposed on the economy in 1991. In the first place, this meant maintaining the "convertibility" of a dollar for a peso, the great accomplishment of the Menem-Cavallo duo. In addition, the opening-up of the economy, the privatization of public services, and the search for a balanced budget as an almost single priority for a greatly reduced state were to continue. None of these objectives was questioned during the electoral campaign. Therefore, democratic scruples and social justice were the shared points of agreement—undoubtedly of a rather vague nature—between the UCR and the FREPASO. Both parties wanted to win, the UCR in order to overcome a long series of defeats and the FREPASO to surmount its status as a party of the progressive opposition and become a governing force. The two parties did not need any more than this minimum consensus to defeat a Peronism divided and weakened by a long recession. Parties and politicians exist to win, after all. Today we might wonder if made any sense that they tried.

In reality, the *Alianza* was not inheriting a successful economy but the failure of the "model." In the Epilogue, I explained the limitations of the "great transformation" of the 1990s and some of the characteristics of the situation existing at the end of 1999. By that point no one could ignore the economic dead-end represented by the existing model. Since mid-1998 the economy had been in a harsh recession. The Convertibility Plan, which in its moment had stablized the peso, had become a rigid strait-jacket. There was no way to abandon it without unleashing a social crisis, such as we are witnessing presently. The dilemma: while the Argentine economy stubbornly clung to Convertibility, it was impossible to become competitive since its costs, measured in dollars, were exorbitantly high. In a word, the country exported little.

For its part, the state had an enormous deficit. It spent a great deal, collected little in taxes, and owed everybody. It had sold the last of what it owned, and no more dollars were coming in from abroad. The economic collapse of Russia and then of Turkey, both before the announcement of Argentina's default on its foreign debt, had eliminated any possibility of international capital flow. The size of the government deficit was kept a secret. Menem's government had declared in 1999 that it was $4.5 billion; the *Alianza's* officials discovered that in reality it was triple that figure, some $15 billion. The party was over and the moment had arrived to pay. Menem's government had left the bill unpaid and the *Alianza* was forced to assume responsibility for the debt, and for all the social and political costs that it implied. There was neither time nor possibilities for doing any of what had been promised in the electoral campaign. Had the win been worth it under these conditions?

Pickets, Peronists, and Brokers

The *Alianza* government lived its brief existence constantly teetering on the edge. The threat came from three sides: the "pickets," the Peronists, and the brokers. The pickets are today the expression of a social protest that is the direct result of the "model." It is a social protest driven by unemployment, which was around 13 percent in 1999 and had risen two years later to 20 percent, to which one would have to add the many who worked only part-time. The situation worsened in these years because of the deepening recession, the cuts in wages, and the difficulties that provincial governments had in paying their public employees as the central government delayed ever more sending federal monies to them. Some 40 percent of the population was by then below the poverty line and the state could do nothing in a consistent fashion to solve the situation; it could offer only palliatives. The government's temporary work programs functioned as a kind of subsidy to the unemployed and are awarded in an arbitrary manner. In such a context, social protest grew to the point of becoming endemic.

This social protest was partly expressed through conventional means. Trade union leaders, especially the most "combative" ones, organized general strikes with protests against the successive austerity measures and budget cuts.

There had been many general strikes during Alfonsín's government and virtu-ally none under Menem, but during the *Alianza* government they reap-peared. In the big cities, these mobilizations grew increasingly intense, with a menacing character that harked back to the 1970s. In some of the smaller provincial capitals, where the payment of public employees was delayed, the protests turned into violent explosions of destructive fury. Such protests were of the sort that Argentina had long experienced. Their participants were workers with a steady income. What was new were the mobilizations of the unemployed. The "pickets" had appeared as early as 1999 in Salta and Neuquén, two provinces with important oil industries that were left pros-trate after the privatization of YPF, leaving a sizable number of workers un-employed. The pickets then spread to the industrial suburbs of the big cities, to the victims of industrial unemployment. In greater Buenos Aires the epicenter was the *La Matanza* district with its two million inhabitants and whose unemployed often cut off access to the capital. Buenos Aires was a city under siege.

These contingents of the unemployed have developed a tactic that became quintessentially theirs: they establish roadblocks, assign pickets to block the traffic, then start bonfires with old tires around which entire families gather. While the men, at times armed, maintain lookout with a menacing de-meanor, the women and children serve as human shields against an eventual repression. The pickets practice direct democracy and everything is resolved by popular assembly. There are among them leftist activists who have not managed to steer the protesters away from their basic demands, which at times are merely food and more often work, a government subsidy in the form of a job in the government's work programs. Throughout these last two years, in protests that were simultaneously spontaneous, menacing, and mov-ing, formal representative organizations took shape, formal committees nego-tiated with the public authorities and then distributed what was obtained, all in accordance with the degree of participation and militancy of each of the pickets who thus saw their combativeness rewarded.

The state essentially subsidizes the hostile mobilization and achieves a kind of compromise—an extremely fragile one—with the pickets. Why should they cease the roadblocks if the government ultimately makes conces-sions? Their actions are continuous, tenacious, and at times explosive. The government can neither satisfy their demands permanently nor repress the protesters. The government has no moral justification to do so nor does it have sufficient strength. As with Buenos Aires, the entire country is under siege.

To govern with the Peronists in the opposition has always been difficult. This has been an established fact since 1955, when Perón was overthrown. In 1999, the Peronists had a great deal of power: they governed many provinces, among them the largest ones, and only the federal districted eluded their control. They also enjoyed a sizable representation in the chamber of deputies, where the *Alianza* held a bare majority. Above all, they controlled the Senate. During the *Alianza's* government, the Peronists lacked a leader, the result of the long and unresolved war between the ex-president, Carlos Menem, and Peronism's defeated presidential candidate, Eduardo Duhalde. Their rivalry complicated things even more, while Peronism did not have a single platform or set of proposals. In the words of Joaquín Morales Solá, an outstanding journalist who covered the Senate, the Peronists were a "coterie of special interests and political bosses."

On the other hand, there were the union leaders, quite discredited by their corruption and their obliging attitude during Menem's government, but skillful in their handling of the social discontent. Their ultimate and non-negotiable objective was to maintain their discretionary control over the copious funds of the *obras sociales*. This was also a point of weakness for them, however, as the government could reduce their participation and even exclude them altogether from administering the union funds, something it threatened to do. Yet the government accepted the union leaders' demands in the negotiations and abandoned, pure and simple, its aspirations to introduce ethical behavior into the political system.

Then there were the governors of the provinces, on the one hand the *caciques* in the smaller provinces—in many cases members of veritable family dynasties—and on the other the powerful figures who controlled the big provinces: Carlos Reutemann in Santa Fe, José Manuel de la Sota in Córdoba, and Carlos Ruckauf in Buenos Aires, all with presidential aspirations for the 2003 elections. Also afflicted with the government's deficit problems, they defended above all their so-called co-participation, that is to say, the quota of the national taxes that was distributed among the provinces. As with the unions and the *obras sociales*, their overriding objective was also a source of weakness. The central government could distribute these funds with a certain degree of discretion and pressure the governors to support its policies, but it could not force them to reduce provincial spending, often earmarked for political clients and constituencies. When the economic crisis worsened, the revenue from the central government took increasingly longer to arrive and the governors—even those of the *Alianza*—began to get nervous and to question the government. This was the second front that the government had to face.

The most secretive of the special interests of the Peronist coterie turned out to be the Senators. The government assumed that it was enough to reach an agreement with each governor in order to gain the acquiescence of the Senators of their province. But it was not to be. During the Menem years, and perhaps from long before, the Senators had become accustomed to selling their votes only at a very high price. Determined to demonstrate to the government that nothing could be done without them, they practiced an unpredictable obstructionist policy, one that proved to be more complicated to handle.

On the whole, the Peronists did not have, during the two years of the *Alianza* government, an unremittingly hostile attitude toward the administration. They were the spokespersons of social discontent, as was the Peronist tradition, but did not abuse their power, given that they too were governing provinces that were under siege by social protests. Indeed, every time that the government needed support to approve legislation, it was able to reach an agreement. Yet the Peronist opposition made the *Alianza* government pay dearly, in more ways than one, and above all blocked any attempt at in-depth reform. Only at the very end, when the state's financial crisis put them against the ropes as well, and the political crisis indicated that profound changes were imminent, did they change their attitude and attempt to prop up the government.

The third threat to the government—the most serious one—was of course the economy, whose representative figure was the broker, that invisible financial operator who handled immense investment funds that in a matter of hours could be shifted from one part of the globe to another. These individuals were the most extreme expression of a capitalism, who, like the proverbial tiger, had escaped from the state's cage and was running amok, devouring everything in its path, even those who sought to ride it to their advantage. In that respect, the world of international finance in 2000 was very different from that of 1990. By the latter date, Argentina's negotiations were predominantly with the U.S. Treasury, the officials of the International Monetary Fund, and those of the Inter-American Development Bank, the two latter institutions being concerned with global economic stability and had medium and long-range policies. The brokers had ties to no one, had little knowledge of the complexities of domestic economic questions, and were given to sudden reactions. In response to immediate problems, they could with the click of a mouse move money from Argentina to Malaysia, Mexico, or Turkey. The results were devastating: the increase of the country's so-called risk factor—the prime rate it paid on its foreign debt bonds and which rose at a dizzying pace during these two years—as well as the drying up of credit and capital flight, with the reserves of the Central Bank declining from $30 billion in 1999 to $15 billion in October, 2001 and to a little less than $5 billion in December of that same year.

The brokers were only the most visible sign of an economic crisis whose full character was even more complicated. Argentina was in debt, on the verge of default, and experiencing a severe recession. The country needed to maintain foreign credit and at the same time jump-start the economy. But it could not do both things at once. Maintaining credit depended, in good measure, on the blessing of the IMF, whose demands were always the same: more "austerity," to reduce rapidly and drastically the fiscal deficit. But austerity measures only deepened the recession, lowered tax collection, which in turn increased the deficit anyway and reduced any possibility of paying the interest on the debt. It was a hopeless situation that exacerbated the other problems previously discussed. Any austerity measures increased social tensions and complicated the dire situation of the provincial governors, in their majority members of the Peronist opposition. Brokers, pickets, and Peronists alternated in exercising an implacable pressure on the government.

The spending of the provincial governors was the national budget's largest black hole. It was very difficult for the central government to make progress in its deficit reduction without adversely affecting the political position of the governors, who naturally resisted. This was precisely the point at which Menem's market reforms had stopped short; de la Rúa barely went much further in the attempt. Indeed, the "austerity" measures were implemented precisely where they were likely to encounter the weakest resistance. Nonetheless, they were insufficient to achieve a reasonable budgetary deficit, much less cover the inherited deficit of $15 billion. The government of the *Alianza* lived in the constant shadow of default. There were plenty of reasons for the brokers to continuously bet against Argentina and frustrate the intentions of the great international monetary organizations.

Administering the Default

In their handling of the economy, the *Alianza* government's directives only managed to delay what was, with hindsight, we can see today as inevitable: Argentina could not meet its service payments on the debt. They fought tenaciously, hoping for a recovery of the economy that as I write has yet to appear, but were frustrated by a series of unavoidable and successive setbacks, leaving the economy spiraling out of control. Each round would begin with an agreement reached with the IMF, granting the country some breathing room in return for fiscal austerity. The announcement of these austerity measures provoked social and political resistance and their implementation deepened the recession. Social protest was calling into question the ability of the government to maintain control of the situation and the recession its incapacity to pay the debt. Both unleashed the knee-jerk reaction of the brokers: the rise of its "risk country" status, the reduction of credit, and new appeals to the IMF.

Thus were the rules of the game. Those who were managing the economy had few options at their disposal, nor did they look for alternatives. Could anyone have been able to find a solution? It is not easy to imagine what kind of social support could have been called upon to chart a new course in economic policy different from those that dominated the current economy. Civic virtue is important for winning elections but is not enough at moments of negotiations when powerful interests are in play. Three decades of neoliberal policies and, above all, ten years of Menem's government had destroyed those business sectors whose interests were in the defense of the national economy. Even the so-called captains of industry, who had thrived during the military dictatorship of the Process, were in retreat. Something similar could be said about the labor movement: the majority of the union leaders were, in effect, now lobbyists for private interests. In the traditional equation, the state mediated between the workers and business; now a state that was virtually destroyed had to live with speculators and the unemployed.

The various ministers of economy did what they could, which was not much. José Luis Machinea, de la Rúa's first minister, was a methodical and efficient technocrat. He began his ministry with the news about the $15 billion deficit, then decreed an enormous tax increase and wage cuts. He negotiated with the IMF and committed himself to carrying forward the two points in his reform agenda that Menem had not completed: labor reform and deregulation of the unions' *obras sociales*. The first, finally approved by the Congress, was intended to make more flexible collective bargaining agreements. Many believed that this would increase efficiency and competitiveness, but the magnitude of the immediate crisis prevented it from ever being signed into law. In the case of the *obras sociales*, the monopoly of unions over their memberships in providing social services was to be eliminated; by introducing competition it was assumed the costs of medical care would be lower. The measure formed part of a reform project but affected the union leaders' most sensitive interest; it was used as a bargaining chip and the government went back and forth on the issue. Today it still remains unresolved.

By November 2000, the government's honeymoon period was over and economic recovery remained elusive. By then, foreign credit had dried up. The government's subsequent negotiation yielded the so-called *blindaje* ("financial armor") an infusion of emergency credit from the IMF to cover the eventual possibility of an inability to make service payments on the debt. It was hoped that this *blindaje* would provide sufficient breathing room to come out of the recession, providing resources for a vast public works and road-building project. This time the condition imposed by the IMF was a fiscal agreement with the provinces consisting of a planned reduction in the revenues-sharing policies with the central government. Congress approved it following a prolonged and difficult negotiation with the governors that abounded in harsh language, angry threats, and dramatic harangues. On the other hand, the IMF demanded a definitive reform in the social security system, partially privatized under Menem, and the elimination of some of the outstanding obligations that the state had with the country's retired community. The measure elicited a strong resistance in the Congress and the government vacillated between following the legislative route or resorting to an "emergency decree," Menem's favorite tactic, harshly criticized by the opposition in its moment and now systematically employed by de la Rúa.

The crisis arrived in March 2001, before any of these plans could take effect, hastened by the collapse of the Turkish economy and worsened by the government's political weakness. In the middle of the crisis, Machinea was removed; his successor, Ricardo López Murphy, lasted barely three days and was dragged down by the inflamed protest that his draconian austerity measures had provoked. It was then that Menem's former minister of economy and the father of the Convertibility Plan, Domingo Cavallo, was summoned by de la Rúa.

Cavallo began with innovation: he increased tariff barriers in order to stimulate production by domestic industry, breaking agreements with Brazil and the *Mercosur*. He also created a highly profitable tax on bank transactions and sketched out an exit for the Convertibility Plan, adding the euro to the dollar as the currency to back pesos, a move that displeased foreign creditors. He then carried out a large swap on the debt (*megacanje*), exchanging bonds on the debt that were fast becoming due for others that could be redeemed at a later date, a complicated operation that nonetheless prevented a default. A "Law of Public Credit," which conditioned all state spending to prior fulfillment of foreign debt obligations, failed in the Congress, above all due to the opposition of the UCR, since by this point the *Alianza* had ceased to exist. But while Cavallo succeeded in passing the "Zero Deficit" law, with which he fulfilled his promises with the IMF, he did not succeed in tranquilizing the brokers, and with reason. In November, he launched another risky idea: restructuring the debt, converting short-term bonds into more attractive and, it was said, secure long-term ones. An accelerated capital flight and a run on the banks, a kind of "market coup d'état," interrupted the negotiations midway and threatened to drag down the banking system along with it. On December 1, 2001, the government ordered the freezing of all bank deposits through what began to be called the *corralito* ("little corral"), which many viewed as a mere confiscation of their savings. By then the government, recently defeated in the October elections, lacked the political strength to defend the measure, or even to defend itself.

The Failure of a Political Leadership

In sum, the possibilities for a successful *Alianza* administration were now remote; nonetheless, there remained a chance. The sold electoral support and broad confidence *Alianza* had elicited in the 1999 elections were not inconsequential things. Perhaps there was some room for maneuver to avoid a cataclysm, provided there was an energetic political leadership, one that was technically competent and that exploited to full advantage potential supporters. In that respect, the *Alianza* government was a total failure. No one was prepared to take any risks. From the beginning, the members of the government were divided between "progressives," who were more concerned about the social crisis, and the "orthodox" group, only concerned with the economy. The two sides lacked a common agenda, perhaps because the original *Alianza* platform had envisioned only the need to make improvements in administering a healthy economy. On the other hand, a political coalition such as this was a new experience in Argentina, where the traditional parties were characterized by their exclusiveness and personalist leadership. What did each of the parties contribute to the failure?

In the FREPASO, a critical wing had quickly emerged, one that did not sympathize with the government's unpopular measures and which distanced itself from the administration and preferred principles to power. That was initially not the case of the FREPASO's leader, then vice-president Chacho Álvarez, who defended the president with resolute faithfulness but a very idiosyncratic style. Álvarez talked constantly and publicly assumed a very prominent role, which contrasted starkly with de la Rúa's diffidence, and ended up throwing off-balance their partnership. Above all, as will be seen, Álvarez became a prisoner of his own words, especially during the debate over corruption in the Senate and the issue of political reform, an issue that he judged he could not compromise on. Ultimately, he too chose principles over power. In the UCR a critical wing emerged as well, but more serious than that was the silent hostility that spread among the party's leaders, annoyed by the scarce portion assigned the party in the division of the government spoils. The UCR became divided in two. One sector grouped around the president, while Alfonsín led the rest, attempting to balance the collective disagreement with his fundamental sense of political responsibility.

Fernando de la Rúa turned out to be a miserable director of this difficult ensemble. De la Rúa was the *Alianza's* candidate without ever believing in it, in reality the most conservative of the UCR leaders. Soon other characteristics of his political personality would reveal themselves: pettiness in his dealings with his FREPASO allies—much more loyal than he to the coalition spirit—mistrust of collaborators, scant ability to delegate responsibilities, and an extreme difficulty in making decisions. These were not traits unknown to those who had anointed him as the presidential candidate. In his cabinet were to be found the best individuals of the *Alianza*, with their diverse abilities, different perspectives and disagreements, but de la Rúa did little to coordinate them. He surrounded himself with a group of young advisers, headed by his son, who sought to strengthen his public image as a leader. To achieve that goal, he removed the experienced leaders of the *Alianza*, who overshadowed him, and replaced them with more loyal and harmless individuals. Along this path, de la Rúa ended up destroying the *Alianza* itself.

The destruction of the *Alianza* was unleashed by the well-publicized Senate scandal in which came together many of the contradictions in the government already noted. In April 2000, in accordance with its pledge to the IMF, the government sent to the Congress the Law of Labor Reform. The negotiation was difficult; there was no clear support coming from the business community and the union leaders resisted it. Determined to get the bill passed, the government threatened to strip the unions of their funds for the *obras sociales*, only to then (in private) negotiate a covert support. By these means, the government won approval for the law in the Chamber of Deputies but encountered an unexpected obstacle in the Senate, where the Senators sought to demonstrate their independence and reestablish the rewards system that had worked fluidly during Menem. The Senators wanted compensation and finally someone from the government offered it to them. Political realism triumphed and the bill was passed.

The problem was that a well-respected journalist exposed the scandal, a Senator brought up the issue in the Congress, and Álvarez, whose constitutional role it was to preside over the Senate, had to enter into battle, obliged both by his principles and by his previous public statements denouncing corruption. Álvarez demanded a full investigation and punishment for those responsible, most of who were quickly identified. He believed that with this issue the great reform of the country's political practices that he had been urging could begin. But he lacked the support, naturally, from the Peronists but also from the UCR—some Senators from the governing party had also engaged in these and other practices—nor did he receive it from the government, which tried to protect the functionary who had actually made the bribe. By this stage, no one doubted that there had been bribes, but all agreed to close the matter. The president even rewarded the guilty party with a promotion to the ministry of labor. Álvarez, trapped by his denunciations and by principle, resigned the vice-presidency.

Álvarez's resignation, and evidence that the government was abandoning one of the major planks in its electoral platform—introducing ethics into politics—marked the end of the *Alianza*. Álvarez continued to support the government from the sidelines, but in May 2001 he announced his retirement from politics. By now, little remained of his FREPASO. Critics of the outcome of the Senate scandal among the FREPASO broke irrevocably with the government, and, together with dissidents from the UCR, threw themselves into establishing a new political party. Those faithful to the president, their hand now strengthened, aimed to improve relations with the most powerful sectors of the business community. They decided to replace Machinea, by now greatly weakened, with an individual from the establishment, Doming Cavallo. His designation as minister of economy precipitated the exodus of the *Alianza* leaders who still held government positions, and only those personally loyal to de la Rúa remained. At that point, the UCR began to distance itself from the president.

The circumstances surrounding the arrival of Cavallo to the government demonstrated the deterioration of de la Rúa's and his team's ability to govern as well as the flimsiness of his political support. In fact, there was assembled a new governing alliance, one with a marked conservative profile. The head of his own small party, *Acción para la República*, Cavallo had been defeated barely a year before by a candidate from the *Alianza* in the Buenos Aires mayor's race. Cavallo was characterized by his strong personality and messianic streak, the latter becoming even more pronounced since 1995, when he left the government. Selected at the high point of one of the country's reoccurring social and political crises—in those very days there were demonstrations and protesters set up road blocks in streets— Cavallo presented himself as the republic's savior and promised to rectify the situation without pain and suffering, all of which the majority of the population believed. Cavallo, it was thought, had the magic solution.

He sought to be the "superminister," with extraordinary powers. Congress, reluctantly, gave him everything he asked for. Yet in the nine months of his ministry he demonstrated more a talent for politics (and not even much for that) than for managing the economy. He perceived from the outset that there would be no solution without a strong executive and demanded the reconstitution of the *Alianza*; Álvarez supported him but the UCR did not. He then made an appeal for a "government of national unity" that included the Peronists, who preferred to witness the government's collapse and prepare to take power. De la Rúa, irritable and in over his head, was incapable of convincing any of his followers to build the necessary alliances. Ultimately, the president and the superminister governed alone, clinging to one another.

In the job of managing the economy, Cavallo made one mistake after another. He probably had lost the knack, the ability to understand fully a situation that had changed drastically since 1991. His former contacts in the U.S. government and the IMF lacked the power they once wielded. He tried various strategies, convinced that he still had the touch, railing against everyone—the banks, Brazil, the business community, even the IMF—and constantly fighting. He earned a reputation for being unpredictable, pulling rabbits out of his hat until the day he discovered that his credibility had disappeared.

But before this outcome, in October 2001, there were general elections for half of the seats in the Chamber of Deputies and all of the Senate. It was a curious and interesting election. The *Alianza's* dissidents established a new party, *Acción para una República de Iguales*, led by a charismatic former UCR congresswoman, Lilita Carrió. This new party aspired to take the place of the expiring FREPASO. The *Alianza*—or what remained of it—ran candidates who strongly opposed the president's policies. Cavallo's party, rebuffed by the *Alianza*, allied with the Peronists. In these circumstances, the president announced that he was supporting no particular candidates in the election; therefore, he could neither win nor lose.

The Peronists did not spark much enthusiasm, governing as they were provinces that were all running deficits, in debt, and behind in salary payments to their public employees. The Peronists were also neutralized by a discontent that teetered on violent protest. Nonetheless, their status as opposition party favored them and they handily won. The *Alianza* lost five million votes compared to the 1999 electoral results, the Peronists one million. The most surprising figure was the number of abstention votes that, added to those who did not vote at all, comprised almost half the electorate. The so-called anger vote was a clear warning to the politicians that, as a group, they were being condemned. The antipolitical discourse was gaining currency and growing stronger.

Meanwhile, the Peronists achieved an ample majority in the two houses of Congress and made preparations to assume power. They did it more as a reflex than with an organized plan, since they still had not resolved their internal conflicts and still lacked a recognized leader. They began by naming a Peronist as Senate president; since there was no longer a vice-president, he was the next in line in presidential succession.

An Unresolved Political Crisis

In December 2001, the political crisis and the economic crisis combined, intensifying one another, dragging down with them the de la Rúa government. The government responded to a run on the banks in late November by freezing all bank deposits, what was referred to as the *corralito*. It was a measure worthy of a revolutionary government; but the government that took it on was in reality in a state of disarray, lacking all international financial support, with a Peronist opposition that had decided to let it fall, and confronting a palpable social tension. Brokers, pickets, and Peronists decided that the time had come for de la Rúa to leave power and it seemed the majority of the UCR concurred.

On December 19 there were supermarket ransackings in greater Buenos Aires. Groups of the poor and unemployed surrounded the supermarkets demanding bags of food or simply enteribng and taking what they could. In general, the police did not intervene and it is suspected that the looters were encouraged by local Peronist ward bosses. At any rate, it was not difficult to mobilize them, both because of their desperate situation and due to the conviction that the government lacked the force to stop them in a systematic fashion.

The supermarket ransackings were something familiar, almost predictable. By themselves, they probably would not have provoked the same horrified reaction as in 1989 when they triggered Alfonsín's final days. But on December 20 something original and more shocking occurred: large contingents of the Buenos Aires middle class—the very people who had voted massively for the UCR and de la Rúa—took to the streets, banging pots in protest. Both rowdy and orderly multitudes gathered at the city's principal street corners, as well as in the *Plaza de Mayo*. They protested for many reasons, but above all because of the *corralito*, which froze their deposits and savings. One of the groups gathered outside the house of Minister Cavallo, who resigned on the morning of December 21.

About the same time, crowds had gathered in the *Plaza de Mayo*. The peaceful middle-class demonstrators were joined by groups of battle-hardened and disciplined young activists who set about systematically destroying everything in sight, especially the shop windows of businesses and banks, and hurling stones at the police. They were not groups easy to identify. For a moment it seemed as if they would launch an assault against the presidential residence when someone gave the order to suppress them. This was done in a brutal manner without distinguishing—was it possible?—the pacifist protesters of the *cacerolazo* from the violent activists. The images transmitted by television were extremely damaging to the government. President de la Rúa made a useless call for a government of national unity and immediately presented his resignation, abandoning the presidential palace in a helicopter.

Between December 21 and January 2, 2002, there was an absolute void of power. Some five presidents rapidly succeeded one another. The Peronist leaders, with a sizable majority in the Congress where the new president would be chosen, only could agree on a minor political figure—Adolfo Rordíguez Sáa, governor of the small province of San Luis—and on a rapid call for elections.

The new president was sworn in on Christmas Day, and had resigned before New Year's. In the interim, Rordíguez Sáa announced, smiling broadly, that Argentina was ceasing payment on its foreign debt, the dreaded "default." Despite the fact he tried to placate everyone, making every imaginable promise, on Friday December 28 there was another *cacerolazo*, perhaps occasioned by the appearance of many of Menem's former collaborators in the new government, perhaps because the *corralito* was beginning to squeeze hard. As on the previous occasion, it was accompanied by supermarket ransackings in the poorer neighborhoods of greater Buenos Aires and by violent protests in the *Plaza de Mayo*. Meanwhile, the principal Peronist leaders did nothing to support the president that they had just selected, having discovered that he intended to stay in power much longer than the two months he had agreed to. Rodríguez Sáa got the message and immediately resigned.

Two days later, the Congress selected as president Eduardo Duhalde, the defeated Peronist candidate from the 1999 elections, who was to serve out the two years that remained of de la Rúa's term. With the support of the Peronist political apparatus of Buenos Aires province and with the consent of the other Peronist leaders, as well as the sympathetic support of Alfonsín and the UCR, Duhalde apparently (who knows) managed to settle into power.

Argentina is presently in the midst of a crisis of incalculable dimensions, the defining characteristics of which have already been suggested in the Epilogue: economic disarray, a greatly weakened state, and tension between a political system that, until recently, had formally been working efficiently but whose politicians are seen as out of touch, increasingly isolated from a society that sinks deeper into poverty. Today the country has reached a nadir on all fronts. The default led to the abandonment of the Convertibility Plan, the most prized achievement of 1990s, and the devaluation of the peso threatens to wreak havoc with savings and incomes. The recession is worse than ever, no one is paying their taxes and it is unclear how the state will pay able to pay public-sector wages. Society continues to mobilize in protest and the proliferating *cacerolazo* protests have taken on an epic quality. It has become common to say that the people finally decided to represent themselves and sweep away corrupt politicians, keeping a close eye on the government's actions, prepared to take to the streets to repudiate any deviation from the public interest, one that is threatened alike by politicians, banks, and foreign companies. It is a powerful social protest but one that still has not decided so much what it is in favor of as what it is against. They are masses in a state of effervescence, fertile recruiting grounds for someone, yet threatened by the excesses of the looters and advocates of violence. The present political leadership has managed to save institutional democracy and constitutional legality, to reach a reasonable agreement among itself and to reconstitute some degree of political authority. Nonetheless, the political class increasingly lacks legitimacy. Today, January 20, 2002, there are many possible outcomes to the present situation. None of them are good.

Glossary of Spanish Terms

apertura   Literally an "opening up," a period of relaxed restrictions, applied to both the economy and society.

arrendatario   A sharecropper, especially in the littoral.

carapintadas   Hard-line faction in the Argentine army, which undertook several rebellions against the government in the late 1980s and early 1990s.

caudillo   In the nineteenth century, a warlord. In the twentieth century, a political boss or charismatic political leader.

chacareros   Small farmers who owned some or all of the land they worked.

clasismo   In the 1970s, a working-class movement devoted to class struggle and the establishment of a socialist state.

colonos   Agricultural colonists, especially in Santa Fe province.

conventillo   Immigrant tenement, especially in Buenos Aires.

criollo   A creole, or native-born Argentine.

desaparecidos   Victims of the state terrorism of the 1970s who were "disappeared."

desarrollismo   Literally "developmentalism," an economic program and political movement associated with President Arturo Frondizi (1958–62) which stressed deepening industrialization through a partnership with multinational capital and reaching a political accommodation with the leading "factors of power."

destape   After the restoration of democracy in the 1980s, the initial euphoric period of restored civil liberties and free artistic and intellectual expression.

foquismo	The guerrilla theory according to which armed struggle can help to create revolutionary conditions.
porteño	A resident of the city of Buenos Aires.
puntero	A political ward boss.
renovadores	The reformist current in the Peronist movement during the late 1980s and early 1990s.
unicato	The period of oligarchical political rule in the late nineteenth and early twentieth centuries.
vandorismo	A current within the trade union movement associated with labor leader Augusto Vandor that employed a pragmatic approach in its dealings with business and politically sought to free the Peronist movement from Perón's direct control.

Bibliography

The following bibliography, though not exhaustive, provides a starting point for the systematic study of the themes dealt with in the text. As with any selection, it represents a personal opinion about the interest and utility of certain studies. The bibliography is presented in four large chronological sections, and the works are grouped according to four thematic areas: general studies and politics; the economy; society; and culture-ideology. Such a classification is rough, and some titles overlap these broad categories. For anglophone readership, I have offered the original English-language titles of the translated works cited in the Spanish-language edition of this book and have added a few titles.

I. To 1930

1. General Works and Politics

Alén Lascano, Luis C. *La Argentina ilusionada, 1922–1930*. Buenos Aires: La Bastilla, 1975.

Alonso, Paula. *Entre la revolución y las urnas*. Buenos Aires: Sudamericana/Universidad de San Andrés, 2000.

Aricó, José A. *La hipótesis de Justo*. Buenos Aires: Sudamericana, 1999.

Bonaudo, Marta. "Society and Politics: From Social Mobilization to Civic Participation (Santa Fe, 1890–1901)." In *Region and Nation: Politics, Economy, and Society in Twentieth-Century Argentina*, ed. James P. Brennan and Ofelia Pianetto. New York: St. Martin's Press, 2000.

Botana, Natalio. *El orden conservador*. 2d ed. Buenos Aires: Sudamericana, 1994.

Botana, Natalio, and Ezequiel Gallo. *De la República posible a la República verdadera*. Buenos Aires: Ariel, 1997.

Cantón, Darío. *Elecciones y partidos políticos en la Argentina: Historia, interpretación, y balance, 1910–1966*. Buenos Aires: Siglo xxi, 1973.

Cantón, Darío, José Luis Moreno, and Alberto Ciria. *Argentina: La democracia constitucional y su crisis*. Buenos Aires: Paidós, 1972.

De Privitellio, Luciano, and Luis Alberto Romero. *Grandes discursos de la historia argentina*. Buenos Aires: Aguilar, 2000.

Falcón, Ricardo, ed. *Democracia, conflicto social, y renovación de ideas (1916–1930): Nueva historia argentina 6*. Buenos Aires: Sudamericana, 2000.

Gallo, Ezequiel. *Carlos Pellegrini: Orden y reforma*. Buenos Aires: Fondo de Cultura Económica, 1997.

Gallo, Ezequiel, and Silvia Sigal. "La formación de los partidos políticos contemporáneos: La ucr (1890–1916)." In *Argentina, sociedad de masas*, comp. Torcuato Di Tella et al. Buenos Aires: Eudeba, 1966.

Íñigo Carrera, Héctor J. *La experiencia radical, 1916–1922*. Buenos Aires: Ediciones La Bastilla, 1980.

Lobato, Mirta, ed. *El progreso, la modernización, y sus límites (1880–1916): Nueva historia argentina 5*. Buenos Aires: Sudamericana, 2000.

Mustapic, Ana María. "Conflictos institucionales durante el primer gobierno radical, 1916–1922." *Desarrollo Económico* 93, 24 (April–June 1984).

Potash, Robert A. *The Army and Politics in Argentina, 1928–1945: Yrigoyen to Perón*. Stanford: Stanford University Press, 1969.

Remmer, Karen L. *Party Competition in Argentina and Chile: Political Recruitment and Public Policy, 1890–1930*. Lincoln and London: University of Nebraska Press, 1984.

Rock, David. *Politics in Argentina, 1890–1930: The Rise and Fall of Radicalism*. Cambridge: Cambridge University Press, 1975.

Rodríguez, Celso. *Lencinas y Cantoni: El populismo cuyano en tiempos de Yrigoyen*. Buenos Aires: Editorial de Belgrano, 1979.

Romero, José Luis. *Las ideas políticas en Argentina*. 5th ed. Buenos Aires: Fondo de Cultura Econímica, 1975.

Romero, José Luis, and Luis Alberto Romero, eds. *Buenos Aires, historia de cuatro siglos*. 2d ed. Buenos Aires: Editorial Altamira, 2000.

Romero, Luis Alberto. *Argentina: Crónica total del siglo xx*. Buenos Aires: Aguilar, 2000.

Romero, Luis Alberto, et al. *El radicalismo*. Buenos Aires: Carlos Pérez Editores, 1969.

Rouquié, Alain. *Poder militar y sociedad política en la Argentina 1: Hasta 1943*. Buenos Aires: Emecé, 1981.

Sábato, Jorge F., and Jorge Schvarzer. "Funcionamiento de la economía y poder político en la Argentina: Trabas para la democracia." In *¿Cómo renacen las democracias?* ed. Alain Rouquié and Jorge Schvarzer. Buenos Aires: Emecé, 1985.

Sidicaro, Ricardo. *La política mirada desde arriba: Las ideas del diario La Nación, 1909–1989*. Buenos Aires: Sudamericana, 1993.

Walter, Richard. *The Socialist Party of Argentina, 1890–1930*. Austin: University of Texas Press, 1977.

2. Economy

Arcondo, Aníbal. "El conflicto agrario de 1912: Ensayo de interpretación." *Desarrollo Económico* 20, 79 (October–December 1980).

Cortés Conde, Roberto. *La economía argentina en el largo plazo.* Buenos Aires: Fondo de Cultura Económica, 1997.

Díaz Alejandro, Carlos. *Essays on the Economic History of the Argentine Republic.* New Haven: Yale University Press, 1970.

Fodor, Jorge, and Arturo O'Connell. "La Argentina y la economía atlántica en la primera mitad del siglo xx." *Desarrollo Económico* 13, 49 (April–June 1973).

Gerchunoff, Pablo, and Lucas Llach. *El ciclo de la ilusión y el desencanto: Un siglo de políticas económicas argentinas.* Buenos Aires: Ariel, 1998.

Giberti, Horacio C. E. *El desarrollo agrario argentino.* Buenos Aires: Eudeba, 1964.

Giménez Zapiola, Marcos, ed. *El régimen oligárquico: Materiales para el estudio de la realidad argentina (hasta 1930).* Buenos Aires: Amorrortu, 1975.

———. *Historia económica de la ganadería argentina.* Buenos Aires: Solar, 1981.

Gravil, Roger. *The Anglo-Argentine Connection, 1900–1939.* Boulder and London: Westview Press, 1985.

Halperín Donghi, Tulio. "Canción de otoño en primavera: Previsiones sobre la crisis de la agricultura cerealera argentina (1894–1930)." In *El espejo de la historia: Problemas argentinos y perspectivas latinoamericanas.* Buenos Aires: Sudamericana, 1987.

Jorge, Eduardo F. *Industria y concentración económica.* Buenos Aires: Siglo xxi, 1971.

Llach, Juan José, ed. *La Argentina que no fue* i: *Las fragilidades de la Argentina agroexportadora.* Buenos Aires: Ediciones del ides, 1985.

Pucciarelli, Alfredo. *El capitalismo agrario pampeano,* Buenos Aires: Hyspamérica, 1986.

Sábato, Jorge F. *La clase dominante en la Argentina moderna: Formación y características.* Buenos Aires: Cisea-Grupo Editor Latinoamericano, 1988.

Smith, Peter H. *Politics and Beef in Argentina: Patterns of Conflict and Change.* New York: Columbia University Press, 1969.

Solberg, Carl. "Descontento rural y política agraria en la Argentina, 1912–1930." In *El régimen oligárquico: Materiales para el estudio de la realidad argentina (hasta 1930),* ed. Marcos Giménez Zapiola. Buenos Aires: Amorrortu, 1975.

Villanueva, Javier. "El origen de la industrialización argentina." *Desarrollo Económico* 12, 47 (October–December 1972).

3. Society

Ansaldi, Waldo, ed. *Conflictos obrero-rurales pampeanos (1900–1937).* Buenos Aires: Centro Editor de América Latina, 1993.

Armus, Diego, ed. *Mundo urbano y cultura popular.* Buenos Aires: Sudamericana, 1990.

Di Tella, Torcuato, et al. *Argentina, sociedad de masas.* Buenos Aires: Eudeba, 1966.

Gutiérrez, Leandro H. "Condiciones materiales de vida en los sectores populares en el Buenos Aires finisecula." In *De historia e historiadores: Homenaje a José Luis Romero.* Mexico City: Siglo xxi, 1982.

Gutiérrez, Leandro H., and Luis Alberto Romero. *Sectores populares, cultura, y política: Buenos Aires en la entreguerra.* Buenos Aires: Sudamericana, 1995.

Korn, Francis. *Buenos Aires: Los huéspedes del 20.* 2d ed. Buenos Aires: gel, 1989.

Moya, José. *Cousins and Strangers: Spanish Immigration in Buenos Aires, 1850–1930.* Berkeley and Los Angeles: University of California Press, 1998.

Panettieri, José. *Los trabajadores.* Buenos Aires: Jorge Álvarez, 1968.

Suriano, Juan, ed. *La cuestión social en Argentina, 1870–1943.* Buenos Aires: La Colmena, 2000.

4. Culture and Ideology

Altamirano, Carlos, and Beatriz Sarlo. *Ensayos argentinos: De Sarmiento a la vanguardia.* Buenos Aires: Centro Editor de América Latina, 1983.

Bertoni, Lilia Ana. *Patriotas, cosmopolitas, y nacionalistas.* Buenos Aires: Fondo de Cultura Económica, 2000.

Halperin Donghi, Tulio. *Vida y muerte de la República verdadera (1910–1930).* Buenos Aires: Ariel, 2000.

Prieto, Adolfo. *El discurso criollista en la formación de la Argentina moderna.* Buenos Aires: Sudamericana, 1988.

Romero, José Luis. *El desarrollo de las ideas en la sociedad argentina del siglo xx.* Buenos Aires: Fondo de Cultura Económica, 1965.

———. "El ensayo reformista." In *Situaciones e ideologías en América Latina.* Buenos Aires: Sudamericana, 1984.

Saitta, Sylvia. *Regueros de tinta: El diario* Crítica *en la década de 1920.* Buenos Aires: Sudamericana, 1998.

Sarlo, Beatriz. *El imperio de los sentimientos.* Buenos Aires: Catálogos, 1985.

———. *Una modernidad periférica: Buenos Aires 1920 y 1930.* Buenos Aires: Ediciones Nueva Visión, 1988.

Terán, Oscar. *Vida intelectual en el Buenos Aires fin-de-siglo (1880–1910).* Buenos Aires: Fondo de Cultura Económica, 2000.

II. 1930–1955

1. General Works and Politics

Bianchi, Susana, and Norma Sanchís. *El partido peronista femenino.* Buenos Aires: Centro Editor de América Latina, 1988.

Caimari, Lila M. *Perón y la Iglesia católica.* Buenos Aires: Ariel, 1995.

Cattaruzza, Alejandro. *Marcelo T. de Alvear: El compromiso y la distancia*. Buenos Aires: Fondo de Cultura Económica, 1997.

Ciria, Alberto. *Partidos y poder en la Argentina moderna (1930–1946)*. 3d ed. Buenos Aires: Ediciones de la Flor, 1975.

————. *Política y cultura popular: La Argentina peronista, 1946–1955*. Buenos Aires: Ediciones de la Flor, 1983.

Conil Paz, Alberto, and Gustavo Ferrari. *Política exterior argentina, 1930–1962*. Buenos Aires: Círculo Militar, 1971.

De Privitellio, Luciano. *Agustín Pedro Justo: Las armas en la política*. Buenos Aires: Fondo de Cultura Económica, 1997.

Del Barco, Ricardo. *El régimen peronista, 1946–1955*. Buenos Aires: Editorial de Belgrano, 1983.

Escudé, Carlos. *Gran Bretaña, Estados Unidos, y la declinación argentina, 1942–1949*. Buenos Aires: Editorial de Belgrano, 1983.

Gambini, Hugo. *Historia del peronismo*. Buenos Aires: Planeta, 1999.

Halperín Donghi, Tulio. *La democracia de masas*. Buenos Aires: Paidós, 1972.

Luna, Félix. *Ortiz: Reportaje a la Argentina opulenta*. Buenos Aires: Sudamericana, 1978.

————. *Alvear*. Buenos Aires: Editorial de Belgrano, 1982.

————. *Perón y su tiempo*. 3 vols. Buenos Aires: Sudamericana, 1986.

Mora y Araujo, Manuel, and Ignacio Llorente. *El voto peronista: Ensayos de sociología electoral argentina*. Buenos Aires: Sudamericana, 1980.

Navarro, Marysa. *Evita*. Buenos Aires: Corregidor, 1981.

Persello, Ana Virginia. *El radicalismo en crisis (1930–1943)*. Rosario: Fundación Ross, 1996.

Potash, Robert A. *The Army and Politics in Argentina, 1945–1962: Perón to Frondizi*. Stanford: Stanford University Press, 1980.

Rapoport, Mario. *Gran Bretaña, Estados Unidos, y las clases dirigentes argentinas, 1940–1945*. Buenos Aires: Editorial de Belgrano, 1981.

————. *Política y diplomacia en la Argentina: Las relaciones con eeuu y la urss*. Buenos Aires: Editorial Tesis-Instituto Torcuato Di Tella, 1986.

Rouquié, Alain. *Poder militar y sociedad política en la Argentina 2: 1943–1973*. Buenos Aires: Emecé, 1982.

Sanguinetti, Horacio. *Los socialistas independientes*. Buenos Aires: Editorial de Belgrano, 1981.

Sidicaro, Ricardo. *Juan Domingo Perón: La paz y la guerra*. Buenos Aires: Fondo de Cultura Económica, 1996.

Taylor, Julie M. *Eva Perón: The Myths of a Woman*. Chicago: University of Chicago Press, 1979.

Tcach, César. *Sabattinismo y peronismo: Partidos políticos en Córdoba, 1943–1955*. Buenos Aires: Sudamericana, 1991.

Torre, Juan Carlos. "Interpretando (una vez más) los orígenes del peronismo." *Desarrollo Económico* 28, 112 (January–March 1989).

————. *La vieja guardia sindical y Perón: Sobre los orígenes del peronismo*. Buenos Aires: Sudamericana, 1990.

Zanatta, Loris. *Del estado liberal a la nación católica.* Bernal: Universidad Nacional de Quilmes, 1996.

———. *Perón y el mito de la nación católica.* Buenos Aires: Sudamericana, 1999.

2. Economy

Barsky, Osvaldo, et al. *La agricultura pampeana: Transformaciones productivas y sociales.* Buenos Aires: Fondo de Cultura Económica, 1988.

Brennan, James P. "Industriales y 'bolicheros': La actividad económica y la alianza populista peronista, 1943–1976." *Boletín del Instituto Historia Argentina y Americana Dr. Emilio Ravignani* 15, 1 (1997).

Dorfman, Adolfo. *Cincuenta años de industrialización en la Argentina, 1930–1980.* Buenos Aires: Solar, 1983.

Fodor, Jorge. "Peron's Policies for Agricultural Exports, 1946–1948: Dogmatism or Common Sense?" In *Argentina in the Twentieth Century,* ed. David Rock. Pittsburgh: University of Pittsburgh Press, 1975.

Llach, Juan José. "El Plan Pinedo de 1940, su significado histórico, y los orígenes de la economía política del peronismo." *Desarrollo Económico* 23, 92 (January–March 1984).

Mallon, Richard, and Juan Sourrouille. *La política económica en una sociedad conflictiva.* Buenos Aires: Amorrortu, 1975.

O'Connell, Arturo. "La Argentina en la Depresión: Los problemas de una economía abierta." *Desarrollo Económico* 23, 92 (January–March 1984).

Panaia, Marta, Ricardo Lesser, and Pedro Skupch. *Estudios sobre los orígenes del peronismo/2.* Buenos Aires: Siglo xxi, 1973.

3. Society

Del Campo, Hugo. *Sindicalismo y peronismo: Los comienzos de un vínculo perdurable,* Buenos Aires: clacso, 1983.

Doyon, Louise M. "El crecimiento sindical bajo el peronismo." In *La formación del sindicalismo peronista,* ed. J. C. Torre. Buenos Aires: Legasa, 1988.

———. "La organización del movimiento sindical peronista (1946–1955)." In *La formación del sindicalismo peronista,* ed. J. C. Torre. Buenos Aires: Legasa, 1988.

———. "Conflictos obreros durante el régimen peronista (1946–1955)." In *La formación del sindicalismo peronista,* ed. J. C. Torre. Buenos Aires: Legasa, 1988.

Durruty, Celia. *Clase obrera y peronismo.* Córdoba: Ediciones de Pasado y Presente, 1969.

Gaudio, Ricardo, and Jorge Pilone. "Estado y relaciones laborales en el período previo al surgimiento del peronismo, 1935–1943." *Desarrollo Económico* 24, 94 (July–September 1984).

Germani, Gino. *Política y sociedad en una época de transición.* Buenos Aires: Paidós, 1962.

———. *Estructura social de la Argentina.* 2d ed. Buenos Aires: Solar, 1987.

Horowitz, Joel. "Los trabajadores ferroviarios en la Argentina (1920–1943): La formación de una elite obrera." *Desarrollo Económico* 25, 99 (October–December 1985).

Matsushita, Hiroschi. *Movimiento obrero argentino, 1930–1945: Sus proyecciones en los orígenes del peronismo.* Buenos Aires: Siglo XX, 1983.

Murmis, Miguel, and Juan Carlos Portantiero. *Estudios sobre los orígenes del peronismo/1.* Buenos Aires: Siglo xxii, 1971.

Recchini de Lattes, Zulma L., and Alfredo E. Lattes. *Migraciones en la Argentina.* Buenos Aires: Instituto Torcuato Di Tella, 1969.

Torre, Juan Carlos, ed. *La formación del sindicalismo peronista.* Buenos Aires: Legasa, 1988.

4. Ideology and Culture

Bianchi, Susana. "Catolicismo y peronismo: La familia entre la religión y la política (1945–1955)." *Boletín del Instituto Historia Argentina y Americana Dr. Emilio Ravignani* 19 (1999).

Buchrucker, Cristián. *Nacionalismo y peronismo: La Argentina en la crisis ideológica mundial (1927–1955).* Buenos Aires: Sudamericana, 1987.

De Ipola, Emilio. *Ideología y discurso populista,* Mexico City: Folios, 1982.

Goldar, Ernesto. "La literatura peronista." In *El peronismo,* ed. G. Cárdenas et al. Buenos Aires: Carlos Pérez Editor, 1969.

Neiburg, Federico. *Los intelectuales y la invención del peronismo.* Buenos Aires: Alianza, 1998.

Plotkin, Mariano. *"Mañana es San Perón": Propaganda, rituales políticos, y educación popular en el régimen peronista (1946–1955).* Buenos Aires: Ariel, 1994.

———. "The Changing Perceptions of Peronism." In *Peronism and Argentina,* ed. James P. Brennan. Wilmington: Scholarly Resources, 1998.

Romero, José Luis. "Martínez Estrada, un renovador de la exégesis sarmientina." In *La experiencia argentina y otros ensayos.* Buenos Aires: Editorial de Belgrano, 1980.

III. 1955–1976

1. General Works and Politics

Altamirano, Carlos. *Arturo Frondizi: El hombre de las ideas como político.* Buenos Aires: Fondo de Cultura Económica 1998.

Balvé, Beba, and Miguel Murmis. *Lucha de calles, lucha de clases.* Buenos Aires: La Rosa Blindada, 1973.

Cavarozzi, Marcelo. *Autoritarismo y democracia (1955–1996): La transición del Estado al mercado en la Argentina.* Buenos Aires: Ariel, 1997.

De Riz, Liliana. *La política en suspenso, 1966–1976.* Buenos Aires: Paidós, 2000.

Gillespie, Richard. *Soldiers of Perón: Argentina's Montonero.* Oxford: Clarendon Press, 1982.

Graham-Yooll, Andrew. *Tiempo de tragedia.* Buenos Aires: Ediciones de la Flor, 1972.

Halperín Donghi, Tulio. *La larga agonía de la Argentina peronista*. Buenos Aires: Ariel, 1994.

O'Donnell, Guillermo. *El estado burocrático autoritario, 1966–1973*. Buenos Aires: Editorial de Belgrano, 1982.

Portantiero, Juan Carlos. "Clases dominantes y crisis política en la Argentina actual." In *El capitalismo argentino en crisis*, ed. Oscar Braun. Buenos Aires: Siglo xxi, 1973.

Pucciarelli, Alfredo, ed. *La primacía de la política: Lanusse, Perón, y la Nueva Izquierda en tiempos del GAN*. Buenos Aires: Eudeba, 1999.

Rouquié, A., ed. *Argentina hoy*. Mexico City: Siglo xxi, 1982.

Seoane, María. *Todo o nada*. Buenos Aires: Planeta, 1991.

———. *El burgués maldito*. Buenos Aires: Planeta, 1998.

Sigal, Silvia, and Eliseo Verón. *Perón o muerte: Los fundamentos discursivos del fenómeno peronista*. Buenos Aires: Legasa, 1986.

Smulovitz, Catalina. *Oposición y gobierno: Los años de Frondizi*. Buenos Aires: Centro Editor de América latina, 1988.

Torre, Juan Carlos. *Los sindicatos en el gobierno, 1973–1976*. Buenos Aires: Centro Editor de América Latina, 1983.

2. Economy

Braun, Oscar, ed. *El capitalismo argentino en crisis*. Buenos Aires: Siglo xxi, 1973.

Canitrot, Adolfo. "La experiencia populista de redistribución de ingresos." *Desarrollo Económico* 15, 59 (1975).

———. *La viabilidad de la democracia: Un análisis de la experiencia peronista, 1973–1976*. Buenos Aires: cedes/Estudios Sociales, 1978.

Di Tella, Guido. *Perón-Perón, 1973–1976*. Buenos Aires: Sudamericana, 1983.

Gerchunoff, Pablo, and Juan José Llach. "Capitalismo industrial, desarrollo asociado, y distribución del ingreso entre los dos gobiernos peronistas, 1950–1972." *Desarrollo Económico* 57 (April–June 1975).

Katz, Jorge, and Bernardo Kosakoff. *El proceso de industrialización en la Argentina: Evolución, retroceso, y perspectiva*. Buenos Aires: Centro Editor de América Latina, 1989.

Katz, Jorge, et al. *Desarrollo y crisis de la capacidad tecnológica latinoamericana: El caso de la industria metalmecánica*. Buenos Aires: bid-cepal, 1986.

Schvarzer, Jorge. "Estrategia industrial y grandes empresas: El caso argentino." *Desarrollo Económico* 71 (August 1978).

3. Society

Abós, Álvaro. *Augusto T. Vandor: Sindicatos y peronismo*. Buenos Aires: Fondo de Cultura Económica, 1999.

Brennan, James P. *The Labor Wars in Córdoba, 1955–1976: Ideology, Work, and Labor Politics in an Argentine Industrial City*. Cambridge, Mass.: Harvard University Press, 1993.

———. *Agustín J. Tosco: Por la clase obrera y la liberación nacional*. Buenos Aires: Fondo de Cultura Económica, 1999.

Brennan, James P., and Mónica B. Gordillo. "Working Class Protest, Popular Revolt, and Urban Insurrection: The 1969 Cordobazo." *Journal of Social History* 27, 3 (spring 1994).

James, Daniel. *Resistance and Integration: Peronism and the Argentine Working Class, 1946–1976.* Cambridge: Cambridge University Press, 1988.

———. "October 17th and October 18th: Mass Protest, Peronism, and the Argentine Working Class." *Journal of Social History* 3 (spring 1988).

Palomino, Héctor. *Cambios ocupacionales y sociales en Argentina, 1947–1985.* Buenos Aires: cisea, 1988.

Palomino, Mirta L. de. *Tradición y poder: La Sociedad Rural Argentina (1955–1983).* Buenos Aires: cisea-gel, 1988.

Schvarzer, Jorge. *Empresarios del pasado: La Unión Industrial Argentina.* Buenos Aires: Imago Mundi-cisea, 1991.

Torrado, Susana. *Estructura social de la Argentina, 1945–1983.* Buenos Aires: Ediciones de la Flor, 1992.

4. Culture and Ideology

Sigal, Silvia. *Intelectuales y poder en la década del sesenta.* Buenos Aires: Puntosur, 1991.

Terán, Oscar. *Nuestros años sesentas: La formación de la nueva izquierda intelectual en la Argentina, 1956–1966.* Buenos Aires: Puntosur, 1991.

IV. 1976-2000

1. General Works and Politics

Abós, Álvaro. *Las organizaciones sindicales y el poder militar (1976–1983).* Buenos Aires: Centro Editor de América Latina, 1984.

Acuña, Carlos, ed. *La nueva matriz política argentina.* Buenos Aires: Nueva Visión, 1995.

Bonasso, Miguel. *Recuerdo de la muerte.* Buenos Aires: Bruguera, 1984.

Cardoso, Oscar Raúl, Eduardo Kirchbaum, and Eduardo van der Kooy. *Malvinas: La trama secreta.* Buenos Aires: Planeta, 1992.

Cerutti, Gabriela. *El jefe: Vida y obra de Carlos Saúl Menem.* Buenos Aires: Planeta, 1993.

Comisión Nacional sobre la Desaparición de Personas (CONADEP). *Nunca más.* Buenos Aires: eudeba, 1984.

Corradi, Juan E. *The Fitful Republic.* Boulder: Westview Press, 1985.

De Riz, Liliana. "Reforma constitucional y consolidación democrática." *Sociedad* 6 (May 1995).

Di Stefano, Roberto, and Loris Zanatta. *Historia de la Iglesia Argentina.* Buenos Aires: Mondadori, 2000.

García Delgado, Daniel. *Los cambios en la sociedad política (1976–1986).* Buenos Aires: Centro Editor de América Latina, 1987.

Giussani, Pablo. *Los días de Alfonsín*. Buenos Aires: Legasa, 1986.

Groisman, Enrique. *Poder y derecho en el Proceso de Reorganización Nacional.* Buenos Aires: cisea, 1983.

———. *La Corte Suprema de Justicia durante la dictadura (1976–1983)*. Buenos Aires: cisea, 1989.

Melo, Artemio. *El gobierno de Alfonsín: La instauración democrática*. Rosario: Homo Sapiens, 1995.

Mustapic, Ana María, and Mateo Goretti. "Gobierno y oposición en el Congreso: La práctica de la cohabitación durante la presidencia de Alfonsín (1983–1989)." *Desarrollo Económico* 32, 126 (July–September 1992).

Novaro, Marcos, ed. *Entre el abismo y la ilusión: Peronismo, democracia, y mercado*. Buenos Aires: Norma, 1999.

Nun, José, and Juan Carlos Portantiero, eds. *Ensayos sobre la transición democrática en la Argentina*. Buenos Aires: Puntosur, 1987.

Oszlak, Oscar, ed. *Proceso, crisis, y transición democrática*. Buenos Aires: Centro Editor de América Latina, 1984.

Palermo, Vicente. "The Origins of *menemismo*." In *Peronism and Argentina*, ed. James Brennan. Wilmington: Scholarly Resources, 1998.

Palermo, Vicente, and Marcos Novaro. *Política y poder en el gobierno de Menem*. Buenos Aires: Norma, 1996.

Pion-Berlin, David. *Through the Corridors of Power: Institutions and Civil-Military Relations in Argentina*. University Park, Pa.: The Pennsylvania State University Press, 1997.

Quevedo, Luis Alberto. "Videopolítica y cultura en la Argentina de los noventa." In *Culturas políticas a fin de siglo*, ed. Rosalía Winocur. Mexico City: Juan Pablos Editor, 1997.

Quiroga, Hugo. *El tiempo del "Proceso": Conflictos y coincidencias entre políticos y militares, 1976–1983*. Rosario: Editorial Fundación Ross, 1994.

Seoane, María, and Vicente Muleiro. *El Dictador: La historia secreta y pública de Jorge Rafael Videla*. Buenos Aires: Sudamericana, 2000.

2. Economy

Azpiazu, Daniel, Eduardo Basualdo, and Miguel Khavisse. *El nuevo poder económico en la Argentina en los años 80*. Buenos Aires: Legasa, 1986.

Basualdo, Eduardo. *Concentración y centralización del capital en la Argentina durante la década del noventa*. Buenos Aires: Flacso/Universidad de Quilmes, 2000.

Beccaria, Luis A. "Distribución del ingreso en la Argentina: Explorando lo sucedido desde mediados de los setenta." *Desarrollo Económico* 31, 123 (October–December 1991).

Bisang, Roberto, Carlos Bonvecchi, Bernardo Kosacoff, and Adrián Ramos. "La transformación industrial en los noventa: Un proceso con final abierto." *Desarrollo Económico* special issue 36 (summer 1996).

Canitrot, Adolfo. "Teoría y práctica del liberalismo: Política antiinflacionaria y apertura económica en la Argentina, 1976–1981." *Desarrollo Económico* 21, 82 (1982).

Gerchunoff, Pablo, and Juan Carlos Torre. "La política de liberalización económica en la administración de Menem." *Desarrollo Económico* 36, 143 (October–December 1996).

Heymann, Daniel, and Fernando Navajas. "Conflicto distributivo y déficit fiscal: Notas sobre la experiencia argentina, 1970–1987." *Desarrollo Económico* 29, 115 (October–December 1989).

Kosacoff, Bernardo, and Daniel Azpiazu. *La industria argentina: Desarrollo y cambios estructurales.* Buenos Aires: Centro Editor de América latina, 1989.

Rofman, Alejandro. *Desarrollo regional y exclusión social.* Buenos Aires: Amorrortu, 2000.

Schvarzer, Jorge. *La política económica de Martínez de Hoz.* Buenos Aires: Hyspamérica, 1986.

———. *Implantación de un modelo económico: La experiencia argentina entre 1975 y el 2000.* Buenos Aires: AZ Editora, 1998.

Smith, William C. *Authoritarianism and the Crisis of the Argentine Political Economy.* Stanford: Stanford University Press, 1991.

Torre, Juan Carlos. "El lanzamiento político de las reformas estructurales en América Latina." *Política y Gobierno* (Mexico City) 4, 2 (April–June 1997).

Viguera, Aníbal. *La trama política de la apertura económica en la Argentina (1987–1996).* La Plata: Ediciones Al Margen, 2000.

3. Society

Beliz, Gustavo, ed. *Política social: La cuenta pendiente.* Buenos Aires: Editorial Sudamericana, 1995.

Brysk, Alison. *The Politics of Human Rights in Argentina: Protest, Change, and Democratization.* Stanford: Stanford University Press, 1994.

Cangiano, María Cecilia. "Reviewing the Past and Inventing the Present: The Steelworkers of Villa Constitución and *Menemismo,* 1989–1992." In *Peronism and Argentina,* ed. James Brennan. Wilmington: Scholarly Resources, 1998.

Minujin, Alberto, ed. *Cuesta abajo: Los nuevos pobres: Efectos de la crisis en la sociedad argentina.* Buenos Aires: Unicef/Losada, 1997.

Silvestri, Graciela, and Adrián Gorelik. "Ciudad y cultura urbana, 1976–1999: El fin de la expansión." In *Buenos Aires, historia de cuatro siglos,* ed. José Luis Romero and Luis Alberto Romero. 2d ed. Buenos Aires: Altamira, 2000.

Torrado, Susana. "La cuestión social." In *Argentina: 15 años de democracia,* ed. Román Lejtman. Buenos Aires: Norma, 1998.

4. Ideology and Culture

Feitlowitz, Marguerite. *A Lexicon of Terror: Argentina and the Legacy of Torture.* New York: Oxford University Press, 1998.

Plotkin, Mariano. *Freud in the Pampas: The Emergence and Development of a Psychoanalytic Culture in Argentina.* Stanford: Stanford University Press, 2001.

Index